A NEW HISTORY OF VIOLIN PLAYING

A NEW HISTORY OF VIOLIN PLAYING:
the vibrato and
Lambert Massart's revolutionary discovery

Zdenko Silvela

Universal Publishers
USA • 2001

A New History Of Violin Playing

Sarasate by Salustiano Asenjo
Cover photo property: Ayuntamiento de Pamplona

Universal Publishers / uPUBLISH.com
USA • 2001

ISBN: 1-58112-667-0

www.upublish.com/books/silvela.htm

To my daughter ELENA

*May this book contribute
to compensate for the unjust neglect
inflicted upon LAMBERT MASSART
and, at the same time, be a token of perennial
homage to the founder of the modern
era of violin playing.*

TABLE OF CONTENTS

FOREWORD

This book will deal only with the most superlative violinists and teachers. This decision has been taken, basically, for two reasons:

a) By selecting only the most salient violinists, we have an advantage: that they concentrate in themselves all the main features and characteristics of violin playing of their time, be them performers, or teachers. It is only by concentrating on the main aspects of performing that we can trace the historical evolution of the art of playing the violin, avoiding to be distracted by minor fiddlers whose style of playing is not always evident.

b) It is from them that we have more data, more anecdotes and more interesting things to tell. Thus the book keeps always awaken the attention of the reader, and facilitates the task to understand the historical changes of this sublime art. By going from top to top, from peak to peak, from tower to tower, from summit to summit, we will have a very bright image on what has been the style of playing on a certain period of time. This book will be the concentrated broth, the "*consommé*" of the violin. Now, if we join with a line these summits from the beginning to the end we will draw a most interesting sky-line of the violin, which will give the reader more than one surprise. But this will come on due course. I cannot reveal it now, for it would be a crime, as if your bookseller would tell you who is the assassin in an Agatha Christie's detective novel you are about to buy.

Nevertheless, should the reader like to have a thorough (but superficial) account of all the fiddlers that played on a certain lapse of time, or on a particular country, or on the whole history, I recommend him to look up in the "*yellow pages*" of the violin, i.e. the voluminous *The History of the Violin* by E. van der Straeten.

The book contains a list of cassette's albums that I have recorded for my personal and exclusive use. They provide me an easy way to identify the works I want to listen to, and in the order that suites me better. But they are not available to anybody for law forbids to dub or duplicate records or cassettes.

Notwithstanding, I have maintained their list and references, for it will give the reader the suggestion of a good recording, adequate, in my view, to illustrate each musician studied herein. To have an absolute understanding on how our fiddlers play, it is indispensable to hear them play. For those violinist that played before the gramophone was invented, I thought it might be a good idea to have, at least, a piece of their composition, to be more familiarised with their musical ideas.

I must admit that some of the recordings are not very easy to find, but if I have managed to find them, so can do my reader.

I have included at the end an ENCYCLOPAEDIA of names and terms used in this book that might be of interest. World-wide known composers, such as Brahms or Tchaikovsky are not included, in the understanding that they are well known by the reader. Names and terms entered in this encyclopaedia are marked with an asterisk in the book text. As for the terms, I have entered the most specific ones, taking for granted that the more general musical terms are known by the reader. Done with loving care it emulates and sometimes excels, its parent, the book.

Names with two asterisks (**) mean that they have their own article in the book.

Finally, this book is within everybody's reach. Written in a plain language, easy to understand, lacking complicated and esoteric musical terminology, it is designed to be understood by everyone, in particular by those who, having little knowledge of music, love, nevertheless, the violin.

A last minute warning: this book is written in English so that it might have the greatest possible spreading all over the world. Written in English by a Spaniard, the reader should not expect a perfectly drafted work with a flawless English-native wording. But this lack of grammatical accuracy adds to it a certain exotic touch, and I would not let it be revised and rewritten by a native English for love or money. The reader, on certain occasions, might have the impression he is reading the owner's manual of a Japanese product, but I do not mind, it is the salt to it, and everybody, English, American or any one who has a certain knowledge of English can easily understand it.

BOOK ONE:

THE BEGINNINGS

GENERAL CONSIDERATIONS

The violin is considered to be one of the most perfect instruments in music. In versatility and in its most attractive musicality it is, indeed, at the top of all instruments. The violin is another human voice, its model, being able to reproduce all kinds of moods, that go from the sorrow and pathetic to lyrical happiness and exhilarating joy. When we arrive to them, we will see how Massart and Kreisler could make their violins cry. It is able to emulate almost all the rest of musical instruments, and depending on the skill of the player, it can produce the most varied emotional feelings. Within the range of its four octaves*, it can play all the tones and microtones of the scale*, and it is within its power to play chords*, as well. The violin is able, also, to imitate all sort of bird singing and animal noises, and in general any other imaginable sound.

It is audible farther off than the gigantic pianoforte, and its tones in a master's hand go to the heart of man. (Charles Reade*. Cremona Violins. Four Letters Descriptive of Those Exhibited in 1872 at the South Kensington Museum. Alexander Broude Inc. New York. N.Y. 1873. p. 6)

To all these possibilities we must add its faculty for brilliant, agile figurations that go far beyond the faculties of the human voice. Its treble, soprano sound, and its deep bass, make of it an authentic replica of the nightingale, to which it resembles even more than to the human voice. Everything in it is attractive, and its sweet, enchanting voice together with its round sensuous curves, resembling those of a pretty young lady, make of it an object to woo rather than an instrument to play. (Reade*, more poetic than me, calls them "the wafer-like sides of its wooden shell" Op. cit. p 5) As he himself says: *Violins are heard by the eye* [1].

They can also stir up ardent passions in connoisseurs, as shown in this anecdote by Charles Reade*: (Op. cit. pag 17)
        <One of the most mythical luthiers*, Luigi Tarisio*, knowing
        that the legendary cello "Bass of Spain" of 1713 by Stradivarius was

---

[1] Charles Reade: Op. cit. Pag. 29.

in Madrid, came here and after many difficult negotiations he managed to buy it for about four thousand francs. And Reade writes: *"He sailed exultant for Paris with the Spanish Bass in a case. He never let it out of his sight. The pair were caught by a storm in the Bay of Biscay. The ship rolled; Tarisio clasped his bass tight, and trembled. It was a terrible gale, and for one whole day they were in real danger. Tarisio spoke of it to me with a shudder. I will give you his real words, for they struck me at the time, and I have often thought of them since:*

-"Ah, my poor Mr. Reade, the Bass of Spain was all but lost"

Was not this a true connoisseur? A genuine enthusiast? Observe! There was also an ephemeral insect called Luigi Tarisio, who would have gone down with the bass: but that made no impression on his mind. De minimis non curat Ludovicus." [Ludovicus (Luigi) couldn't care less about minimal things.]>

To those who might have a certain apprehension to share Reade's view, I recommend them to have a look at web-sites:

- sheila's corner + Soil Stradivari
- sheila's corner + Sauret* Guarneri
And also the spectacular "Prado Museum" in site:
- peterbiddulph.com/publications/violinpics1.htm
In the latter you will see, walking majestically in procession, while they display their ravishing beauty in all its splendour and magic, the following Guarneri del Gesu:

Baltic 1731.
Carrodus 1743.
Dancla* 1727.
D'Egville 1735.
Doyen 1744.
Haddock 1734.
Heifetz**, ex David 1740.
Joachim** 1737.
Kemp 1738.
King 1735.
King Joseph 1737.
Konchanski 1741.
Kortschak 1739.
Kreisler** 1730.
Leduc* 1745.

Lord Wilton 1742. which has been sold in November 1999 for an approximate amount of 4,800,000 dollars (four million, eight hundred thousand), the highest amount ever paid for a violin. It is now called the "ex Jehudi Menuhin".

Ole Bull** 1744.
Paganini (Canon) 1743.
Plauden 1735.
Sauret* 1743.
Stern**, ex Panette 1737.
Stretton 1729.
Vieuxtemps** 1741.
Violon du Diable 1743.
Ysaye** 1740

If after contemplating all these masterpieces of craftsmanship and sheer beauty, the reader does not share Charles Reade*'s opinion, he must stop reading this book now !!

All these possibilities have been profited by composers to write profusely for it, to the extent that we may say that no other instrument has had as many compositions devoted to it, if we consider all the solo and the ensemble music written specifically for it. And it is so indeed because the violins are the main group of the orchestra, and we must take into account all the symphonic literature, as well.

THE ORIGINS

Me préserve Apolon, dieu des arts et de la poésie, d'avoir la téméraire audace de tenter même une simple esquisse, un modeste croquis pouvant ressembler à une histoire générale du violon et des ses origines. <May Apollo, god of arts and poetry, prevent me from having the temerarious audacity to try even to make a simple draft, a modest sketch that might resemble to a general history of the violin and its origins>.

With these words, filled with awe and restrain, begins Arthur Pougin* the chapter devoted to the origins of the violin in his book *Le violon, les violonistes et la musique de violon*, Paris 1924, pag 17.

The violin and the cello have both the same origins, for they belong to the same family. There is, however, a most important difference: whereas the cello is noble by birth, that is to say, that it was accepted straightaway by the courts of nobility, the violin had to struggle his way into them or, what is tantamount, into classical music. As a matter of fact, the violin, until the second half of the 17th century, was an instrument of lowly origin, used mainly by Arabs, gypsies and drunken peasants in their merrymaking (dancing and singing) in the open air; an equivalent of today's mandolin. The beginnings of the violin have much in common with those of jazz and tango, music and dances that were exclusively performed by Negroes, being absolutely forbidden in high society, which considered both most "un-chic" (The film High Society, featuring Louis Armstrong and Bing Crosby, tells us this story) Later tango and jazz acquired universal esteem, thanks to Carlos Gardel* and Louis Armstrong, respectively. In their turn, jazz and tango have exactly the same origins:

Both originate in the mouth of a great river: Mississippi for jazz, Rio de la Plata for tango.

Both are performed only by Black-slaves and have the same dotted, syncopated rhythm.[1]

The idea that the high society and nobility (the consumers of classical music in those days) had on Arabs, gypsies and peasants, was very different than the one we have today, imbued as we are with egalitarian, democratic, tolerant, antiracist and secular elevated principles. In the 17th century these people were thought to be most disgusting and abominable, and the principles of non-discrimination, equality, and the struggle against xenophobia and racism, simply didn't exist. A most accurate account on what gypsies, for example, meant to the well born is given in these Verlaine's* sublime verses:

GROTESQUES (Poèmes Saturniens, V)

Leurs jambes pour toutes montures,
Pour tous biens l'or de leurs regards,
Par le chemin des aventures,
Ils vont haillonneux et hagards.

Le sage, indigné, les harangue;
Le sot plaint ces fous hasardeux;
Les enfants leur tire la langue
Et les filles se moquent d'eux.

---

[1] To savour this assertion hear the tango recordings of Horacio Salgan (p) and Hubaldo de Lio (guit) contained in cas 21, side B. They play classical old tangos but with such a rhythm that one simply cannot say where is tango and where is jazz.

C'est qu'odieux et ridicules,
Et maléfiques en effect,
Ils ont l'air, sur les crépuscules,
D'un mauvais rêve que l'ont fait;

C'est que, sur leurs aigres guitarres
Crispant la main des libertés,
Ils nasilles des chants bizarres,
Nostalgiques et révoltés;

C'est en fin que dans leur prunelles
Rit et pleure-fastidieux-
L'amour des choses éternelles
Des vieux morts et des anciens dieux!

-Donc, allez, vagabonds sans trêves
Errez, funestes et maudits,
Le long de gouffres et des grèves,
Sous l'oeuil fermé des paradis!

La nature à l'homme s'allie
Pour châtier comme il le faut
L'orgueilleuse mélancolie
Qui vous fait marcher le front haut

Et vengeant sur vous le blasphème
Des vastes espoirs véhéments,
Meurtrit votre front anathème
Au choc rude des éléments.

Les juins brûlent et les décembres
Gèlent votre chair jusq'aux os,
Et la fièvre envahit vos membres
qui se déchirent au roseaux.

Tous vous repousse et vous navre,
Et quand la mort viendra pour vous,
Maigre et froide, votre cadavre
Sera dédaigné par les loups!

<GROTESQUES (Poèmes Saturniens, V)

Their legs as their only mount
their only fortune their golden glance
they go ragged and haggard
down the adventure lane

The wise man, indignant, harangues them,
the foul feels sorry for these crazy adventurers
children put out their tongue at them
and girls mock them

And the reason is that hateful and ridiculous
and maleficient indeed,
they look, at dawn,
as if they were a bad nightmare one had

It is also that on their sour guitars
with their liberty clenched hands
they snuffle strange, nostalgic
and rebellious songs

It is, finally, that in the apple of their eyes
it smiles and weep -irksome-
the love for eternal things
for old defunct and ancient gods!

Go, then, truceless rovers,
wander, disastrous and damned,
along chasms and sand banks
under the hidden sun of paradise!

Nature allies to man
to punish, as you deserve,
your proud melancholy
that make you walk with your head high

and avenging on you your blasphemous,
vehement, vast hopes,
bruises your anathematized forehead
with the shocks of the raging elements

Junes burn and Decembers freeze
your flesh to the bones,
and fever invades your limbs that
tear by the reeds.

Everything rejects and grieves you
And when death, thin and cold,
will come to take you, your cadaver
will be by the wolves disdained!>

The first primitive violins, were strung with three strings tuned as the lowest strings of the "true" violin: g, d, a.; the first evidence of it could well be a wall painting by Garofalo* in 1506 in the Sala del Tesoro at the Palazzo di Ludovico il Moro. The existence of the violin and its family is also well evidenced in frescoes by Gaudenzio Ferrari*. The earliest of which is "La madonna degli aranci" in S. Christoforo, in Vercelli, near Milan, painted around 1530. In this painting we can see a little child (an angel) playing a primitive violin, strung with three strings. Ferrari* painted also the whole violin family, cello, viola and the said three strings violin in the cupola of the Saronno cathedral in 1535. But soon this primitive violin will leave way to the modern true one.

The first written account of the true violin, strung with four strings tuned g, d, a, e, is the Epitomé musical des tons, sons et accordz by Philibert Jambe-de-Fer* in 1556.: *"Le violon est fort contraire à la viole...Nous appelons viole c'elles desquelles les gentils hommes, marchantz et autres gents de vertuz passent leur temps...L'autre s'appelle violon et c'est celuy duquel ont use en danceries ..."*

<The violin is quite opposite to the viols...We call viol those with which gentlemen, merchants and other virtuous people pass their time...The other is called violin and is used commonly for dancing...> ["A sensu contrario", those who played the violin must have been for him "non virtuous" i.e. debauched and vicious.]

By the time of Jambe-de-Fer's* Epitomé, the true violin was well know in Europe, but used only for open air dancing.

It is impossible to assert, with absolute certainty, who was the inventor of the violin such as we know it today. This topic has been the source of countless writings and discussions, and oceans of ink have been wasted in defending each of the different ideas on the subject, but there is no evidence of any of the theories that have been stated. This complexity, the absence of written documentation, and the non existence of compositions and scores devoted to the violin, not needed, for it had the simple role to double the vocal parts, that is to say, to play the same notes as the singer, have led to the most varied theories and complex arguments.

The great majority attribute not one but many different predecessors to the violin. So, for example, the New Grove Dictionary says it has evolved from the rebec, the Renaissance fiddle and the lira da braccio. Others like Pasquali and Principe in "il violino" (Edizioni Curci Milano 1926) list nothing less than 20 ancestors of the king of instruments, and similarly Arthur Pougin* in his *Le violon, les violonistes*... believes it has evolved in a two centuries process of improvements of other ancestors that include the crowth, rubebe, rebec, bow vielle, and the viol.

During the last decades of the 20th century a fever for ever more complicated procedures has invaded us in all respects; our civilisation becomes more and more complicated by the day. This complication, often artificial and needless, affects personal computers, cell phones, motorcars, video tape recorders, etc. Even the simplest things have been complicated on purpose without any plausible reason, and thus we have that a fan has become an *electric-fan*, and a witness is not any more a witness but an *eye-witness*. Things have become so complicated that it is estimated that the use we make of modern high technology instruments is only a ten per cent of their possibilities, because we are not able to keep in mind all of them. Our world has become so complex that the man with one of the highest salaries in the world in the present time, interviewed by the BBC in its program *Hard Talk*, whose services are eagerly wanted by all governments and multinational enterprises alike, is one who is specialised in simplifying procedures and bureaucracies of all kinds.

To fight complexity we must practise *simplicity, simplicity, simplicity*. Following this axiom we may say that the cradle of the "true" violin is Cremona (Italy) and that the violin came out of a single act of volition made by the first great luthier* ANDREA AMATI (b.1510 Cremona; d. Id 1580) followed by his two sons ANTONIO (b. Cremona c1540; d. Id ?) and GIROLAMO (b. Cremona 1561; d. Id 1630), by Girolamo's son NICOLO AMATI (b. Cremona 1596; d. Id 1684) and by Nicolo Amati's pupil ANTONIO STRADIVARI (1644-1737).

The use of an additional string towards the treble (E), fourth in the total number of strings used, but called the first, is explained by the need the luthiers* had to give their violins an expanded range of sound, that would counteract the poor response of the lowest (G) string made of gut. [On the violin, strings are call in a descendent order from highest to lowest, (E) first; (A) second; (D) is the third; and (G) is the fourth). The E string will prove to be the most important on the violin, giving it its characteristic soprano, sprightly tone. The French call it "la chanterelle"* (the singing string). La cantarela in Spanish.

MAIN CHARACTERISTICS

The violin has three characteristics: a) It is like a lover, who demands all our attention and devotion. You have to dedicate it the 100% of your time. b) It must become another limb of the body or, as Isaac Stern puts it, a "third arm". c) Amazingly, a significant number of the very, very great fiddlers loose their capabilities, particularly intonation, around the age of 50.

a) The violin as a lover: This statement is almost a truism, for any Art demands our 100% attention.

i) Nietzsche in his "Human too Human", chapter four, paragraph 163, says: *"Avoid speaking of natural gifts, innate talents. We can name great people of all kinds who were little gifted. But they acquired their grandeur, became "genius" (as it is normally said) by means of qualities that those who lack them do not like to speak of them; they all had that robust conscience of artisans, which begins by learning the parts, before risking to make a big ensemble; they took their time for this purpose, because they enjoyed more in the success of the little detail, of the accessory, than in the effect of a dazzling ensemble.* [See in the Encyclopaedia LESCHETIZKY, who had declared: "conducting is not difficult. It is harder to play six bars well on the piano than conducting the whole of Bthvn 9th symphony"]. *"The prescription, for example, for somebody to become a good writer, is easy to deliver, but its fulfilment requires qualities that one usually forgets when it is said: -"I have not enough talent"-*

Devise one hundred or more novel schemes, none of them surpassing two pages, but of such neatness that every single word be necessary; put every day anecdotes in writing, until you learn to give them the fullest form, the most efficient; be indefatigable in recollecting and describing the human types and characters. First of all tell, as often as possible, stories, and listen to the stories of the others, both with a penetrating eye and ear, to catch the effect produced in the others; travel like a landscape painter and like a dress-designer as well; extract for your own use out of every science what, if it is put clearly, produces artistic effects; consider, finally, the causes of human actions without disdaining the slightest indication that might instruct you, and become a collector of such things day and night: Let go by, in this multiple exercise, some ten years; now, what you will create in your atelier can proudly go out to the streets. On the contrary, what does the majority? They do not start by the little part but straightaway by the ensemble. It is possible that once they might succeed in making a hit, drawing the attention on them, and from then on, their works will be worse and worse, for very natural reasons. Sometimes when the intelligence and character lack to conform such an artistic life plan, it is DESTINY and NECESSITY that take their place and carry step by step the future maestro all the way through all the demanding requirements of his métier". (He had in mind Perlman in advance)

ii) Padre Martini* gives us another example: In a letter to Mozart dated in Bologna 18 December 1776, when Mozart was 20, in his prime, and after having received Mozart's latest and best compositions, he says: "*I am delighted particularly to verify that after the day I had the privilege to hear you in Bologna on the harpsichord you have made such enormous progress in composition. But it is necessary that you continue indefatigably to exercise, for it is the nature of music to demand deep exercise and study, for as long as one lives*"

b) On that the violin must become another limb of the body I have a most delightful anecdote: I had an intimate friend, Fernando Paz Heinz, may he rest in peace, who studied the violin for more than 30 years without much progress. He was dilettante, and blamed his lack of improvement to his teachers who, he said, didn't understand him. Until, at last, he decided to go to the most renowned, and most expensive, too, teacher in Madrid. This man told him that if he really wanted to learn how to play the violin he should make this daily easy routine: *go to bed with his violin and leave it on his bed table as near as possible to him. (a close vicinity was essential during the sleeping hours!); on waking up, he should, first of all, hold the violin in the usual way tucked between chin and collarbone, and go in this manner to the bathroom; there, without releasing the violin so held, he should shave the exposed half of his face, then hold the violin on the right hand side, and shave the other half of the face!!*.

My indignant friend, exasperated beyond measure by such a preposterous nonsense to introduce shaving into a violin teaching method,

24

understood clearly that all violinists were absolutely mad, and that the best thing he could do was to give up his studies at once!

> "E pur si muove" as Galileo said: this exercise is, as his teacher rightly told him, ESSENTIAL to become used to hold the violin inadvertently, as if it were a third arm. Giulio Pasquali and Remy Principe, for instance, recommend, specifically, to walk and to do squats frequently everyday with your hands clasped behind you, and the violin tucked under your chin [1]

c) That the large majority of superlatives violinists loose their faculties, particularly intonation, when they approach the 50s is only the result of statistical observation. (On the contrary, old humble violinists, like the typical ragged fiddler beggar in the street, play reasonably in tune, despite their old age) The only plausible reason that occurs to me, might be that by dints of exercising at the maximum their ear to play with such virtuosity and perfect intonation, it gets worn-out, whereas the beggar never did such a titanic effort, and therefore his ear remains almost intact.

The useful musical life of a violinist is very short indeed, and, at best, it won't last more than the span between 25 and the said 50 years of age, that is, 25 years only. Before 25, the violinist is not musically mature enough, and would play only "virtuoso show pieces", and after 50 he looses his faculties. I say that the limit is 50 years of age, to allow a wide margin, but the reader will see, as the book unfolds, first class violinists loosing their faculties much sooner than that. [2] In order to assert firmly this "assertion", we will specifically observe it in all the violinists here studied; those affected by this shortcoming will be called "victim of the 50s". I will give only two examples:

1) Wagner, in his book "My life" (second part, years 1842-1850), when in the year 1843 he is appointed Kapellmeister* of the Dresden orchestra, on the insistent requests of Weber's widow, says that "no sooner had he started, than he elicited the most intense and passionate jealousy of the one who had been, at his epoch, famous virtuoso of the violin, Karol Lipinski, the concertino* of the Dresden orchestra". Lipinski was born in 1790, so when Wagner speaks of him as an ancient virtuoso, it means that by then he was no longer a virtuoso. The words "at his epoch" refer, clearly, to a "remote" past. Lipinski was then 53 years old.

---

[1] Il violino. Edizioni Curci. Milano 1926. Chap. V, pag 107.

[2] This explains why, for instance, it is impossible to appreciate through the gramophone the real quality of certain violinists who recorded after their 50s, such as Szigeti, Sarasate and Thibaud, not to speak of Joachim or Auer.

2) Kreisler** recorded Bthvn's concerto in D when he was 51 in 1926. I have recorded the entry of the violin in the first movement in "C-17" as a testimony. The lapses of intonation are so many that it is almost unbelievable.

Only absolutely rare specimen go beyond that frontier unharmed. So far we have had Hubay, Heifetz, Francescatti, Menuhin and Oistrakh, that I can recall just now. Menuhin lost sharply after 55.

> I am jubilant to the highest degree: By sheer chance, while perusing what Fetis* (Biographie Universelle des Musiciens) has to say about Giardini**, I have discovered, with enormous satisfaction, that the great master is in agreement with me on this very astounding fact. Like the most natural thing in the world Fetis says: *"... in 1763, sa fortune en souffrit d'avantage, ... Pour réparer ses pertes il publia quelques compositions et reprit ses leçons et ses concert. Mais deja il touchait à l'age de cinquant ans... "* (Comme s'il voulait lui excuser de son peu de succès) Le chifre magique, (ou damné), comme l'on préfère!!

> <In 1763, his fortune sustained even more losses…to repair them he published some compositions and resumed his classes and performances, but he was already approaching the age of 50 years…> (As if at 50 he could not have any more successes, his old age being his excuse). The magic, (or damned) figure, as you like!!

FROM THE BEGINNINGS TO THE KING OF INSTRUMENTS

The first one who dared to introduce a violin in classical music, pioneer in this as in so many other fields, was Claudio Monteverdi in his Orfeo in 1607. "C-1". Significantly, violins are played either in the shepherds merry-making or portraying Orfeo's lyre, which at the time was supposed to be a bow instrument; in both cases open air instruments, not courtly ones. Giovanni Battista Fontana* and Biagio Marini* are the first to write sonatas* da chiesa and da camera for the violin around 1630.

Gasparo Florencio Zanetti* was the first to write a didactic book: "Il scolaro per imparare a suonare di violino" Milano 1645, the whole book in first position*. And finally, around 1627, Antoine Furetière*, in his *Dictionnaire Universel* notices already the existence of several writers who distinguish the violin with the complimentary appellative KING OF INSTRUMENTS (a meteoric career). The violin was fully accepted in classical music after only 20 years of its first reluctant appearance.

<Although Furetière's Dictionnaire was published posthumously in The Hague in 1690, he had been working on it since 1620> [1]

This did not mean, however, that it was taken as seriously as it is today. The violin, and music by and large, were not taken really seriously until the continuous and tenacious efforts of Berlioz, of his intimate friend Liszt and of the son in law of the latter Wagner managed to achieve such a mammoth task. So, for example, we know that Franz Clement*, the virtuoso dedicatee of Bthvn's vl conc. who premiered it in December 1806, broke the continuity of the piece and between movements 1 and 2 played several improvisations holding the violin upside-down. This sort of clownish profanation of such a masterpiece seems to us sacrilegious and simply unbelievable, but at the time it was just commonplace.

Berlioz, in his Memoires (Chapter XLVI), tells us how Habeneck*, the best conductor in France and one of the best in Europe, during the première of Berlioz's Requiem, which he was conducting, in the most intricate and difficult part of the whole score, discarded his baton and drew out peacefully his tobacco box, to take a pinch of snuff. (it was a most critical moment, the start of *tuba mirum*, where four groups of brass instrument, stationed at the four corners of the immense orchestra, which with the chorus was placed under the dome in the centre of the building, having to enter successively, chaos was sure to happen if not carefully conducted). Berlioz, who was very near him, jumped hurriedly onto the podium to conduct himself this very intricate part of his work. (This event was determinant in his decision to become himself a conductor). Although Habeneck thanked Berlioz for his timely aid, and admitted that his thoughtlessness might have caused a break-down, Berlioz remained persuaded that there had been no thoughtlessness, and that the break-down was intended, an opinion we, all his admirers, share, being, as he was, the butt of all the envies of Paris.

The hallmark of the total acceptance of the violin in classical music was put by Lully (b. Florence 1632). Himself a great violinist, didn't compose for violin solo, but was more interested in violins as an orchestral mass. Monopolising music in France thanks to the favours of the Sun King*, his influence expanded all over Europe, where there was not a single overture

---

[1] This is the text in the Dictionnaire Universel: *Violon. Instrument de Musique portatif qui n'a que quatre cordes de boyeau, dont la manche est sans touches, et dont on joue avec un archet...Ses sons aigus sont plus gais et font plus d'effet sur l'esprit que ceux de tous les autres instruments, dont il a été nommé le **roi** par quelques-uns.* Violin: Musical portable instrument, that has but four gut strings, whose fingerboard is without frets, and which is played with a bow...Its treble sounds are more agreable and more moving that those of any other instrument, of which it has been named, by some ones, the **king**.

or sinfonia* without the characteristically dotted rhythm he gave to his music. So the violin enters the classical music as a mass of instruments. Later, as time went by, a little group of instruments was selected and enhanced within the orchestra in the concerto grosso*. This group, usually two violins and a basso continuo*, was called "coro favorito or concertino*". (Do not mistake with the title of *concertino** the first violin* of the orchestra has). Later, one of these two violins became protagonist, and so, little by little, appeared the concerto for violin solo.

Attacking in another front, the violin plays solo in the sonatas*, suites* and partitas*. Like any other instrumental music, the sonata for violin, or rather for two violins, derives directly from the vocal music, and more specifically from the CANZONA*. The canzona is distinguished by two main features:

1) It is a four/four time composition, with its typical rhythm: a minim followed by two crotchets, or its variant: a crotchet, two quavers, and two crotchets.

2) It is arranged in fugal* imitations*. These fugues* were basically assigned to two or more treble choirs, supported by one or more basso continuo* choirs. When these canzonas* were transformed into violin sonatas the fugue* was assigned to two violins which dialogued among themselves, supported by a basso continuo* (organ or harpsichord)

The first innstrumental pieces for violin were not for a violin solo but consisted in works for several parts, in what the Germans call, more specifically, *Triosonaten**, works to be played by two treble voices (two violins) in fugal* imitation* and a basso continuo*. We find thus sonatas in trio by Schmelzer*, Valentini*, Fux*, Kerll*, Couperin, Vitali*, Bononcini*, Cazzati*, Rossi*, Ucellini* and Marini*.

But being the organ and the harpsichord polyphonic* instruments in themselves, it soon became evident that the second treble voice of the fugue* could be assigned to their right hand, reducing the two violins to a single one. This origin of the solo violin sonata* has been clearly highlighted by Arnold Schering* in his Zur Gersighte der Solosonaten in der ersten Halfte des 17 Jahrhunderts (Rieman Festschift, pp 309 and following) Notwithstanding, the influence of the triosonata* will be immense, and we can see Leclair** and Gavinies** composing triosonatas* even at a time when the solo sonata was already in full swing. In fact triosonatas will remain alive until Viotti, the founder of the Romantic school.

These sonatas basically consit of compilations and collections of small musical pieces, divided (Italian: partita*) into small parts, generally the transcription of vocal and dance music, disposed in series, that are to be played in succession (French: de suite*), as a whole, in the same sitting. These sonatas are divided into two main groups: 1) Sonata da chiesa. 2) Sonata da camera. These two types of sonatas have something in common, the alternance of a certain number of contrasting movements, so that we may say that they differ more by the type of the pieces they contain, than by their general disposition.

1) The sonata da chiesa is more inspired by the stern polyphonic* style of church vocal music, and is divided into pieces of different tempos that contrast with each other like largo, allegro, adagio* and vivace, and where the use of the fugue* is almost constant.

2) The sonata da camera, on its side, consists mainly on a series of dances, in which the grave, solemn tone of the Sarabande alternates with the more gay of the Courantes and Giges. It will be this sonata da camera which will develop and progress more rapidly. The sonata da camera turns around three main, basic dances: Allemande, Courante and Sarabande, the essential triptych. To it, other dances can be added, such as the Menuet, Bourrée, Gaillard, Gigues and Pavane.

If we make a further effort we will arrive to the sonata for violin solo, without continuo*. Bach during his Köthen period (1717-1723) wrote three suites* and three sonatas* for violin solo which according to Spitta* are the first of their genre [1]. But Adolfo Salazar* [2] singles out those of other composers prior to Bach such as Baltzar*, Walther**, Biber**, Matteis*, Geminiani**, Pisendel**, and Telemann, the excellent characteristics of them all were gathered by Bach, and largely exceeded [3], reaching that greatest possible perfection, the search for which was the ultimate and central concern of Bach's method of composition. Nevertheless the extreme difficulties of these kind of sonatas make of them a rare specimen in the violin literature.

As for the suites* and partitas* we will only say that they are but two more names to designate the same instrumental genre: the sonata*. So sonata, suite and partita are equivalent. Suite is derived from the French "de

---

[1] Spitta, Philipp: J. S. Bach (2 vols., 1873-1880)

[2] Salazar, Adolfo: Juan Sebastián Bach: Alianza Música. Madrid 1985.

[3] Salazar, Adolfo Op cit. Pag 140: *de todas las cuales Bach recoge las características excelentes y a todas supera.*

suite": in succession, in a row; and partita*, from the Italian "partita": split into parts.

THE KING OF INSTRUMENTS

What has the violin to merit the title of King of instruments? Pierre Baillot, in his *L'Art du Violon, Nouvelle Méthode*, 1834, devotes to it a litany of most beautiful compliments: *"One can see in it richness together with simplicity, greatness with delicacy, strength with sweetness; it initiates you to joy and is sympathetic with sorrow. Depending on how you question it, its reply is vulgar or sublime. All melodies are its own...initiated by permanent embracings to all the secrets of the heart, it breaths and palpitates with it. Its tone is a second human voice...it is so varied that you can give it the pastoral character of the OBOE; the penetrating sweetness of the FLUTE; the noble and moving sound of the ENGLISH HORN; The bellicose shinning of the TRUMPET; The fantastic waves of the HARMONICA*; the successive vibrations of the HARP; the simultaneous vibrations of the PIANO; and, finally, the harmonious gravity of the ORGAN"* [1]

This book will deal, in a strict chronological date-of-birth order, with only the best teachers and performers. It is a very selective and snobbish catalogue. We include only superlative musicians. Good violinists are not admitted.

THE VIOLIN ERAS. The history of the violin has three main eras:

1) THE ANCIENT, from the beginnings to Viotti.

2) THE ROMANTIC, from Viotti to Lambert Massart.

3) THE MODERN-VIBRATO ERA, From Lambert Massart to our days.

In this little artisan book we will deal only with the most superlative performers and teachers, and with the violin schools they have created. We may say that until the arrival of the 20th century almost all violinists were, at the same time, great composers, but to do justice to all our performers in this

---

[1] I had selected this paragraph of Baillot right when I started writing this book, in 1990. Today, in May 2000, I realize with great satisfaction that Arthur Pougin*, in his Op. cit., had selected the same text, for the same purpose, in 1924.

very important angle of their careers, would occupy much more space in my work than it is in my power to allow. We will focus only in their performing and teaching aspects, so as to have a better understanding of the evolution of violin playing throughout history. Each violinist studied here will be like the pylon of a high tension electric line, and as the history unfolds we will link them together through their teachings as if through the lines they hold, going from one to the other directly, from teacher to pupil, who becomes the teacher of another pupil, and so on, until we can draw a graph of the different violin schools throughout history.

BOOK TWO:

1) THE ANCIENT ERA

GENERAL CONSIDERATIONS: JUGGLERS VERSUS MUSICALS

Being the violin a new comer into the courts it was only natural that musicians of all kinds would make experiments with it, to draw out all its possibilities. Thus, we find Carlo Farina* publishing in Dresden in 1627 his famous *Capriccio Stravagante*, with a passage played *con il legno*, i.e. striking the strings with the bow stick, and another sul ponticello* and imitating the sound of the cock, the barking of a dog, the flute and the soldier's fife. Biagio Marini* practises the tremolo* and the continuous triple stopping* in his *Capriccio in Modo di una Lira*, and produces remarkable hearing illusions in his *"Echo" Sonata* for Three Violins*, while he makes two violins play a four part piece in his *Capriccio per Suonar con Due Violini Quattro Parti* Op.8 (1626). Matthias Kelz*, in his *Primitiae Musicales* (1658) and *Epidigma Harmoniae Novae* ventures into audacious virtuosity with sudden leaps from the low B to the high G. It is also Kelz who uses frequent double stops* and détaché* in separated strings in his *Passagio Capricioso* in 1669. And Thomas Baltzar* amazed his audience at Oxford in 1658 with his incredible command of the fingerboard. Jacob Walther**, in Germany, in his astonishing *Hortulus Coelicus*, published in Mainz in 1694, produces the most surprising descriptive effects, such as the angels dialogue with the cuckoo (*Scherzo d'Angelli con il Cucu*), the *Nightingale Vocalise*, hens cackling in *Galli e Galline*, carrying his eccentricity to the extreme of making two fiddlers play on the same violin. Biber**, on his side, creates a duality sensation by making happy timbre oppositions, with which, the violin, although it is one, gives the impression of being two. He then untunes his instrument (scordatura*) which instead of the usual g-d'-a'-e'', proceeding by intervals* of 5th, is tuned with the most varied combinations, such as: a-e-a-e // b-f sharp*-b-d // a flat*-d flat-g-d // d-f-b flat-d // c-f-a-c // with which he is able to play octaves*, wider chords* and intervals* with great accuracy.

On the other hand, there were the purists who were concerned only with its musical and expressive resources. Where-from two different and opposite schools:

1) The first did all sorts of pyrotechnics and wizardries with it, and we will call them "jugglers".

2) The second will be called "musicals". (There is a tendency to mistake jugglery with virtuosity. A juggler without musicality is not a virtuoso; a musical without jugglery, neither. So a virtuoso must have both qualities in a very high degree) The only exception, of which he deservedly boasted, was Fritz Kreisler**, who was so exceptionally musical that he needed not to be a juggler, nor to have a great technique, his musicality being more that enough to compensate for his lack of technique. He was the most singular fiddler in history, unique like the Spanish red wine Vega Sicilia.

NON-EXISTENCE AND REJECTION OF THE VIBRATO

A most important characteristic of violin playing in that era was that the continuous vibrato didn't exist. In those days the vibrato was considered as an ornament like the trill* which was to be executed when expressly written in the score on certain conspicuous notes, the continuous vibrato being rejected and ignored.

THE ANCIENT VIOLINISTS

We will present them in a strict chronological order according to their dates of birth. The first indisputable superlative violinist was:

1632 LULLY, JEAN BAPTISTE (b Florence; d. Paris 1687) Musical. French composer, dancer, guitarist, violinist and instrumentalist of Italian birth. He was the founder of the French Ancient school, which will go from him to Viotti.

He was brought from Florence to France at the behest of Mlle. de Montpensier* who wished to practise her Italian. He remained in her household until he was 20, becoming an accomplished guitarist, dancer and violinist. "*Never*" reported the Mercure* Galant in 1687 "*did any man carry so far the art of playing the violin*" His presence at the court of Montpensier* in the Tuileries* gave him the opportunity to meet and hear the best musicians in France. He studied the violin with his compatriot Lazzarini, compositeur de la musique instrumental du roi. After the defeat of the Frondists*, Mlle. de Montpensier* was exiled to her chateau of St Fergeau for her active involvement with the insurgents. But by then Lully had aroused the attention of young Louis XIV as dancer and mime. He requested and received release from her service, returning to Paris in December 1652. On February 1653 the 20-year-old Lully and the 14-year-old Sun King* danced in the same ballet. In that year he was appointed Compositeur de la Musique Instrumental du Roi after the death of Lazzarini.

In 1655 he was commissioned to conduct the "Petits violons" (known also as Petite Bande) which under his discipline soon surpassed its parent orchestra "La Grande Bande" (Les 24 Violons du Roi)

By 1662 he had been appointed "maître de chapelle* de la musique de la famille royale" and a few days later he married the daughter of Michel Lambert*, Madeleine, in Saint Eustache*.[1] The document of his marriage was signed by the most important personalities of the time, not least Colbert* and his wife, and Louis XIV and his Queen Marie-Thérèse of Austria; it is quite a symbol of his burgeoning power at court.

In 1672 the king gave the privilege to *"nostre cher et bien aimé Jean-Baptiste Lully"* (our dear and beloved J. B. Lully) of the sole right to establish an Académie Royale de Musique* (Paris Opera) forbidding performances, without Lully's written permission. Lully's control over music in France was almost absolute, with the power of the throne behind him.

In 1681 Lully achieved his greatest personal triumph when he was appointed Secrétaire du Roi.

---

[1] The second church in importance of Paris (1532-1637). It is here that Mozart's mother is interred. Note worthy are its rose window over the main entrance door in heavenly blue colours, and its singing choir, one of the best in the world. They all sing sight reading any score put before them. Berlioz sang with them to cover his most urgent needs when he had just arrived in Paris, with a ridiculous paternal pension, to study medicine. Berlioz tell us that when he went for the first entry examination, he was asked what song he had prepared to sing, to what he replied: "give me any score and I will sing it for you" Note worthy, as well, is one of the most typical restaurants in Paris, opened 24 hours, with excellent oysters, sea-food, *soupe à l'oignon* and *crêpes suzettes*, just opposite to the main door: *Au Pied de Cochon*. During the 50s and the 60s it was quite in fashion among the *"chic"* people of the City of Light* to mingle with the working classes of a celebrated market, Les Halles, after a night on the town, all in evening dresses, in a splendorous show off of equalitarian, democratic, and brotherly affability, not lacking some affected paternalism, and great doses of sheer vanity, ending, always invariably at dawn, by having a succulent hot *soupe à l'oignon* precisely in this restaurant which was within the market, at 6 rue Coquillière (lane of the shell fish). The site of Les Halles is now occupied by the Centre Pompidou.

At the time of his death Lully had already been enshrined in the French Parnassus and was considered to be the most representative French composer.

In 1687 at the church of Les Feuillants he was conducting an orchestra of more than 150 musicians in a performance of his Te Deum celebrating the King's recovery from an operation. In the heat of the moment he hit his toe with the sharp point of the cane with which he was beating time. An abscess developed and gangrene spread rapidly because he stubbornly refused to allow his physician to remove the toe. Although in the greatest physical distress, he put his financial affairs in order and made his peace with God before dying on the morning of the 22 march 1687. Lully died the possessor of a great personal fortune estimated by Radet to have been 800,000 livres. He owned five houses in Paris. Man of a great vivacity, dancer and choreographer, composer, impresario, business man, courtier, doted with an endless ambition, Lully has reigned with an absolute power over the music of his time, and has marked it with his impulsive genius, and his organisational feelings. The orchestrations, dances, and the kind of overture he had created will be found again in Handel, Telemann and J. S. Bach. Saint-Saëns, writing about Charpentier, says: *"Lully has been an authentic curse for the French school; after having supplanted Perrin* and Cambert* who had to exiled themselves to England, he reigned with unshared power during his long carrier, allowing not a single place near him, and if Marc-Antoine Charpentier could worm his way under his shadow, was because he was his son-in-law and protégé"*. (Au Courant de la Vie. Paris 1914)

Lully's writing for strings is extremely conservative when compared with his Italian contemporaries. The wide leaps, multiple stops* and rapid arpeggios* found in the Italian music as early as Biagio Marini* are alien to his style. Technique and virtuosity were for Lully less important than rhythmic accuracy and finesse in performance.

To end this article we will borrow the words of Bollioud de Mermet* in his, *De la Corruption du Goust dans la Musique Françoise*, Académie des Beaux Arts de Lyon, 1746:

> *"Lulli, que nous proposons hardiment pour le modéle*
> *de la Musique théâtrale, nous a fait goûter dans ses*
> *Ouvrages les charmes séduisants de l'Harmonie. Le beau*
> *tour de ses chants, la noblesse, la force de son expression,*
> *sa manière aisée & naturelle de moduller, le caractère de*

ses symphonies, la mélodie de ses récitatifs, les graces naïves de ses Ariettes & la belle ordonnance de ses Choeurs, lui attireront à jamais le titre de l'Orphée de notre siècle.

Tout plaît dans sa musique, tout charme, tout intéresse. La nature s'y exprime naïvement: l'Art s'y cache habilement. Il y régne, je ne sçais quel air de décence & de dignité peu commun au théatre. Tout y paroît si aisé, si coulant, qu'on seroit tenté de ne lui tenir aucun compte de son travail: tant on est persuadé, par le naturel de ses compositions, qu'elles lui ont peu coûté...La poësie, dans ses mains, prend une nouvelle force; la noble simplicité de ses expressions encherit sur les images & sur les figures du Poëte.

<Lully that we propose boldly as "the" model of theatrical music, made us savour in his works the seducing charms of Harmony*. The beautiful effects of his singing, the noblesse and strength of his expression, his easy & natural modulations*, the character of his sinfonias*, the melody of his recitatives*, the gracefulness of his naïve Ariettas* (little aria*), & the beautiful harmony* of his choirs, have earned him for ever the title of "The Orpheus of our Century". Everything in his music is pleasant, everything charms, everything is of interest. Nature is naïvely expressed in it. Art is skilfully hidden there. There reigns an indescribable atmosphere of decency & and dignity not at all common in theatre. Everything seems so easy, so smooth, that one would be tempted not to value his work: so much one is persuaded, by the natural of his compositions, that they cost him nothing...(1) Poetry, in his hands, gains a new strength; the noble simplicity of his expressions adds more effect on the images & and on the characters of the poet.>

(1) This idea that works of Art must involve a painful hard work and a great deal of knowledge on the part of the artist is absolutely spread all over the world, and few would accept that something done with ease, without any painstaking, could be a master piece. To achieve a masterpiece, according to the general belief, must be as difficult and intricate as to design a petroleum offshore platform, for which you must have a petroleum engineer career. Consequently, to be an artists requires a long carrier in Fine Arts, and his masterpieces must, of necessity, be painstaking.

Here we are confronted with the great argument on modern art, and I will not let the opportunity go by, without saying a few words on it. It is so fascinating!

Simply because, for example, in painting, abstract canvasses do not involve, apparently, hard work or any particular skill, they are not works of art. (Rubbish!, they would say; even a monkey could paint them, if you give it a brush!) Consequently, Picasso, was despised at the beginning, for he painted without effort cubic forms that involved not any hard work, and their fury grew bigger at the total abstraction of painters like Pollock, Kline, Zobel or Rueda, to name a few.

In sculpture it was the same, in particular with assembled sculptures, (that incorporates typewriters, rusty horseshoes, toilets, boilers, etc.) which infuriated them.

Mozart, has never been accepted in his full value due to his extreme easiness to compose. *I write music as pigs piss*, he used to say. And, of course, abstract, atonal music, is despised as a monstrous mixture of disgusting noises. (Or not noises at all, I mean absolute silence, like in the *Requiem por la Libertad Imaginada* (1971) of the Spanish composer Cristobal Halffter, where for some 15 seconds the first violins "play" their part, passing their bows above the strings, but without touching them, in silence, under the careful guidance and meticulous gestures of the conductor [to no avail], to the great scandal of the audience, at the premier in Madrid.)

Modern art has accomplished all its goals, viz.
1)   -"épater le bourgeois", (to shock vividly the middle classes).
2)   -to get rid of all formalisms of the past.
3)   -and to make Art without a previous carrier.

Of course this "loose" art invites to countless "fakes", if I may say so, but at the same time, it becomes more valuable, with such free means, to produce a masterpiece. One goes for the other.

Of Lully I have recorded in "C-1" the orchestral suite of Amadis de Gaula with his characteristic dotted rhythm.

1644 BIBER, HEINRICH IGNAZ FRANZ (b Wartenberg, nr Reichenberg [now Czech Republic]; d. Salzburg 1704) German composer and violinist. Juggler." C-2"

The most outstanding violinist of the 17th century and a first rank composer, little is known about him. He might have studied with the famous Viennese violinist Johann Schmelzer*. After having spent some time in Styria in the service of Prince von Eggenberg he entered the service of the court of Prince-Bishop Karl, Count Liechtenstein-Kastelkorn of Olomouc. In 1670 he left without permission of his patron, who became very angry. This is showed in a letter to Johann Schmelzer* in Vienna to discuss the hiring of new personnel. Liechtenstein-Kastelkorn wrote: "Biber, the fellow who slipped away, played the violin, bass and viola da gamba; he also composed tolerably well". *Played the violin* was said with a certain cynicism, for the violin at the time was not very much appreciated. Nevertheless, Jakob Stainer*, the great Tyrolean violin maker, in a letter to the Olomouc court discussing the sale of some instruments, had spoken of "the formidable virtuoso Herr Biber".

In 1670 he became a member of the Kapelle* at the Salzburg court. His marriage in Salzburg took place on May 1672. By 1677 his duties were extended to include the training of the cathedral's choirboys; in 1679 he was promoted to Vice-Kapellmeister and in 1684 he became Kapellmeister* and dean of the choirboys' training school. In 1690 Emperor Leopold I raised him to the rank of nobility, a most extraordinary case for a musician, that at the time were considered as mere servants.

He used all kind of scordaturas*, particularly in his *Mystery sonatas*, and the *Harmonia artificiosa-airosa*, his two most outstanding sets of musical pieces. These scordaturas allowed him to play intervals* of octave*, 10th and even 12th with great ease and perfect intonation. It is very significant that in the inscription of the Mystery sonatas to archbishop Max Gandloph (1674) he says:"...*you will find here my four-stringed lyre*..." as if he were ashamed even of uttering the word "violin", and he were wishing to introduce it with a more "*genteel*" name.

Biber was the first "great composer" to write music specifically for violin solo, for Lully was more interested, as we have seen, in violins as an orchestral mass.

I have recorded his Mystery sonatas in "C-02". Special attention must be paid to the interpreter, Reinhard Goebel*, splendid violinist, who has just remained at the threshold of this very selective compilation. He is the founder of the group Musica Antique Köln.

1650 WALTHER, JOHANN JAKOB (b. Witterda nr Erfurt; d. Mainz 1717) German composer and violinist. Juggler.

He spent his youth learning in Italy. In 1674 we find him in the service of the elector of Saxony at Dresden as "Primo violinista da camera". In 1681 he moved to Mainz where he was the clerk and Italian secretary at the electoral court, remaining there until his death.

The great rival of Biber, and with him, Walther was the most important and daring of the late 17th century violinists in Germany and Austria, and one of the few who could bear comparison with the most famous Italian players of the time. He cultivated virtuoso techniques involving the use of polyphony*, multiple stops* and very high positions*. Fetis* called him the

Paganini of his century. Whereas in using multiple stoppings Biber was interested chiefly in scordatura*, Walther emphatically rejected it, preferring instead the imitation [1] of other musical instruments and the sound of birds and other animals following the footsteps of Biagio Marini* and Johann Schmelzer* (Biber's teacher). His two works *Scherzi da Violino Solo* and *Hortulus Coelicus* represent the technical summit of the German violin played at that time, both in left and right hand technique. In his Scherzi da violino solo (1676) rapid runs reach the seventh position*, while the bow is used for groups of staccatos* and bounding arpeggios*. But he will push his virtuosity even further in his astonishing Hortulus Coelicus, published in Mainz in 1694, where an immense variety of "variations" go in search of the most unpredictable descriptive effects, such as hens cackling in a courtyard in Galli e Galline (Cocks and hens) Scherzo d'Angelli con il cucu (Angels playing games with the cuckoo) and "treble vocalising of the nightingale". There is not any available recording of this violinist in the market.

<u>1653 CORELLI, ARCANGELO, MARQUIS OF LANDENBURG</u> (b. Fusignano, midway Imola-Ravena; d. Rome 1713) <u>ERA FOUNDER</u>. Italian composer, teacher and violinist. Founder of the Ancient era, which will go from him to Viotti. Musical. "C-1 and 2."

Corelli exercised an unmatched influence during his lifetime and for a long, long time afterwards. This influence affected all aspects of music, style, form, instrumental technique, violin playing, conducting, etc, and was felt not only in Italy, but in the whole Europe, as well. The standards of discipline he imposed in all repects, conducting, teaching method and violin playing, were unusually strict for his time, and they paved the way for the development of violinistic progress in Europe.

Alessandro Scarlatti told Geminiani** that *"he was extremely struck with the manner in which Corelli played his concertos, and his nice management of his band, the uncommon accuracy of whose performance, gave the concertos an amazing effect; and that, even to the eye as well as the ear, Corelli regarded it as essential to the ensemble of a band, that their bows should all move exactly together, all up, or all down; so that at his rehearsals, which constantly preceded every public performance of his concertos, he would immediately stop the band if he discovered one irregular bow"* (Reported by Burney*. General History, vol. 2, pag. 443)

---

[1] Here imitation does not mean the same as the entry in the Encyclopaedia. It means that the violin is used to produce descriptive effects by "imitating" the sound of other instruments or animals, the singing of birds or other sounds.

The Corellis were a family of prosperous landowners, one of the most illustrious families of Fusignano. Corelli received his first lessons from a priest in Faenza, continued his studies at Lugo, and went to Bologna in 1666. This city, which boasted one of the largest church in Christendom in the basilica of S. Petronio, was the home of a flourishing school of composers, the most salient figures being Cazzatti*, Colonna*, Perti, G. B. Vitali* and Torelli**. According to Padre Martini* he took here violin lessons first from Giovanni Benvenuti and later from Leonardo Brugnoli, both pupils of Ercole Gaibara, the doyen of the Bolognese violinists. Burney*, on his side, cited B. G. Laurenti* as his teacher. In 1670, at the age of 17, Corelli was admitted to the Accademia Filarmonica of Bologna. In 1675 we found Corelli in Rome, where he will become soon one of its foremost violinist. In the Eternal City*, where ex-Queen Christine of Sweden, converted to Catholicism, had a real court where musicians where kings, Corelli accumulated the successes of virtuoso, conductor and composer. In 1682 he was appointed chapel* master of the church of Saint Louis des Français, where he published his first 12 sonate a tre (two violins and continuo* ("triosonata*" German). In 1687 he conducted a memorable concert in the Queen's palace with 150 musicians. So far protected by cardinal Pamfili, he went, two years later, under the patronage of another Prince of the church*, cardinal Pietro Ottoboni, nephew of Pope Alexander VIII, who will lodge him till his death. In 1706 Corelli was admitted, with Pasquini and Alessandro Scarlatti, to the Arcadian Academy, receiving the name of Arcomelo Erimanteo.

Corelli's glory suffered no eclipse until 1708, crucial year for him, when he met Handel (one of whose oratorios he conducted) and Alessandro Scarlatti. But it was in Naples where he faced a humiliating failure reported by Burney*:

"At the time Corelli enjoyed the highest reputation, his fame having reached the court of Naples, and excited a desire in the King to hear him perform; he was invited, by order of his Majesty, to that capital. Corelli, with some reluctance, was at length prevailed on to accept the invitation; but, lest he should not be well accompanied, he took with him his own second violin and violoncello (players). At Naples he found Alessandro Scarlatti, and several other masters, who entreated him to play some of his concertos before the King; this he for some time declined, on account of his own band not being with him, and there was no time, he said, for rehearsal. At length, however, he consented; and in great fear performed the first of his concertos. His astonishment was very great to find that the Neapolitan band executed his concertos almost as accurately at sight, as his own band, after repeated rehearsals, when they had almost got them by heart. "Si

suona, (says he to Matteo, his second violin) a Napoli". [They really perform well at Naples]. After this, being again admitted into his Majesty's presence, and desired to perform one of his sonatas, the King found one of the adagios* so long and dry, that being tired, he quitted the room, to the great mortification of Corelli. Afterwards he was desired to lead [1] in the performance of a masque composed by (Alessandro) Scarlatti, which was to be executed before the King; this he undertook, but from Scarlatti's little knowledge of the violin, the part was somewhat awkward and difficult: in one place it went up to F; and when they came to that passage, Corelli failed, and was unable to execute it; but he was astonished beyond measure to hear Petrillo, the Neapolitan leader*, and the other violinists, perform that which had buffled his skill. A song succeeded this in C minor, which Corelli led off in C major; "Ricomminciamo", said Scarlatti, good-naturedly. Still Corelli persisted in the major key*, till Scarlatti was obliged to call out to him, and set him right. So mortified was poor Corelli with this disgrace, and the general bad figure he imagined he had made at Naples, that he stole back to Rome in silence.(General History of Music. Vole 2. P. 439.)

Being extremely sensitive and lacking any fighting spirit, he soon renounced to appear again in public, devoting his efforts to composition.

Hawkins's* description of Corelli as "remarkable for the mildness of his temper and the modesty of his deportment" sums up the impression of his contemporaries, who found those qualities amazing for such a wealthy and famous man. The style of his playing was learned, elegant and pathetic.

The number and eminence of his pupils make Corelli the most outstanding and influential teacher of his century: Italians like Valentini*, Carbonelli, Castrucci*, Gasparini*, Geminiani**, Somis**, Locatelli**, Bonporti*, Mascitti*, and Mossi*; the Frenchman Anet*, the Spaniard Herrando*, the German Stört and the English Edgcumber.

The eminence of Corelli's teaching powers was vigorously stated by Giardini**, who told Burney* that: "*Tartini formed all his scholars on the solos of Corelli's Op. 5*" and that "*of any two pupils of equal age and disposition, if the one was to begin his studies by Corelli, and the other by Geminiani, or any other eminent master whatsoever, he is sure that the first would become the best performer.*" (Burney*: General History of Music. Vol. II. Book III. Chap. IX. Pag. 442)

---

[1] The leader in those days conducted from the desk of the principal violin.

Founder of the Italian school of violin, he founded also, together with Stradella* and Torelli** the concerto grosso*. Corelli's style of playing, perpetuated through his pupils to Viotti**, concentrated mainly on the expressive resources of the violin, counteracting against the prevailing jugglery at the time.

Corelli is buried in the Pantheon of Rome, very near the tomb of Raphael, and a statue was erected at the Vatican with the inscription, CORELLI PRINCEPS MUSICORUM.

The violin as a polyphonic* instrument was born with Corelli and will reach its paramount zenith in the monumental work of J. S. Bach, in the sonatas* and partitas* for unaccompanied violin.

When he reached 40-years of age Corelli bought himself a Stradivarius, the Harrison of 1693, which is now owned by Kyung Wha Chung, and previously by Giardini**. (Chung has given it away very recently to the America's Shrine to Music Museum, The University of South Dakota, 414 East Clark Street, Vermillion, SD 57069, USA, E-mail: smm@usd.edu, and plays now on a Guarneri del Gesu of 1735)

I cannot quit this article without mentioning Arthur Pougin*: "…*It is him (Corelli), finally, who with his talent, his works, and teachings, has founded the first true violin school, which is the origin and the propagator of all the others, so much so, that as a symbol, we may say that Corelli is the father of all violinists, passed, present and future.*[1]

I have recorded a most beautiful concerto grosso* in "C-1" and in the"C-2" his sonata La Folia, in arr of F. David**, played by Enescu**. It is remarkable the incredible spirituality and musicality of Enescu. It is a heavenly version. In Folía all the different bowstrokes in their musical context are displayed systematically. In thanks for a dedication, the Palatinate Elector Philippe-Guillaume honoured him posthumously as Marquis of Landenburg.

1658 TORELLI, GIUSEPPE (b Verona - d Bologna c1708) Italian composer and violinist. Musical "C-1 and 2"

Burney* is particularly unjust and cruel with him: "*Though G. Torelli was an eminent performer on the violin, and a voluminous composer for that instrument, during the latter end of the last century, his productions for*

---

[1] Arthur Pougin*: Le violon, les violonistes et la musique de violon du XVI au XVII siècle. Paris 1924

that instrument are now so superannuated, as almost to cease to be music; for having little original melody, and no uncommon stock of harmony* or modulation*, there is nothing left to make amends for the want of novelty and elegance... [1] (Quite to contrary Torelli's music is very elegant, and his Pastorale per il Santissimo Natale is simply sublime.)

Born in Verona's parish Sta. Maria in Chiavica, he was the son of Stefano and Anna (Boninsegna) Torelli. They were nine brothers and sisters of whom Torelli was the sixth. the youngest, Felice, became famous as a painter. It was him who published the last work of Torelli, his Op. 8. posthumously in 1709, *Concerti grossi con una pastorale per il santissimo natale*, considered his best, and the very first concertos for violin solo. Stefano Torelli was a health inspector for the local customs office who supported his family with ease.

We know little of his beginnings except that he might have studied with Massaroti in Verona. Between 1681 and 1684 he served in the cathedral of Imola, where Padre Martini* lists him as Giuseppe Torelli Veronese Compositore Maestro di Capella* del Duomo d'Imola.

In 1684 he went to Bologna and was admitted as suonatore di violino of the Academia Filarmonica. At the same time he studied composition with Perti with whom he made a good friendship. From 1686 to 1696 he was member of the orchestra of the Basilica San Petronio, first as viola (violetta) player, then as violinist. His frequent absences to give concerts in other cities such as Modena and Parma were noted with displeasure in the records. In 1696 San Petronio orchestra was disbanded because of economic reasons and Torelli left Bologna to seek employment elsewhere in company of the castrato* Pistocchi*. They went to Berlin in May 1697 to perform for the Electress Charlotte Sophie: both subsequently dedicated works to her, Pistocchi his pastorale *Il Narciso* and Torelli his Op. 6. In 1698 both moved to Ansbach where Torelli became maestro di concerto (Konzertmeister*) for the Margrave of Brandenburg and Pistocchi* maestro di cappella (Kapellmeister*). They remained there until the end of 1699, during which time Torelli conducted the orchestra for a rappresentazione dramatica by Pistocchi: *Pazzia d'Amore e dell'Interesse.*

By December 1699 both were in Vienna where Torelli premiered his oratorio *Adam auss dem irrdischen Paradiess verstossen*. Pistocchi wrote that the piece was "pretty as spring, skilfully written". During this period Torelli made serious efforts to obtain recognition for Perti by performing

---

[1] Op. Cit. Book III. Chap. IX. Pag. 436.

some of his cantatas that had been dedicated to the Emperor in 1688: Cantate morale e spirituali Op 1. Their manuscript had been lost, but Torelli located them, amid much court intrigue, and had the satisfaction to obtain for Perti a gold medallion of Leopold I.

By March 1700 Torelli was tired of Vienna and wrote of returning to Italy. He wanted to make a pilgrimage to Loretto, and was desirous of drinking the waters at S Marino "having been so advised by the doctors here because of my cursed hypochondria and melancholy, which torments me greatly, tough I have the look of a prince"

By 1701 he returned as violinist to the newly reformed orchestra of S. Petronio Capella* Musicale, directed by Perti, where he had exceptional treatment due to his friendship with Perti, and also to the fact that he was at the peak of his fame. Torelli died on the 8th of February 1709.

Torelli was well known for his virtuosity both in and outside Italy. In the style of Corelli, he started emphasising one of the two violins of the concertino* in the concerto grosso*, and in his op 6 he requests that sections marked "solo" be played on a single violin; this Op 6 (concerti musicali, dedicated to the Electress of Brandenburg) contains possibly the first solo violin concertos* in the 17th century literature, and we can talk of Torelli as the true creator of the concerto for violin solo, while he shares with Corelli and Stradella* the paternity of the concerto grosso*.

In "C-1" we have the concerto a quatro Op 8-6 con una pastorale per il Santo Natale, and in "C-2" the sonata Op 5-5.

His main pupils were Girolamo Nicolo Laurenti*, Francesco Manfredini** and Pisendel**.

1678 VIVALDI, ANTONIO LUCIO. Italian composer, conductor and violinist. (b Venice - d Vienna 1741) Juggler + musical = virtuoso. "C-1-3".

The most original and influential Italian composer of his generation, he laid the foundations for the mature Baroque concerto. His contributions to musical style, violin technique and the practice of orchestration were substantial.

Vivaldi's father Giovanni Battista, a baker's son, was born in Brescia about 1655. He moved with his widowed mother in 1666 to Venice, where for a while he continued his father's trade before becoming a professional violinist in early adulthood. Antonio was the eldest of six children born to his union with Camilla Calicchio, a tailor's daughter, whom he married in June 1676.

On 23 April 1685 Giovanni Battista was engaged as violinist at St. Mark under the surname of Rossi. Since Antonio had also the sobriquet of "il prete rosso" we may conclude that red hair was a family characteristic.

Ever since his birth Antonio suffered an ailment, "stretezza di petto", as he described it, which has been identified as asthma. Intended to be a priest, he was tonsured when he was 15 and trained for the priesthood by the Fathers of S. Geminiano and of S. Giovanni in Oleo, while continuing to live with his family, profiting from his dispensation for health reasons. He continued to study the violin with his father, for whom he occasionally deputised at S. Mark.

Soon after his ordination on 1703 he ceased for good to say mass adducing his chronicle ailment. In September 1703 Vivaldi obtained his first official post, becoming maestro di violino at the Pio Ospedale Della Pieta in Venice, where he had to teach, direct an orchestra, which soon acquired reputation all over Europe, and compose. To these tasks, already hard for a man incessantly complaining of his bad health, he added in 1713 those of impresario. His fame spread all over Europe, acquiring an unprecedented international glory in music history. All the celebrities of the time passing near Venice went to hear the famous violinist and composer. The governors renewed his post annually until 1709, when a majority voted against retaining him, probably in the interest of economy.

In April 1718 Vivaldi took his recently composed opera *Armide al Campo d'Egitto* to Mantua where he stayed until 1720 as maestro di capella* to the Governor of Mantua, Prince Philip of Hessen-Darmstadt, a music lover. Having briefly returned to Venice, Vivaldi was soon off to the City of the Seven Hills*, where he was invited twice to play before the pope. It was around this time that Vivaldi's association with the contralto Anna Giraud must have began. Daughter of a wigmaker of French origin she became his singing pupil. Between 1724 and 1747 she appeared regularly on the operatic stage, especially in Venice. Being a loyal member of his entourage, it was widely believed that she was his mistress, despite his constant denials.

Between 1733-5 Vivaldi travelled widely visiting Vienna and Prague, and premiering his operas in smaller mainland centres like Verona, Ancona, Reggio and Ferrara.

In August 1735 he was reinstated at the Pieta in Venice as maestro di capella*. The governors now wished to take a firmer line on his travelling, and his renewed absences probably contributed to his failure to gain reappointment in 1738.

Between 1737-39 Vivaldi made frequent journeys to Ferrara, to stage operas of his own. His last, mysterious, journey in 1740 was to Vienna, probably on instigation from Anna Giraud who was to sing an opera in Graz. Vivaldi died in a house owned by the widow of a Viennese saddler in great poverty.

Vivaldi was so unconventional, both as a musician and as a man, that he was bound to elicit much adverse comment in his lifetime; his greed for money knew no limits, and his vanity was notorious.

Vivaldi was praised more readily by his contemporaries as a violinist than as a composer. He was an accomplished juggler, with notorious predilection for extremely high positions*, cadenza*-like passages and multiple stopping*.

Uffenbach* reported his ending the accompaniment to an operatic aria* with "a fantasy which really terrified me, for such has not been nor can ever be played; he came with his fingers within a mere grass-stalk's breadth of the bridge, so that the bow had no room, and this on all four strings with imitations* and at incredible speed" which vividly captures his virtuoso show off capabilities. (New Grove Dictionary)

Venice gossip was his vanity, his excessive preoccupation with money and his hidden love affairs with the contralto, Anna Giraud. All this served as publicity for his music, and explains his sudden decline and death in misery when he committed the imprudence to leave Italy, to escape from so many scandals. He died in Vienna lonely and impoverished.

He composed concertos for violin solo and sonatas. His sonatas are specifically recommended by Baillot** to his pupils.

In "C-1" we have his sonata Op 2-2 played by Heifetz, and in "C-3" the winter and the storm at the sea from the Four Seasons, played by I Musici with Agostini, the last and definitive version (for good, in all senses) of this very difficult piece of music, due to the fact that it has been so much abused that it has become almost vulgar, and it is extremely difficult to give it new breath, like Bthvn's 5th symphony.

<u>1684 MANFREDINI, FRANCESCO</u> (b Pistoia - d id 1762) Italian composer and violinist. Musical. "C-3".

The most prestigious pupil of Torelli and Perti in Bologna, his inclusion in this list is because he ended the definitive construction of the concerto grosso*.

The son of a trombonist, he studied music in Bologna from his childhood, violin with Torelli, and composition with Perti. At an unknown date he joined the S. Petronio orchestra, where he played with Torelli. After the disbanding of the orchestra in 1696 he moved to Ferrara in 1700, becoming first violin* at the church of the Holy Spirit. In 1704, having heard that the S. Petronio orchestra was reconstituted under the direction of Perti, he returned to Bologna to re-enter it. At the same time he became a member of the Accademia Filarmonica and started his first compositions, a set of 12 sonate di camera entitled concertini.

In 1711 he entered the service of Prince Antoine I of Monaco as maestro di capella*, to whom he dedicated his op 3 concerti. In 1727 Manfredini returned to Pistoia to take up the post of maestro di capella* at S. Philip cathedral, where he remained till his death.

I have selected in "C-3" a concerto grosso* that resembles Torelli even in the title. Most sweet and spiritual, it has what I describe as "submarine peace". It submerges you into the depths of the sea where one can enjoy an absolute peace.

<u>1685 HANDEL, BACH, AND D. SCARLATTI.</u> A date to remember. What a remarkable coincidence! Handel and Bach are super first rank composers for violin, and must enter here, but being well known, and since they are not superlative violinists, we do not indulge in their biographies.

<u>1685 HANDEL, GEORG FREDERIC</u> (b Halle, full Halle an der Saale, along River Saale, 35 Km N of Leipzig; d. London 1759)

His sonatas were specifically recommended by Baillot** to his pupils, so I have recorded in "C-16" two sonatas and a pasacaglia by him, played by Heifetz**.

<u>1685 BACH, JOHAN SEBASTIAN</u> (b. Eisenach, at the confluence of Rivers Nesse and Hörsel, 50 Km W of Erfurt, Saxe - d. Leipzig 1750) One cannot speak of music without mentioning, necessarily, Bach, who represents the

ultimate culmination of all the music that preceded him, and the basis and foundation of all the upcoming one. He was, as Bthvn called him, "des unterblichen Gottes der Harmonie" The immortal god of harmony*. (Letter to Breitkopf und Härtel April 22, 1801) And that is so indeed. Everything in Bach is paramount, summit, ultimate perfection, culmination.

The summit of the keyboard literature is the Well Tempered Clavier.

The fugue* reaches its culmination in the Art of the Fugue, or as the New Grove Dictionary rightly says, "fugue reached the apogee of its formal development, technical sophistication and expressive power in Bach". (Voice Fugue)

The concerto grosso* climbs to its zenith in the Brandenburg Concerts.

The supreme MUSICAL composition is Saint Matheus' Passion, because of its colossal dimensions, its grandiose chorales, enchanting recitativos, and the beauty of its music at large. Because it allows each instrument to show off its abilities by designing for them small parts in concertante* relation with the orchestra, and for the enormous drama of the whole work, impregnated with an intense "stilo rappresentativo*" that, here again, reaches its ultimate perfection.

In the violin it could not be less. The paramount zenith of the violin's polyphony* is represented by the monumental sonatas* and partitas* for unaccompanied violin. I have recorded some of them played by Perlman, taking good care that they include what other artists play, to be able to compare him with the others, particularly with Joachim in his bourrée, partita* 1 BWV 1002, and his adagio* of the sonata 1 BWV 1001, and with Sarasate in the prelude of the partita 3 BWV 1006. In Sarasate's prelude we can appreciate a great superficiality, preoccupied more in playing at a high speed than with musicality, but jugglery was what the public demanded from him at the time, and that was what he gave them plenty.

Bach is recorded in "C-3, 16 and 19." See index.

1686 SOMIS, GIOVANNI BATTISTA (b Turin - d id 1763) Italian composer and violinist. Musical.

The most prestigious pupil of Corelli, he passed his teachings to Pugnani, who, in his turn, passed them to Viotti, linking directly the Ancient era to the Romantic one. He belonged to a family of illustrious musicians that for generations served in the ducal chapel* of Turin. He was taught violin first by his father Francesco, and as early as 1696 he was admitted as violinist in the ducal orchestra. In 1703 the Duke of Savoy sent him to the Eternal City*, where he studied four years with Corelli. He then went to Venice to study with Vivaldi for a while.

In 1707 he returned to the Turin chapel* of which he was made first violin* and leader* until his death. Somis travelled little. In 1731 he went to Paris to play at the Concert spirituel*. The Mercure* praised the *ultimate perfection, brilliance and precision of his play.* (April 1733, p 816)

His violin technique was not as brilliant and demanding as that of Tartini, being rather in the humble, simple style of Corelli. He was famed by possessing the most majestic bow stroke in Europe. Hubert Le Blanc* [1], a fiery defender of the basse viol against the attacks of new instruments (violin) that threatened the family of the viol, succumbed under the magic bow of Somis, writing these beautiful words:

Somis parut sur les rangs, il étala le majestueux du plus beau coup d'archet de l'Europe. Il franchit la borne où l'on se brise, surmonta l'ecueil où l'on échoue, en un mot vint à bout du grand oeuvre sur le violon: "la tenue d'une ronde". Un seul tiré d'archet dura au point que le souvenir en fait perdre haleine quand on y pense, et parut semblable à un cordage de soie tendu qui, pour ne pas ennuyer dans la nudité de son uni, est entouré des festons d'argent, de filigranes d'or entremèlés de diamants, de rubis, de grenates, et surtout de perles; on les voyoit sortir du bout de ses doigts. La musique descendit de l'Olympe, et, ayant son dessein, mit dans l'esprit aux dames de faire accueil à Somis. Il fut reçut tantôt ches les unes, tantôt chez les autres, et ce, dans l'espace d'un mois sans que durant ce temps il fut mention de porter un jugement, ou que l'on songeât seulement à lui opposer un rival".

<Somis entered the competition, and displayed the majesty of the most beautiful bow stroke in Europe. He jumped over the boundaries beyond which nobody can go, he surmounted the hurdle against which others crash, in a word, he was victorious over the greatest challenge of the violin, i.e. to hold a semibreve. A single bow direction (bow up or bow down) lasted so long, that its mere remembrance makes you loose breath, and it seemed similar to a tightened silk stringing that in order not to bore with the nudity of its single coloured uniformity, would adorn itself with festoons of silver, and gold felegree, intermingled with diamonds, rubies, garnets, and, above all, pearls;

---

[1] Defense de la basse de viole contre les entreprises du violon et le prétentions du violoncel. Hubert Le Blanc, "docteur en droit" Amsterdam, Chez Pierre Mortier, 1740.

they were actually visible emerging from the tips of his fingers. His music came down from Olympus, and accomplishing its purpose, it introduced itself even in the minds of the fashionable ladies (who never applaud) who gave Somis a warm clap. He was acclaimed here and there, and all this for a whole month, without even daring to judge him, nor even dream to oppose him a rival>.

Somis most famous pupils include his nephew Chabran* and Felice Giardini**. His fame spread all over Europe thanks to his foreign pupils like Guillemain*, Leclair** and Guignon* (Leclair's most fearful rival, he was the only one to overshadow him), all of them residing in Paris. But his most prestigious pupil was Gaetano Pugnani**, teacher of Viotti, founder of the romantic era of the violin.

Somis was just another victim of the 50s. See Van Loo*, Madame* in the encyclopaedia. (Somis's daughter Anna-Maria-Cristina Somis, married to Carle Van Loo*, Madame Vanloo*, was one of the best singers and teachers in Europe, very active in Paris. Her main pupil was Marie Fel*.)

1687 GEMINIANI AND PISENDEL

1687 GEMINIANI, FRANCESCO (b Lucca; d Dublin, Ireland 1762) Italian composer, teacher, theoretician and violinist. Musical. "C-3".

Overshadowed by Corelli, and his contemporaries Vivaldi and Handel, he was, nevertheless, one of the greatest violinists of his day. He studied the violin first with his father, violinist in the Signoria Theatre; he moved then to Milan to study with Carlo Ambrosio Lonati, commonly called Il Gobbo (the hunchback); later he went to Rome to study with Corelli, and to Naples with Alessandro Scarlatti (composition). No doubt his most influential teacher was Corelli, his idol and his model. He succeeded to his father's place in the Signoria Theatre orchestra in Lucca. In 1711 he moved to Naples as leader* of the opera orchestra, not a good job for him, as Burney* reports: "...He was soon discovered to be so wild and unsteady a timist, that instead of regulating and conducting the band, he threw it into confusion; as none of the performers were able to follow him in his *tempo rubato*, and other unexpected accelerations and relaxations of measure" (General History. Vol. 2. Pag. 991.)

In 1714 he left Italy for London. His success there as a virtuoso was instantaneous, and he had the good fortune to be supported by several of the most powerful patrons, the countess of Orrey, the duchess of Burlington, the earl of Essex, his pupil and good friend, the duchess of Marlborough, and last, but not least, Baron Kilmansegge, chamberlain to King George I. Besides his musical career he devoted to dealing with works of art, and in one occasion, if not more, he was imprisoned for debts, although the influence of his patron, the earl of Essex, rescued him. On the recommendation of Baron Kilmansegge to the king as an "exquisite performer" Geminiani played at the court accompanied by Handel. After 1730 he made lengthy visits to Ireland, giving a staggering concert in the Concert Room in Spring Gardens with phenomenal success (Flood*). Geminiani travelled a good deal with frequent excursions to Italy, France and the Netherlands.

His music, theories and style of playing were based upon the theory of "good taste" consisting in expressing with strength and delicacy the intention of the composer, and in using ornamentations within the limits of good judgement:

It is really difficult for us today to imagine that in that time all musicians, fiddlers, pianists, flautist, singers, etc. would deviate from the score and introduce, in the middle of their performance, at the slightest opportunity, ornamentations and improvisations of their own fancy, in a cadenza* like manner, to show off their virtuoso abilities, as well as their refined good taste. These kind of deviations from what was actually written were made by everybody: Gavinies** used them profusely, being much celebrated for them, (see 1728 Gavinies) and also Liszt, who in order to produce greater effect on the audience, accelerated or relaxed the tempo in such serious and uniform passages as the adagio* of Bthvn's Moonshine sonata (1); or play in octaves*, what was written for single notes in Bthvn's piano concerto Nbr. 5, "The Emperor" (2); or Giardini**, who improvised some ornamentations on the representation of an opera by Jomelli*, only to receive a violent slap on the face from the author, who was near him (3); or such a grotesque clown as Franz Clement*, dedicatee of Bthvn's violin concerto, who during his premier, broke the continuity of the piece by playing some improvisations with the violin upside down (4). We will analyse them one by one:

1) (Liszt distorts the adagio* of the "Moonshine" sonata) Berlioz describes thus his interpretation: *There is a work by Bthvn known as the sonata in C sharp* minor*; the adagio* is one of those poems that cannot be described with words; its means of execution are very simple: the left hand plays softly wide accords* of a solemn, gloomy character, the duration of which allow the vibrations of the piano to fade away gradually over each of them; on the treble, the first fingers of the right hand arpegiate* an accompaniment design, with tempo "ostinato"*, the form of*

which remains almost the same from the first to the last bar, while the other fingers play a sort of lament, melodic efflorescence, melancholic harmony*. Once, seven or eight years ago, M. Liszt, playing this adagio* in a small gathering where I was present, had the idea, as it was fashionable at the time, to distort it for the sake of effect, to get the applause of an elegant audience: instead of those solemn scales* in the lows, and of those agonising voices in the treble, instead of that severe, strict uniformity of rhythm and movement that I just spoke of, he introduced the tremolos*, accelerated and relaxed the tempo, disturbing in this manner with passionate accents the calm of melancholy, and making thunders roar in a sky without clouds, which cast only a shadow upon sunrise. I suffered cruelly, more even than when I heard our poor singers embellishing upon the monologue of Der Freischütz [1]; because to this suffering was added the sorrow of seeing an artist fall into the extravagances into which normally fall only the mediocre. But, what to do? M. Liszt was then like those children who without complaining get on their feet by themselves after falling down, wanting it to go unnoticed, and getting offended if you try to give them a hand (Berlioz. Beethoven. Espasa Calpe. Colección Austral. N. 992. pag. 120)

2) (Liszt plays the "Emperor" in octaves*). It is insinuated, with hidden venom, in Sir Charles Hallé's* Autobiography. Commenting on his own performance of Bthvn's piano concerto 5, "Emperor", at the Paris Conservatoire in 1844, he says: "…after the performance a much respected member of the orchestra, Urhan, the principal viola, apostrophised me with: "why do you change Bthvn?" I had not really changed anything in the text, but, misled by the example of Liszt [2], I used then, for the sake of effect, to play some passages in octaves* instead of in single notes…"

3) (Giardini** improvises near Jomelli*) What happened to Giardini is related by Burney* in his General History of Music, Vol. II. Book IV, Chapt. 6, pag. 896, and transcribed by me in the article, 1716, Giardini.

4) (Clement*, the clown) Clement has been immortalised by Bthvn's inscription of his violin concerto, with this fond pun in Italian: *Concerto par clemenza pur Clement, primo Violino e Direttore al Theatro a Viena dal L. van Bthvn.,1806.* He had also the honour of premiering it on the 23rd of December of 1806 in Vienna, when he was 26-year-old, under Bthvn's baton. The performance was an absolute failure, due to several things: a) Bthvn's excessive revolutionary novelty was not understood easily, and so, for example, the Wienner Theaterzeitung of January 8, 1807 says that "endless repetitions of commonplace phrases are fatiguing…One fears that if Bthvn pursues his present path, he and the public will come to no good end…Any listener who was not completely conversant with the rules and difficulties of the art, would find virtually nothing to enjoy, for it contained an excess of unconnected ideas and a continual uproar of certain instruments which leaves the listener with nothing other than an unpleasant sensation of exhaustion". b)

---

[1] Yet another example of deviation from the score.
[2] An easy and utterly bad taste excuse of his own fault. Very childish !

the concert room was not sufficiently heated and everybody suffered from excessive cold, which did not predisposed them in favour of the concert. c) but most of all because Bthvn, typically, handed over the manuscript only in the very last minute, the day before, and there was no room for such luxuries as a rehearsal, having to be played at sight. To top it all, Clement had the audacity to brake the continuity of the work, and between movements 1 and 2 played a set of variations of his own, with his violin upside down and on a single string. This sort of sacrilegious profanation of such a masterpiece, seems to us just unbelievable, but it was of common use at the time. A musician of the calibre of Czerny*, praised warmly Clement's feat, while the Allgemeine musikalische Zeitung* was less concerned with the values of the work itself than to applaud the "elegance and grace" of the performer. Nevertheless, Bthvn did not seem to have liked it particularly, for when he sent the manuscript to the publisher he changed his dedication to his friend Stephan von Breuning. The premiere's failure was a sort of damnation, a curse, and although it was subsequently played by such superlative artists as Tomasini* (Berlin 1812), Baillot** (Paris 1828) and Vieuxtemps** (Vienna 1834) the concert did not quite catch the general approval until the legendary concert of prodigy child Joachim**, aged 12, in London, under Mendelssohn's baton in 1844, winning, overnight, a permanent place in the international repertoire. (38 years in oblivion).

To acquire "good taste" Geminiani recommends the performer who is ambitious to inspire his audience to be first inspired himself; which he cannot fail to be if he chooses a work of genius, if he makes himself thoroughly acquainted with all its beauties, and if while his imagination is warm and glowing he pours the same exalted spirit into his own performance.

<Here comes the eternal debate on who is first, the composer or the performer, the hen or the egg: without the score the performer cannot render his version of the composition, and a score which is not performed is not music, but a mere music project, as much detailed as that of the architect, but not music, a lifeless fossil, just as the architect design is not a building.

On the other hand, an egg cannot not exist without the hen that had laid it, and a hen would not exist without the egg from which it has hatched out.

Until the arrival of the gramophone the general belief was that the interpreter should submit totally to the composer, i.e. to the score, in the believe that the composer's intentions, as laid down in the score, are the best and only ones. But after the arrival of the gramophone, and particularly of the computer, the fallacy of this assertion has become evident. It used to be said that nobody can play Mozart better than Mozart himself, and since it could not be proved, it was just gospel. But with the phonograph we have realized that composers are not "necessarily" the best interpreters of their own works. And it is so, simply because they are not supreme interpreters. There are conductors and interpreters of all kinds that play their works better than them, and it is only natural.

As for the absolute fidelity to the score, none can be better that the computer. But its interpretations are empty, mechanical, frigid, and above all, inhuman. Behind any musical interpretation there must lie, always, a human being, with a soul, who expresses himself with his own emotions, human errors, or achievements, with his art, which is entirely personal to the interpreter. It is true that every composer has a style of his own, a characteristic way to write music, as unmistakable as the style of a painter, or of any other artist. But this style allows for a wide margin of interpretation and here comes the inalienable liberty of the interpreter. The only composer who does not admit any margin of interpretation, whatsoever, is J. S. Bach. As Arnold Schering* says, to play Bach is *an unattainable endeavour, for Bach is essentially awe inspiring and impenetrable, and therefore difficult to translate in music, for he lies somewhere in the middle of his two, far away, opposite extremes: his inflexible, almost mechanical tempo (strict time) on the one side, and on the other, his extreme, passionate "stilo rappresentativo*". To follow the strict time without falling into a frigid, heartless measurement, and to reflect passions and feelings without the exuberant excesses of Romanticism, here lies the secret.* (see Schering in the encyclopaedia). Some examples would help us to understand my viewpoint:

-Mozart has often been accused, unjustly, of being too superficial, too gallant, too joyous and lively, too childish, and in no other work has this been more reiterated than in his symphony 40, K 550, composed in Vienna in 1788 when he was 32-years-old, in his full maturity: It is so widely known, and it has been so much repeated, that it is almost a bore. Its most abused part is the beginning of movement 1, reproduced in tunes for alarm clocks, mobile phones, toys, etc. But Mozart was not always childish and merry, he was also mature, deep, sad and unhappy. If we exploit this less frequent side of his nature we would be amazed with the results we will obtain: a piece of music filled with sorrow. The reason for its wide misinterpretation is twofold: a) The general and most common gallant, happy Mozart seems to ask for a merry interpretation. b) Mozart himself made a misleading notation in the score by setting it Molto Allegro. It is sufficient to slow down the tempo to Allegro Moderato, and to let ourselves become immersed in the sorrow of its g minor* mode* to make it appear in an absolute new, deep, mature version.

-If Bach would resuscitate and see the DVD of Glenn Gould* playing his Goldberg variations, he would die again out of sheer wonder and amazement.

-And continuing with the metaphor, if Chopin, the great Chopin, one of the undisputable gods of the piano, would resucitate and hear MICHELANGELI play his own scherzo Op. 31, he would shoot himself on the spot.

-Horowitz plays Rachmaninof much better than him, and I would also dare say that his Mozart sonatas could not be matched by the composer, simply because they are unbeatable.

-Perlman plays Sarasate better than him, and Szigeti plays Hubay (his teacher) better than him.

-The syncopated rhythm passage immediately after the Arietta* in Bthvn piano sonata n 32, Op 111, marked l'istesso tempo, in demisemiquavers and hemidemisemiquavers, is played by Backhaus, to put an example, in a classical, so to speak, recital style, whereas Julius Katchen* plays it with an amazing jazz rhythm that makes you think it is being played by the very Fats Waller* himself. Who is better? No one, each in his style, very different indeed from each other.

-Bthvn relates this anecdote about one of his piano sonatas played by a good friend of him, Maria Bigot, née Kiene, a formidable amateur pianist. After having heard her play the sonata in question Bthvn said: "*this is not quite the character I have meant for this piece, but even if it is not mine, it is better than mine*". (this citation, attributed to Fetis, can be found in Ludwig van Beethoven. Jean y Brigitte Massin. Turner. Spanish translation, 1987. p. 175. note 2) This is the pure essence of music: that it must needs be interpreted to be fully fulfilled (the fact that it is written in the score is not sufficient, it has to be played into sounds, ephemeral sounds, by interpreters) and interpreters there are many who surpass the composers, be it because of a better skill to conduct or to play the instrument, or because they transmit to the audience feelings, passions, emotions, in a word: ART, that keep their mind beguiled. Good interpreters do what the London Morning Chronicle said of Viotti: *astonish the hearer, awake emotions, give soul to the sound and lead the passion captive.*

One needs not be very daring to affirm that Wagner and Furtwängler have interpreted the ninth Symphony of Bthvn better that he might have done. And it is not a question of whether Bthvn was deaf or not;

it is simply that I consider both to be better interpreters of this work than Btnvn himself.

And Burney*, commenting on the magic powers of Giardini** says that he was astonished when he heard him "*playing some of my own music, and making it better than I intended, or had imagined it in the warm moments of conception*" (G. History. Vol. 2. Pag 896)

I cannot quit this too long incidental discourse without the words of Liszt: *"the virtuoso is not a bricklayer who, hammer in hand, painfully and consciously cuts the stone according to the design of an architect...he creates just as the composer created"* (or even better, I add. Do not forget that Liszt was, at the same time, a supreme composer and performer.) >

Geminiani was a great theorist writing among others, *Rules for Playing in a True Taste, A Treatise of Good Taste in the Art of Music, The Art of Playing on the Violin*, and the *Guida Armonica* ("Guida Armonica o Dizionario Armonico, being a guide to harmony* and modulation*, in which are exhibited the various combinations of sounds, progressions of harmony, ligature, and cadences, real and deceptive) illustrated by numerous pieces of music. By far the most influential and famous of his treatises was The Art of Playing on the Violin, published in London in 1740 considered by Burney* "a very useful work in its day; the shifts and examples of different difficulties, and uses of the bow, being infinitely superior to those in any other book of the kind, or indeed oral instruction, which the nation could boast". (General History, p. 992) Here he repudiates the imitation [1] which was so much in vogue since the Hortulus Coelicus of Walther, to try to extract the peculiar characteristics of the violin. "If we were to imitate anything" -he says- "it would be the human voice, but not the less harmonious, or even shocking, cuckoo and drum sounds."

He then describes the way to hold the violin, and the bow, with special care on the possibility to increase or decrease the sound with the help of the bow pressure on the strings. He divides the finger board into seven positions*, which he calls "orders", that must be practised without the bow, only with the left hand until the student is perfectly in command of them; the glissando*, and other ornaments like the mordente*, détaché* or staccato*, and the use of Piano* and Forte* are also discussed in full.

---

[1] Here imitation does not mean the same as the entry on the encyclopaedia, but to use the violin to produce descriptive effects by imitating other sounds, such as those of animals, birds, other instruments, etc.

Another ornament specially studied is the "close trembling" which amounts to the vibrato of our days, which he favours greatly, recommending to use it as often as possible. He describes it as a "close trembling" or "tremolo*". He says: "To perform it, you must press the finger strongly upon the string of the instrument, and move the wrist in and out slowly and equally; when it is long, swelling the sound by degrees, drawing the bow nearer to the bridge, and ending it very strong, it may express majesty, dignity, etc. But making it shorter, lower and softer, it may denote affliction, fear, etc. and when it is made on short notes, it only contributes to make their sound more agreeable and for this reason it should be made use of as often as possible" (What differentiates the ancient from the modern vibrato is that the first is, as Geminiani says, "a close shake or tremolo*" whereas the latter is wide and intense reaching almost a whole tone like the trill*, being more sensuous than the ancient, which resembles an electric quaver.) As a rule, he recommends a moderate use of these ornaments, and to follow the script as closely as possible. For Geminiani the ultimate goal of music is to express feelings, passions. Good music is that which conveys a meaning to the soul of the audience, a bad music is that which lacks feelings, and has no expression. Geminiani's ideas found, nevertheless, little favour.

Geminiani's style of playing had both extremes, very brilliant and exuberant, with "overwhelmingly technical audacities" (Burney*) and tender and pathetic in the style of Corelli.

He was one of the most celebrated virtuosi and teachers of his days, having renowned pupils such as Michael-Christian Festing*, famous for his numerous compositions for violin (12 concertos) and Matthew Dubourg*.

We have recorded a concerto grosso* Op 2-5 "C-3" and a sonata for vl. and p. in A Major "C-3".

1687 PISENDEL, JOHANN GEORG (Cadolzburg, 20 Km W of Nürnberg; d. Dresden 1755) German violinist and composer.

His father was Kantor* of Cadolzburg. Pisendel was admitted at the court's chapel* in Ansbach as chorister and remained there for six years, during which he had the best teachers of the time: Pistocchi* for singing and Torelli* for violin. He met Bach at Weimar, and travelled to Leipzig where he directed the Collegium Musicus and the opera orchestra deputising their director, Hoffman, who had gone for a concert tour in 1710. From 1712 he was employed as a violinist at the Dresden court orchestra, becoming Konzertmeister* in 1730. During this period he made frequent journeys to

France, Berlin, Rome, Naples and Venice, where he developed a good friendship with Vivaldi.

Pisendel was the most renowned violinist of his time in Germany, obtaining the praises of Hasse* and Quantz**, who particularly complimented him for his adagios*.

He was honoured with the dedication of works by leading composers such as Albinoni, Telemann and his friend Vivaldi. He was also a superb orchestra conductor, with a special precision and sense of tempo, which characterised him. His rehearsals were famous for the meticulousness of his remarks on tempo, precise bowing and musical expression.

Among his pupils we should mention J. G. Graun* (also pupil of Tartini)

1690 VERACINI, FRANCESCO MARIA. (b Firenze - d id 1768) Juggler + musical = virtuoso. Italian composer and violinist, he was one of the best of his time, with loud and clear tone, and just intonation.

Member of a family of reputed musicians, both his grandfather and his uncle Antonio Veracini*, were among the greatest violinists in Florence. Ironically, his father was one of the few Veracinis who was not a musician, not even an amateur. He was a druggist instead.

Francesco's first teacher was his uncle Antonio, studying later counterpoint* and composition with G. M. Casini* and his assistant Francesco Feroci*. A prodigy, he started playing with his uncle Antonio. In 1711 he went to Venice where he was soloist at the Christmas masses of St. Mark. He made frequent journeys to London and Düsseldorf, performing with great success. In 1717 he travelled to Dresden where he was made violin solo to the court by King August of Poland, who was at the same time Prince elector of Saxony. King August had bought a Stradivarius of 1715, the "King Augustus", which was played by his two most important first violins*: Veracini and Volumier*. Veracini had here a very high salary, and both musicians made of the Saxon orchestra of Dresden one of the most celebrated in Europe, which attracted the praises of Quantz**: "I never heard an orchestra better than that of Dresden under Volumier*".

In 1723 he returned to Florence and soon re-established his high reputation. Burney* says: *"Veracini and Tartini, his contemporary, were regarded as the greatest masters of their instrument that had ever appeared...but whatever resemblance there may have been in the* *professional skill of these two masters, it was impossible for any two men to be more dissimilar in disposition: Tartini was so humble and timid, that he was never happy but in obscurity; While Veracini was so foolishly vainglorious as frequently to boast that there were but one God, and One Veracini.*

Being at Lucca at the time of la Festa della Croce, which is celebrated every year on the 14 of September, when it is customary for the principal professors in Italy, vocal and instrumental, to meet, Veracini, entered his name for a solo concerto; but when he went into the choir, in order to take possession of the principal place, he found it already occupied by Padre Girolamo Laurenti* of Bologna; who not knowing him, as he (Veracini) had been some years in Poland, asked him where he was going? Veracini answered, to the place of first violin*. Laurenti then told him, that he had been always engaged to fill that post himself; but that if he wished to play a concerto, either at vespers, or during high mass, he should have a place assigned. Veracini, with great contempt and indignation, turned his back to him, and went to the lowest place in the orchestra. In the act or part of the service in which Laurenti performed his concerto, Veracini did not play a note, but listened with great attention. And being called upon, would not play a concerto, but desired the hoary old father would let him play a solo at the bottom of the choir, desiring Lanzetti, the violoncellist of Turin, to accompany him; when he played in such a manner as to extort an "e Viva!" (bravo) in the public church. And whenever he was about to make a close, he turned to Laurenti and called out: "cosi si suona per fare il primo violino" (this is how one should play to be first fiddle). Many silly stories of this kind are handed about Italy concerning the caprice and arrogance of this performer, who was usually qualified with the title "capo pazzo" (mad master).[1]

In 1733 he returned to London where he had a great musical activity, to the point that Burney* commented that "there was not concert now without a solo on the violin by Veracini" (General History. Vol. 2. Pag. 1003). He also saw and heard Veracini play at Hickford's room in 1745 (he was aged 55) where *he led the band at a benefit concert...in such a bold and masterly manner as I had never heard before.[2]* From 1755 on Veracini remained in Florence, where he was maestro di capella* of S. Pancracio and of S. Michele agl'Antinori.

---

[1] General History. Vol. 2. Chapter IX. pag 450
[2] Id. Vol. 2. Chapter IX. pag 451

The peculiarities of his performances, according to Burney*, were *his bow-hand, his shake (trill*), his learned arpeggios*, and a tone so loud and clear that it could be distinctly heard through the most numerous band of a church or theatre.*[3] All agreed that he was the first, or at least one of the first, violinist in Europe.

Another reliable statement on the style of playing of both Antonio* and Francesco Veracini is a most complimentary review of his teacher Casini*: "the heart, rather than cleverness, guided and accompanied the fingers and bow of these virtuosi"

Among his pupils stands out conspicuously Locatelli**.

As a person he was rather eccentric, sometimes bordering madness, with an arrogant independence, and an absolute originality. This personal originality was transferred also to his style of playing.

Veracini played on two famous violins by Stainer* reputed to be superior to those made by the luthiers* of Cremona and Brescia. Their absolute reign lasted more than 150 years after the first Stainer was made in 1638, until the greater volume obtainable from the Guarnerius, Amatis and Strads. met the demands of the new concert halls of the late 18th century. Veracini lost his two Stainers on a shipwreck in 1745. He humorously call them St. Peter and St Paul.

As we have said, during his stay at the court of King August of Poland he played on the Strad King Augustus of 1715.

1692 TARTINI, GIUSEPPE (Pirano, Istria; d. Padua 1770) Italian composer, teacher, theorist and violinist. Juggler + musical = virtuoso.

One of the main contributors to the virtuoso sonata and concerto, he made a style of his own, which spread all over Europe.

His parents destined him for a monastic career and sent him to study under clerics of Capodistria and Pirano. In 1708 he renounced the cloister and went to Padua to study letters. During his first years here, he led a life of debauchery, being a well known swordsman. He married in secret Elisabetta Premazore in 1710 which elicited the fury of her uncle the Bishop of Padua, cardinal Giorgio Cornado, who accused him of abduction. The cardinal formally charged him before the magistrate, and the police began to chase

---

[3] Id. Vol. 2. Chapter IX. pag 451

him. Tartini left his wife in Padua and run away to Rome in disguise. But finding no safety anywhere, he erred from city to city, until he took refuge in the monastery of the Friars Minor Conventual of Assisi. It is during this secret period of his life that all sort of speculations have been made about him. It is said that he was taught the violin by a Czech friar, and that he received the apparition of the devil, who suggested him the instrumental effects that he later used in his sonata "The devil's trill*". The story of this sonata, that has become legendary, is so romantic that we must reproduce it here in the very words of Tartini himself, as reported by Lalande*:

<One night (in 1713) I dreamt that I had a deal with the devil and that I took him into my service. Everything I fancied turned out well for me. My new servant anticipated all my wishes. I imagined I gave him my violin, to find out whether he would be able to play for me some beautiful tunes; but my astonishment was enormous when I heard a sonata so exceptionally beautiful, performed with such superiority and intelligence, that I had never imagined anything that could be comparable. I felt such a great surprise, delight and pleasure, that I lost my breath. Awakened by this violent sensation, I took immediately my violin in the hope to replay, at least partially, what I had heard; but it was in vain. I then composed a piece that is in fact the best I ever wrote, and I still call it the *Devil's Sonata*; but it is so much below the one that had moved me so deeply, that I had broken my violin and abandon music for ever, had I been deprived of the pleasures it (the dreamt sonata) gave me> [Lalande*: Voyage d'un Français en Italie. Paris, 1769.]

From 1714 to 1720 he frequented Assisi, Ancona and Venice, attending the circles of Corelli and Geminiani. In 1706 after having heard Veracini** play the violin, he decided to perfect his own technique in an absolute lonely exile. In 1721 he was appointed primo violino[1] e capo di concerto[2] at the Basilica of S. Anthony in Padua, with an extraordinary salary and the benefit to accept outside engagements, of which he made use very extensively, particularly in Prague where he stayed from 1723 to 1726 attached to the court of prince Kinsky, Chancellor of Bohemia.

Tartini's style was praised for its flexibility, dexterity, the magic of his bow, and above all, his just intonation. As a man he was extremely shy, but in good company he was brilliant and witty. We have a valuable testimony in an account that President de Brosses* wrote in a letter to M. de Maletest from Bologna on September 6, 1739 which shows him as an artist and as a man. (Tartini was 44, in his prime):

---

[1] Primo violino: first violin*

[2] Capo di concerto: see Konzertmeister* = Leader or first violin.

"...Au bout de vingt-cinq milles, nous revîmes Padoue et notre amis le marquis Soleni, qui nous renouvela ses politesses. Il fallut séjourner le 31 pour entendre Tartini, qui passe communement pour le premier violon d'Italie. Ce fut un temps fort bien employé. C'est tout ce que j'ai ouï de mieux, pour l'extrême netteté des sons, dont on ne perd pas le plus petit, et pour sa parfaite justesse. Son jeu est dans le genre de celui de Leclair, et n'a que peux de brillant; la justesse du toucher est son fort... mais il n'a pas son pareil pour le bon esprit. Ce garçon...est poli, complaisant, sans orgueil, et sans fantasie; il raisonne comme un ange..."

<After 25 miles we saw again Padua and our friend the marquis of Soleni, who renewed his politeness to us. We had to stay till the 31st to hear Tartini, who is commonly considered the first violin of Italy. The delay was well worth it. It was one of the best performance I ever heard as far as absolute neatness of sound is concerned, of which not a single one was lost, no matter how soft, and for the perfect intonation. His play is similar to Leclair's, and is little brilliant; perfect intonation is his forte... But he is unrivalled for his wit. This young-man is polite, pleasant, unassuming, and down-to-earth; he reasoned like an angel...>

A renowned English patron and amateur violinist at Rome, Mr. Wyseman*, told Burney* that he had heard him play and that "of all the players he ever remembered , his adagio* was the most *cantabile* (Italian: cantabile: singing) and divine: "Happy was the scholar," cried he, "who could catch any particle of his manner, which seemed a supernatural gift."

Quantz**, who heard him play in Prague (between 1723-26, that is, when he was 31-35 years old, in his prime) says: *Tartini is a violinist of the first rank; he produces very beautiful sounds. His fingers and his bow obey him equally well. He plays with ease the greatest difficulties. He performes with perfection trills* and even double trills with all fingers, and plays often in very high positions*. But his play has nothing of touching; his taste is not noble, and many a time is even contrary to good manners.*

Pougin*, who cites this remark, is utterly scandalised and tears his garment upon such blasphemy, accusing Quantz of being unjust. (op. cit. Pag 107) But it is not that simple. Quantz was not a fool; all on the contrary he was one of the very best connoisseurs of the violin we ever had in history, (see 1697 Quantz) and his opinions are of paramount value, Gospel, I should say. Is it compatible to play the violin with great perfection and yet not move the listener? Yes indeed!

The art of violin playing has three possible ways to approach the audience:

a) To astonish the listener with the dexterity and jugglery of the player.

b) To inspire an artistic admiration as for the neatness, justness of intonation, power of sound, expressiveness, colours, trills*, double stops*, bow strokes, etc.

c) To move the audience. This is a much more subtle conception of beauty, and in my submission, the culmination of art, the top of the pyramid, something that cannot be learnt, that is well inside the player, a divine talent with which he has been born: the supreme gift to transmit sublime artistic feelings to your listeners. This is quite a different thing than the two previous ones. Here the artist transmits emotions and feelings; the listener is transfigured like Jesus Christ, is raptured by the sounds he hears as if they would come from an angel, his soul leaves his earthly body to go in the presence of God, enjoying His divine sight as an advanced payment of what his after life in paradise will be, he is bowled over as if by the most powerful of narcotics, in a word, he is artistically moved.

Bthvn used to move his listeners to tears whenever he improvised at the piano. The Spanish tenor Fleta* moves. The Italian tenor Pertile and the Irish tenor McCormack* move. Liszt moved Berlioz to tears when he played the adagio* of Bthvn's moonlight sonata in the house of Legouvé* (see in the book of Paganini). Massart and Kreisler move.

A very simple method to detect whether the artist is moving you is to verify if you have got the goosepimples. If you have them you are being deeply touched. To summarize:
Violinists who astonish: Paganini, Wieniawski, Ernst.
Violinists who inspire admiration: Heifetz, Beriot, Joachim.
Violinists who move: Viotti, Massart, Kreisler, Enescu, Hassid, Wieniawski, Paganini. (*Never did I hear a singer who touched me as deeply as an adagio* by Paganini. Friederick Wieck*).

To move the audience was, as we will see, the main purpose of Massart, the founder of the Modern school. His motto was: *A violinist should not astonish his listeners with his technique; but he should move. A tear, a smile are better that astonishment.* This motto was followed to the letter by Fritz Kreisler**.

In 1727 Tartini founded in Padua his Academia for violin instruction, called School of Nations where he taught violin, counterpoint* and harmony*, which attracted students from all Europe. Burney*, citing the words of the rich English music patron at Rome Mr. Wyseman*, says that "he formed the greatest school that the musical world had ever known".

Tartini's theoretical system is expounded in his works *Trattato delle Appoggiature*, where he deals with ornaments, in his famous *Letter to Maddalena Lombardini**, addressed to one of his pupils explaining his principles of violin playing and ornaments, and above all in his *Trattato di Musica Secondo la Vera Scienza dell'Armonia*. The harmonic system contained here, highly controversial, in particular on the part of Padre Martini*, is based, among others, on the theory of the difference tone (terzo tono) using the co-ordination of harmonic laws with those of mathematics and physics, as well as with Platonic theories, to explain the generation of harmony*.

He started as juggler accumulating extreme difficulties in his sonatas and concertos, but changed his style in 1744 to graceful and expressive. So juggler + musical = virtuoso. It is not known who taught him the violin. Most of his teachings were pirated by Leopold Mozart for his Violinschule.

He was the teacher of numerous prominent violinists: Italians such as, Stratico*; Alberghi*; Lorenzo Carminati [Cherminati, Burney*], a Venetian who settled in Lyons (France) in 1750 as violin professor (he played at the Concert spirituel* 7 times in 1753 concertos of his composition *"which pleased very much the audience, his style being considered highly just and learned)*; Guastarobba* (teacher of Campagnoli); Domenico Ferrari*, considered one of his best pupils, who settled in Paris; Filippo Manfredini, the friend and devoted companion of Boccherini, whom he followed in his journeys; Angelo Morigi*, who became music director to the court of the duke of Parma; Giuseppe Signoretti, who settled in Paris, like Domenico Ferrari*; Mme. Maddalena Sirmen*, née Lombardini*; Mosel father; Domenico Dall'oglio*; Pugnani**, Bini**, and Nardini**. French such as Pagin* (most famous in Paris, through his appearances at the Concert spirituel*, where he was considered the ultimate perfection in violin technique), Lahoussaye*, Touchemoulins*, Tremais*. Germans such as Johann Gottlieb Naumann*, who besides being a superb composer, was also a distinguished violinist; Johann Gottliebe Graun* and Antonin Kammel*.

Tartini is buried in the church of Santa Catarina in Padua, near the altar of Santa Dolorata.

I have recorded:

- The devil's trill*: Mutter vl "C-04"
- Variations on a theme by Corelli: Neveu vl "C-17"

He played on the Strad Tartini; Lipinski, owned also by Joachim, of 1715.

1695 LOCATELLI, PIETRO ANTONIO (b. Bergamo; d. Amsterdam 1764) Italian composer and violinist. Juggler.

Little is known about his family, except that being owners of a private grave they must have had some good standing. After working some time as violinist at the orchestra of Bergamo's main church, Sta. Maria Maggiore, he asked and received permission to go to Rome to improve his technique, where he might have studied with Giuseppe Valentini*.

From 1717 to 1723 he played at the basilica of S. Lorenzo in Damaso. He then moved to Mantua where prince Philippe of Hesse-Darmstadt named him virtuoso da camera. His fame spread rapidly and he played in Venice, the court of Bavaria (1727) and in Berlin before the king of Prussia. In 1729 he moved to Amsterdam, where he would stay for ever, devoting his efforts to teaching.

He had a traditional reputation as the Paganini of the 18th century using broken chords*, difficult positions* changes and very high positions for the epoch. Great composer, as well, he published 12 violin concertos with their cadenzas* and 24 caprices for unaccompanied violin in L'Arte del violino which vividly called the attention of Paganini who composed himself another set of capriccios. (Locatelli's capriccios are published on CD)

Locatelli's play had the two extremes: powerful and brilliant, often playing with such fury as to wear out many violins per year, on the one hand, and on the other, with great sweetness and delicacy in the cantabile passages. He played like a devil astonishing his listeners with deliberate scratchy tone and left hand pyrotechnics.

He was teacher of great reputation, his most famous pupil being Jean Marie Leclair**.

I have recorded the sonata Op 8-10 for vl, cello and continuo* in "C-4", and an introduzione Op 4-6 in "C-4".

1697 LECLAIR, JEAN MARIE (b Lyon - d Paris 1764) French dancer, composer and violinist. Musical.

Considered to be the founder of the French violin school. Although Lully was the founder of the Ancient violin era in France, with an enormous influence that went over France's frontiers to reach the whole Europe, Leclair is considered, more specifically, the founder of the French violin school. We might say that Lully concentrated more in violins as an instrumental mass, whereas Leclair focuses in the violin as a solo instrument. In the end of this article we will see how De Rozoi, a good friend of him, says that *Lully needed a Leclair to be perfect*.

His first teachers are unknown, but it is most probable that his father, Antoine Leclair, maker of passementerie, who was also a cellist and a dancer, might have taught him the violin and the art of dancing. When he was 19 he already commanded the violin and the dance. In this he followed a French tradition that put together ballet dancing with violin playing. (Remember Lully) In 1722 he went to Turin to study with Somis.

In 1723 he went to Paris and came under the patronage of one of the most rich persons in France, Joseph Bonier. It was here that he published his first set of violin sonatas Op 1, remarkable for their absolute originality. He was the first who, without imitating anyone, created pure Beauty, something new. He had things to say and he said them with unique personality. In 1728 he went to Paris where he was vigorously applauded at the Concert spirituel* playing his own sonatas and concertos.

In 1733 Louis XV named him Ordinaire de la Musique du Roi*. Here he was confronted with the rivalry of another violinist who grew so much as to counter-balance his reputation: Pierre Guignon*, celebrated by the Mercure* as having played with "absolute perfection". Marpurg* relates us an anecdote of them, which vividly describes their rivalry within the Chapelle*-Musique du Roy, happened in 1736: after a short period of time in the Music du Roi none of them was willing to demean himself so far as to become second violin to the other, being both equally zealous to maintain their pre-eminence, as per the saying: "second place is the first looser". So they agreed in changing the first violin* post every month, and Guignon, a smart gambler, left Leclair to be the first. But when the month elapsed, and Leclair had to degrade himself to second violin, according to their agreement, he could not stand it, and preferred instead to abandon and retire from the Music du Roi, which allowed Guignon* to retained the monopoly of first violin*.

Soon after this incident, in 1736, Leclair travelled to London and Holland (1737-43), where he played with Locatelli, of whom he learnt a great deal, something that became evident at his return to Paris. As Fontenai said (Dictionnaire des Artistes, Notice sur Leclair) his knowledge in composition did but encourage him to learn more and more. It is to this end that he made a trip to Holland to meet Locatelli, and he profited a great deal of his wise advises. He was also received at the court of Anne D'Orange, princess of Holland, who honoured him with the cross of the Nederlander Lion.

In 1743 he went to Parma to serve for two years the Spanish Infant Don Felipe, duke of Parma, son of the Spanish king Philippe V as first violin* and conductor of his orchestra. He fixed definitively his residence in Paris shortly afterwards. In 1748 he entered the service of his former student, the duke of Gramont, as musical director of his orchestra in Puteaux, near Paris.

A difficult and gloomy character, of unstable humour, unsociable and misanthrope, he was neither kind nor happy, but his work is of the first magnitude. Leclair was a man of strong contrasts, great virtuoso and juggler, he did not indulge in the exuberant virtuoso show off of Locatelli, but he incorporated all the grace and freshness of the Italian music to the more stern, musical conception of the French tradition, reaching always a happy midway between both, that was very appreciated by his contemporaries. If we had to choose a single word to sum up the works and style of Leclair, it would be BALANCE.

In 1758 he bought a lonely house in the outskirts of Paris (La Courtille, at the end of faubourg du Temple) where he lived alone with no servants. His patron, the duke of Gramont, was very worried about his solitude, and had urged him several times to come to live in his house. Leclair did not accept his invitation, and the worries of the duke seemed to be a sort of premonition: early on the morning of the 23rd October 1764 a gardener found him assassinated at his house entrance, his body having been stabbed three times in the chest.

In the article devoted to him in the New Grove Dictionary, it is said that although his death was said to be shrouded in mystery, the evidence against his nephew was so clear, that the "only remaining mystery is that he was never brought to trial". Notwithstanding, Lionel de la Laurencie*, much more meticulous, is not in agreement.[1] After perusing all the papers of the coroner's inquest, he reached the conclusion that none of the suspects could be arrested due to lack of proofs. The finger of suspicion pointed first at the gardener, but despite some inconsistencies and gaps in his deposition, there were no substantial evidence against him, all the more since the possibility

---

[1] Lionel de la Laurencie*: l'École française du violon. Paris 1922.

of burglary was ruled out as the motive of the crime, having found in a nearby commode drawer four gold Louis of 24 livres each, and two and a half Louis in six francs pieces each.

As for the nephew, it is true that he was envious of his uncle, and even the lover of his separated wife, but having said to everybody that his uncle's death was just what he deserved, and that being such a miser, misanthrope and avaricious man, living in total solitude, like a wolf, he was almost requesting to end murdered, it did not seem logical that the assassin would comment publicly his rejoice over it.

Consequently the charges against them did not seem sufficient for their arrest, and the criminal case was filed and disposed of.

Leclair moved his listeners by the beauty of his tone. He was reputed by the justness, clearness and neatness of his play, as well as for his virtuosity. But contrary to Locatelli, he never indulged in the extremes of virtuosity; his play was elegant, charming and had high thoughts, keeping a balance between jugglery and musicality.

A most interesting account on what Leclair was as a man and as an artist is found in the article of a good friend of him, De Rozoi, in the Mercure* of November 1764. Its beauty compels me to transcribe it all:

> *"Leclair avoit dans les moeurs cette noble simplicité, caractère distinctive du génie. Il étoit sérieux et penseur, n'aimoit point le grand monde, il n'avoit ni cette modestie intéressée qui mendie des éloges, ni cet orgueil qui en rend indigne. Il étoit assez grand homme pour osser dire qu'il étoit content de ses ouvrages, et pour les retoucher s'il croyoit qu'un meilleur avis lui eût découvert des beautés qu'il n'avoit point saisies. L'Europe entière connoit ses sonates; et si la France a des Gaviniés** et des Caprons*, ce sont ses ouvrages qui les ont formés. Il débrouilla le premier l'art du violon, il en décomposa les difficultés et les beautés. Il manqua un Leclair à Lully; il est le créateur de cette exécution brillante qui distingue nos orchestres, et Rameau lui doit autant qu'à son propre génie. La surveille de sa mort il apportat à M. le duc de Gramont un morceau de musique plein de feu et d'enthousiasme. Il fallait le voir, a soixante-sept ans, exécuter avec une vigueur étonnante, communiquer à un orchestre tout son feu, et si près du jour fatal, goûter le plaisir d'être admiré, avec cette joie modeste et pure qui conviendroit si bien à un jeune homme qu'on loueroit pour la premièr fois."*

<Leclair had in his habits that noble simplicity, the distinctive characteristic of a man of genius. He was a serious and thinking man, and was not attracted by the fashionable society. He had neither that cynical modesty that is fishing for compliments, nor that arrogance that renders you unworthy of them. He was such a great man that he could afford to say, without vanity, that he was happy with his works on the one hand, and on the other, to correct them, if he thought that a better advise had revealed him beauties he had not thought of. The whole of Europe knows his sonatas; and if France has violinists like Gavinies** and Capron*, it is because they have been instructed by his works. He was the first to unravelled the art of violin playing, by individualising its difficulties and selecting its beauties. Lully** would have needed a Leclair to be perfect; he is the creator of that brilliant performances that make our orchestras tower among others, and Rameau is indebted to him as much as to his own genius. Two days before his death he brought to the duke of Gramont a piece of music full of fire and enthusiasm. You had to see him, at his sixty seven years of age, perform with an amazing vigour, and to transmit all this fire to his orchestra, and near his fatal day, to savour the pleasures of being admired, with that modest and pure joy which would be only proper of a young man being praised for the first time.>

Founder of the French school of violin he combined successfully the French style with the Italian tradition. Under a pedagogical point of view his sonatas are very demanding in technique, both for the left and right hands: for the left hand there are three and four-note chords*, all kind of double stops*, double trills* and tremolo* (its first appearance in France) It consisted in conspicuous ornaments for specifics notes, not a continuos vibrato as it is played today. For the right hand he wrote solid staccatos*, difficult articulations and difficult string crossings.

Leclair most renowned pupils were Petit*, D'Auvergne*, Saint-Georges*, Guillaume-Pierre Dupont* (who played often with Gavinies at the Concerts spirituels*), Hauteterre*, J. J. Rodolphe* and L'Abbé le Fils**.

De la Laurencie* (L'Ecole française de violon) names another one: Geoffroy, who followed in his master's footsteps with great speed. (Mercure* December 1764) Geoffroy entered the service of the duke of Gramont, the last protector of Leclair.

I have recorded in "C-2": Sonata for vl and p Op 9-3 by Oistrakh and the vl concerto Op 7-2 played by Franz Joseph Maier* who stands just in the threshold of our list. Co-founder of the Collegium Aureum, he is an excellent violinist. The concerto reminds us much the concerto grosso* we had selected by Manfredini, with that particular "submarine peace".

1697 QUANTZ, JOHANN JOACHIM (b. Oberscheden, nr Göttingen, Hanover – d. Potsdam 1773) PEDAGOGUE. German Flautist, and pedagogue.

Although Quantz is a flautist and a flute maker, his role as pedagogue of the violin is paramount. In his work Versuch einer Anweisung die Flöte Travesieren zu Spielen, Berlin 1752 (An Attempt to Make a Method to Learn How to Play the Transverse Flute) he devotes a whole section (section II, chapter XVII) to a deep analysis of violin playing and music interpretation, full of the most meticulous details and specifications. We will try here to give a concise account of them all.

Quantz reviews all the main factors contributing to a good performance, particularly the ornaments, chords*, pizzicato* and the use of mute. But the whole section turns around the bow stroke and its importance in the aesthetics of violin playing.

For Quantz, musical notes, by themselves, reduced to their simple rhythmic architecture, speak quite a different language than when we establish among them subtle links and intimate, penetrating, connections. It is through the bow stroke that the performer can give new life to the written notes, that combine in a thousand ways to bring alive the music on the stave*. With the innumerable different bow strokes at his disposal, the performer gives individuality to each note group, underlying the melodic line with ever changing accentuations and slurs*, that introduce light and shadow to the work, forming a moving kaleidoscope, incessantly renewed[1]. "It is the bow stroke -says Quantz- which is the most important on the violin...It is it that makes the violin sounds, good or bad; that makes notes come into life, that Piano* and Forte* are performed, that passions are released; that sadness is distinguished from gaiety, seriousness from joyfulness; the sublime from the vile; modesty from courage; ...it is the means to give true expression to music, and to vary a certain thought in different ways..."

1709 BENDA, FRANZ: SCHOOL FOUNDER (b Althenatka, Bohemia – Neuendorf, nr Potsdam 1786) German violinist and composer of Bohemian origin.

---

[1] When we will speak of Viotti, we will see that this was just his main characteristic as a performer. See 1755 Viotti.

The most outstanding of all violinists known to his days in Germany, he is considered to be the FOUNDER OF THE GERMAN SCHOOL.

It was in Prague that he had his first studies with a violinist, Bohemian as well: Koniesek. Belonging to a large, modest family of musicians, he entered as choir-boy at the church of St. Nicholas in Prague. His beautiful soprano voice was noticed soon, and he was invited to join the choir of the chapel* of the Elector of Saxe in Dresden. When an accident made him loose his voice he was dismissed. On his return to Prague he recovered it, this time as contralto and he entered the choir of the Jesuits* in 1723. Some time later, Benda started to tour around serving at the courts of several central European nobles. In 1726 he went to Vienna where he organised with Hoeckh, Weidner and Czarth a musical group with which he toured all Europe, ending in Warsaw, where he stood two years at the service of king Frederick August. When this monarch died he moved to Dresden where he met Quantz, who completed his musical studies. Quantz, who was at the service of prince Frederick, the future king Frederick the Great, sent him to the prince's residence at Rheinsberg. Comfortably established at the prince court, with no worries, Benda devoted to improve his violinistic talent, described as follows by Burney*: "*his style was neither that of Tartini, nor the one of Veracini; he had a style of his own, with great originality, which he had acquired from his deep studies of the great masters*". And Hiller*, a devoted admirer, praised the quality of his sound, *of the most beguiling beauty, the purest and most harmonious that one can imagine.*

Besides his two sons Karl Hermann and Friederich, and his brother Joseph, we should mention as his pupils Fodor*, Bodinus*, Leopold Abel*, Friederick Wilhelm Rust*, Veichtner*, Johann Wilhelm Hertel* and Karl Haack*. But the influence of Benda does not limit itself to his direct pupils; it extends to a whole school of brilliant violinists, what is called the Benda School.

THE BENDA SCHOOL OR THE GERMAN SCHOOL.

Making an exception on the general strict date of birth order, we are going to give here a flash of lightning of its main virtuosi, studying them all as a whole under a single article, ending with a global outline of the German school. We will consider them in strict chronological order:

-The two Cannabich, father and son (Christian –1731-and Carl -1771]
-1739 Dittersdorf
-1751 Haack
-The two Eck brothers (Friederich (1767) and Franz (1774)

-1774 Möser
-1789 Maurer.
-1789 Kayseder.
-1801 Kalliwoda.

1731 Cannabich, Christian. (Mannheim, Baden-Württemberg land, SW Germany, by the Rhine River at the mouth of the canalised River Neckar, halfway Mainz – Stuttgart; d. Frankfurt am Main, 35 Km NE of Mainz, upon River Main, Germany 1798) Member of a distinguished family of musicians at the courts of Munich and Mannheim. Violinist, composer and conductor. He was one of the most illustrious composers of the Mannheim school. Studied the violin with Stamitz** and harmony* with Jomelli* He was admitted to the Mannheim orchestra in 1744, becoming its director and conductor after the death of J. Stamitz. He went several times to Paris, where he was acclaimed as conductor and violin virtuoso at the Concert spirituel*. He made a good friendship with the Mozarts.

1739 Dittersdorf, Carl Ditters von: (Vienna – château de Rothlhotta, Bohemia, 1799) Austrian composer and violinist. His father had enough money to procure him a good education on the violin, French language and religion. He entered the renowned orchestra of Prince Sachsen-Hildburghausen in Vienna in 1751. He undertook a journey with Gluck to Bologna. He succeeded Michel Haydn as Kapellmeister* to the court of bishop Grosswardein in Hungary. He frequented Haydn and Mozart in Vienna. He has left a prolific number of works, instrumental, vocal and operatic, of which *Doctor und Apotheker* has survive to our days. He died in misery.

1751 Haack, Karl (Potsdam – id 1819) German violinist and composer. Direct pupil of Benda, joined the orch. of the prince of Prussia in Potsdam and in 1796 became leader* of the royal chamber ensemble. He was very appreciated in Berlin and Potsdam, perpetuating Benda's school through his pupils, mainly Möser* and Maurer*.

1767 Eck, Friederich J. (Schwetzingen, 10 Km W of Heidelberg, 20 Km SE of Mannheim – id 1838) Member of an important German family of musicians, he studied the violin from the age of seven with Danner. He entered the Mannheim orchestra. in 1778 as supernumerary, and moved with them to Munich. He served there also as director of music of the small court theatre, and in 1788 he was promoted to Konzertmeister*. He had a beautiful tone and the good taste of his performances made a great effect on the public.

1771 Cannabich, Carl (Mannheim, Baden-Württemberg land, SW Germany, by the Rhine River at the mouth of the canalised River Neckar, halfway Mainz-Stuttgart; d. Munich 1806) German composer and violinist, son of Christian. He first studied with his father, and later he learnt the violin with Friederich Eck. He served at the orch. of his father in Munich, and was promoted to Konzertmeister* in 1798. At the death of

72

his father in 1800 he replaced him as court music director in Munich, i.e. Kapellmeister*.

1774 Eck, Franz (Mannheim, Baden-Wurttemberg land, SW Germany, by the Rhine River at the mouth of the canalised River Neckar, halfway Mainz-Stuttgart; d. Strasbourg 1804) Violinist, brother of Friederich. He entered the Munich orch in 1789. In 1801 he made a virtuoso tour through Europe. In 1802 the young Spohr** became his pupil and both travelled around Germany, and to St. Petersburg. Here, Eck became famous and was appointed solo virtuoso to the court orch. In the words of Spohr he had a controlled and powerful tone, exceptional technique, rich in ornamentation and nuances, total command of his intonation, having always "irresistible charm" He developed madness in Russia and died in an asylum in Strasbourg.

1774 Möser, Karl (Berlin – id 1851) German composer and violinist. Pupil of his father and Karl Haack*, he played in Friederich Wilhelm II private chamber ensemble. He toured to London and met Rode and Viotti!!. The effect was so astounding (no doubt it was, Rode in his prime, and Viotti who never lost a bit of his talent, were the best violinists in history, after Paganini, of course) that he retired to perfect his technique. From 1807-11 he settled in S. Petersburg. Back in Berlin he was promoted to Konzertmeister* of the Hofkapelle*. He was a reputable conductor.

1789 Maurer, Ludwig (Potsdam – St. Petersburg 1878) German violinist and composer. He studied with Carl Haack*, Friederich the Great's Konzertmeister*, a direct pupil of Benda. He was admitted to the royal chapel* in 1803. He travelled through Germany, Russia, and Paris. Met Rode in Mitau, and Baillot in Moscow. He was director of the opera in Hanover from 1824 to 1832. He had a great command of the violin technique, and a surprising dexterity as virtuoso.

1801 Kalliwoda, Johann Wenzel (Prague – Karlsruhe, 60 Km W Stuttgart 1866) Bohemian violinist and composer. He entered the newly founded conservatory of Prague in 1811, and graduated with honours in 1816. He played at the orch. of the Stavovske Theatre under Weber. In 1822 he started touring Germany, Holland and Switzerland. In 1822 he entered the service of prince Karl Egon II in Donaueschingen. He elevated the musical life of the city and famous artists like Liszt, Thalberg, Robert and Clara Schumann* performed there. Later he had important posts in Cologne, Mannheim orchestra, Leipzig and Prague. He was a prolific composer with more than 240 Op. numbers.

The last figure in the Benda's school is Spohr, who has an article devoted to him. Spohr is a super-star that brights by itself, and must be considered apart.

We have had a quick glimpse of the major fiddlers of the German school, and have seen how Benda has been the head of a school of violinists, that for more than a century have maintained honourably the renown that their founder had obtained through his talent.

What is the importance of this school in the history of violin playing? Fetis*, in an article about music in Germany says: *"the violin school founded by Franz Benda has engendered first class violinists; if Eck*, Fränzel* [1], Maurer*, Möser*, Spohr and Bohrer are inferior to the great artists of the French and Italian schools, they are, nevertheless, men of a remarkable talent"* (Revue Musicale, 1821, t I, p. 361)

And Henri Blanchard*, in a substantial study entitled Psychology of the Violin, expressed himself as follows: *"Stamitz and Leopold Mozart, father of the author of Don Giovanni, contemporaries of Leclair and Gavinies, were the representatives of the German school, that has always been inferior to the Italian and French schools, despite the efforts of Andreas Romberg*, brother of the cellist, Mayseder* and Spohr**, one of the most salient man of learning of our time."*(Revue et Gazette musicale, 11 August 1839)

On his side, Arthur Pougin*, is not much more benevolent with the Germans, and in agreement with the two precedent writers, says: *"if the so called Benda's school has produced absolutely distinguished virtuosi like Eck*, Fränzl*(foot note 1), Cannabich, Stamitz**, Ditter von Dittersdorf*, and successively Möser*, Maurer*, Bohrer, Kayseder*, Kalliwoda*, and Spohr**, it has not given birth to the superlative artists Italy has formed like Somis**, Pugnani**, Lolli**, Giardini**, Campagnoli**, and the greatest of them all, Viotti**. One could not, hence, I said it before, establish a comparison between both schools, and Italy keeps over Germany an overwhelming superiority, not only for the number, but also for the quality of the artists that it brought to light in addition to its well known masters, and we cannot deny that virtuosi of the calibre of Torelli**, Veracini**, Vivaldi** and so many others make vanish the prowesses of Baltzar*, Biber**, Westhoff*, or any other of their disciples."* (Le Violon, les Violonists et la Musique de Violon du XVI au XVIII siècle. Paris 1924, p. 254). And in a foot note he adds: *"It is certain that the most skilful and reputed German fiddlers would not stand comparison with Corelli, Geminiani, Tartini, Viotti, on the one side, and on the other, with Leclair, Gavinies, Rode, Kreutzer and Baillot."* (Op. cit. p. 255)

THE ANCIENT ERA, CONTINUATION

1714 GLUCK, CHRISTOF WILLIBALD (b Erasbach, nr. Berching, Upper Palatinate, Bavaria [Germany]; d. Vienna 1787) Austrian composer.

The influence of Gluck in all the upcoming music is so great that we must include him here. For example Mozart's scene in Don Giovanni, where the Commendatore requests him:

---

[1] They were two, Ignaz Fränzel* (father) and Ferdinand Fränzel* (his son), but they do not belong, specifically, to the Benda school, but rather to the German school by and large, through the teachings of Johann Stamitz** and the orch. of Mannheim.

"-Pentiti
-No, no"

is an impudent photocopy of Orfeo's plea to the Spirits in Gluck's
Orfeo ed Euridice:

-"Laissez vous toucher par mes larmes
-Non, non."

<-"Let yourselves be moved by my tears.
- No, no.">

Bthvn, who idolised him, took inspiration in this same scene for the 2nd
movement of his piano concerto nbr 4, although, in this particular instance,
Gluck seems slightly superficial as compared with:

a) The unexpected and irrational outcry of the orchestra, menacing and
awesome, all in unison, supremely forceful and utterly pitiless, that fills the
piano with great anxiety and terror.

b) The most tender and sweet entreaties of a horrified, frightened piano,
rendered almost speechless with fear {pianissimo}, inclemently replied by
the orchestra with harsh and renewed roars, until it is finally tamed by such a
naïve, insistent ingenuousness, in the characteristic contrasts of opposite
extremes, so dear to Bthvn.

Berlioz was also bewitched by him and used to go to the library of the
Paris Conservatoire* to learn by heart all his masterpieces.

Finally, Burney* joins the hosts of his admirers and calls him the
MICHELANGELO [1] OF MUSIC:

*In some scenes of great distress, in which the human heart is torn by
complicated misery, by "horrors accumulated," it is then that M. Gluck,
transported beyond the bounds of ordinary genius, gives such energy and
colouring to passion, as to become at once poet, painter and musician. He
seems to be the Michelangelo of music, and is as happy in painting difficult
attitudes, and situations of the mind, as that painter was of the body;*

---

[1] "Michelangelo" is a name predestined to make men number one in the world: besides him,
we have MICHELANGELO Antonioni, one of the best film directors in history, and Arturo
Benedetti MICHELANGELI, the best pianist of all times, except Liszt, who is a legend, with
whom we cannot compare him, for he left no recordings. Liszt is in the piano what Paganini in
the violin.

indeed, his expression of passion may sometimes be too strong for common hearers: but,

Il échappe souvent des sons à la douleur,
Qui sont faux pour l'oreille, & sont vrais pour le coeur (Dorat*).

<Grief often gives vent to sounds, that are false to the ears, but true to the heart. (Dorat*>
(The Present State of Music in Germany, etc. Pag. 289)

I have recorded in "C-04":
- Overture to Ifigenia in Aulide
- Sinfonias* to La Danza and La Corona.
- Orfeo ed Euridice's "J'ai perdus mon Euridice" sung by Maria Callas. Any excuse, whatsoever, is good to hear Callas again; besides, the violins, as a group, have a very important role in this piece.

<u>1716 BINI, PASCUALE</u> (b Pesaro - d id 1770) Italian composer and violinist. Musical.

He started his first years under the patronage of cardinal Olivieri, who in 1731 sent him to Padua to study with Tartini. Tartini's lessons lasted more that three years, and in 1734 he went to Rome, but returned soon after to Padua for further studies with Tartini. Tartini admired him greatly, and on a letter of presentation to the English patron, Mr. Wyseman*, in Rome, said: *Io lo mando a un mio scolaro che suona piu di me, e me ne glorio per essere un angelo di costume e religioso.* "I recommend you to a scholar who plays better than myself, and I am proud of it, as he is an angel in religion and morals"

After cardinal Olivieri's death in 1738, Bini entered the service of another Prince of the Church*, cardinal Acquaviva Troiano in the eternal City*. When Acquaviva died in 1747 Bini suffered many persecutions and endured several disasters that forced him to return to his native Pesaro. There he taught and played at the Teatro del Sole. In 1754 he entered the service of the young duke Carl Eugene of Württemberg, with a high salary as director of concerts and chamber music of what was the most reputed orchestra of all Europe: the Stuttgart orchestra under the direction of Jomelli*. (we will see more than one of our superlative violinists playing in this orchestra as first fiddle [erste Geige, German]) In 1759 he returned to Pesaro where he remained until his death. Bini was a superlative player who owed much of his reputation to the enthusiastic support of Tartini.

<u>1716 GIARDINI, FELICE</u> (Turin; d. Moscow 1796) Italian composer, harpsichordist, cellist, maestro of singing and violinist.

Burney*, in his General History of Music, writing on Giardini's teacher Somis**, says: *(Somis) was regarded as one of the greatest masters of his instrument of his time; but his chief professional honour is having formed among his scholars such a performer as GIARDINI.*(Book III. Vol. II. Chapt. IX. Pag. 446).

Giardini's father sent him to Milan to sing at the choir of the cathedral. Here he studied singing, harmony* and harpsichord with Giusseppe Palladino. Having showed a special talent for the violin his father recalled him to Turin to study with G. B. Somis.** This master showed him all the beauties of Corelli, and made of him one of the best violinists of the world.

Notwithstanding, he had also great talent for the harpsichord, and he will develop equal genius as singing teacher, and the violoncello, as we will see later. As for the harpsichord Burney* says: *But though his preference to the violin, upon which he soon became <u>the greatest performer in Europe,</u> seems a lucky circumstance, yet he had talents which would have made him a superior harpsichord player, had he continued to practice that instrument; but he told me himself, that he was perfectly cured of that vanity, at Paris, by the performance of Madame de S. Maur, a scholar of Rameau, who played in such a manner , as not only made him ashamed of his own performance, but determined him never to touch the instrument again in serious practice.* (General History. Vol II. p. 895)

After having played sometime in the orchestra of the Teatro della Opera in Rome he went to Naples as violinist of the Orch. of the Teatro S. Carlo in Naples, being promoted very soon to the position of deputy leader*. His most salient feature was his ability for embellishment, ornamentation and improvisation, wich he did with very good taste and which pleased very much his audiences, both for their novelty and for their intrinsic charm. Burney* says: *"I well remember my pleasure and astonishment in hearing Giardini, in a solo that he performed at the oratorio, 1769, play an air at the end of it with variations, in which, by repeating each strain with different bowing, without changing a single note in the melody, he gave it all the effect and novelty of a new variation of the passage."* (Burney*. A General History of Music. Vol. II. Book III. Chap. IX. Pag. 443.)

But one evening he had a nasty experience during the performance of an opera, which he reported to Burney*:

"One night, during the opera, Jomelli*, who had composed it, came into the orchestra, and seating himself close by me, I determined to give the Maestro di Capella* a touch of my taste and execution; and in the symphony (see in the encyclopaedia "sinfonia") *of the following song, which was in a pathetic style, I gave loose to my fingers and fancy; for which I was rewarded by the composer with a violent slap on the face; which... was the best lesson I ever received from a great master in my life."* (Burney*. General History of Music. Vol. II. Book IV. Chapt. VI. Pag. 896)

In 1748 he started a virtuoso tour which took him to Frankfurt and Berlin where he had a staggering success. He then played 3 times in Paris at the Concert spirituel* with equal success (1750), and was well received by the French court, *being disputed among the fashionable ladies both as an artist and as an agreable man.* (Fetis*).

On the Spring of 1950 he went to London, where he made his debut at a benefit concert for the soprano Francesca Cuzzoni.* (it was her farewell, pathetically shameful, concert: *the last I will ever trouble them [the public] with, and is made solely to pay my Creditors* (said she). Burney*, who was present reports that "she sung (sic) in it with a thin cracked voice, which almost frightened out of the little theatre in the Hay-market, the sons of those who had perhaps heard her at the great theatre in the same street, with ecstasy" And Burney goes on–"But when Giardini played a solo and concerto, though there was very little company, the applause was so loud, long, and furious, as nothing but bestowed on Garrick* had ever equalled. I had met him the night before at a private concert, with Guadagni* and Frasi*, at the house of Napthali Franks, Esq., who was himself one the best dilettanti performers on the violin at that time; and we were all equally surprised and delighted with the various powers of Giardini at so early period of his life; when, besides solos of his own composition of the most brilliant kind, he played several of Tartini's, in manuscript, at sight, and at five or six feet distance from the notes, as well as if he had never practised any thing else. His tone; bow; execution; graceful carriage of himself and his instrument; playing some of my own music, and making it better than I intended, or had imagined it in the warm moments of conception; and, lastly, playing variations, extempore, during half an hour, upon a new but extraordinary kind of birth-day minuet, which accidentally lay on the harpsichord – all this through into the utmost astonishment the whole company, who had never been accustomed to hear better performers than Festing*, Brown* and Collet*! Of his academy, scholars, manner of leading* at the opera and oratorio, performance in private concerts, compositions vocal and instrumental, I shall say nothing here, lest my praise should be too much for others, and too little for himself." (General History. Vol. 2 p. 896)

This debut made him soon famous, his gay embellishments and ornamentations making a strong sensation among the English public, somewhat tired of the old fashioned style of Festing*, who was already very ill, Brown* with his monotonous and ever repeated same solo of Tartini, the only piece of music he played during his seven years stay in England, and the stern manners of Geminiani. He also had the good fortune to be supported by several of the most powerful patrons, viz. Lady Bingley (Mrs. Fox Lane), the duke of Cumberland, the duke of Gloucester, and not least, Frederick, Prince of Wales, at whose houses they organised famous academias. One of these elegant *academias* or private concerts is meticulously described by Burney*:

Giardini performed seldom in public, but he preferred to play at the fashionable private concerts in London. " The next remarkable *Academia*, that I remember to have occasioned much curiosity and speculation, was established at the house of Mrs. Fox Lane, afterwards Lady Bingley, on the arrival of Giardini in England. The superior talents of that performer were always warmly patronised by this lady to the time of her death; and not content with admiring him herself, she contrived every means that could be devised to make him the admiration of others. As Giardini was seldom to be heard in public after his first arrival, she invited very select parties of the first people in the kingdom to hear him at her house, for which happiness she did not suffer them to remain ungrateful at his benefit.

When Mingotti* arrived in this kingdom, having united her interest with those of Giardini in the conduct and management of the opera, Mrs. Lane espoused her cause with great zeal; entering into the spirit of all her theatrical quarrels as ardently as if they had been her own. With two such performers, the concerts she gave to her choice friends were subjects of envy and obloquy to all those who were unable to obtain admission. At these concerts Mrs. Lane played the harpsichord herself; as did Lady Edgcumbe, and the late Lady Milbanke, both admirable performers on that instrument. Lady Rockingham, the Dowager Lady Carlisle, and Miss Pelham, scholars of Giardini, and Mingotti* used to sing; and the difficulty, or rather impossibility, of hearing these professors and illustrious dilettanti any where else, stimulated curiosity so much, that there was no sacrifice or mortification to which fashionable people would not submit, in order to obtain admission. And *la padrona della casa* lost few opportunities of letting them know the value she set on her invitations, by using them like dogs when they were there. Whenever a benefit was in contemplation for one of her *protégés*, taking care of the honour of her guests, she obliged them to behave with due gratitude and munificence on the occasion. "Come" would she often say to her friends, "give me five guineas" -a demand as implicitly obeyed as if made on the road. Nor had anyone, who ever wished to be admitted into such good company again, the courage to ask the occasion of the demand; but patiently awaited the Lady's pleasure to tell them whether they should be honoured with a ticket for Giardini's or Mingotti's* benefit." (G. History. Vol. 2. Pag. 1013)

His teaching activities were famous, as were his morning musical gatherings at his house where his pupils of harpsichord, violoncello, violin and singing, and himself, displayed their skills. All this feverish activities made him earn a great deal of money becoming one of the most distinguished "dandies" in London. His 20 concerts with the oboist Thomas Vincent and his participation at the Bach-Abel* (Carl Friederich) concerts gave him fame and wealth. In 1751 he started directing the Italian Opera in London, imposing a degree of discipline not known till then, and he imposed a new style of playing which spread all over the U.K. He remained attached to the Opera for more that 40 years. He also directed the orch. for the Three Choirs Festival (1770-76), and led the Orch of the Pantheon at Oxford Street.

Giardini is thus described by Burney*: (Giardini) *whose great hand, taste, and style of playing, were so universally admired, that he had soon not only a great number of scholars on the violin, but taught many ladies of the first rank to sing; and after he had been here a few years, he formed a morning academia, or concert, at his house, composed chiefly of his scholars, vocal and instrumental, who bore a part in the performance. This continued, while he was still augmenting the importance of his instrument and our national partiality for the taste of his country* (op. cit. Vol. 2. Pag 1012)

Everything seemed to go smoothly and, more than that, marvellously well for Giardini, and a promising old age was assured for him, until he committed the imprudence of becoming impresario of the Italian Opera in 1756 in association with the Italian soprano Regina Mingotti*. The following year, his losses were so considerable that he was forced to renounce to his enterprise. He restarted it in 1763 but his losses were even higher, and everything he had earned till then disappeared by the end of the year. In vain tried he to rebuild his fortune with new concerts, but he was approaching the age of the 50s and had lost most of his faculties. Disenchanted he came back to Naples in 1784. An attempt to return to England directing the opera La Ninetta of Cimarosa was a failure. He then went to S. Petersburg in great poverty, but had no success. Another attempt in Moscow was a blunder and he died in extreme poverty and total self-abandonment.

Giardini was a man of many talents, performer and teacher of cello, harpsichord and violin, and maestro of singing, as well. Fetis* speaks of his charm in executing the adagios* with "good taste and expression" and of his absolute command of intonation. Among his didactic works we must cite *Metodo di canto* (school of singing) London 1854; and two manuscripts: E*sercizii per il cembalo e il violino*, and *Instruzioni ed esercizii per il violino*.

Giardini treasured three valuable instruments:

1) A violoncello Strad. Aylesford of 1696, owned later by Piatigorski* and Starker*. There is an anonymous watercolour of the XVIII century of Giardini in the Museo Teatrale della Scala, in Milan, where we see him with an aristocratic appearance, beautifully cut cloths, and graciously dainty figure, lying on a stylish sofa, (which in the antics jargon is called "Récamier*" after a well known painting of Madame Récamier* by J. L. David.) having this cello *Aylesford* at his feet. This painting duly accounts for the powerful attraction he exerted on the fair sex.
2) The Strad. (violin) Aylesford of 1683.
3) And his most valuable, the Strad of Corelli, the Harrison of 1693. It was bought for him by Mr Avison, and has been owned, also, until very recently, by Kyung Wha Chung**. In order to defray his expenses for his last journey to Russia he was forced to sell this Strad. to an amateur violinist of Como named Ciceri.

1717 STAMITZ, JOHANN ANTON (b Nemecky Brod, now Havlickuv Brod, Czech Rep. – d. Mannheim, Baden-Wurttemberg land, SW Germany, by the Rhine River at the mouth of the canalised River Neckar, halfway Mainz-Stuttgart 1757) German composer and violinist.

The phenomenal building erected by Gluck was crowned by Stamitz, the father of all symphonic music, the heart of which is the violin mass, so much so that the leader* of the first violins is considered the head of the orchestra and honoured with that beautiful title of *concertino**. Under his direction the Mannheim orchestra became the most reputed in Europe. Its discipline was absolute, and it was particularly famous for its *crescendos** and *diminuendos**, two devises that made a spectacular effect on the public. He was the first to introduce clarinets and horns in the symphony orch.

And Burney* adds: "and the Piano*, which was before chiefly used as an echo, with which it was generally synonymous, as well as Forte*, were found to be musical *colours* which had their *shades*, as much as red or blue in painting." (Present State of Music in Germany. p. 94)

He first studied with his father, and next at the Jesuit* gymnasium of Jilhava. By 1741 he was engaged at the Mannheim orch. becoming first violin* in 1743, and Konzertmeister* in 1746 and director of instrumental music in 1750. He spent the year of 1754 in Paris, performing several times at the Concert spirituel* as soloist and conducting his own instrumental music. He was engaged by Le Riche de la Pouplinière*, a "rich" protector of music, to direct his own private concerts in his house. This wealthy man was a true patron of music and his private concerts were most appreciated in the whole Paris, on which he spent fortunes. This kind of private concerts were very fashionable among the great figures in Paris, like the duke of Noailles, Mollier, the duke of Aumont, Mlle. Maes, Monseigneur de Clerambault, the prince of Condé, the count of Clermont (who had at his service no one less that Pagin*), and Louis François de Bourbon, prince of Conti. [1] (There is at The Louvre in Paris a famous painting of a concert at the house of prince of Conti with young Mozart playing the harpsichord). La Pouplinière's* concerts became extraordinarily successful under Stamitz's direction.

Stamitz is considered the propagator of Tartini's school, and had a huge influence in Mozart.

Two works have I brought from him:

- Symphony Op 7-6 in D "C-4"
- vl concerto in C major "C-4"

1719 MOZART, LEOPOLD (b Augsburg; d. Salzburg 1787) German violinist, TEACHER and theoretician. Musical.

He received a solid formation from the Jesuits* of S. Salvator of Augsburg in humanities, violin playing and music theory. Upon his father's death he was directed to a clerical career and was sent to Salzburg where he studied at the Benedictine University.

In 1739 he entered the service of Count Thurn und Taxis, and thanks to him he became fourth violin at the orchestra of the prince – archbishop, then

---

[1] This custom to organise fashionable concerts at their houses derived from the impossibility of hearing any music other than that of the Opera, according to the sole privilege to stage music in France granted to Lully** and his successors by Louis XIV. See Concert spirituel* in the encyclopaedia.

violin teacher of the choirboys of the cathedral and in 1757 he was appointed composer to the court and chamber the following year second violin and in 1763 vice Kapellmeister*.

The birth of Wolfgang changed completely Leopold's life who dedicated all his efforts to promote the miraculous gifts of his son.

As theorist Leopold is well known by his *Violinschule*, 1756, a treatise strongly influenced by Quantz and C. P. E. Bach that has many passages pirated from Tartini, but it evidences a deep knowledge of all the available theorists of the turn of the XV century. It transmits the Italian method to the German style, particularly from Tartini and Locatelli.

Leopold Mozart acknowledges the presence of continuous vibrato among some players, but he despises it and notes: "Performers there are who tremble consistently on each note as if they had the palsy"

In "C-02" we have several duets played by Kremer and Grindenko.

1722 NARDINI, PIETRO (b Livorno - d Firenze 1793) Italian composer and violinist. Musical.

In 1734 he went to Padua to study with Tartini for six years. In 1740 he returned to Livorno where his fame as violinist and teacher was great. From 1760 to 1762 he travelled to Vienna and other German cities.

In 1762 he entered as solo violin and leader* of the STUTTGART ORCHESTRA, famous under the direction of Jomelli* (as we will presently see this post was shared with Antonio Lolli). Leopold Mozart heard him play and said that the beauty, and purity of his tone and his cantabile could not be surpassed.

Nardini was particularly praised for his adagios* and cantabile passages, the sweetness of his play, and the tenderness of his bow. He was distinguished by an intense melancholy that made his public cry.

Hearing of Tartini's grave illness he went to Padua to care for him with filial affection. After Tartini's death he accepted the appointment as music director of the orchestra of the ducal court in Florence, where he remained till his death.

Nardini was the best pupil of Tartini, and Burney*, for example, says: "Nardini played in such a manner as to leave nothing to wish; his tone is even and sweet; not very loud, but clear and certain; he has a great deal of expression in his slow movements, which, it is said, he has happily caught from his master Tartini. As to execution, he will satisfy and please more than surprise: in short, he seems the completest player on the violin in Italy; and, according to my feelings and judgement, his style is delicate, judicious, and highly finished". And in a foot note he adds: "Whoever has heard the polished performance of the celebrated Madame Sirmen* *may form a pretty just idea of Signor Nardini's manner of playing."* [1]

And Schubart* says: "the tenderness of his playing is indescribable ...one has seen ice-cold aristocrats cry when he performed an adagio* ... his melancholic manner was such that one did not always enjoy hearing him, for he was capable of transmuting the most extravagant fantasy into a funeral mood. His bow stroke was slow and solemn; yet, unlike Tartini, he did not tear out the notes by the roots but merely kissed their tips. He detached the notes very slowly, and each seemed a drop of blood from his soul. Those who heard him in younger years insist that his style was very bright and rose-coloured"

Nardini's best pupil was Thomas Lineally a friend of the Mozart's.

I have managed to find a violin concerto in E flat* major* played by Edward Melkus, in "C-5".

1725 LOLLI, ANTONIO (b. Bergamo -d Palermo 1802) Italian composer and violinist. Juggler+musical = virtuoso. He enjoyed the highest reputation until Viotti.

On Padre Martini's* recommendation he entered as solo violinist at the STUTTGART ORCHESTRA from 1758 to 1774. As the successor of the brilliant Bini he must have been, already, an extraordinary performer. In a few years time he had a salary equal to that of Nardini who was also at the orchestra in his same post for several years. He was allowed to have long periods of absence to tour in concert. His first Vienna concerts took place in 1762. Dittersdorf* described the lasting influence of Lolli's highly successful Vienna concerts. His fame grew even higher with his appearances in the Concert spirituel* in Paris in 1714 all criticised in superlatives by the Mercure* de France.

By 1767 the Stuttgart orchestra underwent grave economic and political pressures and had to reduce drastically the number of its musicians and

---

[1] The Present State of Music in France and Italy. P. 249.

dancers. Jomelli* himself was dismissed, but Lolli retained his post, what gives us an idea of his extraordinary importance.

In 1769 he made another tour visiting the main European cities (Paris, Palermo, Madrid, Naples, Vienna) From 1774 to 1783 he entered the service of Catherine the Great in St. Petersburg as Chamber Virtuoso, but continued to travel in concert. Lolli's last years were spent in impoverished retirement in Palermo.

Of Lolli's stay in England Burney* gives us this account:

"The celebrated performer on the violin, Lolli, came into England in the beginning of 1785; but by a caprice in his conduct equal to his performance, he was seldom heard. And then so eccentric was his style of composition and execution, that he was regarded as a madman by most of his hearers. Yet I am convinced that in his lucid intervals he was, in a serious style, a very great, expressive, and admirable performer. In his freaks nothing can be imagined so wild, difficult, grotesque, and even ridiculous as his compositions and performance. After playing at the oratorio, and making the grave and ignorant laugh at very serious difficulties upon which he had perhaps but ill bestowed his time, he suddenly left the kingdom, *à la sourdine*; perhaps, at last, to shun difficulties of another kind."

Lolli's importance as a performer was highlighted by Schubart*, who called him "the Shakespeare among violinists" He wrote: "his octave* passages on the unwieldy instrument were as pure as if they had been played on the best-tuned clavichord", and that he played both octaves and 10ths with the greatest precision". The Allgemeine musikalische Zeitung* wrote that "the most dangerous leaps from depths to the uttermost heights were child's play for him". For the French there has always been a before and an after Lolli.

His extraordinary ability to play octaves* and twelves was due to a little secret of his own: he untuned the fourth string* (G) by lowering it a fourth interval*, from g to d which resulted in an interval between strings fourth and third of an octave* instead of the conventional fifth, resulting in the "scordatura*" ($d - d' - a' - e''$). This scordatura was dubbed "in the style of Lolly" and was used among others by Bertheaume* in his "sonate dans le style de Lolly", Tremais* and Cartier*.

1727 L'ABBÉ LE FILS, JOSEPH-BARNABÉ SAINT-SEVIN (b. Agen; d. Paris 1803). French composer and violinist. Musical.

One of the finest of the mid 18th century, he was an accomplished composer and teacher. He belonged to a family of prestigious musicians; a prodigy child, he won a position in the orchestra of the Comédie Française at the age of 11, a feat that attracted the attention of Jean Marie Leclair, who gave him lessons between 1740 and 1742, when he joined the Paris Opera* Orchestra, in which he served for 20 years. His debut as soloist was in the Concert spirituel* in 1741 when he played a duo composed by his teacher Leclair with the 13-years-old Gavinies**.

But L'Abbé was also a naughty boy, as de la Laurencie* reminds us: three years after his brilliant success in the Concert spirituel*, his father requested to the *Lieutenat général de police* that his son be interned in a reformatory (The Fathers of Saint-Lazare), for having broken a wardrobe and robbed him 12 gold Louis, that were all his fortune. This internment proved to be "miraculous" ("*la purga de Benito*" as we say in Spain) and after only one month, the Fathers of Saint-Lazare, being very happy with his behaviour, had recommended his freedom. L'Abbé returned thus to his family, his violin and his exercises, and never misbehaved again, except for another trouble he got into in 1753 (being 26), related by de la Laurencie* in loc. cit. He had rented a house in Montmartre in company of one of his colleagues of the Opera and the Concert spirituel*, the singer Laurent Poirier. When the lease ended the owner took legal action against them for damages in his propriety. As a matter of fact they had practically devastated his house, destroying door and window casings, damaging ceilings, breaking into pieces six pottery vases that surrounded the terrace overlooking the garden, and razing down to the ground five trees of that garden. The ghost of the old boarder of the Fathers of Saint-Lazare revived once again, but it was only once, and never again.

Several performances at the Concert spirituel* established him as one of the finest violinists in Paris.

During the Revolution he lost his fortune, dying alone, poor and forgotten.

He was a great pedagogue and published a treatise: the *Principes du violon pour apprendre le doigté de cet instrument, et les différens agrémens dont il est susceptible*, 1761, which ranked just behind those of Leopold Mozart and Geminiani. He was the first to study the pronation (1) - the modern fashion to hold the violin - multiple stops* (2) - half position* (3) - and the application of sons filés (4) - and arpeggios* to the violin, and was the first since Mondonville* essay on *Les sons harmoniques* (1738) to discuss the production of harmoniques*.

1) Pronation is the rotation of the forearm in the elbow joint around its own lengthwise axis so that it can turn the hand, without any assistance from the upper arm, from a position with the palm facing the floor to one facing the ceiling. This is the movement used so much in daily life for turning keys in their locks or door knobs. The technical terms for these turning motions are: a) Pronation: palm turning to the floor. b) Supination: palm turning to the ceiling.

2) Multiple stops: to stop* two or more strings to play them simultaneously.

3) Half position: Basically the fingerboard is divided into seven positions*, that go from the lowest pitch, first position, closest to the scroll, to the highest one, the seventh, nearest to the bridge. But he introduced an intermediate position, called half position: that between the scroll and the first position.

4) Son filé: (in bel canto *filato*) Consists on prolonging as much as possible a sustained tone or musical phrase on a single bow stroke without having to change bow direction. Somis and Nardini were specially praised for their son filé. See 1686 Somis and 1722 Nardini. (in bel canto the filatos of the Spanish tenor Miguel Fleta* have never, ever, been equalled)

1728 GAVINIES, PIERRE (b Bordeaux - d Paris 1800) French composer, teacher and violinist. Juggler + musical = virtuoso. He was Leclair's successor as teacher of the French school. Viotti dubbed him "the French Tartini". Mainly autodidact, he taught the violin in the Paris Conservatoire* from its establishment in 1795 until his death. He was most profusely complimented for his expressiveness and for the purity of his tone.

The son of a luthier*, he heard violins from his cradle, carrying in his blood the sounds of the instrument, with which he grew up. He spent his first years hearing his father's clients testing his violins; later, he too started playing them, receiving spontaneous free teachings from his father's customers, who were delighted to help such prodigy child. Although Gavinies is taken for autodidact by the great majority of his biographers, the violin is so difficult "per se" that he must have had some sort of help at the beginning. I, therefore, subscribe to the opinion of François Fayolle*, that his father must have taken a teacher to give him lessons at home in his early years in Bordeaux.[1] Gavinies was taken to Paris by his father in 1734, and it

---

[1] François Fayolle*: Notices sur Corelli, Tartini, Gavinies, Pugnani et Viotti (Paris 1810)

is probably here that he might have received also several lessons from Leclair, as De la Laurencie* suggests.[2]

Be it as it were, all his biographers coincide in saying that after the age of 13 Gavinies could do without any teacher. He devoted ardently to hard work and deep studies, and thus he became, in a few years, the most renowned virtuoso in the Ville Lumière*.

At the age of 13, in 1741, he made a sensational debut at the Concert spirituel* in Les Tuileries* playing a sonata for two violins by Leclair with L'Abbé le Fils. (Probably one of the sonatas of Leclair's Op. 8).[3] He appeared again that same year in the Concert spirituel* at All Saints' Day playing in soloist Vivaldi's Spring with great success. (Gavinies performances of The Spring remained legendary, and Boisgelou,[4] in his Catalogue, says: "Refreshing and agreeable singing in The Spring, a concerto very much applauded when it was played with all the grace and charm of Gavinies' style."

From then on, the name of Gavinies does not figure anymore in the Concert spirituel*, and it is only in 1748 that he reappears at them. The cause of this gap is not known, but de la Laurencie*, citing Mme. de Salm[5] and Bernadau,[6] says that it would not be hard to believe that his feats might have attracted the attention of the great protectors of the capital, and that the duke of Orleans or the Grand prieur d´Orleans might have taken him as their private musician between 1742-1748.

On April 10, 1748 Gavinies returned to the Concerts spirituel*, playing often as soloist, but also in association with other famous musicians of the time. We will try to single out the most relevant of them:

In 1748 he plaid frequently with **L'Abbé le Fils**, already studied in the preceding article.

---

[2] Lionel de la Laurencie: L'Ecole française de violon. Vol. II Chapter. XI
[3] L. De la Laurencie. Ibid.
[4] Boisgelou: Catalogue des livres de la Bibliothèque du roi qui traitent de la musique. Paris 1787
[5] Mme. de Salm (Mme Constance Pipelet, princesse de Salm) *Éloge historique de Gavinies*. Speech given at the Lycée des Arts. Paris an X (1802)
[6] Bernadau: Notice sur un célèbre musicien-composituer originaire de Bordeaux. Histoire litteraire de la ci-devante provence de Guyenne. Bulletin polymatique de Musée d'instruction publique de Bordeaux.

88

In 1749 he shared his concerts with the famous flautist **Blavet***, already at the peak of his career, and with **Guignon***, Leclair's nightmare, whose playing he matched and even surpassed many times, to the extreme jealousy of the latter.

Blavet*, Michel (Besançon 1700 – Paris 1768) French flautist and composer. Autodidact, he mastered the bassoon and the flute. In 1726 he made his debut at the Concert spirituel*, which marked the beginning of his brilliant career. Blavet appeared at the Concert spirituel more that any other musician, and he was unanimously praised by the purity of his singing tone, dazzling technique and just intonation. Frederick the Great, while still Prince, offered him a place at his Prussian court, but he declined. In 1738 he was appointed first flute of the Musique du roi*, and in 1740 of the Paris Opera*. Blavet attracted the admiration of Voltaire, Telemann, Hubert le Blanc*, and last, but certainly not least, QUANTZ**.

Guignon, Jean-Pierre [Ghignone, Giovanni Pietro] (1702 Turin – Versailles, 1774) Italian violinist very active in France, where he was made French in 1741. One of the best pupils of Somis, he made his debut in Paris at the newly founded Concert spirituel* in 1725, playing a sort of contest between him and Baptiste Anet*, both considered by the Mercure* to be the best violinists in the world. He played very frequently here for the rest of his career. In 1733 he was named Ordinaire de la musique du roi*. Leclair, who was also first violin* of this ensemble, unable to stand his exasperating competition, just resigned his post out of shear jealousy. Guignon, in company of Mondonville*, made several triumphant tournes in France. His virtuosity and agile bow made him surpass all the violinists of his time in Paris, like Anet*, Mondonville*, LECLAIR, and Guillemain*.

In 1750 we see him playing with the cellist **Canavas**, whose performances were praised by the Mercure* as "much elegant".

Canavas, Jean-Baptiste [Canavasso] (Turin 1714 – Paris 1776) Italian cellist. He appeared frequently at the Concert spirituel*, and was very active in France. In 1745 he joined the Musiciens de la Chambre du Roi, and in 1765 the 24 Violons.

1751 is a year of numerous successes, sometimes shared with the violinist **Jean-Baptiste Dupont***.

Dupont, Jean-Baptiste (Very active in Dunkirk and Paris between 1773-83. His dates of birth and death are unknown) He made his debut at the Concert spirituel* in 1746, on the Ascension Day, playing with L'Abbé le Fils. By 1774 he was first violin* of the Dunkirk Orchestra. He played often at the Concert spirituel, both alone and in duo with Gavinies.

On the 24 December 1751 Gavinies obtained this complimentary review from the Mercure*: *"It was a long time since M. Gavinies had not extracted from his violin as beautiful sounds as those we heard yesterday"*.

Similar triumphs expect him in 1752, when he plaid, together with **Mademoiselle Fel**, a mixed concerto for voice and violin, where both played in imitation*, in what happened to be a most successful combination. (A creation of Mondonville*, who had earlier made the same experience playing himself with the same Marie Fel on May, 1747).

Fel, Marie (1713 Bordeaux – 1794 Chaillot) French singer. One of the most famous singers of the Académie Royale de Music*. She studied in Paris with Madame Van Loo*, a celebrated Italian teacher, daughter of SOMIS. In her brilliant career, besides performing over a hundred operas, she appeared 284 times in the Concert spirituel*, where she sang with the violinists Mondonville* and Gavinies**. For over 35 years she reigned unimpaired at the Académie royale de musique* and the Concert spirituel*. (1733-1769). She was most celebrated for her flexibility, expressiveness and clear articulation, with a natural voice of total equality in all her notes, from the lowest to the highest, along two and a half octaves*, having all the same loudness and round sound, as if they were a collar of precious pearls. (Those who are familiar with the art of singing, or "bel canto", know that it is precisely the equalisation of the notes of a singer throughout all his *tessitura** [range of voice between the lowest to the highest pitch] what matters most to a singing maestro) This equality and evenness, she possessed as a natural gift, without any effort or study. This was her most salient characteristic, and made the writer Grim to say in the Mercure*: "What she has by nature, nature denies the others, who must make up for the lack of this gift with hard work" J. J. Rousseau dedicated his Salve Regina to her.

Mondonville*, Jean-Joseph Cassanéa de (1711 Narbonne – 1772 Belleville, nr. Paris) French violinist and composer. He was taught by his father, an organist. He played first at the Concert spirituel* in 1734. His play at the Concert spirituel on Passion Sunday of 1739 is reported as "admirable and singular" by the Mercure*. Singular because of the harmonic* sounds that he produced in the sonatas Op 4 he had played, the first time ever to produce such particular sounds on the violin. Mondonville* was the first to study these harmonics*, and therefore their inventor. He played frequently at the Concert spirituel* with the flautist

Blavet*, with Guignon* and Marie Fel*. His operas, motets and instrumental music, had deserved fame.

In 1752 his playing was thus described in the Mercure*: "We dare say that this young virtuoso lacks nothing of what nature can grant. Fire, beautiful sound, boldness, [1] precision; he has got all talents; but, at 24, it is impossible to have all the instruction. Arts are infinite; a journey of a few years would be very useful to Gavinies..." (January 1752. Pag. 181)

In 1753 he played frequently at the Concert spirituel*, and at Easter he stood his own! (Mercure*) in face of Pugnani's fearful competence. Gavinies continued to give ever more successful concerts, and in 1760 the Mercure says: "we admire always his astonishing easiness to perform; nothing seems difficult for him. He makes infinite variations that are always new and fresh".

In 1762 he obtained this review in the Mercure*: "we say nothing about his performance for it is today matchless, and his celebrity needs not to be re-stated"

In 1763 Gavinies reached the peak of his career and several musicians dedicated works to him:

-Jean Godefroy Eckhard his sonatas Op. 1.
-Leduc* L'Ainé his sonatas Op. 1.
-The cellist Berteau* named a sonatas of his Op. 2 "La Gavinies"
-Rodolph Kreutzer** inscribed to him his 3rd violin concerto.
-Romain de Brasseur his Op 1 sonatas for violin solo and bass.

In 1765 Gavinies (aged 37) ceased playing in the Concert spirituel*. A most premature victim of the 50s, de la Laurencie* tries to excuse him by saying that he could not stand the competence of Lolli, but as we well know, an artist does not retire while he is in full possession of his talent; quite to the contrary, there are abundant examples of artists who do just the opposite, they continue to play after they have lost their faculties, in a blind pursuit of vanity and ever lasting success.

Applause and glory (the golden calves* of musicians) are much more strong than a mere competence of another violinist. In addition, those who continue to play beyond their natural limits, are incapable to make a self-

---

[1] When we arrive to them, we will see that boldness is one of the most salient characteristics of Wieniawski, David Oistrakh and Isaac Stern.

criticism of themselves, and they keep on performing in the believe that they are doing well, whereas, on the contrary, they are falling into the most abject ridiculousness, buoyed up by their misleading vanity and by the advise of perverse, so called "friends", abhorrent flatterers, who incite them to carry on indefinitely. In the course of this book we will see some disgraceful examples of this.

In 1773 together with Gossec* and Leduc* he was co-director of the Concert spirituel*. In 1795 Gavinies was admitted through competitive examination as professor of the Paris Conservatoire*. He was an affable and charming professor with pupils of such renown as Paisible*, Capron*, Guénin*, l'Abbé Robineau*, Baudron*, Leduc*, Bertheaume* and, his favourite, Imbault*.

As a person he had the art to charm ladies, being particularly kind with the fair sex, who returned him in "kind". He seemed to live exclusively for them, and, as his biographer Mme. de Salm said, [1] his attitude yielded him very good dividends indeed, not least a hand written will of Mme. Marie-Anne Merlet Franqueville in 1778, which bequeathed him with a life annuity of 1,500 Livres.

Another remarkable virtue of Gavinies was his easiness to read music at sight. Bernadau, in his *Notice sur un célébre musicien-compositeur, originaire de Bordeaux* refers to an anecdote happened in the house of the wealthy financier De la Pouplinière*. In order to set him a trap Gavinies was asked to play at sight a manuscript concerto, filled with difficulties, that an Italian violinist had brought, well prepared, to measure himself against our maestro. Gavinies, full of modesty, refused, and said that he would play it the following day after having studied it, which was taken by his enemies, ironically, as a sign of cowardice. Gavinies's friends, offended by such an outrage, insisted so much on him, that eventually he played it at sight without missing a single note.

As a pedagogue his most influential work is the *Vingt quatre matinées*, 1794. This compilation of études, which marks a capital date in the history of violin technique, has its essential goal in the development of the bowing discipline in combination with the use of all positions*. The easiness, flexibility and facility of the bow are its main goal. It was the most demanding work of the 18th century. More difficult that those of Tartini, it

---

[1] Mme. Constance Pipelet, Princesse de Salm: Eloge historique de Gavinies. Lecture at the Lycée des Arts in 1801

uses extreme leaps and very complex passages mainly between the fourth and seventh position*. They were unsurpassed until Paganini.

Gavinies was best known to his contemporaries as a violinist; very praised were his expressiveness and purity of his tone. He had extremely facile technique, with a very flexible bow. His improvisations and his sight-reading facility were famous.

1731 PUGNANI, GAETANO (b Turin - d id 1798) Italian composer, teacher and violinist. Musical. And so we arrive to the greatest of all: Pugnani.

The essential of his studies were made with Somis and Tartini. At the age of 10 he was admitted to the last chair of the second violins of the Teatro Regio at Turin. In 1749 he went to City of the seven hills* to study composition with Ciampi*. Back in Turin he was promoted to the head of the second violins in 1763. By that time he had acquired an international reputation after his first appearance the 2nd of February 1754 at the Concert spirituel* in Paris, playing one of his own compositions. The Mercure* wrote: "the connoisseurs insist that they have never heard a violinist superior to this virtuoso". (March 1754 p. 193)

He played at the Concert spirituel* again on March 25, 1754, a concerto of his composition. And finally that same year, on Ascension day, May 23, another concerto of his composition.

He went to London on 1767 where he conducted the King's theatre until 1769.

In 1771 he returned to Turin and achieved his dream to be first violin* of the Turin orchestra, the post of his first teacher Somis, being at the same time the leader* of the Teatro Regio. In 1776 he became general director of instrumental music, and in 1786 supervisor of the military bands. From 1780 to 1782 he undertook a lengthy concert tour through northern Europe, accompanied by his favourite pupil Viotti**. On his return to Turin, the Royal Orchestra had been disbanded because of the war with France, so Pugnani ended his days in sad inactivity. He was, without doubt, the best fiddler that ever played a violin to his day.

He was a capital link between Corelli and Viotti. His importance throughout Europe was great and he left many pupils of renown such as Polledro*, Borghi* and Bruni*. But the most important one was Viotti, the founder of the romantic era.

His playing was known by his power, eloquence and rich cantilena. He made important improvements in the bow, influencing the conception of the modern one.

I have found two works by him: an overture n 3 in B flat* major* "C-7" a most beautiful largo espressivo played by Enescu in "C-16" Noteworthy is Enescu's sublime tenderness and spirituality.

1751 CAMPAGNOLI, BARTOLOMEO (b. Cento, bordering the Reno River, 25 Km NW of Bologna; d. Neustrelitz, 100 Km N of Berlin, 1827) Italian composer and violinist. Musical.

His first teacher was Dall'Occa, pupil of Lolli in Bologna. He then went to Modena to study with Guastarobba*, a prominent pupil of Tartini. In 1763 he returned to his native town and got a position in the local orchestra of Cento. In 1770 he performed successfully in Faenza and Rome. After that he settled in Florence for five years to study with Nardini while he was the head of the second violins of the Teatro della Pergola orchestra.

In 1775 he had the same post in the Teatro Argentino in Rome, but he only remained there one year; he left Italy to enter the service of the Bishop of Freysingen. The next year he toured in concert Scandinavia, Germany and Poland. In Stockholm he was elected member of the Royal Swedish Academy. He then moved to Dresden to serve under the Duke of Courland, with frequent leaves of absence to tour in concert Italy, Prague, where he stood two months, and finally Berlin. At the Duke of Courland's death in 1797 he became leader* of the Gewandhaus* in Leipzig, where he remained until 1816. From then on he dedicated his life to accompany his two daughters, who were opera singers. As a performer Campagnoli's style stems entirely from Tartini.

His pedagogical works include fugues* for violin solo, which helped entire generation of pupils, the 41 caprices for viola and the Nouvelle Méthode, 1824 which are systematically organised with graded exercises that enjoyed great popularity.

1755 VIOTTI, GIOVANNI BATTISTA. He ends the Ancient era and starts the Romantic one. So, before talking of him, we must make a compilation and draw some conclusions of the period.

MUSICALS

1. Lully
2. Corelli
3. Torelli
4. Manfredini
5. Handel
6. Bach
7. Somis
8. Geminiani
9. Pisendel
10. Leclair
11. Gluck
12. Giardini
13. Bini
14. Stamitz
15. Leopold Mozart
16. Nardini
17. L'Abbé le Fils
18. Pugnani
19. Campagnoli

JUGGLERS

1. Biber. No significant school
2. Walter. No significant school
3. Vivaldi. Great teacher
4. Veracini. "   "
5. Tartini   "   "
6. Locatelli. No significant school
7. Lolli. No significant school
8. Gavinies. No significant school

All the musicals were great teachers having huge influence in all countries. Of all the jugglers only formed school five: Vivaldi, Veracini, Tartini, Locatelli and Gavinies.

If we take a quick look into the Ancient era, we will see that at the beginning it was jugglery which prevailed both in Germany with Biber and Walther, and in the primitive Italian school of Fontana* and Marini*, of whom we have not talked, because they were not superlatives, but we know by references that they filled their works with innumerable difficulties.

But from Corelli on, an opposite school, that of pure musicality, gathers importance, and will dominate the period until the end of the era.

The only great masters of the juggler tendency that could have made a school of their own, namely Veracini, Locatelli and Tartini, built up a superb playing technique for their pupils, but their pupils did not limit themselves to jugglery, but they blended it, instead, with a most sensitive musicality, preferring always expressiveness and purity of tone, to the virtuosistic audacities of their teachers.

In the French school the jugglery of the first Italians and Germans was absent, being more worried to obtain a just, musical and expressive interpretation, than to perform with dazzling virtuosity. The French, "chauvinists" as usual, believed they were the sole depositories of good taste and musicality.

If at the beginning the violin was the subject of all kinds of experiments, fiddlers rivalling on who was the most skilful, played more difficulties and at a greater amount of speed, there was an opposite current, that of the musicals, which tried to draw out of the violin its most expressive and musical tones. Initiated by Corelli and going through the 19 musicians shown in the column "musicals" up to 1755 (two centuries) it made the balance incline definitively to the musical side. The theory of good taste had won the competition, and the harmonics*, pizzicatos*, scordaturas*, unbelievable multiple stops*, dangerous leaps from depths to the uttermost heights, and extremely high positions* sank into oblivion.

The rules of good taste were well established, and the school teachers body of all the ospedales, basilicas, musical academies, maîtrises, cathedrals, and the rest of musical tuition centres, including the royal and nobility courts, all in the same direction, were proud of the highly beautiful violin building they had erected within two hundred years. This teachers' establishment was well consolidated, "law and order" prevailed, and there were no breaches in it.

This was the panorama Viotti found when he arrived in Paris. But soon there was to come a tremendous hurricane that would shake the whole building down to its very foundations. This happened in 1782, and like all hurricanes, it had a name: Paganini.

I have drawn a graph of all the schools of the ancient era for a better understanding.

96

GRAPH OF THE ANCIENT ERA

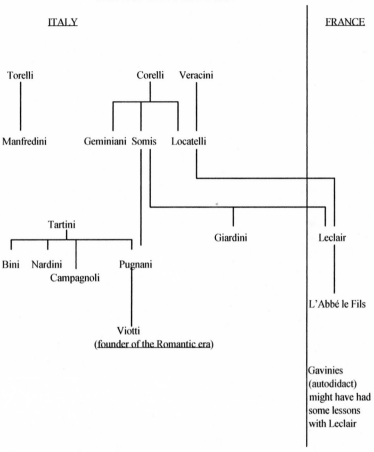

ITALY   FRANCE

Torelli   Corelli   Veracini

Manfredini   Geminiani Somis   Locatelli

                Tartini   Giardini   Leclair

Bini   Nardini   Pugnani
          Campagnoli

                                                                   L'Abbé le Fils

          Viotti
(founder of the Romantic era)

                                                        Gavinies
                                                        (autodidact)
                                                        might have had
                                                        some lessons
                                                        with Leclair

BOOK THREE

2) THE ROMANTIC ERA

GENERAL CONSIDERATIONS.

The following characteristics dominate the period:

a) The vibrato continues to be rejected, not only for the violin, but for the voice as well. Spohr (Violinschule 1832) called the vibrato by the singer's name "tremolo*" and said: "the deviation from the perfect intonation of the tone should hardly be perceptible to the ear."- He added - "avoid, however its frequent use, or in improper places", and his examples show that he restricted it to notes of certain length and of an expressive character. The rejection of the vibrato was extended, as we have just said, to the voice (tremolo*) being both considered of an utterly bad taste, as a grave defect that jeopardises the authentic, pure sound of the note, and should be avoided and eradicated as soon as they were detected.

b) Another device that was formally prohibited, both in voice and in violin, was the glissando* (portamento* di voce) These ornaments are of the most beautiful effect if they are used properly and with good taste, (the greatest examples of most beautiful glissandos are Fritz Kreisler in violin, and Carlos Gardel* in singing, without forgetting those of Andrés Segovia on his guitar and the most romantic vibrato and glissandos of Anton Karas on his zither in the immortal film "The Third Man" by Sir Carol Reed), but become horrendous if misused. (The French call them "degueulando": vomiting disgusting). The glissando is a devise most appropriate to facilitate position* changes, for it indicates (by sound degrees) the precise intonation, but it must be used within the strict limits of the most absolute and exquisite good taste. In view of the impossibility to teach good taste to the then prevailing bad taste, a taste that was sugary, affected and lacking the most indispensable minimum rigour, teachers opted for prohibiting it altogether.

c) The violin becomes more and more the protagonist as soloist.

d) The violin's centre of gravity is transferred from Italy to the Franco Belgian axis.(conservatories of Paris, Brussels and Liège)

e) The whole Romantic era cannot be understood without a deep study of Paganini, the King and head of all the Romantic period. Paganini made everybody wish to play like him, but as the teachers's establishment never accepted him, there was an ever increasing gap between teachers, who stuck to orthodoxy, and those who only wanted to imitate Paganini's wizardry. It is the time of phenomenal jugglers who reached heights that just fall short of that of Paganini, like Lipinski, Ole Bull, Ernst, and Sarasate, who dazzled their publics with their wizardry and incredible speed. It is the time of the great virtuosi who made fortunes with their performances.

f) It is the time of the advent of the middle classes, very numerous and wealthy enough to fill up the concert rooms, and willing to pay their money to hear their heroes. Concert halls were not ample enough to house these multitudes and new bigger ones had to be built. The wealthy virtuosi did not confine themselves to the performances of existing music; the audience demanded from them compositions of their own that should contain some ingredient of the new romantic feelings, namely the new preoccupation with nature, the struggle for national identity and unity, the search for individual identity, the expression of moods, of deep feelings, the domination of imagination over form, of instinct over reason.

g) THE CREATION OF THE MODERN CONSERVATORIES. The eager anti-clerical feelings that ravaged France in the years preluding the French Revolution had put an end to the French "maîtrises", traditional religious institutions for the musical education of males (Church choir schools). The Napoleonic invasions and their radical secularisation ended the religion-based music schools in Europe, particularly those of Italy, where the ospedali (hospices) of Naples {Santa Maria di Loreto, the most ancient one, founded in 1587} and the four existing in Venice, the most famous of them being the Ospedal della Pietá, where Vivaldi taught, came to an end. This closing of religious houses disrupted their charitable foundations, and a new idea of a secular school of music (conservatory) aroused interest in Europe. The first one was the Paris Conservatoire*, founded by the law of the Convention National of 16th Thermidor an III (3rd August 1795). See calendar* of French Revolution)

The Paris conservatoire* digs its roots into two older institutions (its forerunners) that merged to become the conservatoire: i) the *Ecole royale de chant* et de déclamation* and ii) the *Ecole supérieure de musique de la garde nationale*.

Until the Revolution, musical knowledge was taught in the "maîtrises", choirs and music schools, looked after by the clerical chapters of the different local churches. Upon their closing by the Revolution, another system had to be put in place to substitute them. This reform took two ways, that of the *Ecole royale de chant*, and that of the *Ecole supérieure de musique de la garde nationale*.

i) The *Ecole royale de chant et de déclamation* was founded as part of the Académie Royale de Musique* (Paris Opera) in 1784, thanks to the efforts of the French musician François-Joseph Gossec* (b. Vergnies, Hainaut 1734; d. Passy, annexed to Paris, XVI arrondissement 1829) who was its first director. Its aim, as its name implies, was the training of opera singers and theatre declamation, to which the teachings of string and keyboard instruments were added.

ii) The *École superior de musique de la garde nationale*. The task to replace the old church schools by secular ones was entrusted to the formidable musical administrator Bernard Sarrette*, who became the head of the Ecole supérieure de musique de la garde nationale, and later, the first director of the Paris conservatoire. His nation-wide plan included the creation of 30 [first degree- musical schools], 15 [second degree-ones], in replacement of the maîtrises, and a few [third degree] others, providing refreshment courses, plus an Ecole supérieure in Paris. All of them should provide free tuition. None of them were created with the exception of that of Paris: the Ecole supérieure de music de la garde nationale. One day prior to the demolition of the Bastille by the populace, the 13th July 1789, Bernard Sarrette* was named captain of the National Guard, entrusted with the responsibility to organise a band within the regiment, which he did by creating the *Ecole supérieure de musique de la garde nationale*, with the double task to give open air concerts in patriotic and civic festivities, and to train the musicians of the Garde nationale. This new body of the Garde nationale took part in many public, patriotic events, as well as in the main civic festivities, not least, the transference of Voltair's ashes to the Paris Panteon in 1791.

At the end of the Franco Prussian* war, the Commune de Paris* disbanded the Garde Nationale. When the amazing spontaneous communist experiment of the Commune was over, Sarrette* profited of the occasion to request a new institution that would produce new recruits for the band, increasing its size. Sarrette* drew up a plan for a school of military music, which was accepted in 1792, founding the Ecole gratuite de la garde nationale, where 120 pupils, sons of soldiers of the Garde nationale, were given free tuition, establishing the first school for wind instruments in France. In order to increase the size of the Ecole supérieure de music de la garde nationale, to reaffirm its goals, and redefine its statutes, Sarrette* obtained a decree (1793) transforming it into the Institut national de musique*. Sarrette*, wishing to extend the teachings of the Institut to singing, and string and keyboard instruments, took-over the existing Ecole royale de chant et de déclamation*, incorporating it to the Institut, in 1794. The next year this enlarged Institut national de musique* became the Conservatoire de Paris*.

The Ecole supérieure de music de la garde nationale* passed successively by several denominations which make its identification very confusing: Ecole gratuite de la garde nationale (1792), Institut national de musique* (1793), Conservatoire national de music et de déclamation (1795). Under the Restoration it changed to Ecole royale de music, then it became again Conservatoire de music et de déclamation (1822), until it took its definitive name: **Conservatoire national supérieur de musique et de danse de Paris**, located in the Cité de la musique, 209, avenue Jean-Jaurès, 75019 Paris.

As far as the violin is concerned, the conservatoire started with eight violin classes, being their teachers selected in the following manner: 4 among the teachers of the Garde nationale* and the Ecole de chant et de déclamation*, and the remaining 4 recruited through competitive examination. The eight first teachers of the conservatoire were recruited as follows:

Teachers coming from the Garde nationale: Frederic Blassius, Pierre Blassius and Rodolph Kreutzer.

Teachers from the Ecole de chant: Alexandre Guénin*.

Teachers selected through examination: Pierre Gavinies, Henri Guerillot, Pierre Lahoussaye* and Pierre Rode**.

This conservatoire was soon imitated by the one of Leipzig (1843), where Mendelssohn, Ferdinand David, Schumann and Joachim attracted hundreds of pupils. To them followed Munich (1846), Berlin (1850), Dresden (1856), Frankfurt (1861) Weimar (1872) and Hamburg (1873) In Russia the first was St. Petersburg (1862) then Moscow (1866) Similar conservatories were founded in the USA, Italy, and the rest of the world.

IMPORTANCE AND INTERNATIONAL ROLE OF THE PARIS CONSERVATORY*

As a matter of fact, the conservatoire de Paris*, as the reader will realize along the following pages, was not only the first to be created, as far as time is concerned, but it was also the first in importance of them all, to the point that we may say that all the different national schools have amalgamated into just one: the world-wide school of the Paris conservatory*. This universal pre-eminence does not come only from the capital importance of the MASSART school, that we will study in depth on book six, but also from other most influential teachers within the conservatoire. As professor Josef Gingold* says in a recent opened letter to the students of the Paris conservatoire, the Parisian teachers spread all over the world their influence, and we have thus Wieniawski**, pupil of Massart, teaching in St Petersburg for twelve years, who formed innumerable pupils who, in their turn, became teachers in Russia, making of the Russian school a perpetuation of the Paris school, or more precisely, of the Massart school.

Ysaye*, Wieniawski's pupil, did the same in Brussels. Isidor Lotto*, pupil of Massart, became teacher of the Warsaw conservatory, spreading the Parisian school in Poland.

Sarasate, the Spanish genius, toured all over the world the teachings of Alard, professor in Paris. Similarly Kreisler disseminated around the globe the teachings of his master Massart in the Paris conservatoire.

Another pupil of the conservatoire, Capet*, who won first prize under professor Maurin*, was the teacher of nobody less than Ivan Galamian**, teacher of Zukerman**, Perlman**, and Kyung-Wha-Chung**.

Persinger**, on his side, taught in the USA the teachings of his professors Ysaye and Thibaud, both of the Parisian school. Persinger was the teacher of Menuhin, Ricci and Isaac Stern, all studied in this work.

Digging deeper, Gingold* finds the Parisian influence on Heifetz , pupil of Auer**, pupil of Joachim**, who, in turn, was taught by Boehm**, pupil of Rode**, one of the inaugurating teachers of the Paris conservatory.

Two other giants of the violin in Paris, Emile Sauret* and Henri Marteau* succeeded Joachim at the Hochschule in Berlin.

Finally, Gingold*, himself, acknowledges his Parisian strong influence, having studied with Ysaye from 1927 to 1930. As he vividly puts it: *"because, like every violinist in the world, my roots trace back to the Paris Conservatoire"* and he adds *"...if I have had many honours bestowed on me in my long carrier, I cannot think of any other having filled me with greater personal satisfaction, than that of being invited to teach regularly as guest-professor in the Paris conservatory during the last four years."*

THE ROMANTIC VIOLINISTS

As usual, we will proceed by strict date-of-birth order:

1755 VIOTTI, GIOVANNI BATTISTA (b Fontanetto da Po, Piedmont; d. London 1824) Juggler + musical = virtuoso. ERA FOUNDER. founder of the Romantic era, which will go from him up to Auer, (1845-1930). Almost exactly one century (two more years) after the birth of Corelli, Viotti was born in Italy.

Italian composer, teacher and violinist, his compositions are among the finest examples of the Romantic violin school. In Viotti everything was Romantic, even his own life, which shows how unjust life is: He was pupil of Pugnani, who in turn was pupil of Somis and through him direct heir of Corelli. The son of a humble blacksmith, Viotti showed his musical aptitudes remarkably soon. In 1766 he was taken to Turin where he lived in the house of Prince Alfonso dall Pozzo della Cisterna who protected him. In 1770 on the return of Pugnani from London he entered his classes.

In 1775 Viotti entered the orchestra of the Royal Chapel* in Turin, where he occupied during five years the last desk of the first violins, with one of the lowest salaries of the orchestra. In 1780 he and his master Pugnani set out on a tour over Europe, presenting him always as the "pupil of the celebrated Pugnani" But he parted with Pugnani in Berlin and proceeded alone to the *well worth a mass** city...and it proved to be much worth than just a mass!!

Viotti made his staggering debut at the Concert spirituel* on Good Friday, the 17th of March, 1782, playing a concerto of his composition. (this date must be well remembered for it constitutes one of the most phenomenal events in history) His success was instantaneous, and he was unanimously and without exception acclaimed, at once, as the best violinist in the face of the earth. Thus, in just one evening, he was skyrocketed from the last desk of the Turin orchestra to violinist number one in the world. The general recognition that took Paganini 15 years to acquire, from 1813 when he triumphed in Milan until 1828, when he played in Vienna and definitively established his world-wide reputation as the best violinist alive, was obtained by Viotti on a single evening.

What had Viotti to be acclaimed in such a manner? To know that, we must consult the journals of the time, and the opinion of key connoisseurs in the matter. So, for example, *Le Journal de Paris* (March, 23 1782, p. 2) *wrote:*

"After the famous Lolli, there had not appeared a violinist of the calibre of Viotti. He surprised at the first movement of his concerto by the unbelievable easiness and neatness with which he performed the greatest difficulties; he won all the votes with his finished manner to play the adagio*; it was in this passage that we felt really how precious is the talent of this artist."

The Allgemeine musikalische Zeitung*, 3rd July 1811 informed us that Viotti's style was based on three main pillars:

1) A large, strong, full, tone.
2) The combination of this with a powerful, penetrating, singing, legato*.
3) Variety, charm, shadow and light, were brought into play through the greatest diversity of bowing.

If we go back now to Quantz (1697 Quantz) we will see that Viotti was exactly the reincarnation of Quantz teachings, and that what the Allgemeine musikalische Zeitung's* reviewer writes, without knowing it, repeats almost to the letter, word by word, what Quantz had said half a century ago on violin playing and bow stroke.

The *Mémoires secrets* (t XX, March 20, 1782) said: "Viotti has maintained the reputation he had already acquired from the very beginning in this country. A performance in a true manner, a precious finish and a quality in his admirable adagio* make this artist to be placed at the first range of the great musicians. It has been said that after the famous Lolli, there has not appeared a violinist of his calibre."

On its side, the London Morning Chronicle, 10th March 1794 reported: "Viotti, it is true, astonishes the hearer, but he does something infinitely better: he awakens emotion, gives soul to the sound and leads the passion captive"

Baillot, who had heard both Viotti and Paganini, does not hesitate to say that Viotti is the best of the two. In his L'Art du Violon Nouvelle

Méthode, Paris 1834 he says: "If among all these geniuses (violinists) who offer such an enormous and happy variety, there is one who particularly suits better your way of feeling, study him, imitate him; but to imitate does not mean to copy, do not let yourselves be misled by this. In Art to choose a model does not mean to copy this model; It is rather to follow the steps of this master and benefit from his experience; take profit of everything that is right. Wise-man is he who learns from every body, say the Orientals. Just look at all the eminent geniuses: they have started by doing what others did, before envisaging to build a new avenue for themselves. If the admiration for all of them could be fixed in one single violinist, we would say that the violin has never been so great, more beautiful, than under the bow of Viotti, who in his brilliant career that he has toured in triumph, has shown the noble and touching simplicity of his style, the grandeur and magnificence of his concertos"

For a year and a half he played frequently, (at the Concert spirituel* 24 times, 1782-83) but in 1783 he retired abruptly and entered the service of Marie Antoinette at Versailles. He was also leader* of Prince Rohan-Guéménée's orchestra for a short period. In 1788 he came under the patronage of the Count of Provence (future King Louis XVIII) and he established a new opera house called the Théâtre de Monsieur (in July 1791 Théâtre Feydeau). In this new post he proved to be an ambitious and vigorous administrator, creating one of the most excellent companies in Paris. Under his direction a good number of new operas were produced, particularly Italians and French, including the operas of his friend and associate Cherubini. By mid-1792 the Revolution had made Viotti's situation untenable, and in July he escaped to London. Here he turned again to performance, becoming musical director of the New Opera Concerts. He played at Haydn's benefit concerts, and was frequent performer in private wealthy homes including that of the Prince of Wales.

In 1798 the British Government, suspecting Viotti of Jacobean* activities, ordered him to leave the country. and he took refuge in Germany. But in 1800 he returned to London. He then retired almost entirely from music and devoted his energies to a wine business. In 1802, 1814 and 1818 he visited his old friends in Paris and played for them in private. Baillot reported his wonder that his playing had lost none of its power!

In 1813 he was one of the founders of the Royal Philharmonic Society.
The failure of his English business in 1818 left Viotti deeply in debt to his English friends. the Count of Provence, his former patron, was now Louis XVIII and Viotti applied for the position of director of the Paris Opera*, which he obtained. But after only four months the Duke of Berry*

was murdered at the entrance of the Opera, which aroused the antipathy of the public and the royal patrons, forcing him to tender his resignation. In 1823 he retired to London to live with his closest friends, Mr. and Mrs. William Chinnery, in whose home in Portman Square he met his unhappy end.

He composed 29 vl. concertos, introducing many novelties such as not always following the dictates of the sonata form* in the initial allegro to the letter, in emphasising the melody, often given to the first strings, and in sometimes echoing operatic and popular progressions, thereby reaffirming the essential Italian character of the composer, who was more inclined in inspiration than towards academic formalism of his foreign colleagues.

Viotti was a splendid teacher, as well, to judge by his pupils Rode, (his pet) Baillot and Kreutzer. The three were magnificent fiddlers and have their place in this book. The recently founded Paris Conservatoire* asked them to lay the basis of violin teaching by writing a treatise. Their task was not an easy one, the only methods they had available being those of Geminiani, Leopold Mozart, Duppont and L'Abbé le Fils. They had to make deep and numerous studies, and it required a great deal of imagination and creativity to print the first rigorous violin book: Méthode du violon. Baillot, Rode, Kreutzer. Paris 1803. They had decided to revise the work every 30 years, but when the time came, Rode and Kreutzer had died, so it was Baillot alone who made it: L'Art du Violon, Nouvelle Méthode Paris 1834, much more advanced and perfected than its predecessor.

Let us hear what Baillot has to say on the vibrato (L'Art du violon) page 138. (We are today so used to it that it seems inconceivable that one can play without it) To start with he didn't call it vibrato but undulation produced by the left hand "...this undulation, made more or less slow by the finger, may have an animated, tender or pathetic expression; but this rocking of the finger alters momentarily the justness of intonation. In order that the ear does not suffer from this and becomes consoled at once, you must start and end by playing the just and pure intonation ...this expressive device is very powerful, but if it were often used, it will soon loose the virtue of moving emotion, and will only have the dangerous disadvantage of denaturalising the melody..."

From Viotti we have brought his most famous vl concerto, the nr 22, played by Menuhin in "C-5"

Viotti had no less than ten Strads:

1690 Telaki, owned also by Ole Bull
1695 Sopkin
1700 Jupiter, which he passed on to Rode
1704 Viotti
1709 Viotti; Hall
1710 Viotti; Magaziner; Fuchs
1712 Viotti
1716 Viotti; Colossus, which he passed to Baillot, and owned later by Thibaud
1718 Viotti
1729 Viotti; Libon, owned also by Suk
-Also a Guarneri del Gesu "Viotti" of 1730.

<u>1766 KREUTZER, RODOLPHE</u>. (b. Versailles - d. Genève 1831) French composer, pedagogue and violinist. Musical. Disciple of Viotti.

Son of a wind player from Breslau, his father played in Versailles in the orchestra of the Swiss Guards in 1760. Rodolph received his early lessons from his father, and in 1778 he went to study with Anton Stamitz. Although it is not documented, the influence of Viotti was such that we have to consider him, at least, as one of his disciples.

Kreutzer's debut in Paris was at the Concert spirituel* on Corpus Christi, the 25 May 1780 with 14 years of age as a prodigy child, playing a concert by Anton Stamitz. "he heralded the most rare talents, amazing because of his age and even among the most skilful" (Mercure*, June 1780, p 40). After that he appeared at the Concert spirituel* 12 times. In 1784 he performed his own violin concerto at the Concert spirituel with great success. After the death of his father and mother in the same year, he came under the patronage of Marie Antoinette.[1]

Kreutzer was a member of the Ecole supérieure de musique de la garde nationale*, which was integrated into the Institut National de Musique* in 1793, which turned into the Paris Conservatoire* in 1795. He was selected among the first teachers of the conservatoire, among those belonging to the Garde nationale. He taught there until 1826, and was member of its council from 1825 to 1830. In 1796 he made a successful tour in Italy, and in 1798 he joined the party of Bernardotte, named ambassador to Vienna. There he met Bthvn. who liked him very much and said: "I prefer his modesty and

---

[1] For more details see "Sur un évantaille de Marie-Antoinette et des musiciens liégeois de Paris" by Joseph PHILIPPE Extract from Si Liège m'était conté. Liège nbr 8. 1963

natural behaviour to all the exterior without any interior, which characterises most virtuosi"

Spohr wrote "from all the Parisian violinists, the Kreutzers (Rodolph and his brother Auguste) are the most cultivated"

On his return to Paris he had a very successful concert season at the Théâtre Feydeau. When Rode went to Russia in 1801 he took his post as solo violin of the Opera; in 1802 he entered Napoleon's chapel* orchestra and four years later his private orchestra.

In 1810 he had a carriage accident and broke an arm, ending his violinist career. Nevertheless he retained his official posts. After the Restoration he was named Maître de la Chapelle* du Roi, and in 1817 overall director of the Opera. In 1824 he became Chevalier de la Légion d'honneur*.

Much have been speculated on the famous Bthvn's sonata *a Kreutzer*. It is absolutely false that he never had any notice of this dedication, all on the contrary, he knew it very well. The story goes that the reason why he never played it was his ignorance of such an inscription. Not at all. The reason is simply that he utterly detested Bthvn's music. We have an invaluable witness of this fact: One day, during a rehearsal of Bthvn's 9th symphony by Habeneck* in Paris where Berlioz was present, he saw Kreutzer rushing out of the theatre in horror, covering his ears with his hands. (Berlioz adds in his defence that the same horror was shared by the 99% of the French population at the time) <Hector Berlioz. Beethoven. Chapter I. La Sociedad de Conciertos del Conservatorio, y la introducción de Beethoven en Francia. Pag 21. Colección Austral. N° 992. Espasa Calpe. Cuarta edición. 1979. ISBN 84-239-0992-1> After all there is nothing strange on it. We all know Weber's exclamation after hearing the 7th symphony: "Bthvn is ready to be interned in a lunatic asylum!"

Together with Baillot and Rode he formed, we know already, the founding Trinity of the French school. He composed 42 studies for unaccompanied violin that occupy an almost unique position in the literature of violin studies.

Under Kreutzer I have recorded two pieces:

- A composition by himself, a duo for two violins in B flat* Major* Op 2-3 in "C-7"

-The famous sonata in A minor* "Kreutzer" which he never played, comes here magnificently played by Francescatti and Casadesus* in "C-5"

Kreutzer had the following Strads:

1701 Van Houten
1708 Wetherill, owned also by Ole Bull
1720 Kreutzer, which he passed to his pupil and protégé LAMBERT MASSART
1721 Kreutzer; Kruse, owned also by Isaac Stern
1727 Kreutzer; Lupot
1731 Kreutzer; Lotto*

Kreutzer's pet pupil and protégé was no one less than LAMBERT MASSART, the founder of the modern-vibrato era of the violin.

1771 BAILLOT, PIERRE (b Passy, annexed to Paris: XVI arrondissement; d. Paris 1842) French composer, teacher, pedagogue and violinist. Musical.

He showed remarkable talent when very young; he was taught first by Polidori and later by Saint-Marie. On the death of his mother and father in 1783 Baillot was placed under the care of a high government official, M. de Boucheporn, who sent him with his own children to Rome, where he was placed under the tuition of a pupil of Nardini, Pollani. In 1791 he returned to Paris. At an unknown date he became pupil of Viotti whom he admired ardently for the rest of his life.

Baillot's violinist career began in 1791 when he entered the orchestra of the Théâtre Feydeau. He was named professor in the newly created Conservatoire de Paris* in 1795. In 1805 he joined the private orchestra of Napoleon.

From 1805 to 1808 he toured with great success Russia and Vienna where he met Haydn and Bthvn.

Baillot was also a superb chamber music player, and he was founder of one of the very first quartet groups in France; their performances were praised enthusiastically by Spohr, Berlioz and Mendelssohn. By 1814 Baillot's fame spread all over Europe, and he toured England, Belgium and Holland between 1815–16. In 1821 he entered as leader* of the orchestra of the Paris Opera*, a position he retained until 1831. In 1825 he was also leader* of the Chapelle* Royale. His final tour was in 1833 through Italy and Switzerland.

As pedagogue he wrote the first edition of the Méthode du violon together with Kreutzer and Rode in 1803. This work had to be revised by all of them every 30 years, but when the time came the other two had already died. The revision, made all by himself, bears the title L'Art du Violon. Nouvelle Méthode Paris 1834, which improves its predecessor in all respects.

Besides being an exceptional pedagogue and teacher, Baillot was a superlative performer whom all Parisians idolised. There is an anecdote by Berlioz that we cannot miss. (Berlioz. Memoires, chapter XV) Berlioz used to go to the Paris Opera* surrounded by a group of unconditional supporters, something similar of today's soccer hooligans or tifossi. Their admiration for their favourite composers had no comparison but with the extreme hate they felt for those whom they disliked. The Pontifex Maximus of this dilettante group was, of course, Berlioz. They used to go one hour in advance to select well their places and all, score in hand, listened with fervour the Pontifical explanations of Berlioz. As the musicians came out to the platform he told them who they were and which were their particular abilities. When Baillot came out he said: Here comes Baillot! He does not do like other solo violinists who reserve themselves only for the intermezzo of the Ballet (an instrumental piece between opera acts where the singers are silent and the orchestra plays alone, very appropriate for good soloists to show off their abilities) He does not feel dishonoured to accompany an opera by Gluck. You will presently hear a song he plays exclusively on the fourth string*; he is audible over the whole orchestra.

One day, this pretty dangerous gang of dilettanti managed to inflame the populace with their fury: Baillot was announced to play a solo in the intermezzo of the ballet Nina. But due to an indisposition Baillot couldn't come, and the administration put only a little notice on the bill, so small, that nobody paid attention to it. The great majority of the public expected, consequently, to hear their idolised violinist. But when the moment came and Baillot didn't appear, it was Berlioz who shouted the war-cry: "Hey, hey there, what about the violin solo?" To which all the public cried out "Baillot!, Baillot!" The turmoil became greater by the moment, the members of the orchestra, seeing the magnitude of the revolt flew in panic and the infuriated masses stormed the stage destroying everything they met: desks, drums, double basses, chairs, etc.

Unfortunately, I haven't been able to find anything by Baillot or in connection with him, except, of course, his L'Art du violon, Paris 1834, which is one of my treasuries.

Baillot had the following Strads:

1694 Baillot
1709 Baillot; Thibaud
1716 Baillot; Colossus, which he inherited from his teacher Viotti
1732 Baillot, owned also by Kreisler

On the article devoted to Viotti we said that Baillot liked Viotti more than Paganini. Let us have a closer look into it.

In his L'Art du Violon he devotes a whole section to Paganini: "to insert in this work the name of Paganini, in the moment when his successful performances in Paris, that he has just given, confirm and justify his reputation, is for us a duty and an honour. Besides the pleasure we have in rendering him justice, we have seen from the first moment that his way to play the violin was, in general, very particular to himself and that it had very little resemblance to the rest of virtuosi. This difference gives his play the excitement of the novelty, and nevertheless this style relies almost entirely on the use of certain difficulties which have been used before, such as harmonic* sounds, pizzicatos*, scordaturas* that were in disused since a long time ago; to say the truth, Paganini has added more effects to those named previously, he has extracted so much of the double harmonics* and of the exclusive use of the fourth string*, that the violin in his hands becomes a different instrument like the very artist who has placed himself out of the borders."

And two pages latter he affirms: "If the admiration on all players could be fixed just on one fiddler, we would tell you that the violin has never been greater, more beautiful, than under the bow of Viotti..." (Baillot is yet another example of the long list of teachers of the violin establishment that never accepted Paganini, repudiating him as a sacrilegious profaner of the orthodox principles of the violin)

Baillot's infatuation and love for his teacher Viotti were such that he was unable to recognise the evidence. The very magnitude of Viotti's tree did not allowed him to see the wood. LATER HISTORY HAS PROVED HIM WRONG. Any Chinese or Japanese would know who Paganini was, but only the very professional European connoisseurs of the violin know who was Viotti. To Baillot we should sing that famous Jerome Kern's song "Smoke Gets in your Eyes", which comes here recorded in a most beautiful version of Dinah Washington in "C-17", where you can listen to the lyrics as well.

<u>1774 RODE, PIERRE</u> (b Bordeaux - d Chateau de Bourbon 1830) French composer, teacher, pedagogue and violinist. Musical.

He received his first violin lessons from Fauvel aîné that started when he was six and lasted eight years. His first public performance was in Bordeaux when he was 12. Next year Fauvel brought him to Paris, where he will become a pupil of Viotti. In a short period of time Rode became Viotti's favourite pupil. His first appearance was at the Concert spirituel* in Paris in 1790, playing Viotti's concerto no 8. Viotti had ceased to play, and he entrusted Rode for the first performances of his concertos, that used to take place in the Théâtre de Monsieur, of which Viotti was the musical director. The premiers of Viotti's concertos nos. 17 and 18 in 1792 had, in particular, an immense success.

Rode was named professor at the new Paris Conservatoire* in 1795. But soon he embarked on a concert tour through Germany and Holland. He then went to London to play on a single concert that was not particularly successful. There he met his former teacher Viotti, but both were expelled from England in 1798 because of suspected Jacobean* activities. We know already that Viotti went to Germany, whereas Rode returned to Paris to resume his duties at the Conservatoire. The next year he came to Madrid, where he made a good friendship with Boccherini. Here he played with enormous success Viotti's concerto no 6 dedicated to the Spanish Queen Maria Luisa of Parma, wife of Charles IV, so many times painted by Goya.

1803 was the year of his journey to Russia, playing several concerts in Germany, where Spohr heard him, and was captivated by his art. From 1804 to 1808 he was solo violinist to the tsar in St. Petersburg. At the end of 1808 he returned to Paris, where he played with little success, his faculties having deteriorated greatly. (an catastrophic precocious loss of faculties at only 35 years of age!)

He went to Vienna in 1812 where he gave the first performance of Bthvn's vl sonata Op 96, which disappointed very much the composer. (It comes to us superbly played by Perlman in "C-6") In 1814 Rode got married and settled in Berlin, where he devoted to composition. A last attempt to play in public in Paris in 1828 resulted in a complete blunder. By the end of his life he was stricken with paralysis.

In his prime Rode was the most distinguished violinist in the world. As pedagogue he has left us 24 caprices, and we know already that he was co-author with Baillot and Kreutzer of the first serious French didactic publication: Méthode du violon.

I have managed to find out a composition by him:

- Minuet-caprice played by Thibaud in "C-16".

His Strads:

1696 Vormbaum; Weinberger
1700 Jupiter, inherited from Viotti, and owned also by Joachim.
1715 Rode, owned also by Auer.
1722 Rode (decorated instrument)
1727 Rode; Nestore

BOOK FOUR:

PAGANINI

1782 PAGANINI, NICOLO (b. Genoa – d. Nice 1840) Italian composer, violist, guitarist and violinist. Juggler + musical = THE VIRTUOSO PAR EXCELLENCE

INTRODUCTION

Paganini cannot be considered as being part of this very selective list of virtuosi. This list deals with human beings, and Paganini is a god, and has to be considered apart. He is a planetary star around which turn, in orbital circulation, all the rest of fiddlers.

Together with Liszt they centred and commanded the whole life of the Romantic era. Paganini's violin dominated all the rest of the instruments of the great "Romantic tutti" of 1830. His effigy was reproduced in tobacco boxes, and in cane pommels, his name was given to hats, shoes, and fabric fashions. He was admired by the connoisseurs, regarded with awe by the superstitious and cheered enthusiastically by all who were lucky enough to have heard him play. The extraordinary wizardry of Paganini, which revolutionised the violin technique was, no doubt, the product of natural unequalled talents, but, most of all, of a steady perseverance in his studies that perhaps nobody else has been able to imitate. (Paganini is just one more living example of Nietzsche's article reproduced at the beginning of this book. <violin's main characteristics:1) The violin as a lover>). During his youth in Genoa, when he started writing for the violin, he accumulated in his works such difficulties that he was forced to exercise them without rest and sometimes he spent more than ten hours repeating a few bars to obtain a single effect. Here Paganini concentrates on the little detail, as Nietzsche wrote: "*they all had that robust conscience of artisans, which begins by learning the parts, before risking to make a big ensemble...*"

His virtuosity was such that, people supposed him to be in league with the Devil. Rumour had it that his fourth string*, from which he could draw ravishing sounds, was made out of the intestine of his mistress, whom he had murdered with his own hands. It was whispered that he had been jailed for twenty years as punishment for this crime, totally isolated from the outside world with the sole company of a violin, and with nothing to do he entertained his solitude by wresting from the instrument its innermost secrets. The letter Paganini wrote to the Revue Musicale in April 23, 1831, in which he denied murdering his mistress and being incarcerated, vividly brings in sight his anger. Paganini even identified the source of his misfortune, in a vain attempt to silence his slanders. It seems that a violinist called Duranowski, who was in Milan in 1798, was induced to accompany several ruffians to a nearby village where they intended to assassinate the local priest, who was reputed to be rich. One of their numbers shrank from committing this crime and denounced his companions. The police arrived and arrested Duranowski and the others as they walked into the priest's house. For this attempted crime they were condemned to twenty years in a galley-ship. Two years after receiving this sentence Duranowski was pardoned. "Will you credit it!" exclaimed Paganini. "Upon this groundwork they have constructed my history. It was necessary that the violinist's name ended in "i", to conclude that Paganini was the assassin".

No other musician had more fantastic stories to his name, but knowing the value of good publicity, he took not much trouble to refute them, but, being very smart, he almost encouraged this kind of rumours to spread.

Paganini has fascinated all the Romantic artists, violinists, pianists, composers, painters and writers. Schumann, Liszt, Rachmaninof, Chopin, T. Gauthier, Goethe, Heine*. His wizardry, and musicality as well, mesmerised the audiences. After having heard him play in Paris in 1832, Liszt retired from the concert platform to perfect his already phenomenal technique. As a matter of fact, Paganini didn't invent all the difficulties he played. We already know that by the end of the Ancient era all the hazardous difficulties performed by the primitive jugglers had sunk into oblivion, giving way to a more poised and musical concept of violin playing; but, endowed with an extraordinary power of synthesis, he compiled in a whole artistic system, very suitable for the then way of thinking and feeling, what already existed before him. Paganini's most salient effect on his audience was, therefore, his revolutionary way of playing, his novelty. But there were much more than that. He explored all the acrobatic possibilities of the violin, like nobody else had done, acquiring an absolute command of all its possibilities. He mesmerised his audience by going down to the highest positions*, using hazardous glissandos*, passing without transition from the lowest to the highest tones and vice versa at incredible speed; he was the first to use at its maximum the fourth string* (Although Berlioz in his Memoires -Chapt XV- noticed already: "...here comes Baillot...you will presently hear a singing he executes on the fourth string; he is audible over the sound of the whole orchestra") Paganini's interest on the fourth string aroused during a performance he played for the 28-years-old Princess Elisa Bacciochi, sister of Napoleon Buonaparte. He improvised a scena amorosa (love scene) using only two strings of his violin, the E string portraying the lady, the G string the man. After that, many other pieces came for the forth string: sonatas Majestueuse, Militaire, Maria Louisa, Sonate Sentimentale, three themes variés, Napoleon. He practised the scordatura* and long pieces in chromatic* sequences. Thanks to an extraordinary extensibility of his left hand he played the most perilous extensions, octave* and unison trills*, he was audacious with the staccato*, jeté*, double, triple and quadruple stops*, and chords* that required complicated positions*, crossing fingers and extensions that were double difficult due to the enormous speed of tempo. He extended the use of harmonics*, pizzicatos* with both hands, etc.

Schumann called the difficulties of the capriccios "the solstitial point of virtuosity". He displayed a phenomenal command of the fingerboard, and could move from the first to the highest position in lightning speed either on one string or in four octave* arpeggios*. His double stops* and chords* showed infinite variety. His most striking effect was the left hand pizzicato* (doubtless derived from his guitar playing)

They have inspired numerous composers such as Schumann (two sets of piano studies and piano accompaniment for the originals), Liszt (Six Études d'exécution transcendantale d'après Paganini and the 12 Études d'exécution transcendante), Brahms (Paganini variations Op 35), Rachmaninof (rhapsody), Casella*, Castelnuovo Tedesco, Lutoslawski, Dallapicolla and Boris Blacher (Orchestervariationen), all of them well known.

Chopin and Ernst wanted to add their contribution to this list, by composing both a set of variations on Paganini's variations on "O mamma, mamma cara" Op 10, of 1829, on the opera by Campra* "Le Carnaval de Venise". (The Carnaval de Venise is an opera by André Campra*, premiered at the Paris Opera* in 1699. In this work the composer deviates himself from the French tradition of the mythological opera imposed by Lully, and presents us with a contemporary subject, of comic and light tones, funny and ever varied, in which the author releases his tendency for melodic music. This masterpiece had little favour among the public, who had ears only for Lully's music). Both are recorded here.

Ernst's <Variations burlesques sur la canzonetta "Cara mia mamma" Op 18 (Leipzig 1844)> were the delight of Berlioz. "…You had to hear him, when, after having performed in his great style his own works so passionately and so masterly conceived, he took leave of his audience, under a storm of applause, by playing a set of variations on the air of the Carnaval de Venise which he dared to write after those of Paganini but without imitating them.

In this exquisite, good taste, fantasy, the caprices of the inventor blend so gracefully and at such great speed with the eccentricities of the prodigious technique, that one ends by not being astonished any more, and allows the melody to rock yourself with the monotonous accompaniment of the Venetian air, as if out of the violin there would not stream down the most gracefully coloured melodious cascades, with the most astonishing, unforeseeable bounds. In this curious feat of strength show-off, constantly melodious and performed with such ease that one could be mislead to think they are played with negligence, almost in a clumsy manner, Ernst always charms and fascinates his audience. He simply juggles with diamonds. …These variations that I often heard him play impress me now in a very peculiar way. As soon as the Venetian theme appears under his magic bow, it becomes midnight for me, and I find myself again in Saint Petersburg in a large hall lit up by day-light, feeling that strange and sweet nervous fatigue that one feels at the end of every splendid musical soirée; there are enthusiastic clamour and glinting laughter pervading the air; I fall into a Romanesque melancholy to which I cannot resist, and to which it will be even harmful for me to resist" (Berlioz. Memoires. Chapter LVI. Pag. 515-16)

These variations Op 18 composed by Ernst in 1844 for violin solo were later arranged by the author for violin and piano. Gidon Kremer, on his turn, transcribed them for two violins in the 1970s and are played in "C-19" by himself and Grindenko.<here Gidon Kremer is out of his depth, and we can hear many lapses of all kinds. Ernst was too much a violinist to be emulated>

Those of Chopin are recorded in "C-17" beautifully played by Fou T'Song*. They have not Op. number and are entitled "Souvenir de Paganini" They are included in the Chopin Complete Works edited by Paderewsky* in The Fryderyk Chopin Institute MCMXLIX seventh edition ISBN 83-224-1177-4 Vol. XIII Page 51.

Paganini was born into a poor family, although with enough resources to live with dignity. His father, Antonio, was a cargo handler and a shipping clerk who played the mandolin as a hobby; Paganini's first studied this instrument, although soon he turned to the violin. His father, seeing in him a possible source of important earnings for the family, like Mozart, would make him practice the whole day, depriving him of food whenever his diligence seemed to falter. When Paganini knew everything his father had to taught him, he was sent to Antonio Cervetto, a violinist of the Genoa theatre orchestra. The following year he went to study with Giacomo Costa, a leading violinist of Genoa. But Paganini's progress was so fast that it was decided to send him to the most renowned teacher in Parma: Alessandro Rolla*.

He made his debut at Genoa when he was 9-years-old playing a set of variations composed by himself on la Carmagnola. In 1797 he made a tour in the Lombardy accompanied by his father. Between 1801 to 1804 he devoted himself to study the guitar. He was director of music of princess Bacciochi, sister of Napoleon.(1805-1813) After his enormous success in Milan (1813) he toured all Italy in triumph. But it was not until 1828 that he had the international recognition in Vienna. Between 1828 to 1834 he toured all the main cities of Europe. In 1834 he went to Paris were he made friends with Berlioz, to whom he asked to compose a concerto for viola which he played as well. Berlioz replied that no one better than Paganini himself to accomplished this task, but Paganini decline on the grounds that he wasn't in the best of moods to compose, due to the advanced state of his larynx cancer. Thus the Harold was born; Paganini was very excited with the composition and came almost every day to Berlioz's house to see its progress, but when the score was about to be finished he refused to play it, for the viola was too integrated in the orchestra and he could not show off his virtuoso gifts. And everything was forgotten.

Paganini heard Harold for the first time by mere chance four years later, in 1838, during a journey he made to Paris to supervise his new Casino Paganini, and he liked it so much that, when Berlioz was retiring after the last applause, he dragged him back to the stage, and before all musicians and audience, he kneeled down and kissed his hand.

The next morning he sent his son Achille to see Berlioz, who was ill in bed, with this notice [1]: *"Mio caro amico, Bthvn spento non c'era che Berlioz che potesse farlo rivivere; ed io che ho gustato le vostre divine composizione degne di un genio qual siete, credo mio dovere pregarvi a*

---

[1] Berlioz. Memoires. XLVIII. Flamarion. Paris, 1991. Pag. 292

voler accetare, in segno del mio ommagio, venti mila franchi, i quali saranno rimesse dal signor baron de Rothschild dopo che gli avrete presentato l'acclussa. Credetemi sempre

Il vostro affezionatissimo amico, Nicolo Paganini"

<My dear friend, Bthvn departed, there was nobody else than Berlioz who could make him revive; and I, who have enjoyed your divine compositions, worthy of a genius such as you are, deem it my duty to pray you to be willing to accept, as a token of my homage, twenty thousand Francs, which will be handed over to you by Monsieur the baron of Rothschild on submission of the enclosed. Believe me always your most affectionate friend, Nicolo Paganini>

And Berlioz goes on: "I Know enough Italian to understand such a bill, but due to the unexpected of its contents, it caused me such a surprise that my ideas became quite confused and I could not make any sense of it all. But an envelope addressed to M. de Rothschild was enclosed, and without fancying I could make an indiscretion I hurriedly opened it. It contained these few words in French: *My dear Baron, I pray you to kindly hand over to M. Berlioz the 20,000 Francs I deposited with you yesterday.*

Then, and only then, I began to see a light, and it seems I got so pale that my wife, who entered in that moment, finding me with a letter in my hand and my face utterly convulsed, exclaimed: <Come on!. What's new again?. Something wrong once more? You must be brave! We have had worse than this! – No, No, On the contrary! – What then? – Paganini… - And…? – he sends me…twenty thousand francs… - Louis! Louis! cried out Henriette, beside herself with joy, running to fetch my son who was playing in the next room. Come here, come with your mother, come to thank God for what He has done for your father! And mother and son came to prostrate themselves by my bedside, the mother praying, the child, astonished, joining his little hands to hers… Oh! Paganini… What a scene!…if only he could have seen it!!!

(20,000 FF were the equivalent of 300,000 Euros value year 2001). Rather than giving figures, which should always be corrected by the intervening inflation, we have a better way to find out its purchasing power. On a letter of congratulation of Jules Janin* [1] dated in Paris, the 20th December 1838, he says: "My dear Berlioz, It is absolutely necessary for me to let you know my happiness on reading this morning on the newspaper about that bill of exchange and of the Glory that you have received from the illustrious Paganini. I am not talking only of the fortune he has given to you – three years of leisure…" <Three years in which he had to maintain his wife, his child and himself>.

---

[1] Berlioz. Correspondance G. Vol. II. Flamarion. Paris 1975. Letter 608 bis. Pag 497.

The reader has another means of calculating the enormous amount of money Paganini gave Berlioz: See in the encyclopaedia Legouvé. This man gave Berlioz two thousand Francs, which was considered by Berlioz an immense fortune, so great that he would not dare ask anybody. Well, Paganini gave him ten times that "fortune".

Genius and disorder. This is the résumé of Paganini's life. Inveterate gambler, adventurer without scruples, womaniser, he lead an existence full of vicissitudes. According to his enemies he acquired his performance perfection thanks to the long idle periods he spent in prison. But the truth is that he was an ailing man, who would disappear from time to time to study the guitar or to practice agriculture at the farm of one of his lady admirers.

Paganini was a rebel. Having been formed outside the academicism of schools, he was denigrated by the Establishment of scholar teachers who, after the manner of the Romans, tore their garments in sign of disapproval of such a sacrilegious heretic. But they were the only ones, and their opposition was futile.

All the rest, musicians or public, admired him, and it continues to be so, and so will it be SICUT ERAT IN PRINCIPIO, NUNC ET SEMPER ET IN SECULA SECULORUM, AMEN.

We have seen the opinion of Baillot when we spoke of him: *a yes but not, extraordinary but heretical, old fashioned, mesmerising audiences with obsolete tricks...*this is the insight reading of Baillot's paragraph.

Another member of the Establishment, Spohr, the Sancta Sanctorum in Europe, not only in violin, but in music in general, who used to give his opinions like the Pope: "ex catedra", was decidedly unimpressed: "In composition and in his style there is a strange mixture of consummate genius, childishness and lack of taste that alternately charms and repels"

Paganini was unequalled in wizardry, but he was also unrivalled in his adagios*, what true musicians look for. There is a little story very appropriate for this:

Berlioz in a letter to Liszt (Paris 6th August 1839) reminds him of this story: "Te rappelles-tu notre soirée chez Legouvé*, et la sonate en ut dièze mineur, (sonate quasi una fantasia Op 27-2 au Clair de Lune de Bthvn) et la lampe éteinte, et les cinq auditeurs couchés sur le tapis dans cette obscurité, et notre magnétisation, et les larmes de Legouvé* et les miennes...? Mon Dieu, mon Dieu, que tu fus sublime ce soir-là!" <Hector Berlioz. Correspondance Générale. Vol. II. Flamarion. Paris 1975. Letter 660. Pag. 565>

<"Do you recall our evening at the house of Legouvé*, and the sonata in C sharp* minor* (Bthvn sonata quasi una fantasia Op 27-2. Moonshine) and the lamp out, and the five listeners lying down on the carpet in that darkness, and my tears and those of Legouvé* ...? My God, my God, that you were sublime that evening!">

The evening in question was being spent in the house of a famous writer, Ernest Legouvé*, in Paris. He had invited some friends of the very cream of the cultural world of the Ville Lumière*, namely: Victor Schoelcher*, Prospère Goubaux*, Eugène Sue*, Berlioz and Liszt. Liszt arrived late at night [1] when they were already arguing heatedly about the value of a work by Weber, which either due to the mediocre performance of the orchestra, or to any other reason, did not quite catch the public's favour in a recent concert. Liszt sat at the piano to reply to the antagonists of Weber by making his point in his way, i.e. playing it on the piano; this argument was just conclusive, and left no room for reply.

Everybody had to admit that it had been a brilliant piece of music that went unnoticed. When he was about to finish the lamp which was lighting up the room started to run out of fuel; Goubaux* hurried to refuel it.

"Don't do anything ! -said Berlioz- *if the maestro is willing to play for us the adagio* of Bthvn's sonata in C sharp* minor*, (moonlight sonata) this twilight will be very suitable"*

Two things to remark here:

1) Berlioz and Liszt were hand and glove with each other, so much so, that they addressed mutually by "tu" (a most extraordinary thing for that time), instead of the usual "vous", which was used even to address ones parents. But here, before such renowned personalities, Berlioz calls him, most respectfully, maestro.

2) Although being such a good friend of him, Berlioz had not had many occasions to make a request to Liszt at the piano; but he does not ask for the Etudes Transcendentales après Paganini or a Hungarian rhapsody; he wanted, instead, the adagio*.

---

[1] Yet another example of Liszt's design to centre everybody's attention on himself. He knew that by arriving late they all would miss him and long for his arrival. This divo like behaviour, which he did on purpose all along his lifetime was one of the most characteristic aspects of Liszt's personality, and is discussed in the encyclopaedia under Lisztomania*

-"Delighted -replied Liszt- but then put out the lamp completely and put out the fire, as well, so as to have a total darkness".

They all lied down on the carpet, and I can imagine Berlioz securing for himself a place right under the grand piano to catch as much harmonics* as possible.

When the gloomy, awesome darkness was complete, and after several, anguishing, endless moments of concentration, he played it. And Berlioz continues: "the great elegy raised shrouded in its sublime simplicity; we were hearing the great voice of Bthvn, evoked by the pianist as if he were his shadow. In silence we trembled, astounded with respect, with religious fear, with admiration, with poetical grief; and were it not by the beneficial tears that came to our rescue, I guess we would have died of asphyxia" At the end Berlioz, on the brink of suffocation, was weeping copiously. <H. Berlioz: Beethoven. Espasa Calpe. Madrid 1950. Colección Austral. Nbr. 992. Pag 121> [this is just one more example of the charismatic, supernatural effect and hysteria that Liszt provoked among those who surrounded him. For more details see Lisztomania* in the Encyclopaedia]

Paganini has received lots and lots of compliments, but among all, I prefer those of these two connoisseurs:

1) Friederick Wieck*: *"Never did I hear a singer who touched me as deeply as an adagio* by Paganini."*

2) Franz Schubert: "When he heard Paganini for the first time, he wrote me to Graz: *I heard in the adagio* an angel singing*" (Souvenirs d'Anselm Hüttenbrenner*)

Schubert heard Paganini for the first time the 29th of March 1828 in Vienna. Paganini was then very busy composing his concerto n 4 in D minor*, so it is more than probable that for his debut in Vienna he used his concerto in D minor Op post. No 6, which was the first he had composed and with which he was most familiar, being, no doubt, his battle-hoarse. That is why I have recorded it in "C-6"

Paganini was also a superlative sight reader, and he would, as a stunt, sight-read any composition put before him at the end of a concert.

The easiness to read music at sight is something that just cannot be learnt; it is a gift God confers to His chosen few, like perfect pitch. None of these two gifts mean, however, that the person endowed with them is necessarily a good musician, although it helps a great deal. Perfect pitch had Mozart and Berlioz, and a similar easiness for sight reading was enjoyed by Liszt, for example. We will presently discuss more closely Paganini's easiness when we describe his encounter with the famous teacher Rolla*. As for Liszt's sight reading easiness, there is an interesting anecdote referred by the American singer Lillie Moulton (Franz Liszt. Alan Walker. Faber & Faber. Vol. 3. P. 98) that we cannot miss: *"Just before dinner, Liszt spotted a manuscript which Auber* had brought with him. After picking it up and glancing briefly at it, he put it down again with the words "c'est tres jolie!" (it's very pretty) The company then went on to dinner, and after Liszt had dined and smoked his usual cigar, he went over to the piano and played the "jolie little thing" of Auber from memory"* [1].

On the other hand, we can find true idols of the violin who had real difficulties in reading music: so, for instance, Kreisler** was not admitted to the Vienna Opera orch. (later Vienna Philharmonic) due to his poor sight-reading. Another example is Corelli, in his disgraceful performance in Naples. See his article p. 34.

I have left on purpose for the end another virtue of Paganini. Besides the great number of them that we have named, there is an additional one: he is the patron saint of all autodidact. This has a lot to do with his own life, so there we go: A violinist of such calibre, the best in history, must of necessity have had (so the academicians would say) the best teacher, one as good as a Corelli, Pugnani or Viotti. Who taught Paganini the violin? His father who was a shipping clerk. Amazing, isn't it? True that the father enjoyed playing the mandolin in his spare time, but that was all. Fantastic! These family lessons started when Paganini was seven years old and lasted for three years. Then he turned to Servetto, an obscure violinist of the Genoa's theatre orchestra, for two more years, and one more year with a Genoa violinist called Costa, maestro di capella* of St Lorenzo's cathedral. But in the meantime Paganini had started giving concerts with ever increasing success. In view of this prodigious progress, his father decided to send Nicolo to a really good teacher in Parma, but it was too late, Paganini knew already everything about the violin. The story is worth telling:

In order to raise funds for the trip, Paganini gave two more concerts, and father and son set out for Parma in 1795. The teacher in question was the famous maestro Alessandro Rolla*. When they presented themselves at

---

[1] Alan Walker. Franz Liszt. Vol. 3: the final years, 1861-1886. Faber and Faber. 1997. Pag 98. Extracted from Lille de Hegermann-Lindencrone. In the Courts of Memory, 1858-1875. Contemporary Letters. New York. 1925.

Rolla's house, they were told that the maestro was ill in bed and that they had to wait. Nicolo noticed a manuscript of one of Rolla's latest concerto, picked up a violin and played it at sight with such perfection that Rolla jumped out of bed and asked: *Who of the two has played this?* And when they said it had been the boy, he exclaimed: *"I can teach you nothing, my boy, go to see Paer*!"* (composition)

So by the time his father decided to take him to a real good teacher he knew already everything. Paganini's teachers had been two obscure violinists from the age of 11 to 13, and his father, a cargo handler, from 7 to 11. It seems that we are joking. Where was the secret of all that? In the Nietzsche method; remember: "... When the intelligence and character lack to conform such an artistic life plan (poor little Paganini was physically unable to have neither the intelligence nor the character) it is Destiny and Necessity that take their place and carry step by step the future Maestro..." In this particular instance Destiny and Necessity were Nicolo's father who was a brute beast, that made little Nicolo practice from morning till night, and would deprive him of food whenever his diligence seemed to falter. In other words, by practising at the Nietzsche style, all by himself, he became what he was: Paganini.

For us the peoples of the Western developed countries, who live in a ridiculous "softy" society, this brutality seems atrocious, but we must not forget that:

a) It was the normal way of educating in those days.

b) That thanks to that brutality mankind had the good fortune to be endowed with at least two gods of music: Paganini as a violinist and Bthvn as a musician.

Paganini played in two different, opposite, ways, according to circumstances:

a) With pyrotechnics and wizardry for the public, the great masses.

b) In a very serious and musical manner when he was in the intimacy of his good friends, as for example the French painter and excellent fiddler Jean August Dominique Ingres* (the French call one's favourite hobby *le violon d'Ingres**) with whom he delighted in playing what delights us all, namely, the Bthvn's string quartets.

During his year's stay in Parma (1795, when he went to see Rolla*)
Paganini gave two concerts, one at the Royal theatre and the other for the
Royal family. Late in 1796 he returned to Genoa. He became very interested
in the guitar; he also met Kreutzer, who played in Genoa in 1796-7. But his
strongest impact came from his discovery of Locatelli's half forgotten *L'arte
del violino* (1733) which contained 24 caprices for violin solo; they incited
him to play all the incredible difficulties he added to his works creating a
whole world of intricate wizardries, never before heard, particularly his own
24 caprices. Caprice no. 1 is a tribute to Locatelli's no. 7.

During the years of Napoleon's Italian campaign, Antonio Paganini
moved his family out of Genoa to save his son from possible conscription.
He took Nicolo to Livorno in 1800; that year the son gave several highly
successful concerts in Modena and Livorno. In 1801, at the age of 18,
Paganini succeeded in freeing himself from paternal supervision, going to
Lucca where he decided to remain after successful public appearances. In a
typical pendulum reaction, being now freed from the restraint of his home,
he sowed his wild oats, felling into bad companies, and taking to gambling
and other vices, the most natural result of his father's harsh training showing
itself in lack of moral stamina.

For a time his careless life had its allurements, but the young virtuoso
was frequently reduced to great straits, and on one occasion, if not more, he
pawned his violin. This happened at Leghorn, where he was to play at a
concert, and it was only through the kindness of a French merchant, M.
Livron, who lent him a beautiful **Guarneri del Gesu ("Canon")** of 1742
that he was able to appear. When the concert was over, and Paganini
brought back the instrument, its owner was so delighted with what he had
heard that he refused to receive it. "Never shall I profane strings which your
fingers have touched" he said "the instrument is now yours". This Guarneri
became his pet instrument for all his life.

In 1805 Princess Elisa Bacciochi, the 28-year-old sister of Napoleon,
was installed as ruler of Lucca. She disbanded the two existing orchestras
and formed a chamber sized orchestra where Paganini soon found a place.
But in 1809 he decided to embark on a career of "free artist"

During the first three years he travelled a great deal, until 1813 when he
triumphed in Milan giving more than 12 concerts in two months. From 1816
to 1822 he toured all Italy; in Milan he was stricken by an illness that proved
so serious that his mother, lawyer and friends were summoned from Genoa.
His recovery was very slow, and ever since he retained a cadaverous look.
In 1824 he played mostly in northern Italy. It was in this year that his liaison

with the singer Antonia Bianchi started; the following year their son Achille was born. In 1827 Pope Leo XII created Paganini a Knight of the Golden Spur, an honour very highly considered by him.

The Milan success spread Paganini's fame through Italy. Yet he needed other 15 more years to embark into an international career.

So far his concerts have been mainly addressed to the great public, the masses, which he mesmerised with his dazzling thechnic. But the international reputation could not rely only on this, his violin playing should consist in more serious and musical performances. So, for example, he coincided with Spohr in Venice in 1816, but he declined to play before him arguing that his play was only for the great masses.

He knew also that in order to triumph in the European capitals he could not limit himself to play existing music; that he should prove to be a valuable composer as well, and he started composing.

PAGANINI COMPOSER

The first violin concerto he composed carries the no 6 Op post, discovered in 1972 in London. He composed it before 1815 under the title of Grande concerto di Nicolo Paganini. Then he continued with his no 1 (1817) the six works of the Op 1 including the Caprices, proudly dedicated "to the artists" (1820); his sceptical colleagues dismissed them as unplayable, but they were soon proved wrong. Concerto no 2 was written in 1826 and so on in a large composer's career which include numerous sonatas both for violin and guitar, variations, chamber music, sonatas for the fourth string*, etc.

THE INTERNATIONAL CAREER

His international triumphs began in Vienna in 1828. Here his personal relationship with Antonia Bianchi became untenable and they were officially separated; Paganini was awarded the full custody of Achille, upon whom he lavished his most tender care.

Paganini's stay in Prague in 1828 was rather unhappy. In October he underwent two jawbone operations in which all his teeth were removed. This gave his face his peculiar sunken appearance.

From 1829-31 he toured Germany with immense success comparable to that of Vienna. Critics Rellstab* and Marks ascribed more importance to his emotional appeal that to his technical wizardry (which proves them to be true musicians; we return once more to the eternal tug of war between jugglers and musicals) while the young Ernst followed him from city to city copying by ear his as yet unpublished compositions to seize his style. Paganini, in order to preserve what he considered to be his professional secrecy, published only very few of his compositions, giving to his manuscripts prohibitive prices to deter inopportune editors. <Important notice: I understand by true musicians those who love and understand well music, be them performers, critics, music-lovers, composers, autodidacts, painters or whatever, in a word: ARTISTS.

A good example is the French painter Jean Auguste Dominique Ingres* who after having played on the violin the Kreutzer sonata with Liszt was enthusiastically embraced by the latter in spite of the enormous respect Liszt felt for the old painter. (Lettres d'un Bachellier ès Musique: A Berlioz) How many star violinists would give a fortune to see, for example, Horowitz embracing them like this after performing the sonata in A minor*. On the contrary "official" musicians i.e. those who have a conservatory diploma, but who do not love deeply music are called by me music "civil servants", people who approach music to make a living from, not as an art. In this respect I share fully the Jambe- de-Fer's* opinion: (Epitomé Musical Lyon 1556) on those who make a living from music through their labour regarded as servants, as opposite to artists who approach art independently, for the sake of art, not for money. I cannot help having the impression that a certain number of professional musicians are actually music workers in the very sense of Charlie Chaplin's film Modern Times, with a time clock and them punching their time cards at entry time, playing the music they are ordered to play and punching again at closing time, without the slightest motivation. If, as it happens nowadays, great artists earn a great deal of money, so much the better. In these times we generally confront professionals to amateurs, the first being considered better that "simple" amateurs. But, is there anything more serious and sublime than to give our love to our hobby? (AMATEUR is he who loves.(From Latin *amator*, a lover). For the Spanish philosopher Don José Ortega y Gasset there is no other nobler effort than that wich is done for nothing, without any reward or gain. It is, as he puts it, the supreme sport.>

I feel constrained to transcribe and translate Liszt's letter to Berlioz from San Rossore, September 2, 1839 (Lettres d'un bachelier ès musique. Le Castor Astral, 1991. Pag 161):

"...Un jour que je n'oublierai pas, nous (Ingres* et un group d'ammis inclu Liszt) visitâmes ensemble les salles du Vatican; nous traversâmes ces longues galeries ou l'Etrurie, la Grèce, la Rome antique et l'Italie chrétienne sont représentées par d'innombrables monuments. Nous passion avec respect devant ces marbres jaunis et ces peintures à demi-effacées. Il marchait en parlant; nous l'écoutions comme des disciples avides. Sa parolle de flamme donnait une nouvelle vie à tous ces chefs-d'oeuvre; son éloquence nous transportait dans les siècles passés; la ligne et la couleur s'animaient sous nos yeux; la forme altérée par le temps et par la main des profanateurs renaissait dans sa pureté première, et se montrait à nous dans sa jeune beauté. Tout un mystère de poésie s'accomplisait: c'était le génie moderne évoquant le génie antique. Puis, le soir, lorsque nous rentrâmes, après nous êtres assis sous les chênes vertes de laVilla Médicis*, après avoir causé longtemps coeur à coeur de toutes ces grandes merveilles, je l'entraînai à mon tour ver le piano ouvert, et lui faisant doucement violence: "Allons maître, lui dis-je, n'oublions pas notre chère musique; le violon vous attend; la sonate en la mineur (Kreutzer) s'ennuis sur le pupitre, commençons."

Oh, si tu l'avais entendus alors! Aveque quelle réligieuse fidélité il rendait la musique de Bthvn! Avec quelle fermeté plein de chaleur il maniait l'archet! Quelle pureté de style! Quelle vérité dans le sentiment! Malgré le respect qu'il m'inspire, je ne pus me défendre de me jeter a son coup, et je fus heureux en sentant qu'il me pressait contre sa poitrine avec une paternelle tendresse."

<One day, that I will never forget, we (Ingres* and a group of friends including Liszt) visited together the halls of the Vatican; we went through those long galleries where Etruria, Greece, the Ancient Rome, and the Christian Italy are represented by innumerable monuments. We respectfully passed in front of those yellowed marbles, and paintings worn away in the course of time. He talked while walking; we heard him like avid disciples. His inflamed words gave new life to all those master-pieces; his eloquence projected us into the passed centuries; lines and colours became full of life under our eyes; their shapes, altered by time and the profaner's hand, displayed themselves in their young beauty. We were attending to the accomplishment of a whole poetry mystery: it was the modern genius evoking the ancient one. Then, in the evening, when we returned, and after having sat under the green oaks of Villa Medicis*, after having chatted at length, heart to heart, of all those great marvels, I led him, on my turn, towards the opened piano, and exercising on him a soft violence I said: "Let us go, maestro, we must not forget our beloved music; the violin is waiting for you; the sonata in A minor (Kreutzer) gets bored on the music stand, let us start".

(As for the visit to the Vatican halls, I have been lucky enough to have had the same personal experience when visiting the Munich Kunstmuseum with a renowned Spanish painter friend of mine, Gerardo Rueda, and the impression that caused me was such that I will never forget it)

Oh, if you had heard him then! With what religious fidelity he rendered the music of Bthvn! With what warm firmness he handled the bow! What pureness of style! What truth in his sentiment! Despite of the enormous respect he inspires me, I could not help jumping onto his neck to embrace him, and, fortunately, my fears were dissipated when I felt that he was pressing me paternally against his breast.>

(He could as well have been talking about Paganini, couldn't he? This highly eulogistic report contrasts sharply with what is related about him by other relevant musicians like Gounod, or Charles Hallé. Gounod in his Mémoires d'un Artiste, Paris 1886, p. 87, says: *"M. Ingres played the violin. He was not a professional, even less a virtuoso, but he had played, in his youth, at the orchestra of the theatre of his native city, Montauban."* And Hallé, in his Autobiography, says: *[Ingres] Great artist as he was, with an immense reputation, he thought less of his paintings than of his violin playing, which, to say the least of it, was vile.*) For a more detailed view of Ingres see the encyclopaedia.

Hostility and triumph were Paganini's fate in Paris in 1831. Said Boerne: "it was a divine, a diabolic enthusiasm...the people have all gone crazy" and Castil-Blaze*: "there is no comparison possible between him and the others who have gone before him" Yet an ugly press campaign started when Paganini refused to play at a benefit concert, and the public began to see him as an avaricious miser. Renewed scurrilous rumours were revived, and not put to rest by Paganini's long and careful denial in the Revue Musicale of 21 April 1831. That same year he went to London, where he was greeted by another adverse press campaign led by The Times, accusing him, once more, of being a miserable greedy who gave his tickets exorbitant prices. But after the first concert the repentant Times had to admit: *"He is not only the finest player that ever has existed on that instrument, but he forms a class by himself"* He toured England, Ireland and Scotland in a staggering successful number of concerts.

THE DECLINE

The year 1834 (he was 62) saw the decline of Paganini's international career. His six years of international tours had made him rich and famous, but had shattered his health. In 1835 he settled in Parma where he had bought the Villa Gaione. The Grand Duchess Marie-Louise of Austria, then ruler of Parma, was an excellent amateur pianist and very hospitable towards artists; she knew Paganini from his first stay in Vienna, and was obviously delighted to acquire such an illustrious citizen. Paganini was given exclusive direction of music of the orchestra of the ducal theatre. In 5 January 1836 he wrote: "I am delighted at having obtained everything I could wish"

In 1837 Paganini embarked on a totally different venture. He backed the *Casino Paganini* in Paris, which was supposed to provide musical entertainment as well as gambling opportunities. He went to Paris to supervise the affair and stayed there until December 1838. It was during this period that the famous story of Harold happened. It was also in 1837 that he played in Marseilles in successful competition with young Ernst (23 in his prime, against a Paganini in his total decline) Paganini's presence in Paris could not save the casino; its operations were in violation of the law, and he was forced to close it after two months. Paganini, betrayed by his friends and advisers, sustained great losses.

The last years of his life saw the steady deterioration of his health. A larynx cancer was undermining his health, and at the end he could not speak at all. Only his son Achille understood what he said, acting as his interpreter. He stubbornly refused to see a priest, and the Church gave him up as a hopeless renegade. On these grounds the bishop of Nice denied permission for burial, and for several years his coffin was kept in a cellar. In 1845 the Grand Duchess of Parma authorised an interment at the Villa Gaione, until finally, in 1876, his remains were transferred to a cemetery in Parma. By his will, made three years before his death, he left an immense fortune and the title of baron, which had been conferred on him in Germany, to his son Achille. The fortune amounted to four hundred thousand US$ of 1899. Paganini never devoted himself to teaching. He had no teachers, he had no pupils, only his faithful worshipers. At the time of his death Paganini owned 22 valuable instruments including 10 Strads (3 violas and 2 cellos) two Amati and four Guarneri del Gesu. His pet one was the Guarneri del Gesu of 1742 "Canon" bequeathed to the city of Genoa, where it is kept in the Palazzo Civico. No artist might posses it after him, but it is customary that the most illustrious violinists could give special concerts with it.

List of the Strads of Paganini:

1690 Paganini; Boni; Hegar (cello)
1736 Paganini, owned also by Mendelssohn (cello)
1721 Paganini (viola)
1723 Paganini (viola)

1731 Paganini (viola) owned also by Berlioz, Joachim, and Mendelssohn.

VIOLINS
1680 Paganini
1722 Paganini; Earl of Westmoorland
1724 Paganini; Bentinck; owned also by Sarasate
1727 Paganini
1732 Paganini; Taylor; owned also by Spohr and Joachim

We have recorded:

- Variations on "nel cor piu" by Mullova "C-05"
-vl conc. 2 "la campanella" . "C-18"
- vl concerto 6 adagio* and rondo. Accardo. "C-06"
- Capriccios 1-12 Perlman. "C-06"
-      "   13-24   "   "C-07"
- Several movements of guitar sonatas by Zigante (guitar) "C-07"

BOOK FIVE

THE ROMANTIC ERA (CONTINUATION)

1784 SPOHR, LOUIS (b. Brunswick - d. Kassel 1859) German composer, teacher, conductor and violinist. Romantic. Musical.

He was, I said it under Paganini, the Pope of the musical life in Europe. He is the largest figure of the Benda's German school, that brights by itself.

Son of Karl, a doctor, he had his first lesson from his father who played the flute and his mother, an accomplished singer and pianist. In 1790 a successful concert at the court of Brunswick impressed vividly the Duke Karl of Brunswick who help him financially. In 1802 he became pupil of Franz Eck*, violinist of the Mannheim orchestra, who built anew his whole technique of violin playing.

After a long tour with Eck* which took them to Russia, Spohr returned to Brunswick in 1803. Here he heard Rode play, who left in him a long life impression, becoming his hero ever since. From 1804 to 1805 he toured Germany, giving concerts in Halle, Magdeburg, Berlin, Dresden and, above all, in Leipzig, where he had a staggering success at the Gewandhaus*. With his fame established in Germany he was named Konzertmeister* in Gotta.

During his years in Gotta, from 1805 to 1812 he devoted himself to composing and to conducting the orchestras of the festivals of Erfurt and Frankenhausen. In 1806 he married Dorette Scheidler, a virtuoso harpist, and he composed several pieces of music for them to play in joint concert tours that took them to London, Rome, Paris and Vienna, where he played with Rode in successful competition. (This victory over his life-long hero must not surprise us: Rode had lost catastrophically his faculties at a very premature stage, around 1808, when he was only 34 years old. His victory must have occurred around this date)

From 1813 to 1815 he directed the orchestra of the Theater an der Wien. From 1817 to 1819 he directed the orchestra of Frankfurt am Main and its Opera. In 1821 he settled in Dresden where he continued composing until 1822 when he was appointed Kapellmeister* of the Kassel orchestra for life. Under his direction the musical life of Kassel progressed greatly. After a long period when he became one of the best composers in Germany, he was appointed Generalmusikdirector at Kassel in 1847.

As teacher he received pupils from all over the world, among which stand out Ries* (Hubert); Ferdinand David**, Hauptmann* and Ole Bull**.

Spohr was considered the best violinist in Germany in his youth. As pedagogue he wrote a Violin Method in 1831 of great help for his students. He opposed the juggler trend and most specifically Paganini, of whom he had declared: *"In composition and in his style there is a strange mixture of consummate genius, childishness and lack of taste that alternately charms and repels"*. He over-lived his own epoch and became antiquated in his last years, like Cherubini.

I have selected from him the concerto n 8 Op 47 by Heifetz "C-7"

His Strads:

1700 Kempel
1718 Spohr; Bennett
1721 Spohr
1725 Spohr; Bott; Cambridge
1732 Spohr; Taylor; owned also by Paganini and Joachim

1790 LIPINSKI, KAROL (b Radzyn - d Urlow nr. Lwow 1861) Polish composer, conductor, teacher, violist and violinist. Romantic. Juggler + musical = virtuoso.

Lipinski had his first violin lessons with his father Feliks, conductor of the orchestra of the Potocki family. In 1799 Feliks was named conductor of the Orchestra of Count Starzenski, where he gave a post to his son Karol. In 1809 Lipinski became first violin* and later conductor of a theatre orchestra in Lwów. After a special journey to Vienna to meet Spohr in 1814, who encouraged him to continue, he resigned from the orchestra of the theatre and devoted to practice and composition. In 1817 he went to Italy to hear Paganini, giving concerts on his way in Croatia and Hungary. He met Paganini in 1818 in Padua, and even played with him.

In 1819 he started a career of concert tours that took him to Germany, Poland and Russia. In 1819 he met Paganini again in Warsaw, during the coronation of Nicholas I of Russia as King of Poland. Paganini's impression on him was so great that he retired from the concert platform for further studies and practice. From 1835 to 1839 he toured through Germany, Paris, Manchester, London, Vienna, Prague, and several cities of Russia, including St. Petersburg, Kiev and Moscow. In 1839 he was appointed Konzertmeister* in Dresden, where he settled. Besides his duties in the royal orchestra he formed his own string quartet, that had reputed fame.

Lipinski represents the orthodox romantic school of Viotti and Spohr. He played several times the viola, of which he was a virtuoso, as well, for Berlioz in his Harold.

He lost faculties much earlier that the barrier of the fifty years of age.

I have recorded from Lipinski his vl concerto 2 in D Major "Militaire" played by Igor Ivanov "C-8". (The performer is not at all at the level of our players, but it is not always possible to find a recorded piece played by one of the great. And it is always good, from time to time, to compare the bad with the good to see the excellence of the latter).

Lipinski played on a Strad of 1715 Lipinski; Tartini, owned also by Joachim.
1795 BOEHM, JOSEPH (b Pest; d Vienna 1876) Hungarian violinist and TEACHER Romantic. SCHOOL FOUNDER.

Boehm enters here as a superlative teacher, founder of the Vienna Romantic school. He received his first lessons from his father who was the violin leader* of the orchestra of the Pest Theatre. He then studied for a short period of time with Rode who impressed him greatly, becoming his idol. Rode's influence on Boehm is paramount to asses the importance of the Paris conservatory* influence all over the world, that we have singled out at the beginning of the Romantic era.

Boehm made his first public performance in Vienna in 1816. In 1819 he was appointed professor of violin of the new Vienna conservatory. He combined his conservatory duties with those of violinist of the imperial orchestra from 1821 to 1868. He had deserved fame as soloist and quartet player, being selected by Bthvn to play one of his string quartets. He premiered also several quartets by Schubert.

Boehm is the father of the Viennese violin school, having among his pupils violinist of such prestige as Joachim**, Ernst**, Remenyi*, Hellmesberger Sr. (Georg), and Jacob Dont* (teacher of Auer).

He played the Strad Khevenhueller of 1733, owned later by Menuhin.

1800 HELLMESBERGER, Sr, GEORG (b. Vienna; d. id. 1873) Austrian conductor and violinist. TEACHER. Romantic.

The XIX century awakens with the birth of another father of the Viennese school.

After having received lessons from his father at an early age, he played for the emperor at the age of five. He entered then the choir of the Hofkapelle* where he sang with Schubert, whom he replaced as soprano soloist voice. Intended to follow an ecclesiastical career he entered the Cisterciensis monastery of Heiligenkreutz, but he soon devoted himself to music. He was taught the violin by Joseph Boehm, and composition by Förster.

He made his public debut in 1819. He entered the Vienna conservatory first as Boehm's assistant in 1821. In 1826 he was named titular professor and in 1833 active professor, a post that he considered as a sacred task and which he held until his final retirement in 1867.

Hellmesberger became soon famous as virtuoso soloist, eventually displacing Boehm and Mayseder* as the most distinguished player of Austria. But his musical career included also other fields of the musical world, becoming Konzertmeister* at the Hofoper in 1830 and shortly afterwards member of the Hofkapelle*. He founded also the Philharmonic Concerts, which he conducted regularly, and was an enthusiastic player of chamber music, organising frequent concerts at is house.

As pedagogue he formed pupils of the importance of Joachim**, his son Joseph Hellemesberg jr**, Ernst** and Auer**.

1802 BERIOT, CHARLES AUGUSTE DE (b. Louvain-d. Bruxelles 1870) SCHOOL FOUNDER Belgian composer, teacher, pedagogue and violinist. Romantic. Musical.

Founder of the Belgian Romantic school. He received his first lesson from Jean-François Tiby who became his guardian after the premature death of his father. He advanced so quickly that at the age of nine he performed successfully a concerto by Viotti. His next teacher was André Robberechts, a pupil of Viotti. He travelled to Paris in 1821, where he played for Viotti. He wanted to have lessons with him, but since Viotti had all his time busy, he turned to Baillot. After a few months he made his debut in Paris, with enormous success. In 1826 he played in London with equal fortune. On his return to Brussels he was appointed solo violinist to King William I.

In 1829 he met the stunningly beautiful, most elegant and famous prima donna Maria Malibran*, daughter of the superb Spanish tenor and maestro of singing Manuel García* Sr, the best bel canto teacher of his day (being her maiden name, consequently, Maria García). Malibran was the name of her first husband, whom she had married as a means to escape the cruel harshness of her father. Her marriage was a complete failure and they fall apart in 1827. For the next six years Beriot and Malibran* travelled together giving joint concerts in England, Belgium, France and Italy. This liaison led to their marriage on 1836, when her first marriage was annulled. But it lasted only six months, Malibran dying from a sudden heart attack. The inconsolable Beriot gave up his concert tours and secluded himself in Brussels. (not the most appropriate place to cure a depression: with 90% humidity, almost perennial dark, cloudy skies, cold, and gloomy, it brings to my mind Jacques Brel's immortal song, "Le plat pays" which goes:…"*Avec un ciel si gris, qu'un canal s'est pendu*" <With such a dark sky that a canal hang itself>

In 1838 Beriot resumed his concert tours playing in Italy and Austria with the younger sister of Malibran*, Paulina Viardot* (maiden name Paulina García*).<here again, Paulina took her artistic name from her husband Louis Viardot, a distinguished French writer>. In 1842 De Beriot married again, this time Marie Huber, daughter of an Austrian judge. That same year he performed in Russia.

On the death of Baillot in 1842, his post as professor at the Paris Conservatoire* was offered to him, but after ten long years of hesitation, he declined, accepting instead an appointment to the Brussels Conservatoire. This ten-year laps of time was providentially vital in the history of violin playing, for it allowed Massart to grow up from the "supposedly" [1] 18 years of age he had then, to 29, an age deemed by the directors of the Conservatoire mature enough to consider his request to replace Baillot's vacancy. This fact is extremely important for us, for it brought about nothing less that the acceptance of LAMBERT MASSART as professor of the Paris Conservatoire, opening thus the new modern era of the violin.

---

[1] Massart had been made two years younger by his mother, in an effort to render more prodigious his prodigy child qualities.

Beriot was the founder of the Belgian school of violin. He was the opposite extreme of jugglery. In his Méthode 1858 he says: *"A fever for technique has mesmerised the violin, deviating it from its true mission, to imitate the accents of the human voice (without vibrato, as we will presently see) noble mission which has won for it the title of King of instruments."*

As a pedagogue he wrote a *Méthode du violon en trois parties* 1858, and *École transcendental de violon* 1867.

Let us see what he has to say on the vibrato: *"Of the vibrating sound: We understand by vibrating sound a certain undulation or tremor of sustained notes which in singing denotes the soul emotion transmitted through the voice The vibrated sound is a quality in the artist who knows how to use its effect on the adequate moment and knows how to abstain from it on purpose, but it becomes a failing if used too frequently. This habit, inadvertently acquired, deteriorates into a nervous tremulousness or quaver which one cannot command any longer, which produces a tiring monotony. The voice of the singer, like the beautiful quality of the violin tone, becomes altered by this capital flaw. This evil is even more dangerous as it is influenced and increased by the natural emotion which seizes the artist when he appears before the public. In the art of performance there is no other good emotion than that which the artist feels, but if he cannot master it, it goes always beyond the limits of truth. Whether he is a singer or a violinist, the vibrated sound is nothing but a convulsive movement on the side of the artist dominated by this fever to produce effect, which denaturalises the accuracy of intonation, making it fall into a ridiculous exaggeration. Therefore one should not use the vibrating sound but when the drama of the action demands it; but the artist must not try to acquire this dangerous effect, of which the use must be done with the most absolute soberness. Almost all the fiddlers who make a frequent use of the portée de voix (portamento*; glissando*) abuse also of the vibrating sound. One of these failures drags along the other inevitably. This great affectation introduced by the use of these elements renders the artist's playing mannered and exaggerated, for it gives the piece more expression than truth demands"*

I have translated literally the whole article for it is of the most relevant importance. Issued in 1858 it will be proved wrong by Lambert Massart and his pupils who played with vibrato at the same time of its appearance. Massart since 1830, Wieniawski since 1858, the year when Beriot's Méthode is printed, and Ysaye since 1878. The vibrato had the best against the arguments of Baillot, Spohr, Beriot and the rest of the orthodox. But on the other hand, and in that particular moment of history, Beriot was partially right. A virtuoso of the calibre of Sarasate, in the long sustained notes, had a sort of electrical quaver, a very fast, short in scope tremor, very disagreeable indeed; and his sugary glissandos* were of the most horrendous "mal gusto" (hear his nocturne by Chopin in "C-15"). Now, if this happened with nobody less than Sarasate, you can imagine with the rest of violinists.

Beriot's favourite pupils were Vieuxtemps** and Monasterio**.

Beriot favourite instruments include:

-Guarneri del Gesu "De Beriot" of 1744
-Strad of 1700 Berger, which he passed to his pupil Vieuxtemps;
-Strad of 1708 Regent; Superb.

1810 BULL, OLE and DAVID, FERDINAND

1810 BULL, OLE. [Ole Bornemann Bull] (b. Bergen- d. Lyso, nr Bergen. 1880) Romantic era. Norwegian composer and violinist. Romantic. Juggler + musical = virtuoso.

Belonging to a cultivated family, he was the son of a pharmacist. He took a violin for the first time when he was five-years-old. His first teacher was Niels Eriksen, and he made such rapid progress that when he was eight he was able to play at his home's musical soirees. He then entered the orchestra of the Bergen Harmonic Society, the statutes of which had to be altered to admit such a young member. He was then taught by two leaders* of the Harmonic Society orchestra: Poulsen, pupil of Viotti, until 1820 and Ludholm, pupil of Baillot, from 1820 to 1827. His father did not intend him to be a musician, and send him instead to Christiania to study theology in the university, but he did not pass the entry examination. He was then offered the posts of conductor of the theatre orchestra and the Musical Lyceum to substitute their leader*, Thrane, during his illness; but Thrane having died a few months later, he was appointed to succeed him as conductor. In 1829 he made his first tour abroad to Kassel and Copenhagen. In 1831 he went to Paris where he met the young Ernst. Here he contracted a serious illness, but was lucky to be nursed by his landlady, Madame Villeminot, whose grand-daughter he married in 1836. His performances in Paris had little success; he went then to Switzerland and to Italy, where he gave concerts in Venice, Milan and Trieste. He then went to Bologna where he had his first sensational concerts, and was appointed honorary member of the Accademia Filarmonica. For his journey to Italy Bull had made important modification in his violin, making the bridge flatter, and the bow heavier and longer, which allowed him to play difficulties never before heard and long polyphonic* passages that were a legendary feature of his technique. Bull met in Bologna Beriot and his future wife Malibran*, and both praised him greatly. After giving concerts in Naples and Rome, Bull returned to Paris giving a soloist concert in the Opera. He went to London in 1836 where he had a sensational success in the Philharmonic Society, becoming the greatest violinist of his time. Bull made a tour through the British isles giving no less that 270 concerts. He next went in triumph to Russia and Germany, returning to Norway in 1838, where he was received as a national hero. From 1839 to 1843 he gave more than 300 concerts in Austria, Germany, Sweden, the Netherlands and Denmark, playing with Liszt, Mendelssohn and David; in November 1843 he embarked for the USA, where he stayed for two years giving many successful concerts and being welcomed by the Americans like one of their nationals.

In 1846 he returned to Europe playing in France, Algeria, Portugal and Spain. Back in Norway he backed the idea of preserving the Norwegian art and founding a national theatre. After two years he inaugurated the Norwegian theatre in Bergen. Its business being not as good as he hoped, Bull was forced to tour again in 1852, going once more to the USA, where he got involved in the establishment of the "*New Norway*", a colony centred on a city which was to be called *Oleona*. He bought for this purpose more that 11,000 acres in Potter County, Pennsylvania, and in 1852 the new settlers began to come. After only one year it became evident that the land was better for timbering and industry that for farming, and in 1853 the whole scheme collapsed, and Bull sustained considerable losses that forced him again to tour to pay his debts.

In 1857 he returned to Bergen devoting his energies to the theatre, and to promote the career of several Norwegian dramatist, and musicians. He also tried, unsuccessfully, to create a conservatory. From 1866 to 1867 he made a long tour of Poland, Germany, and Russia. He returned to USA, where he married for the second time the 20-years-old daughter of a Wisconsin senator.

Bull knew not the barrier of the 50s, playing to perfection until his death.

He had an impressive personality that towered above all others. He was a consummate connoisseur in the violin making art, working closely with luthier* Vuillaume* when he was in Paris. Schumann regarded him as equal to Paganini. He could toss off from his violin the most hazardous juggleries, and at the same time play Mozart with the sweetest simplicity.

His Strads:

-1687 Bull Ole
-1690 Bull Ole; Telaki; it was presented by king Leopold II to Viotti. Wagner also owned it and it has his name stamped on it. Count Telaki presented it to the National Museum of Budapest in 1899.
-1708 Bull Ole; Wetherill owned also by Kreutzer.
- Also a Guarneri del Gesu *Ole Bull* of 1744.

1810 DAVID, FERDINAND (b. Hamburg - d. Klosters, [Switzerland] 25 Km E of Chur, 5 Km W of the frontier with Austria, 1873) German composer, conductor, teacher and violinist. Romantic. Musical. He was born in the same house as Mendelssohn.

He studied first with Spohr between 1823-25 in Kassel. From 1826 to 1828 he played in several German cities in company of his sister Louise. During this same period he was violinist at the Königstadt Theater; he made a good friendship with Mendelssohn with whom he played chamber music.

For the next six years he was leader* of the string quartet of Karl von Liphart. In 1836 he went to Leipzig to be leader* of the Gewandhaus* orchestra under the direction of Mendelssohn, a post that he kept for the rest of his life. He combined his duties here with those of leader* of the Stadttheater and director of church music in Leipzig. During this period he married the daughter of his old patron Sophie von Liphart. From 1839 to 1841 he visited twice England, where he met Moscheles*. At the opening of the Leipzig conservatory in 1843 he was appointed professor of violin. His first important pupil was Joachim**, who went to him on Mendelssohn's advise.

He also was a significant advisor in the composition of Mendelssohn's violin concerto, of which he gave the first performance on March the 13th 1845, playing his Guarneri del Gesu of 1742, and which was subsequently dedicated to him. From 1851 to 1866 he remained in the Gewandhaus* being increasingly active as conductor. His health deteriorated considerably in his last years, but when advised by his doctor to give up his performances he replied "my heart would stop beating if I cannot play the violin"

David was not a virtuoso in its fullest sense, but he played with great musicality and intelligence; his command of the finger board was good but he lacked stamina and speed. He was an excellent leader* of the violins and a good conductor as well.

140

As pedagogue he gave a great impulse to the Leipzig conservatory. His most important pupils were Joachim**, Wasielewski* and Wilhelmj*. He published numerous musical works like his Violinschule (1863) and many studies by Rode, Kreutzer, Gavinies, Fiorillo*, and Paganini. He edited the first practical volume of Bach's unaccompanied violin works, and several didactic études.

He has been dedicated also the sonata vl, p. Op 121 of Schumann.

His favourite instruments:

Guarneri del Gesu "David" 1740 owned later by Wilhelmj* and Heifetz**. It was on this instrument that David premiered Mendelssohn's concerto in 1845.
Guarneri del Gesu Ex David 1730
Guarneri del Gesu Ex David 1735
Strad of 1698 Lark.

I have recorded an arr. by him of La Folia, sonata by Corelli, played sublimely by Enescu in "C-2" and, as a remembrance of his Mendelssohn's dedication of the vl concerto, the same played by Grumiaux, in "C-8".

BOOK SIX

THE RISE OF THE MODERN ERA.

THE GREAT REVOLUTION OF THE VIBRATO.

THE NEED TO OBTAIN A LOUDER SOUND FROM THE VIOLIN

The appearance of the vibrato was the fruit of a need of the times, which called for an intensified expressiveness, a higher communication with the public through the transmission of musical sensations, much more moving, that would unburden the romantic, passionate, vibrant feelings of the author's soul, by means of an externalisation that, trespassing the limits of his intimacy, and of the rigid tight rules of classicism, would reach the ears of the public vivid and full of light as a gigantic spiritual vent.

We are in the midst of Romanticism. There were also practical reasons: the new concert halls were much wider, the writing style of the musical literature around 1830, was much more colourful through the wind instruments (Weber, Rossini) which demanded more string instruments, and more sonorous ones. (This sonority would be given by the vibrato) Last, there was also the Romantics' proclivity to pathos, very specially Meyerbeer and Berlioz

Be it as it were, they all felt the need for a louder sonority in the string instruments. The need was there, but no one knew how to satisfy it. The Massart's vibrato bridged this gap. The new vibrato, originally dubbed the "*French vibrato*", met all the previous requirements. This explains the enthusiastic support of Vieuxtemps to the Marsick's (pupil of Massart) and Ysaye's interpretations of his own works, with an intensified vibrato the existence of which and, above all, its effects, he never had imagined, although he anxiously yearned for them. The vibrato adds changes in frequency level <recognised by the ear as pitch changes> Intensity level

<Loudness> and variations in the harmonic* structure of the sound. These variations cause the aurally pleasing changes in the quality of the sound notes played with vibrato. For further details see Fletcher and Sanders. "Quality of Violin Vibrato Tones" Journal of the Acoustical Society of America xli (1967) 1534.

MAIN CHARACTERISTICS:

a) The continuous vibrato becomes an organic part of the left-hand technique and is embraced by the 100% of violinists. So far the words that appeared unceasingly under the pen of the critics to describe the performance of their contemporary violinists were "grace, elegance, charm, easiness and variety of bowing" and also "power, amplitude, intensity of bowing expression". The bow was the main part in violin playing, the left hand having the only task to stop* the strings at the correct note, which unfortunately was not precisely the case in the ancient or romantic era. The lapses of intonation, on the contrary, were of common use. How should one cover his lapses of intonation? Through jugglery: the greater the speed, the less probabilities there were that listeners could detect intonation's lapses.

From Massart on the words tender, sensuous, melancholic, dramatic, sweet, prevail, all deriving from the effect produced by the vibrato in the violin tone.

b)The violin's tone becomes much louder and full of emotion, and at the same time, much easier to play in tune: i.e. since the modern vibrato is more intense and much wider that the ancient and romantic ones, having an oscillation of roughly a full tone, like the trill*, if the performer doesn't stop* the string in the just place, (and supposing he hits within plus-minus a tone of difference) with the help of his left hand rocking he can shift his position* to the correct intonation at a fraction over dictation speed, all within the tremor of his vibrato, without being noticed by the listener.<It is what professor Ivan Galamian calls "instant adjustment" which he considers to be a part of the violin technique. Says Galamian: *"The artist must be extremely sensitive and should have the ability to make instantaneous adjustments in his intonation. (The best and easiest way to make such adjustments is by means of the vibrato)>* (Principles of violin playing & teaching. Second edition. 1985, 1962. Chapter two. The left hand. Intonation. Page 22. Prentice-Hall, Inc. A Simon & Schuster Company. Englewood Cliffs, New Yersey 07632. Printed in the USA. ISBN 0 - 13 - 710 773 - 0)

c)The founder's idea was that *the violinist must not astonish his listeners with his technique, but he should move,* (a reaction against the, then, prevailing jugglery). But the technique has developed so much since then that today players astonish and move at the same time, in what has become the sheer perfection in music. It is the "desiderata" of every musician.

THE COEXISTENCE OF, AND THE STRUGGLE BETWEEN, THE ROMANTICS AND THE MODERNS

From Massart on we will have to attend to an enormous dissociation between the orthodox, who stubbornly prohibited the vibrato, and Massart and his legions of disciples who used it. This dissociation would have last almost for ever due to the fact that it was very difficult, in those days, to listen to each other. This ever lasting war between the followers of one group and the others ended, finally, abruptly with the invention of a sort of atomic bomb, that stopped the struggle once and for all in benefit of the beauty of the continuous vibrato: the gramophone. This occurred in 1912 when Ysaye started recording.

Even after the invention of the gramophone there were orthodox, antiquated teachers, who would condemn the vibrato as an abominable defect, in particular Pougin* and Auer**. For these, and for many others, the vibrato was simply unbearable, and they kept on complaining of the intolerable abuses of the vibrato made by many contemporary violinists. Not really very smart, instead of profiting of the great occasion they had to hear at the same time the best Romantic and Modern performers, they kept on complaining.

But their pupils, following the example of the great violinists of the beginning of the 20th century, namely Ysaye, Carl Flesch, Kreisler, Enescu, Elman, Heifetz and Francescatti, all available through the gramophone, would not pay any attention to their romantic teachers, and against their will and prohibition, they would continue to use the vibrato. On the divorce pupil-teacher think, for example, of Ysaye. He learnt his most beautiful vibrato when he was very young from Wieniawski (direct pupil of Massart) in Brussels, and later he went to Paris to study with Vieuxtemps who opposed frontally the vibrato. But Vieuxtemps' efforts (if any) to eradicate the vibrato from him were in vain; Ysaye learnt a great deal with Vieuxtemps' lessons, of course, but he continued with his vibrato as a precious treasury, such as it had been taught to him by Wieniawski. Later Vieuxtemps accepted the vibrato, as it is evident through his enthusiastic support of Marsick's. (pupil of Massart) and Ysaye's interpretations of his own works, all with vibrato.

Similar divorce existed in singing, between the orthodox, who were in favour of prohibiting the tremolo*, and the progressists, who advocated for it. Wishing to determinate de Beriot's assertion that the vibrato (tremolo) was also a capital flow in singing, I have bought the most important and influential singing method of the period, that of the Spanish maestro of singing *Manuel (Patricio) García* *(Sitches)*, (Manuel García Jr.) teacher of Jenny Lind*, Mathilde Marchesi*, Julius Stockhausen* and Charles Santley* among others. He was brother of the two gigantic Prima Donnas Paulina Viardot* and María Malibran*. Both took their artistic names from their husbands. In his *Traité complet de l'art du chant*, Paris, published as late as 1878, García* says: Quote. The tremolo* must only be used to describe feelings that in real life move us deeply: the anguish of seeing some beloved person in an imminent danger, the tears that we shed in certain states of anger or revenge, etc. Even in these circumstances, its use must be strictly regulated by buon gusto and restraint; as soon as one exaggerates its expression or duration, it becomes tiresome and disgraceful. Apart from the special instances we have just given, one must abstain from altering in the least the just intonation of sound, for the reiterated use of the tremolo* renders the voice quavering. The artist who has acquired this intolerable defect becomes unable to phrase any kind of sustained singing. That is the way that many beautiful voices have been lost in the art of singing. The voice quaver is, in any case, but an affectation of the sentiment that certain people believe to be a truly feeling. Certain singers wrongly believe that through this means they render their voices more vibrant, just as several violinists try to increase the loudness of their instrument by the undulation of its sound. The voice cannot vibrate but by the effect of the brilliance of its timbre and the air emission power, and not by its trembling. Unquote.

(Despite García's diatribe against the tremolo* in 1878, the voice followed the violin's footsteps very closely, finding its way into the opera in an astonishing short period of time of less than 20 years, and thus, for instance, we can hear Caruso through the gramophone in 1910 with a splendid, wide, sensuous tremolo*.)

Ysaye took his vibrato from Wieniawski, who in his turn had taken it from Lambert Massart. Ysaye's recordings ended the war instantaneously like the atomic bomb in the 2nd World War, and nobody cared of the orthodox teachings, but all embraced the new vibrato.

The only exception to the vibrato in violin playing is jazz, where you can find some fiddlers playing without it, and, of course, in good versions of all the ancient baroque and romantic music, which should follow the uses of the time, when there was no vibrato. For example Mutter plays the piece for vl solo by Bach without vibrato in "C-3".

LAMBERT MASSART FOUNDER OF THE MODERN SCHOOL

A) THE LOGICAL ARGUMENTS

That Massart is the real founder of the vibrato school is the conclusion of three different tracks of investigation: 1) A letter from Liszt to Massart himself. 2) The teachings of the Bible. 3) The original name of the vibrato.

1) The Liszt's letter. In an invaluable letter that Liszt wrote to him from Milan on the 2nd of September of 1838 (Lettres d'un Bachellier ès Musique) the vibrato is mentioned explicitly for the first time in the XIX century to describe a violin performance, and it is precisely that of Massart. Says Liszt: "...Votre pensée vient-elle parfois chercher l'ami absent pour le faire asseoir à vos côtés, partager vos travaux, applaudir à vos succès, sourir à vos joies? Oh! dites qu'il en est ainsi. Dites que rien n'est changé. Dites qu'à mon retour je retrouverai ma place à votre foyer, mon abri dans votre coeur. Dites aussi que j'entendrai de nouveau mes accords energiques et VIBRANTS, ces chants plein de tendresse et de mélancolie que je n'ai jamais pu écouter sans me sentir profondément ému, et qui restent pour mois l'ideale expression de votre bienfaisante et fidèle amitié".

<..."Do your thoughts sometimes go in search of the absent friend to make him seat near you, to help you in your work, applaud your successes, smile with your joys? Oh! Do tell me it is so. Say that nothing has changed. Say that on my return I will find my seat around your fire, my shelter in your heart. Tell me, as well, that I will hear once again my energetic and VIBRANT chords*, those songs full of tenderness and melancholy that I could never listen without feeling deeply moved, and which continue to be for me the ideal expression of your beneficial and faithful friendship.">

These tenderness and melancholy were very contagious and all his pupils and descendants, to use a more affectionate word, became infected with them, in particular Wieniawski and Kreisler.

2) The teachings of the bible. But we have other proofs. Says the Bible: "by your deeds shall ye be known"

Which were the deeds of Massart? An impressive roster of laureates coming out of his classes, among which we have two stars that bright with

146

special intensity: Wieniawski and Kreisler, his most renowned pupils. The two played with an intense vibrato, and we have irrefutable evidence of it:

a) Wieniawski: Unfortunately he died before the gramophone was invented, but we have the testimony of his condisciple Kreisler: "He could toss off technical fireworks, but also move his listeners to tears. The emotional quality of his tone was heightened by an intensified vibrato which he brought to heights never before achieved"

b) Kreisler is quite a different thing. We can hear him play in "C-10 and 11". I like to think of him as the mirror of his teacher: his vibrato, tenderness and melancholy are indescribable. The cassettes are just to show that. It cannot be that both, Kreisler, and Wieniawski, each one on his own, decided independently to play with vibrato. They must have had something in common, and this was Lambert Massart, the teacher of the two, or, to use a more familiar term, their "father".

3) The original designation of the vibrato. The first indisputable notice we have on the vibrato was that of Wieniawski, through the testimony of his condisciple Kreisler, that we have seen in paragraph 2.

The next we know for certain who played with vibrato was Ysaye from his gramophone recordings. During this first period the new vibrato was dubbed the "FRENCH" vibrato. But paradoxically none of the players who used it were French, so there is an apparent contradiction between the players' nationalities and the vibrato's dubbing as "French"

David Boyden* in Die Musik in Geschichte und Gegenwart, vol. 13, col 1979-1980, Im 19en Jahrfundert, relates Wieniawski with Ysaye and Vieuxtemps. The similitude with Ysaye is patent through the gramophone. That with Vieuxtemps is much more questionable.

To begin with, Vieuxtemps was the favourite pupil of Beriot, whose diatribe against the vibrato as a most abhorrent defect, we have seen in his article, so it is not very probable that his pet pupil might have played with it. Vieuxtemps heard the Wieniawski's vibrato for the first time in St. Petersburg in 1848, when he was already 28-years-old and in full possession of his technique. Much as he praised Wieniawski, it was not question to rebuild anew his whole violin career to acquire the vibrato technique; it clashed frontally with his deep principles of non vibrato playing. On the other hand he was too mature to go to the Massart classes. (Nevertheless we will soon see a violin teacher of the Berlin Conservatory, in full maturity, who implored Massart to enter his classes: Rappoldi)

147

i) Being Wieniawski Polish and Ysaye Belgian, it would have been absurd to dub the vibrato the "French" Vibrato. Where is that French component of it? In that it came from and was originated in, France, more precisely in the Paris Conservatoire* where Massart was the violin professor.

ii) By locating the vibrato in Paris the apparent contradiction disappears, for it took its name from its place of origin: the Paris Conservatoire. Now everything is clear. All the first players of the new vibrato were pupils of Massart, or pupils of his pupils as Ysaye who learnt it from Wieniawski.

iii) There is a third violinist (incidentally Austrian) who played with vibrato, and most curiously, he is also a direct pupil of Massart: Kreisler. Gentlemen: it is as plain as a pikestaff.

B) THE DOCUMENTED EVIDENCE: THE MANUSCRIPT LETTERS TO MASSART

So far, so good. Up to now we have been working with presumptions, assumptions, deductions and suppositions. But I wanted something more clear, more specific, more straightforward; some documented evidence which might refer directly to the vibrato, or else that might name specifically Massart as founder of the modern era.

So I started looking for some descendants of him that could have some documents in which I would be able to base my assumptions; and I managed to find out in Belgium a family, collateral to Massart, that has kept with scrupulous good care a great amount of letters written to him; and there I went. A large majority of them consist of letters of invitation, gratefulness, social life and the like, many addressed to his wife, Aglaé Masson, formidable pianist, professor at the Paris conservatory* and most beautiful and attractive indeed, to whom Berlioz writes what amounts to be true love letters with absolute impudence and piquant coquetry. And after having perused with great difficulty more than eight hundred manuscript ones, lo and behold, I finally found exactly what I was looking for: an inestimable letter of Kreisler to him in which he declares him to be the founder of the vibrato.

The letter is dated in Vienna the 31st of December 1890, And says "...it is to the plain and frank truth that I render homage when I assure you that I hold you in great esteem, that I love you, and that I consider you as the founder of my talent (Kreisler was then in full possession of his talent ever since he had won the Paris first prize in 1887.) Notice that Kreisler had been

148

taught first by Jacques Auber, and then three years by Hellmesberger Jr., both Romantic; but he recognises only Massart as the founder of his talent.

How is Kreisler's talent? Upon what is it built?

Any one who hears him play will notice at once that Kreisler's sublime, divine Art, is built upon two main pillars:

a)   his continuous vibrato
b)   his glissandos*

The combination of both give his play that insaissable tenderness and melancholy that characterises him as well as Massart himself. (remember Liszt's Lettres d'un Bachelier ès Musique addressed to Massart) Kreisler is the mirror of Massart, his alter ego, the branch that stems from Massart's tree, his reincarnation. We shall have a closer look at it when we talk about Kreisler.

These pillars, these two ornaments, were precisely those that were specifically forbidden in writing, as the most abhorrent sacrileges, by all the teachers of the time (see de Beriot's work Méthode de violon 1858 in which he recommends the teacher to punish and repudiate any attempt by the pupils to play with vibrato or make any glissando*; and he added that the vibrato defect drags inevitably the performer to the other defect, the glissando, both being intolerable shortcomings that had to be eradicated as soon as they were noticed) See also Baillot, Spohr, Auer, Flesch.

So Kreisler admits in writing that Massart is the founder of the vibrato and the glissando*. This honours him greatly, for there are few pupils who would admit, once they have acquired fame, that all they are, almost in its entirety, is due to their teacher.

The reader will presently find two letters of Kreisler addressed to Massart and their translation.

Kreisler's first letter to Massart

Vous raconter de mes succès, que je ne dois qu'à vous

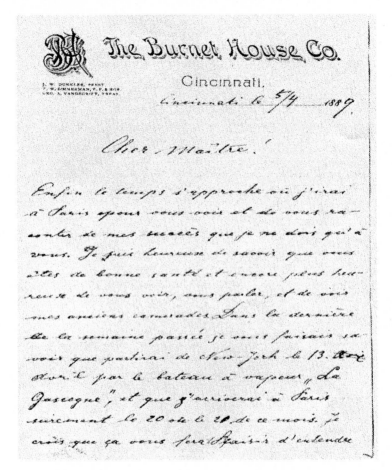

raconter de la Chûte du Niagara, du Mississippi et aussi de votre ancien élève Bannet qui, un charmant garçon, duquel je faisais connaissance à New-York. Pour maintenant peu revoir en 14. jours, mon cher maître, Espérons que je passerai la mer en revenant aussi bien qu'en allant. En vous priant d'accepter l'expression de mon estime je reste

Fritz Kreisler

151

TEXT OF KREISLER'S FIRST LETTER to Massart

(vous raconter de mes succès, que je ne dois qu'à vous)

Cincinnati le 5/4 de 1889

Cher Maître!

Enfin le temps s'approche où j'irais à Paris pour vous voir et de vous raconter de mes succès, que je ne dois qu'à vous. Je suis heureux de savoir que vous êtes de bonne santé et encore plus heuruex de vous voir, vous parler, et de voir mes anciens camarades. Dans la dernière de la semaine passée je vous faisais savoir que partirai (sic) de New York le 13 d'avril par le bateau à vapeur "La Gascogne" et que j'arriverai à Paris surement le 20 ou le 21 de ce mois. Je crois que ça vous ferat plaisir d'entendre raconter de la chûte di Niagara, du Mississippi et aussi de votre ancien élève Banner, un charmant garçon, duquel je faisais connaissance à New York. Pour maintenant au revoir en 14 jours, mon cher maître. Esperons que je passerai la mer en revenant aussi bien qu'en allant. En vous priant d'accepter l'expression de mon estime je reste   Fritz Kreisler

* * * *

TRANSLATION OF KREISLER'S FIRST LETTER
To tell you about my successes that I only owe to you

Cincinnati the 5/4 1889

Dear Maestro!

At last the hour has come for me to go to Paris to see you and to tell you about my successes that I only owe to you. I am happy to learn that you are in good health and even more happy to be able to see you, to talk to you, and to see my old comrades. In my last letter of the week before I informed you that I'll leave New York the 13th of April in the steamship "La Gascogne" and will arrive in Paris surely the 20th or the 21st of this month. I hope it will please you to hear me tell you about my experiences in the Niagara falls and the Mississippi, and my encounter with your old pupil Banner, [1] a charming boy, whom I met in New York. That's all for now. I'll see you in 14 days, my dear maestro. Let us hope that I'll cross the sea on

---

[1] Banner: born in Sacramento (Ohio) USA the 20th August 1868, won first prize under Massart in 1884

my return as smoothly as I did when I came here. Praying you to accept the expression of my high esteem I remain

yours sincerely

Fritz Kreisler

Kreisler's second letter

Que je vous aime comme fondateur de mon pouvoir

s'étende au-delà des bornes ordinaires en s'écoulant tranquillement.
C'est à la franche et simple vérité
que je rends hommage quand je
vous assure, que je vous estime,
que je vous aime comme fondateur
de mon pouvoir et que j'en fais
mon possible p afin de me rendre
plus digne de vous et qu' un jour
vous trouviez un artiste perfectionné, qui soit regardé avec fierté
par vous en votre.
    élève et ami

Fritz Kreisler

Vienne, grosse Schiffgasse 21.
    Schiffasse   21

TEXT OF KREISLER'S SECOND LETTER to Massart
(Que je vous aime comme fondateur de mon pouvoir)

Répondu de Nice
de Nice le 6 Février (ècrit par Massart)   Vienne e 31/12 1890
        1891

Cher Maître, Vous serais surpris, Monsieur Massart, en ouvrant ma
lettre car je parais penser si peu à vous tandis que j'y songe plus que vous en
doutez. Il aurait été trop commun de vous écrire une foule de phrases
banales, plongées en devotion et des felicitations; mais puis-je m'aquitter
(sic) avec cela à votre égard? Je ne puis qu'esperer et souhaiter que votre vie
si utile au monde s'étand au-delà des bornes ordinaires en s'écoulant
tranquillement. C'est à la franche et simple vérité que je rend hommage
quand je vous assure que je vous estime, que je vous aime comme fondateur
de mon pouvoir et que j'en fais mon possible afin de me rendre plus digne
de vous et q'un jour vous trouviez un artiste perfectionné, qui soit regardé
avec fierté par vous en votre

        Élève et amis.   Fritz Kreisler
                        * * * *

TRANSLATION OF KREISLER'S SECOND LETTER
(that I consider you as the founder of my talent)
Vienna the 31/12, 1890
Answered from Nice
        from Nice   written by Massart
        the 6th February 1891

Dear Maestro, You will be surprised, Monsieur Massart, on opening
my letter, for I seem to think of you very little, whereas I do it much more
that you can imagine. It would have been too pedestrian to write you a letter
brimming with trivial praises, apologies and best wishes for the New Year;
but will it acquit me in your judgement? I cannot but hope and wish that
your life, so useful to this world, continues to flow peacefully beyond the
normal boundaries of life. It is to the plain and simple truth that I render
homage when I assure you that I hold you in great esteem, that I love you,
and that I consider you the founder of my talent, and that I do my best to
become worthy of you so that one day you will find an accomplished artist
of whom you could be proud. Your pupil and friend, Fritz Kreisler

MASSART AS A PEDAGOGUE

Massart was a phenomenal pedagogue with an impressive list of laureates coming out of his classes, which we will see shortly afterwards, that confirm him to be the best teacher in history. But among them there are two stars that bright with special shine: Wieniawski and Kreisler. These two "sons" of Massart give evidence of his extraordinary pedagogical faculties.

a) Wieniawski was, everybody agreed on that, the foremost virtuoso of the age.

b) We cannot say the same of Kreisler, for it would not be true. He lacked a lot of technique and he boasted of it. "I need not practice -he used to say- just dipping my hands in warm water is enough", but it was not, indeed. In this he followed the teachings of his maestro who had declared: "a violinist should not astonish his audience with his technique, but he should move: a tear, a smile are better than astonishment" But he was unique, and he probably moves more than any other violinist in history.

Among the manuscript letters I had the opportunity to read in Belgium, there are many that refer to Massart's renown as teacher. A great amount of them are of recommendation, coming from the most outstanding musicians of the time.

a) So, for instance, VIEUXTEMPS, in a letter dated in Frankfurt 11 August 1856, says: "I have a violin student, who has won the first prize in this conservatory, Adolf Gross, who desires to improve his knowledge, and I, quite naturally, have thought of you..."

b) LEO DELIBES recommends him Charles Kaese, first prize of the Vienna conservatory, in a letter dated in Vienna 30 November 1855.

c) ERNST's letter, dated in Marseilles 8 March 1865, is very juicy indeed. *"...I have learnt that three of your pupils have won the first prize this year. Are you aware that you are very lucky with your pupils? But rather I should say, indeed, that they are very lucky too, to have found such a good teacher as yourself.*

Wieniawski and I have met a lot last summer in London. I have found him just colossal in his musical talent, and sweet and charming as a friend. He has improved a lot in every respect."

<In 1865 Ernst was 51-years-old, and, as we know, one of the best, if not the best, violinist alive. Berlioz compares him unflatteringly with Joachim. By that time Wieniawski was 30 at the peak of his career. The fact that Ernst says he is "just colossal" speaks clearly of Wieniawski's superhuman talent.>

d) One of the best violin teachers in Germany, professor of the conservatory of Berlin, where Joachim** was the director, EDOUARD RAPPOLDI*,[1] writes from Berlin the 19 May 1874 imploring Massart to allow him to enter his classes!! (a teacher longing to become a pupil? it has to be seen to be believed) or to spend some two months with him wherever he would like, because *"I wish to be informed on several matters relative to the art of violin playing from whom I consider to be the greatest pedagogue of the world"* Coming this statement from a connoisseur of the importance of Rappoldi it only corroborates what we already know: i.e. that Massart was indeed the greatest in the world. (If he had with him as director Joachim, the best violinist of his time, what was he looking for in Massart? Indeed something new, not known until then, that Massart knew well. I leave the reader full liberty to guess what could it be.

1811 MASSART, (JOSEPH) LAMBERT (b Liège - d Paris 1892) Belgian teacher and violinist. Most musical. FOUNDER OF THE MODERN ERA. Massart was born on the 19th of July 1811 in Liège.

His birth certificate of the following day says: "The year one thousand eight hundred and eleven on the twentieth day of the month of July, at eleven hours in the morning, before us, Frédéric Rouveroy, deputy mayor of the city of Liège, department of Ourte, deputised by the said mayor, chevalier de la Légion d'honneur*, according to his decree of last December 31, ordering us to fulfil the duties of public officer of the registry office, has appeared before us Joseph MASSART, aged 46 years, musician, with domicile in this municipality, rue de l'Agneau 418, south district, who has presented us a child of masculine sex, born yesterday near midnight, from the said declarer and from Marguerite Schreders, his spouse, and to whom he has declared to wish to give the names of LAMBERT – JOSEPH..."

Three days later he was baptised in the church of Saint-Denis in Liège being his godfather Jean Joseph Massart (eldest brother of his father, who would later taught him to play the violin) and his godmother Marie

---

[1] Rappoldi* was reputed to be one of the best teachers of Austria and Germany, and had been one of the most salient pupils of Hellmesberger, and as such he is mentioned in this book. For more details see L. Rappoldi*: *Memoriem* (Dresden 1929).

Josephine Guillaume, spouse of Gerard Thonnard, giving him the names of Lambertus Josephus.

The Massart family, all composed of musicians, is so numerous that it became an enormous anthill, terribly complicated, that has discouraged many a musicologist on its study, having more than 30 musicians in a lapse of three generations. Still in 1914 one could hear in Liège to speak of the "Massart's tribe"

The eminent Liège Conservatoire musicologist, José Quintin, started very seriously the matter in 1963 but eventually had to give up his investigations due to the enormous difficulties it involved. Nevertheless he has been so kind as to send me a résumé of all his inquiries:

"the first one, a cargo handler, was
-<1> Jean Marie (b 1729-d after 1807) married to Mme Delva had 8 children (6 girls and 2 boys <8> and <9>)
- 8> Joseph Marie, father of Lambert (b Liège 1761 - d 1830) married to Mme Jacob, had 9 children (8 boys <10-14> <16-17> and one girl <15>) All the boys were musicians.
- <17> LAMBERT MASSART, married to Aglaé Masson, piano professor at the Paris Conservatoire*. No children.
- <13 bis> Victor M. Son of <13> (b Liège 1799 - 1883) Doblebassist, professor at the Liège Conservatoire, married to F. A. Hérode, had 4 children <30 - 33>
- <30> Jean-Victor-Leopold (b 1832)
-<31> Alphonse, great friend of Berlioz, primo violino of the Orch de la Société Philharmonique de Paris.
- 32> Nicolas-Louis-Leon (b 1836 - d 1910) Cellist, prodigy child, professor of the Liège Conservatoire (1859-1909)
- <33> Hubertine. Singer. The 2nd of August 1847 Hubertine gave a concert in Spa (Belgium) with her brothers Alphonse(violinist), Léopold (pianist) and Leon Massart (cellist). The orchestra was conducted by their uncle Louis Massart. Louis conducted the Spa's orchestra from 1839 to 1849, settling then in Saint Quintin (France)
- <11> Hubert M. (b Liège 1793 - d 1858) Married Mme M. Th. Touvenot. Hubert was horn player, professor of the Liège Conservatoire (1827-1856) They had 4 children (3 boys and 1 girl, among them <23>
- <23> Joseph (b 1818 - 1897) Violinist and pianist, piano professor at the Liège Conservatoire (1858-1897) married to Ch. E. Raveau, had at least 2 boys <23 a >
- <23 a> Rodolphe M. (1840 - 1914) violinist, professor of the Liège Conservatoire, teacher of Ysaye."

When Massart was born in Liège, the city was attached to France ever since the decree of the Convention of the 9th Vendémiaire of the year IV See calendar* of French revolution (1st. October 1795), being therefore part of the French Empire. Liège remained French until January 1814, when the first treaty of Paris detached it from France.

Lambert Massart was taught music first by his father Joseph Marie and later he was put under the tuition of his father's eldest brother Jean-Joseph (b. 1790 d 1818) disciple of the famous teacher Gaillard. After the premature death of his uncle Jean Joseph in 1818, when Massart was 7-years-old, young Massart passed under the tuition of Delaveux (b Liège 1787-d id 1849) also pupil of Leonard-Joseph Gaillard (b Huy 1766 - d Liège 1837). Delaveux, being at the same time professor and impresario, presents his pupil, prodigy child, to the Liège public in March 1821 at the Société d'Emulation. Lambert Massart is eight-years-old.[1]

Several successful concerts followed in Liège, Gand, Bruxelles and Aix-la-Chapelle. Here the young virtuoso performed two pieces written to his intention by the violin solo to king Louis XVIII, Fontaine: one andante and a rondo. In 1823 he played in Paris, and in 1824 in Liège in the same Salle de l'Emulation. In January 1826 Massart obtains a sensational success in his second concert in Paris. He is only 15 and he had made a name already. In 1831 in the Paris Conservatoire*, he played a piece for solo violin composed by Auguste Kreutzer. But the first great concert of the young virtuoso was in Liège in 1834, where he played an original theme with variations composed by himself, and a concertino (Italian: small concert) for violin composed by Auguste Kreutzer to his intention. Massart was 23. A Parisian critic praises "the vigour, the grace, the infinite variety and the agility of his bow, the exquisite and delicate expression, the quality of his sound"

Delaveux got a scholarship for his pupil from the Ville de Liège and from the king of the Low-Countries William I, to go to complete his studies in Paris, but his entrance in the Conservatoire* is blocked by Cherubini on the grounds that he was a foreigner. Nevertheless Rodolphe Kreutzer made him his favourite pupil and protégé. Massart entered into the Kreutzer

---

[1] In order to increase the value of his condition of prodigy child, his parents decided to make him two years younger than he really was, pretending that Lambert was born in 1813. This lie was believed by everyone included Massart himself, who in his two letters requesting the vacancy of Auguste Kreutzer as professor of the Paris Conservatoire, says that at the death of Auguste Kreutzer in 1832 he was only 18-years-old.

family the 21 February, 1827. He soon became another member of the family, being nicknamed "Pouff".

Born French in Liège, "Pouff" will make in Paris a first magnitude French carrier. He received both the teachings of Rodolphe Kreutzer and those of Auguste Kreutzer, his younger brother, who replaced Rodolphe as teacher in the conservatory at his death.

In 1829 he was finally admitted to the Conservatoire* as foreign student of counterpoint* and fugue*. First he was admitted to the preparatory classes given by M. Millault, assistant professor to M. Fetis*, where he remained till the 17 December 1831 (two years and two months). He passed then to the special class of counterpoint* of M. Fetis, remaining there until his voluntary exit on the 11 June 1832.

His talent perfected with the aid of his perseverance in his studies; unfortunately, he gave very few public concerts, and lived retired with the Kreutzer's family, where he had found a devoted affection. The result was that his natural shyness, far from diminishing with time, did but grow; (it is absolutely necessary for the artist-performer, the frequent exhibition of his talent, if he does not want to loose his self-confidence).

Massart used to withdraw, also, to his own cosy drawing room, in which the musical soirées, accompanied by his wife, the superb pianist Aglaé Masson, had deserved fame.

During the winter of 1841 Massart gave several highly successful concerts in Paris and a staggering one in Brussels, where the King honoured him as Chevalier de L'Ordre de Léopold de Belgique.

The last time Massart gave proof of his talent was at the Société du Conservatoire* the 23 of May, 1843, playing with Liszt the Bthvn sonata in A minor, "Kreutzer". To play with Liszt was a very hazardous undertaking, indeed, and we will presently see the reason for it.

Sir Charles Hallé* was among the audience in this concert and, in his autobiography, tells us what happened: (Sir Charle's account is very succinct and bare; but with the help of a little imagination, and of what we know on the Lisztomania*, we can arrange a well adorned scene) No sooner had the first sound of the violin started, when a voice from the audience called out "Robert le Diable!". This call was repeated by many others and the sonata had to be interrupted, or as Sir Charles beautifully says, the cries *drowned the tones of the violin*. Robert le diable was a fantasia that Liszt had composed recently based on themes of the opera of the same title written by Meyerbeer which was at the top of its fame. This fantasia, on its turn, had been played by Liszt with staggering success many times, and was all the rage at the time. Liszt rose from his stool, bowed to the public and said: "I am always the humble servant of the public; but do you want to hear the fantasia now or after the sonata?"; to which new and more intense cries of Robert were the only reply. Liszt turned to Massart to dismiss him, and sat at the piano. The fantasia under Liszt's magical fingers turned the audience into an absolute frenzy; they all became crazy, and stormed the platform to congratulate and embrace him, profiting of the confusion to try to steal off from his garment, as a trophy, a button or any badge or decoration Liszt might wear. On their side, swooning lady admirers would try to cut a few locks from his hair. All this hysteria that Liszt used to provoke, ~~on purpose~~, all along his life was dubbed by Heine* *Lisztomania** and is discussed more deeply in the encyclopaedia.

Berlioz gives us a complementary view of the same scene[1]: *"There were cries of admiration, heated moments in which the orchestra, so far quiet, took the main part; a deluge of flowers that flooded the stage, and Bravos! from ladies who never applaud. In a word, all the necessary to constitute one of the greatest triumphs, so scarce and ridiculous when they are not sincere.*(refers to Liszt's previous interpretation of Bthvn's piano conc. 5) *Massart overcame the many difficulties of the sonata, increased by the fast rhythm Liszt gave to the allegro, which on certain moments was so quick that it was hardly possible to follow him with the violin."* (Berlioz. Beethoven. Espasa Calpe. Colección Austral. 992. P. 125)

When all this turmoil came to a rest, Massart, most dutifully, returned and played the Kreutzer sonata, which fell entirely "flat" after the dazzling display of the great pianist, or as Sir Charles puts it, *the Kreutzer sonata somehow no longer seemed in its right place.* (Try this: fill a glass with Coca Cola and put in some ice on top; you will know what I mean: all its bubbles vanish and it becomes "flat"). Massart hardly could follow the frenzied, diabolic, fast rhythm Liszt imposed to the sonata, (enraptured as he was with his staggering triumph). This event proved to be the last straw for Massart's career of virtuoso violinist. This humiliating and bitter blow on Massart's proud was too much for him, and he promised never again to play in public. He devoted instead all his energies to teaching, and thus is how he became the ~~best teacher in history~~. This is not the only example where an apparent

---

[1] Hector Berlioz
. Beethoven. Espasa Calpe. Colección Austral. 1979, Madrid. Pag. 124

misfortune turns up to be a magnificent fortune for the welfare of mankind. We will find it again when we talk about Perlman.

[this kind of abuse of force was a frequent artifice of Liszt, whereby he showed off his pre-eminence above others. He did the same thing to Sir Charles Hallé* himself, one day that he made him the honour to ask him play a duet for two pianos with him, at a concert at the house of Princess Czartoriska. After having said they will give a *moderate* pace to the theme and variations, he played it in octaves* at a diabolic speed, to the horror of Hallé who reports: "I did not conceive the possibility of getting through my portion of them alive"

On the other side, Liszt was extremely kind and sensitive when he played the Kreutzer sonata with Ingres* {the scene is described in Paganini's book} adapting himself to the naturally limited faculties of the great painter, which resulted in one of the best versions of the sonata Liszt had heard in his life]

HIS EFFORTS TO BECOME A PROFESSOR AT THE CONSERVATOIRE

At the death of Auguste Kreutzer in 1832 Massart was too young (18) to occupy that chair, and although he applied for it, the Conservatoire's director, Cherubini, refused to accept it on grounds of his early age, and finding no other violinist good enough for the post, the class was suppressed. Ten years later, and only after knowing that de Beriot, to whom it had been offered, had refused to accept it, Massart requested the vacant post in two letters dated in Paris the 29 December 1842 and 11 January 1843 respectively.

In both Massart is obsessed with one single idea, a "Leitmotif"*, if I may say so: The need that the Conservatoire* should have another school of violin playing, other than the old, French, romantic one, represented by Habeneck* and his pupil Alard**. He wants to introduce at any price his new modern school, taking advantage of the prestige of both the Kreutzer brothers, even if it were for the price of sharing the same chair with Alard. But let us read how Massart "sells" his own artistic image. Massart is so anxious to enter as professor in the Conservatoire* that within two years, 1842 and 1843, he writes two letters requesting to be admitted.

163

M. Thornton — P. 1. P. f° 51. n° 335. Paris, 29 Décembre 1842.

Monsieur (le Directeur Auber)

Ayant appris que M. de Bériot avait définitivement renoncé à la
place que vous lui aviez offerte au Conservatoire et que vous en étiez informé,
je me suis présenté plusieurs fois chez vous sans être assez heureux pour
vous rencontrer. Malgré mes droits incontestables à la classe laissée
vacante par la mort de M. Baillot, j'ai cru devoir rester à l'écart tant
qu'il y a eu incertitude sur l'acceptation de M. de Bériot; mais cette
incertitude n'existant plus, je viens, Monsieur, vous rappeler tous
les droits, bien convaincu que votre impartialité et votre justice
vous feront accueillir ma candidature.

Envoyé à Paris en 1823 par le roi des Pays-Bas, et à la demande
de la ville de Liège ma patrie, je fus confié aux soins particuliers
de M. Rodolphe Kreutzer, le célèbre violoniste et compositeur, qui écrivit
exprès pour moi différents morceaux, que j'exécutai aux grands
Concerts Spirituels de l'Opéra. Je recevais en même temps les
conseils de M. Auguste Kreutzer, son frère, qui lui succéda en 1825 ou 26
comme professeur de violon au Conservatoire. La santé de ce dernier
étant très délicate et l'obligeant à de fréquentes absences, je fus
chargé de le remplacer par votre prédécesseur, Monsieur Cherubini.

Mr Auguste Kreutzer est mort en 1832 et pendant les dernières
années de sa vie j'ai dirigé presque constamment les études
de la classe. il serait trop long de mentionner ici tous les excellents
élèves qui en sont sortis. Je ne citerai que MM. Leudet, Sagarin,
Lecorbeiller etc. et Mr Artot qui remporta à cette époque le
second et le premier prix et dont les études m'avaient été particulièrement
confiées par notre maître commun. à la mort de Mr Auguste Kreutzer
j'avais 18 ans. Mon âge ne permettant pas que j'occupasse une
position aussi importante et aucun autre violoniste n'étant alors
assez marquant pour l'obtenir, cette classe fut supprimée,
mais avec la promesse que me fit Mr Cherubini de me proposer
à la première qui viendrait à vaquer. Tous ces faits, Monsieur, sont
d'une entière exactitude : les feuilles de présence ainsi que le témoignage
des professeurs de cette époque, ne vous manqueraient pas au
besoin.

Aucune vacance ne s'est présentée depuis dix ans et je ne
pense pas que cet espace de temps ait amoindri ma réputation ;
j'en puis en donner pour preuve les succès que j'ai obtenus
l'hiver dernier à Paris et plus récemment encore en Belgique où
le roi m'a accordé la décoration de son ordre -

Tout incontestable qu'en soient les droits sur lesquels je m'appuie,
je voudrais cependant, Monsieur, devoir en abandonner une partie,
reconnaissant le poids que doit avoir auprès de vous une auguste
recommandation en faveur de Mr Allard, qui d'ailleurs n'a même
pas encore obtenu son second prix au conservatoire où j'y remplissais
déjà les fonctions de professeur. Je viens donc, Monsieur, dans le but de

concilier en même temps les intérêts de Mr. Allard et la justice
de madame, qui ne peut être niée par personne, vous propose de
partager la classe entre nous deux, bien persuadé que ma
nomination obtiendrait l'approbation des Artistes. Une autre considération
doit aussi, ce me semble, vous faire désirer que Mr. Allard ne soit
pas nommé seul; car, dans ce cas, étant élève de Mr. Habeneck,
les deux seules classes de violon seraient alors dirigées par
la même école.

Puis-je espérer, Monsieur, dans la supposition où vous
auriez quelques objections à faire à ma candidature, que vous
voudrez bien me donner l'occasion d'y répondre. Si l'on
m'opposait ma qualité de Belge, je vous prierai d'observer
que la place avait été offerte à Mr de Bériot qui, lui même,
est Belge; que je suis né sous la domination française en
1813 et que d'ailleurs, habitant Paris continuellement
depuis vingt ans, je crois pouvoir être considéré comme
français.

Veuillez, Monsieur, me pardonner cette
trop longue lettre et recevoir en même temps que mes
excuses l'assurance de ma haute considération.

Vendredi, 9 Décembre 1842.   Lambert Massart

                                        rue St georges 18

Document conservé au Centre historique des Archives nationales à Paris.
Cote AJ/37/71 and AJ/37/217
CHAN-CARAN/SR/VZ/13/12/99/R-8613

166

TEXT OF MASSART'S FIRST LETTER (to the director of the Conservatoire Auber*)

Monsieur,

Ayant appris que M. De Beriot avait définitivement rennocé à la place que vous lui aviez offerte au Conservatoire et que vous en étiez informé, je me suis présenté plusieures fois chez vous sans être assez heureux pour vous rencontrer. Malgré mes droits incontestables à la classe laissée vacante par la mort de Baillot, j'ai cru devoir rester à l'ecart tant qu'il y en a eu incertitude sur l'acceptation de M. De Beriot; mais cette incertitude n'existant plus je viens, Monsieur, vous rappeler tous ces droits, bien convaincu que votre impartialité et votre justice vous feront accueillir ma candidature.

Envoyé à Paris en 1823 par le roi des Pays-Bas et à la demande de la ville de Liège, ma patrie, je fus confié aux soins particuliers de M. Rodolphe Kreutzer, le célèbre violonist et compositeur, qui écrivit expres pour moi différents morceuax que j'exécutai aux grands Concerts spirituels* de l'Opéra. Je recevais en même temps les conseils de M. Auguste Kreutzer, son frère, qui lui succeda en 1825 ou 1826 comme professeur de violon au Conservatoire. La santé de ce dernier étant très délicate et l'obligeant à des frequentes absences, je fus chargé de le remplacer par votre prédécesseur, Monsieur Cherubini.

M. Auguste Kreutzer est mort en 1832 et, pendant les dernières année de sa vie, j'ai dirigé presque constamments les études de sa classe; il serait trop long de mentioner ici tous les excellents élèves qui en sont sortis. Je ne citerai que M.M. Leudet, Lagarin, Lecorbeiller, etc. et M. Artôt* qui remporta à cette époque le second et le premier prix et dont les études m'avait été particulièrement confiés par notre maître common <Rodolphe Kreutzer>. A la mort de M. Auguste Kreutzer j'avais 18 ans. Mon age ne permettant pas que j'occupasse une possition aussi importante et aucun autre violoniste n'étant alors assez marquant pour l'obtenir, cette classe fut supprimée, mais avec la promesse que me fit M. Cherubini de me proposer à la première qui viendrait vaquer. Tous ces faits, Monsieur, sont d'une entière exactitude: les feuilles de présance ainsi que le témoignage des professeurs de cette époque ne vous manqueront pas au besoin.

Aucune vacance ne s'ést présentée depuis dix ans et je ne pense pas que cet espace de temps ait amoindri ma réputation: je puis en donner pour preuve les succès que j'ai obtenus l'hiver dernier à Paris et plus récemment encore en Belgique ou le roi m'a accordé la décoration de son ordre.

Tout incontestables que soient les droits sur lequels je m'appui, je crois cependant, Monsieur, devoire en abandonner une partie, connaissant le poids que doit avoir auprès de vous une auguste recommendation [1] en faveur de M. Alard, qui d'ailleurs n'avait pas encore obtenu son second prix au Conservatoire que j'y remplisais dèja les fonctions de professeur. Je viens donc, Monsieur, dans le but de concilier en même temps les intérèts de M. Alard et la justice de ma cause, qui ne peut être niée par personne, vous proposer de partager la classe entre nous deux, bien persuadé que ma nomination obtiendrait l'approbation des Artistes. Une autre consideration doit aussi, ce me semble, vous fair désirer que M. Alard ne soit pas nomme seul; car, dans ce cas, étant élève de M. Habeneck*, les deux seules classes de violon seraient dirigées par la même école.

Puis-je espérer, Monsieur, dans la supposition où vous auriez quelques objections à faire à ma candidature, que vous voudrez bien me donner l'occasion d'y répondre. Si l'on m'opposait ma qualité de Belge, je vous prierez d'observer que la place avait été offerte à M. De Beriot qui, lui même, est Belge; que je suis né sous la domination française en 1813 et que d'ailleur, habitant Paris continuellement depuis vingt ans, je croi pouvoir être considéré comme français.

Veuillez, Monsieur, me pardonner cette trop long lettre et recevoir en même temps que mes excuses l'assurance de ma haute considération

Vendredi 9 Décembre 1842   Lambert   Massart
    Rue St. Georges 18

* * * *

TRANSLATION OF MASSART'S FIRST LETTER

To Monsieur the Director of The Conservatoire (Auber*)

Monsieur,

Having learnt that M. De Beriot had renounced for good to the place offered to him in the Conservatoire and that you had been briefed of it, I have called on you several times, but I was not lucky enough to be received by you. Despite my indisputable rights to occupy the chair left vacant at the death of Baillot, I deemed it my duty to keep out of the way so long as there

---

[1] With all probabilities from King Louis-Philippe d'Orleans, himself.

was uncertainty about the acceptance of M. De Beriot; but since this doubt does not exist any more, I come, Monsieur, to remind you of all my rights, in the understanding that your impartiality and justice will make you accept my candidacy.

Brought to Paris in 1823 by the king of the Low Countries and at the request of the city of Liège, my homeland, I was put under the private tuition of M. Rodolph Kreutzer, the celebrated violinist and composer, who wrote and dedicated specially for me several pieces of music that I played at the great Concerts spirituel* of the Opera. At the same time, I received the lessons of M. Auguste Kreutzer his brother, who substituted him as violin professor in the Conservatoire in 1825 or 1826. But being his health very delicate, he was forced to frequent absences, and I was asked by your predecessor, Monsieur Cherubini, to replace him. M. Auguste Kreutzer died in 1832 and during the last years of his life I have directed almost constantly the studies of his class. It would be too long to mention all the excellent pupils who had come out of this chair. I will only quote M.M. Leudet, Lagarin, Lecorbiller etc. and M. Artôt* who won at that time the second and first prizes, whose studies had been very particularly entrusted to me by our common maestro. (Rodolphe Kreutzer) At the death of M. Auguste Kreutzer I was only 18-years-old. My young age did not allow me to occupy such an important position, but as there was not any other salient violinist to obtain the place at that time, this class was suppressed, but with the promise made by M. Cherubini to propose me for the first chair that would be vacant. All these facts, Monsieur, are totally exact: the attendance register as well as the testimony of the teachers of that period will corroborate them, if needed.

Since there has not been any vacancy for the last ten years I do not think that this lapse of time might have diminished my reputation: the success I had last winter in Paris and, more recently even, in Belgium, where the king has honoured me with the decoration of his order, give proof of it.

No matter how indisputable may be all these rights upon which I relay, I believe, nevertheless, Monsieur, that I should abandon some of them, knowing the power that must have upon you an august recommendation[1] in favour of M. Alard who, incidentally, had not yet won the second prize of the Conservatoire, that I was exercising already the functions of professor. I, therefore, Monsieur, propose to reconcile the interests of M Alard and the justice of my cause, that cannot be denied by anybody, by sharing the chair between the two of us, fully persuaded that my nomination will obtain the approval of the Artists. It seems to me that another consideration must also

---

[1] with all probabilities from king Louis-Philippe d'Orleans, himself.

make you desire that M. Alard should not be nominated alone, for in that case, being him a pupil of Habeneck*, the two only chairs of violin would be directed by the same school.

May I hope, Monsieur, that on the case that you would have any objection to my candidacy, you would grant me the opportunity to defend myself. If I would be objected on the grounds of my condition of Belgian citizen, I would pray you to consider that the place had been offered to M. De Beriot who is Belgian himself, that I was born under the French domination in 1813, and that besides that, having lived in Paris continuously during the last twenty years, I think I could be considered as being French.

I pray you, Monsieur, to excuse me this too long letter, and to receive, together with my excuses, the assurances of my high regard.

Friday 9th December 1842   Lambert Massart
Rue St. Georges 18

In his following year's letter, dated in Paris the 11 January 1843, apart from repeating the same list of illustrious pupils coming out of the classes of both Rodolphe and Auguste Kreutzer, and repeating the same historical record that headed his precedent letter he says:

11 Janvier 1843

[lettre manuscrite]

Document conservé au Centre historique des Archives nationales à Paris.
Cote AJ/37/71 and AJ/37/217
CHAN-CARAN /SR/VZ/13/12/99/R-8613

TEXT OF THE END OF MASSART'S SECOND LETTER (to the director of the Conservatoire and the members of the Teaching Committee)

"Je termine, Messieurs, cette trop long lettre en vous priant d'apprecier la necessité qu'il y a de reunir dans le Conservatoire differentes écoles de violon. Celle de Rodolphe Kreutzer est européenne et aucun n'a produit un plus grand nombre de violonistes distingués. J'ajouterai aux noms précédement cités, ceux de M Auguste Kreutzer*, Lafont*, Vidal, Charles et Auguste Tolbecque*, Battu, Tilman et tout d'autres qu'occupent ou ont occupé des places importantes soit en France soit à l'étranger.

Puis-je espérer, Messiuers, que vous êtes maintenant persuadés de la validité de ma demande et que vous ne la jugerais pas trop présumtueuse en m'accordant l'hommage de vos suffrages.

Veuillez, Messieurs, agréer l'assurance de ma consideration respectueuse

Paris 11 Janvier 1843   Lambert Massart"

* * * *

TRANSLATION OF MASSART'S SECOND LETTER

"...I end, Messieurs, this too long letter by praying you to recognise the need there is in the Conservatoire to include the different violin schools. That of Rodolphe Kreutzer is European and no one has produced a higher number of distinguished violinists, I would add to the names previously cited those of M. August Kreutzer*, Lafont*, Vidal, Charles and Auguste Tolbecque*, Battu, Tilmans and many others who occupy or had occupied important places in France or abroad.

May I hope, Messieurs, that you are by now convinced of the validity of my request and that you will not find it too presumptuous, granting me the honour of your approbation."

* * * *

Eventually the Conservatoire created two independent new violin chairs, one for Alard, the other for Massart; they were appointed professors on the same day, the 24 February, 1843. Their pupils came from all over the world, as the administration of the Conservatoire no longer barred foreigners from being admitted.

MASSART'S LONG LIST OF FIRST PRIZE LAUREATS

Even before becoming professor of the Paris Conservatoire* Massart managed to make one of his pupils win the first prize in it: After the death of

Rodolphe Kreutzer his violin chair was taken by his brother Auguste Kreutzer in 1825; but his bad health forced him to very long absences and the Conservatoire's director, Cherubini, requested Massart to replace him. One of his best pupils was M. Artôt*, whose education had been particularly entrusted to him by Rodolphe Kreutzer. Massart managed to make Artôt* win the first prize by unanimous vote in 1828.

After only three teaching years Massart started his long list of first prizes with the most phenomenon violinist of his time, nobody less than WIENIAWSKI, when he was 11 years old. This feat was never surpassed, and was only equalled by Ginette Neveu, in the same Conservatoire de Paris*, with another premier prix in 1930 when she was 11, as well. Neveu is a direct successor of Massart through Enescu and Flesch, pupils of Marsick, direct pupil of Massart. (She is, therefore, a grand-grand daughter of Massart, artistically speaking). But this was only the beginning. The palmarès of PREMIERS PRIX of his pupils is really impressive: their brand new vibrato was en vogue and caused a sensation, and they won their first prizes with astonishing flying colours. If we discount 1871, the year of the Franco Prussian* war, when the violin class was suspended, he got an average of more than one premier prix per year, surpassing not only all his colleagues in the Paris Conservatoire, but any other teacher in history.

This is the list of them:

1828 1) ARTÔT* (Joseph) by unanimous vote. Born in Brussels 25th January, 1815
1846 2) WIENIAWSKI** born in Lublin (Poland) 1835
1848 3) REYNIER (Leon) Born in Saint-Cloud (Seine et Oise) 15-years-old
1849 4) CHERY (Victor CIZOS) born in Auxerre (Yonne) 19-years-old.
1850 5) LABATUT
1851 6) FLORENS (Juan) born in Mahon (isla de Menorca, Spain) 5th Nov. 1834
1853 7) FOURNIER (Hyppolite-Henri) born in Paris (Seine) 7th June 1829
1853 8) LOTTO* ISIDORE
1858 9) GROS (Victor-Aimé) born in Lyon (Rhône) 11th March 1837
1861 10) WILLAUME (Jules-Louis) born in Villore-Cotterete (Alene) 24-3-1847
1861 11) JACOBI* (Georges) born in Berlin (Prussia) 13th February 1840
1861 12) WILLAERME
1863 13) DESJARDINS (Leon-Charles-Edouard) born in Paris (Seine) 5 April 1847, professor at the Conservatoire, 1890-190?
1864 14) CHOMANOWSKY (Jean-Désiré) born in Warsaw (Poland) 23 May 1846
1865 15) FRIEMAN* (Narcisse-Gustave) born in Lublin (Poland) 17th October 1844
1866 16) TAUDOU* (Antoine Antonin Barthèlemy) born in Perpignan (Pyrènèes-Orietales) 24-8-1846, professor at the Conservatoire 1883-1913.
1866 17) Miss CLOSET (Marie-Alexandrine) born in Lyon (Rhône) 15-4-1853

1867 18) LEVÈQUE (Marie-Jean-Baptiste) born in Hem (Somme) 10 July 1846

1868 19) RIES* (Franz-Wilhelm) born in Berlin (Prussia) 7th April 1846

1869 20) MARSICK** (Martin-Pierre-Joseph) born in Jupille (Belgium) 10 March 1847, who will be his successor as professor in the Paris Conservatoire, and who will play a decisive role in the transmission of the modern school to the 20th century.

1871 <There was no contest due to the Franco Prussian* war>

1872 21) SEIGLET (Victor-Joseph) born in Lyon (Rhône) 15th August 1847

1873 22) HOLLANDER (Benôit) born in Amsterdam (Holland) 8th June 1853

1874 23) LEFORT (Narcisse-Augustin) born in Paris (Seine) 18th June 1852, professor at the conservatoire 1892-1929.

1877 24) BERTHELIER (Jean-Baptiste) born in Limoges (Haute-Vienne) 27th Dec. 1856, professor at the Conservatoire 1896-1915.

1878 25) ROEMY or Rémy* (Guillaume-Antoine) born in Ongrée (Belgium) 26th August 1858.(Ysaye's rival at the Liège Conservatoire, and professor in the Paris Conservatory*, 1896-1929)

1879 26) ONDRICEK* (Franz-ONDRICEK) born in Prague (Bohemia) 29 April 1857

1879 27) MENDELS (Israel) born in Brussels (Belgium) 19th August 1859

1880 28) TUA*, TERESINA (1866-1956)

1881 29) WOLFF (Jean-Louis) born in The Hague (Low Countries) 12th May 1861

1882 30) MELBERNAK

1883 31) HAYOT, professor at the Conservatoire, 1894-1896.

1883 32) GELOSO

1884 33) BANNER (Michael) born in Sacramento, Ohio (USA) 20.8.1868

1885 34) SICARD (Michaël) born in Odessa (Russia) 7th December 1867

1886 35) BRUN, professor at the Conservatoire, 1896-1929.

1886 36) SINAY

1886 37) MORET

1886 38) ROSETTI

1887 39) KREISLER** Friederich-Max, (better known as FRITZ) born in Vienna (Austria) 2nd February 1875

1887 40) WONDRA (Charles-Henri) born in Constantinople (Turkey) 29th August 1868

1887 41) PELLENC (Leon-Darius-Herbenval) born in Toulon (Var) 23-11-1866

1887 42) RINUCCINI (Charles-Louis) born in Cluny (Saône et Loire) 15   Sept. 1873

1887 43) GAUTIER

1889 44) DURIEUX (Edouard-Charles-François) born in Lille (Nord) 10 May 1873

1889 45) DUPORT (Marie-Amélie-Josephine) born in Lyon (Rhône) 23 January 1867

1889 46) BARACH (Emile) born in Vienna (Austria) 8th Sept. 1870

1889 47) BOURGAUD (Auguste-Jeanne-Mario) born in Lyon (Rhône) 24-2-1875

1890 48) Miss SCHYTTE (Frida) born in Copenhagen (Denmark) 31st March 1871

1890 49) KOSMAN (Elkan) born in Rotterdam (Holland)

1891 50) QUANTÉ [1]

---

[1] Although Quanté and Wormèse won the first prize under Garcin, the bulk of their formative period, the first four teaching years, were given by Massart.

And I have discovered another first prize among the famous letters in Belgium. Gounod in a letter dated in Saint Cloud 4 August 1867 tells Massart that his son JEAN GOUNOD has obtained the premier prix thanks to his teachings. Gounod will be first prize number 52.

IN TOTAL, 52 premiers prix in 46 teaching years, an average of more that one first prize winner per year. I challenge the reader to name any other professor in history with a higher average. At year's end the pupils of every professor of the same instrument competed with each other for the premier prix. Massart's pupils had to deal with those of the following teachers:

François Habeneck* 1841-1860.(Pupil of Baillot, won premier prix in 1804)
Paul Guérin 1841-1860 (Got prix d'encouragement in 1813)

Delphin Alard** 1843-1875. (Pupil of Habeneck*, got premier prix in 1830)
Charles Dancla* 1860-92. (Pupil of Baillot and Guérin, won 1st prize in 1833)
Eugene Sauzay* 1860-1892 (Studied with Baillot. Got premier prix in 1827)
Jean-Pierre Maurin* 1875-1894. (Pupil of Baillot and Habeneck*, won premier prix in 1843 under the latter).

CONTINUATION OF MASSART'S STUDY

Massart wrote no original didactic work, nor did he need to do so, in view of the phenomenal results he got as teacher without doing it: the spectacular list we have just given proves it. No other teacher had ever had such remarkable achievements. A glory to boast of.

His motto was, we said it before, *"a violinist should not astonish his listeners with his technique, but he should move: a tear, a smile, are better than astonishment"*

Massart, as founder and pioneer of a new era, a totally different way to play the violin, deserves, at least, the same importance as the other two era founders: Corelli and Viotti. But with this important difference: whereas Corelli and Viotti had, say, a 60% of followers, the remaining being dissidents to a more or less extent, Massart had the 100% of followers, all accepting unanimously the modern vibrato without a single exception. And what is more, this feature tends to perpetuate itself instead of diminishing.

If we take a panoramic view of all the pupils and violinists belonging to the Massart's school (or to put it more affectionately, the Massart's family)

175

we will discover with amazement that all of them are particularly musical, tender and melancholic like the great maestro. None of them is juggler, (with the exception of Wieniawski who was both juggler and musical, i.e. virtuoso, and that of Ysaye who had a certain "penchant" to jugglery) and they all prefer musicality to technique. This very particular feature of Massart, already highlighted by Liszt in the letter to him mentioned above, has perpetuated along history to our days, from his first direct pupils (his sons: Wieniawski, Kreisler and Marsick), going through (his Marsick's grand sons: Flesch, Enescu and Thibaud), up to (his grand-grand sons: Hassid, Neveu, Menuhin and Grumiaux) Here lies, precisely, the grandeur of Massart as teacher: that he has managed to infect with his contagious tenderness and melancholy all his disciples, and the disciples of his disciples, and so on and so forth, or, as I like to put it, all his "family descendants"

Massart was a very daring innovator and just on the time when all teachers condemned, expressly in writing, and without exception, the use of the vibrato, he not only used it in his own playing, but taught it to his pupils, showing an enormous faith in what he was doing and in the future of his teachings.

Massart also devoted himself with great enthusiasm to chamber music and he founded a string quartet which had deserved fame.

He was also a viola virtuoso and played it several times for his friend Berlioz in Harold.

Massart was a great friend of Liszt, and in the latter's separation from the Comtesse d'Agoult*, and the subsequent bitter quarrel over their children, he was the moderator, and go-between, taking care of them during most of 1844-45. Massart's arrangements, at first, worked well, but when their young offsprings became the object of a tug-of-war between their parents, Liszt wrote to Massart a letter on May 2, 1845 urging him to take whatever action was necessary to ensure that the children did not fall into Marie's hands. (Vier, Jaques. Franz Liszt. L'artiste, le clerc: Documents inédits. Paris, 1951) Massart was present, as well, at the famous duel between Thalberg and Liszt, in the salon of Princess Cristina Belgiojoso-Trivulzio, on March 31, 1837. (As a matter of fact the competition was among Thalberg, Liszt, Chopin, Czerny*, Herz and Pixis, each had to play a fantasie on the Marche des Puritains, by Bellini, and each having to perform a piece of their composition.)

In 1849, on the occasion of Massart's marriage to the beautiful and superb pianist Aglaé Masson, Liszt wrote him a cheerful letter of congratulation, not exempted of a certain jealousy: *Vous voici donc marié ! Personne ne saurait vous féliciter plus sincèrement que moi, car personne ne vous porte plus sicèrement envie ! Le mariage, la famille, quels plus doux et plus nobles buts de l'homme ! Et combien n'y aspiré-je pas de toutes les forces vives et harmoniques de ma nature !<"So you are married then! No one could congratulate you more sincerely than I, for no one envies you more sincerely! Marriage, family, what sweeter and nobler aims for a man! And how I would aspire to them with all the vigorous and harmonious forces in my nature">* (Vier, Jaques. Franz Liszt : L'Artiste, le clerc: Documents inédits. Paris, 1950, p. 93) <At that time Liszt was struggling to marry princess Carolyne, as stated by himself: "I dearly wished to call [Carolyne] by the sweet name of wife"> (La Mara, ed. Franz Liszt. Briefe, vol. 5 p.53)

In a letter Liszt wrote to Massart dated in Lyon, the 29th June, 1837, he said: *"You know (or rather, you do not know sufficiently) how much I am totally yours"* (Jacques Vier. Franz Liszt. L'Artiste-Le Clerc. P. 32. Les Editions du Cèdre. Paris, 1950)

Massart's and his pupils vibrato was called at the beginning the French vibrato, but soon it became of necessity the universal vibrato.

Liszt was not the only musician to be highly fascinated by Massart's vibrato: Leon Kreutzer*, composer, pianist and writer on music (son of Jean Nicolas Auguste, brother of Rodolph Kreutzer**, in a letter addressed to Massart, dated in Paris February 21, 1846, tells of his admiration for his dazzling bow and says:*"... You make your Stradivarius tremble"* (Sur un évantail de Marie-Antoinette et des musiciens liégeois de Paris. Extrait de "Si Liège m'était conté" Liège n° 8 (1963) Joseph Philippe)

DECORATIONS AND HONOURS

Massart's decorations include:

-Chevalier de la Légion d'honneur* 1864.
-Chevalier de l'ordre de Léopold de Belgique.
-Palme de l'instruction Publique.
-Caballero de la Real y Distinguida Orden de Carlos III, Spain, 16 March 1865.
-Cavaliere dell'ordine della Corona d'Italia 1882.
-Ufficiale dell'ordine della Corona d'Italia 1890.
-Chevalier de l'Ordre de Danebrog.

HIS SUCCESSION AT THE CONSERVATOIRE

Massart's final and irrevocable resignation as teacher of the Conservatoire, was the cause of the outbreak of one of the most turbulent periods within the conservatory:

1) On the one side there was, so to speak, the natural, statutory successor to Massart: Jules Auguste Garcin*, called **Salomon**. (1830 Bourges – 1896 Paris) Garcin was one of the most illustrious violinists in France. Having won the first prize of the Paris Conservatory* in 1853 as pupil of Alard, he was admitted to the opera orchestra in 1856. Here he soon became solo violinist, then third conductor in 1871 and chief conductor in 1885. His association with the Société des Concert du Conservatoire* started in 1860, becoming solo violinist and in 1885 principal conductor. In this post he promoted with energy German music, particularly Bach's B minor Mass, Wagner and Brahms, whose music was still very controversial in France. He premiered also Cesar Franck's symphony at the conservatoire in 1889. His long teaching career at the Conservatoire began in 1875 leading the preparatory classes until 1890, when he is promoted to violin teacher, to substitute Massart. He was also a founder member of the Société Nationale de Musique in 1871.

He was decorated Chevalier de la Légion d'honneur* in 1889.

2) On the other hand, there were the interests of all pupils to maintain the new technique of the vibrato at any price. When the rumour had it that Massart was going to resign, the pupils, who didn't want him to go for love or money, addressed a letter to the director of the Conservatoire, dated in Paris, 16 September 1890, saying: Quote: *Monsieur, Several pupils of M. Massart are desirous that the committee of the Conservatoire take the necessary steps to approach our old teacher to convince him to continue with his lessons.*

Without challenging the merits of his future successor (M. Garcin) we would prefer that M. Massart should remain our teacher, in the certitude that we will profit from his wise lessons.* Unquote.

Why the students did not want Garcin? Indeed because he belonged to what Massart described as the French school: Baillot, Habeneck*, Alard and Garcin* himself, pupil of Alard. (all of them Romantic) Massart, fearing that his school might be in danger of extinction if his chair was given to any Romantic, antiquated teacher, and desirous to perpetuate it, suggested as his successor one of his old premier prix, Berthelier, but the conservatory's

178

director did not want to inflict injury on the legitimate rights of M. Garcin* to succeed him and didn't accept it. Nevertheless, he proposed another pupil of Massart to occupy the place left vacant by Garcin in the preparatory classes: M. Desjardins, proposition that was accepted by the Minister of Public Instruction and Fine Arts, Leon Bourgeoise, who in his letter from the Palais-Royal of October 29, 1890 to the director of the Conservatoire says "....On the other hand, I am glad to comply with your request by designating M. Desjardins, pupil of Massart, as successor of M. Garcin*, <in his post of professor in the preparatory classes>giving thus Massart, a proof of the great value I confer to the maintenance of the tradition of his excellent teachings in the Conservatoire". The modern era was already unstoppable, and thus it continued to spread all over the world, like wild fire, up to our days. The minister, by arrêté (decree) of the 29 October 1890 accepted Massart's resignation and promoted him to the rank of honorary professor of the Conservatoire, as well, "in token of the regret my administration feels to be deprived of services such as yours..."

In the end the directors of the conservatoire opted for a Solomonic solution for "**Salomon**": he was promoted to his long deserved category of violin professor (after having served in the preparatory classes since 1875 i.e. 15 years) in 1890. Desjardins (pupil of Massart) was named professor of the preparatory classes in that same year of 1890, and six years later, in 1894 Berthelier (the Massart's pupil suggested by him to be his successor) was named violin professor, in replacement of professor Maurin*. Garcin kept his post until 1896, dying that same year.

THE END

Massart died the possessor of a considerable fortune, to judge by the house where he died, the 13th of February 1892, right in the very centre of Paris, in one of its most emblematic and significant streets: rue de la Chaussée d'Antin 58, which starts in the Place de L'Opera and ends in the Eglise de la Trinité. He is buried in the cemetery of Montmartre. From Massart we have the legacy of his "mirror" Kreisler, playing in "C-10 and 11" (Kreisler's violin playing is exactly what we can imagine was Massart's style of playing, as stated in all the accounts of his contemporaries, especially in the famous Liszt's letter to him in "Lettres d'un Bachelier ès Musique": particularly tender and melancholic) He had two Strads to which he, naturally, passed his name:

- 1714 Massart; Vaillant
- 1720 Massart; Kreutzer, undoubtedly inherited from his protector and teacher.

The enormous influence of Massart was such that by the turn of the century ALL the violin teachers of the Paris Conservatory* were his first prize pupils, as per the following list:

Antoine Taudou* from 1883 to 1913
Martin Marsick** from 1892 to 1900 violin.
Narcisse Lefort from 1892 to 1929 violin.
Guillaume Roemy or Rémy* from 1896 to 1929 violin.
Berthelier from 1896 to 1915
Hayot from 1894 to 1896
Brun from 1896 to 1929
Desjardins 1890 to 19..

The two different schools of the Conservatoire de Paris*, viz. the French (Romantic) and the modern ones, had merged into a single one: the universal modern vibrato school, the Massart school.

* * * *

≤As for today, Lambert Massart is a totally unknown violinist:

The French Dictionary Larousse de la Music, in two volumes, does not even mention him, despite of the fact that he was by far the best professor of the Paris Conservatoire.

The Dictionnaire Biographique des Musiciens, J. Baker & N. Slonimsky - Paris, Laffont, 1995, devotes him a ridiculous half column in which it is stated that one of his pupils was Sarasate!!

The English New Grove Dictionary of Music and Musicians, in twenty volumes, devotes him half a column, but, of course, it is ignorant of his main feature: to be the founder of the modern vibrato era.

Another half column is dedicated in the Dizzionario Ricordi Enciclopedico Universale della Musica e dei Musicisti

Fetis*, who was his harmony* teacher, is more generous with him, writing a whole column in his Biographie des Musiciens.>

BOOK SEVEN

THE OVERLAPING OF ROMANTICS AND MODERNS

The foundation of the modern school did not mean that it would be accepted overnight by everybody, and a natural period of coexistence between Romantics and Moderns was inevitable. Several reasons accounted for it:

i) Communications in that time were very short in range and very slow too.

ii) There were many virtuosi of the Romantic school in full swing and at the pick of their career who would not change their mind so easily.

iii) The Romantic principles were so deeply rooted in the minds of everyone that the change from one school to the other was not done without much effort and apprehension. Even some of those who had embraced the new vibrato, like Carl Flesch**, for example, had their scruples, which made him write: "from a purely theoretical standpoint the vibrato, as a means for securing a heightened urge for expression, should only be employed when it is musically justifiable"

iv) The Massart school was so revolutionary that, by its own nature, it was bound to elicit much criticism. It was denigrated, and accused of denaturalising the perfect pitch of the sound, of adding oversentimental accents unnecessary to the musical interpretation; those who taught the vibrato were accused of being unmusical and even ill-intentioned. The vibrato was considered a grave defect and even in such a recent date as 1925 there were still Romantics of the calibre of Auer who would not accept it, despite that since 1910 Ysaye, Wieniawski, Kreisler, Heifetz (his pupil) and Francescatti were at the summit of their glory with their vibrato, that by then was available to everyone through the gramophone. Auer was so impervious to the vibrato that he even dared write in his *Violin Playing as I Teach It* (1925) that it (the vibrato) was the result of a nervous disease!! of the players, so far unknown in medicine.

Let us cite, also, Arthur Pougin*, who in his Le violon, Les Violonistes et la Musique de Violon du XVI au XVIII Siècle, Paris 1924, speaking on the tremblement in the viole mentioned on a work by Pierre Triche, *Traité des instruments de music*, 1640, says: *From these tremblements in the viol* *we may derive that the insufferable vibrato of which our violinists of today abuse so insolently was already used by the viol players, perhaps with more discretion.* (Footnote 1, pag 29)

By and large this overlapping will continue until the invention of the gramophone, that made available to everybody the excellencies of the vibrato. Until then, Romantics and Moderns will coexist like in the French political system *"la Cohabitation"* of left wing and right wing top political positions: the presidency and the prime minister. It must have been a most interesting period of the history of the violin, allowing the listener to hear both schools in the same period of time, represented by colossal virtuosi of each school: Romantics such as Ernst, Vieuxtemps, Joachim, Monasterio and Sarasate, on the one side, and Moderns such as Wieniawski, Marsick, Ysaye and Kreisler, on the other. The trouble is that, due to those inconsistencies of natural behaviour in man, they did not like each other, the Moderns being insufferable for the Romantics, and vice versa. Today it would not be the same, but it is already too late: we cannot hear a piece on the violin without vibrato, and we must content ourselves to imagine how it would have sound. The most approximate is the classical flute, which is played without it.

<u>1814 ERNST, HEINRICH WILHELM</u> (b. Brno - d. Nice 1865) Moravian composer, violist, teacher and violinist. <u>Romantic</u>. Juggler + musical = virtuoso.

He received the first lessons at home, making very rapid progress that allowed him to play in public in 1823. In 1825 he was sent to Vienna to study with one of the most superlative teachers in Europe, JOSEPH BOEHM.

After having heard Paganini play in Vienna in 1828 he decided to follow him on tour to capture his technique and copy by ear his unpublished works, which he did with such fidelity that amazed Paganini. Then he retired for further studies for three years.

Ernst had the privilege to play with Paganini in 1837 in Marseilles. He then began a concert tour through the main cities of Russia and Europe, earning the public acclaim. In 1843 he made his debut in London, with an immense success, being considered by the British press as the best violinist of his day. Such a success made him go to London with regularity, settling there in 1855.

He was a wonderful string quartet player and by 1859 he became leader of the Bthvn society string quartet with Joachim, Wieniawski and Piatti*. (What a quartet of super-stars!!) He played the viola under Berlioz's baton in Harold several times. He was considered second to Paganini. Joachim declared that "Ernst was the greatest violinist I ever heard; he towered above others". And Sir Charles Hallé*, in his autobiography declares: *Ernst was all passion and fire, regulated by his reverence for, and clear understanding of, the masterpieces he had to interpret.*

Berlioz in a letter to Morris Barnett dated in Paris, 28 April 1849 says: "I have learnt that Ernst is in London, do you know him? If you see him give him my best regards. He is one of the artists I like most, whose talent is most agreeable to me". (Correspondance Générale. Vol. III. P. 628)

He was a showman who liked to play for great audiences, comparable to Liszt or Horowitz.

Berlioz in his Memoires, Chapter LVI. Ernst. Nature de son talent. Says: "...he never was more powerful than when he had to tame two thousand people, like Liszt..."

Commenting on Ernst's Variations Burlesques sur la Canzonetta "Cara mia mamma" Op 18 (Leipzig 1844) Berlioz enthusiastically says: *"...You had to hear him, when, after having performed in his great style his own works so passionately and so masterly conceived, he took leave of his audience, under a storm of applause, by playing a set of variations on the air of the Carnaval de Venise which he dared to write after those of Paganini but without imitating them. In this exquisite, good taste, fantasy, the caprices of the inventor blend so gracefully and at such great speed with the eccentricities of the prodigious technique, that one ends by not being astonished any more, and allows the melody to rock yourself with the monotonous accompaniment of the Venetian air, as if out of the violin there would not stream down the most gracefully coloured melodious cascades, with the most astonishing, unforeseeable bounds. In this curious feat of strength show-off, constantly melodious and performed with such ease that one could be mislead to think they are played with negligence, almost in a clumsy manner, Ernst always charms and fascinates his audience. He simply juggles with diamonds. ...These variations that I often heard him play impress me now in a very peculiar way. As soon as the Venetian theme appears under his magic bow, it becomes midnight for me, and I find myself again in Saint Petersburg in a large hall lit up by day-light, feeling that strange and sweet nervous fatigue that one feels at the end of every splendid musical soirée; there are enthusiastic clamour and glinting laughter pervading the air; I fall into a Romanesque melancholy to which I cannot resist, and to which it will be even harmful for me to resist"* (Berlioz. Memoires. Chapter LVI. Pag. 515-16) These variations Op 18 composed by Ernst in 1844 for violin solo were later arranged by the author for violin and piano. Gidon Kremer, on his turn, transcribed them for two violins in the 1970s and are played in "C-19" by himself and Grindenko.<here Gidon Kremer is out of his depth, and we can hear many lapses of all kinds. Ernst was too much a violinist to be emulated>

His Strads:

- 1709 Ernst
- 1725 Ernst; Plotenyi

In "C-9" we have Ernst's variations on "the last rose of summer" played by Midori, and in "C-19" his variations on the Carnaval de Venise, "O mamma cara" played by Kremer.

1815 ALARD, DELPHIN (b. Bayonne - d. Paris 1888) Romantic. French composer and violinist. Musical.

Alard received his first classes of violin from his parents. His progress was so quick that by 1825 he played a Viotti concerto with such perfection that by unanimous vote the people of Bayonne sent him to Paris for further studies. Here he entered as pupil of Habeneck*, a Romantic teacher, studying with him from 1827 to 1830, when he won the first prize of the Conservatoire.

He soon found a place as violinist in the Opera orchestra, continuing his studies of harmony* with Fetis* (1831-3) His debut in Paris was in 1831 with the Société des Concerts du Conservatoire* playing as soloist, being encouraged by Paganini who was among the audience.

After this, his fame grew rapidly, becoming member of the Royal Orchestra in 1840, and on Baillot's death solo violinist. In 1853 he was appointed solo violinist of the Chapelle* Imperial de Napoleon III.

He was also a superb quartet player founding his own string quartet which had great reputation.

As pedagogue Alard entered the Paris Conservatoire* the same day as Lambert Massart, having, according to the Massart's letter of application for the professorship, a very strong, highly influential, recommendation (with all probabilities from king Louis Philippe d'Orleans, himself) of such power that Massart was on the brink to renounce to his application, suggesting even the possibility to share the same violin chair with Alard. Alard was professor at the Conservatoire from 1843 to 1875, writing a Méthode Complète et Progressive (Paris 1844) translated into many languages, several studies, and a set of 24 caprices in all keys* Op 41. He represented the Romantic Italo-French school of Baillot, that he received through his teacher Habeneck*.

Alard's main pupils were Caudella*, Arthur Pougin*, Garcin*, and, above all, was Pablo de Sarasate.

Thanks to his father in law, the famous luthier* Vuillaume*, he owned some of the best Strads of his time.

- 1715 Alard
-1715 Knoop
- 1716 The incomparable Messiah; Salabue.
- 1728 Alard; Artôt*

1820 VIEUXTEMPS, HENRI (b. Verviers, 25 Km SE of Liège, Belgium - d. Mustapha nr. Algiers 1881) Romantic Belgian composer, teacher and violinist. Juggler + musical = virtuoso.

He took his first lessons of violin from his father and next with Léonard-Joseph Lecloux. When he was six he played in public a Concerto by Rode. Next year Beriot, impressed by his innate gifts, shown in a concert at the Société Grétry in Liège, took him to Paris as his pupil. He gave a successful concert there in 1829 that impressed much Fetis*, who described him as a consummate musician.

In 1831 after Beriot's departure to Italy, he started a concert tour in company of his father, playing in the main cities of Germany, which gave him the opportunity to meet Spohr who encouraged him to continue. The tour finished in 1833. In 1834 he went to Vienna where he undertook the study of the Bthvn violin concerto, practically forgotten, and performed it with considerable success (nevertheless this concerto never acquired international fame until it was played by the prodigy child Joachim** under the baton of Mendelssohn) he then went to Leipzig where his play was acclaimed by Schumann as comparable to Paganini. After having spent most of the year 1834 in London where he met Paganini, he settled in Paris in 1835 for further studies mainly in composition with Reicha*.

He resumed his travels through Europe in 1837, giving a very successful tour in Russia. In 1841 he played in Paris one of his own concertos with immense success that made Berlioz say " to his merits as an eminent virtuoso we must now add those of a composer"

His career of travelling virtuoso took him to London (1841), and to America during 1843, 1857, and in 1870 he toured with Thalberg. He was idolised in Russia where he was soloist to the Tsar and professor of violin, teaching from 1846 to 1851, contributing significantly to the development of the Russian school.

After his return from America in 1871 he was appointed professor of the Brussels Conservatory. From 1871-73 he taught in the Brussels's Conservatoire where he had as Pupils Ysaye and the English Georges Haddock of Leeds, who gave his name to the Guarneri del Gesu of 1734 he played. (Ysaye was then 23 years old and in full possession of the violin technique, including the vibrato that Wieniawski had taught him). Vieuxtemps, the pet pupil of Beriot, who forbade the vibrato, did not try to eradicate this monstrous defect from him, but on the contrary encouraged Ysaye to play with it (Vieuxtemps' lessons consisted "mainly of aesthetic advise"); he devoted all his energies to this new task as teacher, which he regarded as a "sacred mission", and contributed decisively to the growing success of the Belgian violin school in which he took great pride.

Unlike Auer, who clung stubbornly to his antiquated, Romantic ideas until his death, well into the 20th century (1930), Vieuxtemps knew how to evolve with modern times, adapting himself to the new vibrato, towards the end of his life, around 1868, when he began to promote enthusiastically the art of the young Ysaye, his pupil, and that of Marsick (20 years old) in their performances (with vibrato) of his own works.

See index to his recordings.

Vieuxtemps' favourite instruments:

Strads:
- 1682 Yardonoff
- 1700 Berger, inherited from Beriot
- 1707 Lvoff
- 1710 Leslie; Tate
- 1710 Duke of Camposelice, owned also by Suk

-Also a Guarneri del Gesu *Vieuxtemps* of 1741. Menuhin, in a letter of 1974 said he preferred its tone to his own superb Strad. the Soil of 1714.
-Also a Giovanni Guadagnini* of 1758.

1828 HELLMESBERGER Jr. JOSEPH (b Vienna; d Vienna 1893) Austrian Conductor, violinist and TEACHER. Romantic.

Just as the French school had a trinity of founders (Kreutzer, Rode, Baillot) the Austrian conservatory has another trilogy of founders, all Romantics: Joseph Boehm, Georg Hellmesberger, Sr. and Joseph Hellmesberger, Jr.

Another superlative teacher, he ended the foundation of the Viennese school; he had also a superlative career as violinist, as a leader of the quartet bearing his name and as a musician by and large. Belonging to an illustrious family of musician he is the son of Georg Hellmesberger Sr. teacher, violinist and conductor of immense fame in Vienna. He first studied the violin with his father at the Vienna conservatory, becoming violin soloist at the Hofoper orchestra when he was 17.

From 1851 to 1859 he was appointed conductor and artistic director of the Gesellshaft der Musikfreunde orchestra which under his leadership became one of the most renowned orchestras in Vienna, transforming it from amateur to a professional one.

He was appointed professor of the violin and director of the conservatory from 1851 till his death. From 1851 to 1859 he was first violin* of the court orchestra and Kapellmeister* to the Emperor. He was also founder of a string quartet bearing his name which enjoyed the highest reputation in Vienna. He was also a conductor of deserved fame.

As teacher he had pupils of the category of Auer**, Grädner*, Rappoldi* [1] the Schrammell* brothers, Brodsky*, Joachim**, Kreisler** and Enescu**.

1831 JOACHIM, JOSZEF (b. Kittsee (Austria) 50 Km SE of Vienna, by the frontier with Slovakia; 10 Km S of Bratislava; d. Berlin 1907) Romantic. Austro-Hungarian composer, conductor, teacher, and violinist. Juggler + musical = virtuoso.

---

[1] It is he who, while being teacher of the Berlin conservatory, wrote a letter to Massart, imploring to be accept as a pupil in Massart's classes. (See book six: Massart as a pedagogue)

The seventh of eight children born to Julius and Fanny Joachim, he started learning the violin at the age of 4 with Serwaczynski*, a teacher in Pest. His progress was so fast that by 1839 he made his first public appearance; during the summer the Joachims moved to Vienna, where he studied with Georg Hellmesberger Sr. and later with Boehm who built up all his remarkable technique. In 1843 he moved to Leipzig to study in the newly founded conservatory under Mendelssohn direction, but he found nothing else to teach him on the violin, procuring him, instead, a splendid general education in music, introducing him to F. David and Hauptmann*.

For his debut with the Gewandhaus* he played some pieces by Beriot accompanied by Paulina Viardot*, Clara Schumann* and Mendelssohn. The next year he went to London where he played with enormous success a fantasy by Ernst; this was followed by other concerts equally successful in London, but there was one, also in London, which particularly rocketed him to international fame: that of the Bthvn violin concerto under the baton of Mendelssohn; Joachim was 12-years-old. The premier of this concerto had been a failure due to the fact that Franz Clement*, its dedicatee, played it without rehearsal and at sight. In addition, Clement, between movements one and two, performed a series of variations playing with the violin upside-down, which provoked the fury of Bthvn who didn't want to hear any more about the concert during his life time, sinking into oblivion for 38 years. Despite of the fact that it had been played with success by Tomasini* (Berlin 1812); Baillot (Paris 1828) and Vieuxtemps (Vienna 1834) it didn't quite catch the general acceptance until our prodigy child played it in 1844.

In 1850 he was appointed Konzertmeister* in Weimar under the general direction of Liszt. Here he profited of Liszt's advises to complete his musical maturity, but when he was named violinist to king George V in Hanover in 1852, his classical basic education made him dissociate from Liszt's conception of the "new music". He developed instead a strong friendly association with the Schumanns and with Brahms. His admiration for Brahms' music made him a propagator of his works, conducting, for example, the premier of Brahms' symphony nr. 1 in 1877 in Cambridge.

In 1868 he was appointed head of the newly formed Hochschule für Ausübende Tonkunst (conservatory) in Berlin devoting all his efforts to it, forming more than 400 pupils. But his reign in the Berlin conservatory took place just within the time of the arrival of the modern era, that began in Paris, with Lambert Massart, in 1843. And we have evidence that at least one of the teachers of his staff deserted his school, to enrol into the Massart's legions: in 1874 Berlin violin professor Edouard Rappoldi* wrote to Massart saying that he needed to enter his classes to discuss different aspects of violin playing with whom he considered the best teacher in the world: Massart. (see the manuscript letters to Massart)

He was the dedicatee of the Brahms vl. concerto, in the composition of which he took a most important role, giving also its first performance. Also dedicated to him were the concertos by Schumann, Max Bruch and Dvorak. In 1869 he founded a string quartet the performances of which have remained legendary. He was the most representative eminence of the traditional German school.

Other dedications include:

Brahms: Double concerto for vl and cello in A minor Op. 102.
Brahms, Schumann and Dietrich: Sonata vl-p. (FAE)
Schumann: Fantasie fur vl and orch. in C major Op 131
Max Bruch: Violin concerto 1.

His playing followed the classical French style of Viotti, Rode and Kreutzer. He placed musical integrity above mechanical virtuosity. His bowing was magnificent and powerful, even when he was over 70 in his recording of Bach's partita* BWV 1041 "C-8" (compare the same by Mullova in "C-3." Do not let you mislead by his intonation faults, just concentrate in his bowing, much more powerful). He played with a conspicuous vibrato that he used only in particular notes, a vibrato of a very high frequency, like an electric quaver.

In "C-8" we can hear him play at 72-years of age.

When it came to my knowledge that a new CD had been released with Joachim playing, I got very excited on the idea that I would be able to hear the best violinist of his time, but when I heard all those monstrous lapses of intonation and all the rest of flaws you can hear on "C-8" I got terribly disappointed. Joachim was too old to play and he should have never consented that recording to see the light, but his egocentricity was stronger.

Bernard Shaw noticed already lapses of intonation as soon as 1890, but dazzled by Joachim's prestige gave a preposterous explanation of this fact, by attributing him a particular German scale* of intervals* (sic) totally different from our modern one: Quote: *this peculiar intonation of Joachim for a long time greatly hindered my appreciation of his art: the Celtic troll in me rebelled against intervals* that were not the same as my intervals.* Unquote.

Shaw started his musical critic career in 1888 when Joachim was already 57, he had passed the barrier of the 50s, and it was only natural that he had lost most of his faculties. The truth is that he played off key* like a beginner, or as we say in Spanish: *desafinaba como un perro.* (His telltale recordings, that do not lie, attest to it.) He also had to retire on time. This is one of the most difficult things to do, for it requires lots and lots of humility and a good conscience of what reality is. This is the reason why God retires by sheer force his favourite and beloved sons, killing them in their prime of their careers, like Neveu or Hassid in violin, Mozart in Music, Jorge Negrete (Mexico) and Carlos Gardel* (Argentina) in singing. Only very, very few violinist can trespass the barrier of 50 unharmed, like Hubay, Heifetz, Francescatti, Menuhin and Oistrakh. Be it as it were, I got so disappointed with the Joachim's CD that it came to my mind a tango "Esta noche me emborracho": "C-08" I cannot translate here the whole lyrics but it tells the bitter disappointment of a man badly in love with his girl friend, who leaves him despite of all his entreaties. Ten years later he finds her again turned into a prostitute, ugly and faded away. In his despair he says: "... this evening I'll get drunk, I'll get pissed, quite pissed, out of my tiny mind." It is sung by Carlos Gardel*, the best baritone tango singer Argentina ever had. (He was killed in an air crash in his prime and world wide glory) I have recorded this tango in "C-08". Any excuse is good to hear again Carlos Gardel* singing. (On the need to retire on time see Liszt's letter to Lambert Massart September 2nd, 1838 in Lettres d'un Bachelier ès Musique) Malibran* was another privileged daughter of God, Who took her away in the prime of her glory.

Berlioz lavished praises and eulogistic comments whenever he wrote about him. So, for example, in Berlioz's Correspondence générale, we have the letters nbr. 1636, 1717, 1726, in which we can read:-

(1636) To Gemmy Bracdus, Brunswick 26 Oct. 1835: "... Joachim has come from Hanover and played at the yesterday's concert, with a magnificent success, a vl concerto composed by himself and a capriccio by Paganini; he has a superb talent."

- (1717) To Franz Liszt Hanover 31 march 1854: "...The King wanted the programme to be exclusively of my compositions. So we gave ... and my romance for violin which Joachim played in young master, three times maestro of his Art..."

- (1726) To his uncle Felix Marmion Brunswick 4th April 1854: "... you would have been marvelled, my dear uncle, if you had listened in this concert the young violinist Joachim (23) Konzertmeister* to the King. He is a phenomenal talent both for his elevation and his deepness. Evidently Joachim is at the present time the foremost violinist in Europe...He has played with an amplitude of style, a soul, a tenderness and an incomparable caprice, and as a musician that we haven't seen since 23 years ago"

Joachim heaped up during his most brilliant career a spectacular collection of Strads, to which he, naturally, passed his name:

- 1698 Joachim; Kortschalk owned also by Weber
- 1700 Joachim; Jupiter owned also by Viotti and Rode
- 1708 Joachim; Morgan owned also by Weber
- 1709 Maximiliam (King Joseph)
- 1714 Joachim
- 1715 Joachim; De Barrau owned also by Mendelssohn
- 1715 Joachim; Cremonese
- 1715 Joachim; Hochstein owned also by Heifetz
- 1715 Joachim; Tartini; Lipinski
- 1715 Joachim; owned also by Mendelssohn
- 1722 Joachim; Elman owned also by Napoleon
- 1722 Joachim; Laurie owned also by Mendelssohn
- 1723 Joachim, owned also by Weber
- 1725 Joachim; Chaconne; Hammig
- 1729 Joachim; Benny
-1732 Joachim; Taylor owned also by Paganini and Spohr

In total 16 Strads.

-Also a Guarneri del Gesu "Joachim" of 1737.

Joachim founded, also, a string quartet bearing his name the performances of which were legendary.

I have recorded:

     i) the Bthvn vl concerto *in memoriam* of his great feat when he was only 12 in "C-8" in a version which for me is the definitive one, that of Francescatti with Bruno Walter.
     ii) A cadenza* he composed for this same concert in "C-8" and
     iii) an arr. made by him of the Brahms' Hungarian dance 5 played by Ysaye in "C-10".
     iv) Finally his arr of Brahms' Hungarian dance 1 played by Joachim himself in "C-8" and the same by Zukerman in "C-12".

v) Joachim performs Bach, Joachim and Brahms in "C-8"

1835 WIENIAWSKI, HENRYK (b. Lublin - d. Moscow 1880) Polish composer, teacher and violinist. The first great pupil of Massart enters with full rights in the modern era. Juggler + musical = virtuoso.

Wieniawski was born to a family of excellent musicians, his mother Regina Wieniawska, (née Wollf) being a professional pianist, sister of the famous pianist Edward Wollf*. His exceptional talent for the violin was discovered very early by his teachers in Poland. First Serwaczynski* (teacher of Joachim) then by Hornziel (both Romantic).

After a brilliant audition in Paris he was allowed to enter the Conservatoire in 1843 where he was taught first by Clavel and the next year he entered the classes of Lambert Massart. After only three years of lessons he was awarded first prize in the violin in 1846, when he was 11 years old, a feat that nobody else equalled, (except Neveu) and continued his studies as Massart private pupil for two more years.

His apprentice years completed, he embarked on a career of travelling virtuoso. He spent the years 1851-3 in Russia and gave more than 200 concerts in company of his brother Josef (pianist). In 1853 he achieved his first great success in Germany, at the Leipzig Gewandhaus*; soon he became famous internationally giving in 1858 a memorable concert in Paris with Anton Rubinstein*.

On the behest of Rubinstein*, who was making efforts to improve the musical conditions in Russia, Wieniawski joined him, settling in S. Petersburg from 1860 to 1872 exerting a decisive influence on the growth of the Russian violin school, teaching there for the first time the Massart's vibrato. In 1862 he played his second violin concerto under the baton of Rubinstein*. Cui*, a severe critic, reported two days later: "I still haven't recovered from the impact of that first allegro."

Wieniawski resumed his world travels in 1872, starting with a two-year tour on North America. He gave more than 200 concerts with Anton Rubinstein*. Upon his return to Europe, he accepted the offer in 1875 to replace Vieuxtemps as professor of the violin at the Brussels Conservatory. This did not prevent him from making extensive tours; although suffering from a severe heart condition, he went to Germany in 1876. In 1878 he went to play in Paris, and then to Berlin, as well. Here he collapsed during a concert. Joachim who was in the audience hurried to replace him. Despite his shattered health he continued to tour in 1879 with the singer Desirée Artôt*, but had to be interned in a hospital in Odessa.

Wieniawski was also a keen performer of chamber music appearing several times with the Bthvn Quartet society, formed by him, Joachim, Ernst and Piatti.*

He rivalled in wizardry with Paganini, but he could also move his audiences to tears "thanks to an intensified vibrato" according to the testimony of his condisciple Kreisler.

His best pupil was Ysaye, the first to record on the gramophone with the modern vibrato in 1910.

Anton Rubinstein*, who accompanied Wieniawski on tour several years, called him "without doubt the greatest violinist of his time" This admiration was reciprocated by Wieniawski who declared that his best music teacher had been Rubinstein. His motto was "il faut risquer" (one must take risks) and occasionally he missed, like Perlman or Oistrakh do, but it is so impressive to hear a violinist who does not fear intonation nor any other difficulty, and plays with full energy and courage, that the occasional lapses are forgiven or even unnoticed.

From Wieniawski I have recorded several of his compositions: See index.

His Strads:

- 1712 Schreiber
- 1719 Wieniawski; Bower
- 1720 Wieniawski
- 1725 Wieniawski

We arrive, now, to the two most famous Spanish violinists, Monasterio and Sarasate. Being both my compatriots the reader will allow me the little vanity to indulge in them lavishly.

1836 MONASTERIO, DON JESÚS (b. Potes, 75 Km SW of Santander, by the majestic sierra Picos de Europa, (Santander) - d. id. 1903) Romantic. Spanish composer, conductor, teacher and violinist. Musical.

Don Jesús de Monasterio y Agüeros was born in the Liébana mountains, in the village of Potes (Santander) in 1836. His father, a retired judge, played the violin as a hobby. One evening that Mr. Monasterio was playing a rather melancholic tune on the violin, when little Monasterio was not quite four years old, he saw his son, who had crept into the room, weeping copiously.-*Why are you crying, my boy?* He asked him - *I cry-* replied the child- *because that music makes me cry.* His good father noticed at once that those weeps were the sign of a not at all common sensitivity, and he decided to encourage his son in this vocation. Profiting the first journey he made to Valladolid, he bought his son a second hand small violin, which he made restore for him, and which our fiddler kept for ever as a precious relic. At the age of five he played before queen Isabel II. He later went to Madrid where he was put under the teachings of Don José Vega, Don Juan Ortega and Don Antonio Aroca, all the three professors of the Royal Chapel*, to whom, later, Beriot sent a letter of compliments for the good job they had done with their pupil. Monasterio made a tour on the main cities of Spain, gathering many applause and compliments, but his father, who was always with him, could have said what Mozart's father in a letter to Herr Haguenaguer of Salzburg: "We would be very happy if all the kisses they give to my children, and particularly to Wolfgang, were cash money; but neither innkeepers nor carriage drivers accept this kind of gracious currency"

The death of his beloved father in 1845 put an end to these tours, and Monasterio retired to his natal village of Potes to console his mother and sisters, and there he would have stayed for ever, were it not for one of those rare men, enthusiastic about arts, dear to the extreme for his pupil, who came across in his path, and with firm, decided will, took Monasterio out of that obscure little village: Don Basilio Montoya. This tutor, with a most paternal love for his pupil went to Paris and Brussels to see by himself their conservatoires, and finally left Monasterio in Brussels under the classes of Beriot, to whom he asked to give Monasterio private lessons in his own house, besides those of the conservatoire. After only two years Montoya received a letter which filled him with joy. An enthusiastic friend of him, who later became director of the Conservatoire of Brussels, Gevaert*, announced him that despite the prejudices of the jury, "not because of the merits, but because of the short age of the pupil, Monasterio had won, together with his condisciple Bömer, the PRIX EXTRAORDINAIRE in violin".

On his return to Madrid Monasterio was named honorary violin to the Royal Chapel*, and honorary member of the Academia Pontificia in Rome. Soon after, he received the invitation to participate in a tour that Louis Jullien* used to organise every year through England and Scotland. This tour was an uninterrupted series of triumphs, although with a frightening episode which embarrassed much our maestro. It was in Scotland in the theatre of Edinburg. He had played a fantasia on Spanish themes (which later won him the cross of Carlos III). In the end, after a few applause, a whistling and booing storm broke out at him. Monasterio was disconcerted and upset, and would not return to the platform until his impresario forced him to do so; then the hissing was replaced by the most enthusiastic hurrahs and renewed hissing... He later learned that the Scottish, when they reach the top of their enthusiasm, do not clap, but hiss and boo instead.

On his return (1857) he was named professor of the Conservatorio de Madrid. Soon after he embarked on a tour of Europe, mainly Belgium and Germany. Here he met Meyerbeer who willing to hear him play accompanied him at the piano in the "Adios a la Alhambra" composed by Monasterio, which pleased so much the author of Le Robert that he would not stop exclaiming "c'est ravissant! C'est ravissant!"

Monasterio went then to Weimar to meet his Brussels' conservatory mate and old friend Lassen*, Konzertmeister* in that court. Lassen arranged a concert for the grand dukes in which both were to play, not before having worn Monasterio that the grand duke was very stern and austere with the court protocol, that he never expressed his enthusiasm and that he might not even address a word to him. After the concert the grand duchess was very enthusiastic particularly with the Adios a la Alhambra, while the grand duke was as imperturbable and silent as Lassen* had predicted. There was, however, an impertinent gentleman who at every moment would interrupt the conversation he was having with the grand duchess, besieging him with all kind of questions, to which our artist replied more laconically as the besiege grew in intensity. After the court had gone Lassen* came to congratulate his friend. Said Monasterio:

-*"As for the grand duchess, she is a model of good manners and elegance, but as for her august husband, you were right in warning me, I have not merited a single word from him"*

-*What?* -replied Lassen*- *I never saw him more loquacious in my life. Do you find he has been little talkative?* In short, that impertinent gentleman who had harassed him so much the previous evening was no one else than the grand duke; the silent, stern person, was an Austrian diplomat who dared not speak in the presence of the dukes. The reader may well imagine the many apologies Monasterio gave to the grand duke the next day when he was summoned to his palace.

The grand duke offered him the post once held by Joachim as first violin* to the court, but Monasterio declined. When De Beriot died he was also offered to replace Beriot as professor at the Brussels's Conservatoire but he declined as well, preferring to stay in his own land. With his 1719 Stradivarius in hand (a precious present of Don Juan Gualberto Gonzalez to which he passed his name and is called *Monasterio*) Monasterio drove the audience after him, and either he infused it with the sweet and quiet calm of Haydn's music, either he filled them with melancholy and drove them to tears in Mozart's quintet, either he oppressed their hearts and moved them in a Bthvn passage. Of Monasterio one could say what Giacomo Ferrari* tells in his "Anedotti Piacevole" [1] of Celeste Coltellini* when she sang the role of La Molinara by Paisiello: "era un giogello...faceba piangere...et toglieva quasi il respiro a chi l'ascoltava e vedeva" (She was a jewel...she put her audience to tears...and she took the breath away from everybody who heard or saw her).

Monasterio sang rather than play, and at the same time his face showed the sensation he was experiencing, either a pleasant smile which anticipated a graceful delicate passage, either frowning his brows announcing in advance his listeners the arrival of a dramatic sequence. (We will see this same feature when we will talk of Perlman)

Monasterio was a superb conductor as well, what made a high politician of the time say that "the most respected power he knew in Spain was that of Monasterio over his orchestra."

Monasterio was most important as teacher and above all as an organiser and promoter of instrumental music in Madrid, which at the time, was overshadowed by Italian opera.

Monasterio endowed his Strad with his name: Monasterio of 1719, later owned by Milstein** and Ricci**.

---

[1] Annedotti piacevoli e interessanti accorsi nella vita di Giacomo Gotifredo Ferrari* de Rovereto (London, 1830)

1844 SARASATE, PABLO DE <Pablo Martín Melitón de Sarasate y Navascués> (b. Pamplona - d. Biarritz 1908) Romantic. Spanish composer, and violinist. Juggler.

A prodigy child and one of the most dazzling musical personalities of his time, Sarasate is Spain's greatest violinist.

Originally baptised Martín, after his God father, and Melitón, after his birth saint's day, he added later to them the artistic name of Pablo with which he has been known. (This occurred before 1855 as it is deduced from his mother's letter to her husband from Madrid to La Coruña: "The maid we had in Valladolid is hearing Pablo, totally transfixed, stunned...") The change of name was of common use at the time, and so did Gayarre* and Arrieta* who changed their original names of Sebastian and Pascual, respectively, for the more commercial ones of Julián and Emilio. But Sarasate's substitution was not official until much later, as it appears in his Paris Conservatoire* first prize diploma of the 8th of December, 1857, awarded to Martin Sarasate in 1857.

His father, Miguel Sarasate, was Pamplonese, and violinist and conductor of the band of Regiment "España 30", in garrison in Pamplona. As it is usual with all military families, Miguel Sarasate's regiment was transferred to La Coruña. Don Miguel, who had discovered the precocious gifts of his son, sent him to take lessons with the 17-years-old José Courtier, concertino* of La Coruña's cathedral. But the true musical carrier of Sarasate, whose name was still Martín Melitón, started in La Coruña with Blas Álvarez, concertino* of the theatre orchestra, when he was five-years-old. Sarasate started giving public concerts at 8 in La Coruña, El Ferrol and Vigo, and then he went to Madrid in company of his Mother Francisca Javiera Navascués. Here he was taught by Manuel Rodriguez Saez, first violin* of the Teatro de la Zarzuela*. In his daily going to classes, violin under arm, Sarasate used to pass by the window of a confectioner's shop, and he would stand there, for a long while, contemplating, absorbed, those cakes, the sight of which made his mouth water with greedy yearnings. This attitude called the attention of the shop's owner, who offered him a cake on condition that he played his violin. When the confectioner noticed that his shop filled up with customers when Sarasate played, he repeated this improvised commercial advertising many a time.

1856 was a crucial year for Sarasate. After a series of concerts in Madrid, his fame reached the Royal Palace and he was invited to play before the court. In June it was decided that Sarasate should go to Paris, the musical capital, and there he went in company of his mother. This journey

197

would prove similar to that of Mozart and his mother to the same city. With the aid of a pension granted to him by Queen Isabel II he started his long journey, with stops in Pamplona and San Sebastian, to give several successful concerts. After crossing the French border, another stop at Bayonne, where his mother got infected with the cholera epidemic which ravaged Europe in those days. Lodged in a humble boarding-house, with the added difficulty of not knowing French, Sarasate witnessed, powerless, his mother decease in just a few hours. Totally devastated, Sarasate would have succumb to despair, if good fortune, which never forsook him, had not wanted that his boarding-house owners got in touch with the Spanish consul general, another Pamplonese, Don Ignacio García Echeverría, a wealthy banker, who took charge of everything, included a request to the regional Committee of Pamplona to obtain a new, increased pension for him. García Echeverría also got in touch with Delfin Alard, whom he had known in Bayonne (Alard's native city), professor of the Paris Conservatoire, and sent the child to him.

With the natural scepticism, Alard received the boy as an insignificant provincial youngster, from a foreign country. With the help of his new protector, Ignacio Echeverría, Sarasate found lodging in Paris, in the house of M. Lassabathie, administrator of the Paris Conservatoire, who had no children and welcomed him as his own son. Alard had to acknowledged he had nothing to correct or to teach Sarasate, who in the next year obtained the premier prix. (1857). He was 13-years-old. Sarasate gave many successful concerts in Paris, until 1861, when Lassabathie, in agreement with Sarasate's protector Don Ignacio Echeverría, deemed it convenient that the child should go to Spain to visit his father. Here, Sarasate played for the royal court in the Palacio de Aranjuez, and it provoked such admiration that Queen Isabel II decorated him with the cross of Carlos III, making an exception, for the order statutes forbade the entrance to anyone younger than 20 years of age. That same year (1861) he returned to Paris, and started his long carrier of international performer, first in London, then Constantinople, Vienna, Budapest and Bucharest. He went later to the USA playing in New York and Boston, going later to Chile, Peru, Brazil and Argentina. In 1871 he went to England for a series of uninterrupted successful concerts.

So far Sarasate had focused mainly on his artistic facet, to the prejudice of its economic-commercial side, which allowed substantial profits for his impresarios. But all this was going to change in February 1877 when he met the person who would find a solution to all his economic and programming worries. This happened in a railway travel to Frankfurt, where he met by sheer chance the German pianist Otto Goldschmidt*, (they happened to have contiguous seats in the train) who would become his "artistic agent" and made him earn a great deal of money. Years later Goldschmidt* married - for the second time - the, as well pianist, Berta Marx, who would become Sarasate's inseparable accompanist in all his concerts. (Goldschmidt had been married first with the magnificent soprano Jenny Lind*, who died precisely that year of 1887) The first tour of this new stage started in Germany, where he played for Emperor William I. Year 1877 was dedicated to a tour of all the main Russian cities.

In 1884 his father Don Miguel died while he was absent on a concert tour. Again Sarasate crossed the Atlantic for a triumphant tour in America, going to the USA and Mexico. On his return to Europe he passed as usual by England where he gave a memorable sell-out concert in company of his friend, and county fellow, the incomparable tenor Gayarre*.

Sarasate was always triumphant, and his good luck never abandoned him. He had just what the public of his era demanded. The high speed with which he played, his perfect intonation and his astonishing dexterity with his bow and fingers were *"music to his listners' ears."*

SARASATE AND PAMPLONA

Sarasate was a great lover of his county, Navarra, and in particular of Pamplona, his birth-town, where he never failed to attend the renowned "fiestas de San Fermín" the 7th of July of every year, coming from wherever he might be in the world, with the only exception of 1884, in his entire career. It has been soundly said that Sarasate's heart was Pamplonese and his violin universal.

Every year, upon his arrival for San Fermín, Sarasate was greeted at the railway station by the whole of Pamplona, and he and his horse carriage were carried shoulder high to his hotel. There, an open door serenade was organised in his honour. From then on Sarasate would give very low priced concerts, many in company of the most extraordinary tenor Gayarre*, county fellow of Sarasate, Navarrese, and born in the same year as him. Sarasate's concerts in San Fermín reached the number of 93. The last one took place on the 12th July, 1908, at the end of which Pamplona's mayor decorated him with the Great Cross of Alfonso XII.

It was precisely during one of these Sanfermines, while Sarasate was strolling about the streets of Pamplona in company of his friend Gayarre*, that he came across a blind beggar playing his old, down-at-heel violin.

Sarasate borrowed it and played in his stead, earning a fabulous amount of money for the poor old man.

By his will, made in Paris in the presence of the notary E. Delorme, Sarasate bequeathed to the town council of Pamplona "in full ownership my watches, tiepins, rings, diamond jewels, decorations, crowns, palms, diplomas, certificates, bronzes, paintings, souvenirs,..." With all these treasures Pamplona has founded a Museum in 1991 in the street del Mercado.

On its turn Pamplona has honoured Sarasate lavishly:

1) FAVOURITE SON :On February the 10th, 1900, the town council, in plenary meeting, honoured him as "favourite son" of the city of Pamplona, with the unanimous vote of all the councillors, "in gratefulness for the many favours received...and for the many proofs he always gave of his special love for his native town, and for his donation of a superb collection of jewels and decorations to constitute a municipal museum" (City Golden Book)

2) PASEO DE SARASATE In 1903 the city council named Paseo de Sarasate the old Paseo de Valencia.

3) INTERNATIONAL VIOLIN CONTEST. In 1991 the government of Navarra created the International Violin Contest Pablo Sarasate.

4) THE MONUMENTS OF LA TACONERA AND LA MEDIA LUNA The city has built a monument for him in la Taconera in 1918 and another one in the Jardines de la Media Luna in 1959.

5) SARASATE MUSEUM. Located in 11 Mercado street, it houses Sarasate's legacy to Pamplona

THE END

By his will, Sarasate bequeathed his two Strads to the conservatories of Paris and Madrid.

-The Strad of 1713 Sarasate; Boissier, to Madrid.
-The Strad of 1724 Sarasate; Paganini, to Paris.

In his recordings (1904, when he was 60) we hear him play with a conspicuous vibrato, of a very high frequency, a sort of an electric quaver. His intonation was perfect, and he was able to play at an enormous amount of speed, with great accuracy, and incredible wizardry. To judge by these recordings his style was rather superficial, lacking emotional involvement, but the truth is that he was already 60 years old, had gone beyond the fatal barrier of the 50s, and consequently had lost his abilities, so these recordings are not reliable to judge him.

But those who heard him in his prime say that his play was distinguished by a tone of unsurpassed sweetness and purity, produced with a "frictionless" bow stroke. When he played the Bthvn concerto in Berlin (1880s) he was compared unflatteringly with Joachim's, which angered him greatly.

Saint-Saëns said: "...those who attended formerly my Mondays *soirées musicales* will never forget the full brilliancy that Sarasate brought into them, such that for several years no other violinist would consent to play in them for fear of any comparison. And he not only shined in his talent, but in his wit and conversation as well, always interesting and enjoyable." (Saint-Saëns, Au Courant de la Vie. Paris 25th January 1914, p. 38)

And Carl Flesch says: "...With awe, as if he was a supernatural phenomenon from a wonderland for ever inaccessible to us, we boys looked up to the small, blacked-eyed Spaniard with the well-trimmed, coal-black moustache and equally raven, curly, over-carefully arranged hair... It was a unique experience to see this little man stride to the platform with genuine Spanish grandeur, superficially calm, even phlegmatic, to witness how, after some stereotyped movements, he began to play with unheard-of sovereignty and, in a rapid climax, put his audience into astonishment, admiration, and highest rapture"

See index for his recordings.

Sarasate's Strads:

-1713 Sarasate; Boissier, bequeathed to the Conservatorio de Madrid.
-1724 Sarasate; Paganini, his favourite, bequeathed to the Paris Conservatory*.

Sarasate was the dedicatee of many pieces:

-Alexander Mackenzie: vl concerto
-Bruch: (vl conc. 2, and Scottish fantasy)
-Saint-Saëns: *Il y a bien longtemps de cela, je vis arriver chez mois, frais et jeune comme le pringtemps, Pablo de Sarasate, déjà célèbre, dont un subçon de moustache ombrageait à peine la lèvre. Il venait gentiment me demander comme la chose la plus simple d'écrire un concerto pour lui.*

Flatté et charmé au dernier point, je promis et tins ma parole avec le Concerto en la majeur auquel on donne, je ne sais pouqois, le titre de Concertstück. J'écrivis ensuite pour lui le Rondo Capricioso en style espagnol et plus tard le Concerto en si mineur, pour lequel il me donna de precieux conseils auquels est due certainement en grand partie la faveur dont jouit cette oeuvre auprès des exécutants. (Au courant de la vie. Pag. 37. Paris 1914)

<"A long, long time ago, I saw one day calling on me, as fresh and young as spring, Pablo de Sarasate, already famous, on whom a faint shadow of a moustache could scarcely be glimpsed over his lip. He was coming most gently to ask me, as the most simple thing in the world, to compose a concerto for him. Flattered and enchanted to the highest degree, I promised, and kept my word, to compose for him my conc. 1 in A major*, which is dubbed, I do not know why, with the German title of Concertstück. Later, I wrote for him the Rondo capriciosso, in Spanish style, and still later, the conc. 3 in B minor*, for which he gave me many precious advises, to which, to a great extent, is certainly due the favour that this work enjoys among performers" (Saint-Saëns. "Au courant de la vie". Pag. 37 Paris 1914.)>

-Lalo: (vl conc. in F minor and symphony espagnole)
-Joachim: Variations for vl and orch.
-Wieniawski: vl conc. n 2 in D minor, Op 22
-Dvorak: Mazurek Op 49

Sarasate incorporated all these works into his repertoire and played them superbly, contributing largely to the success of those composers. Saint-Saëns expressly recognises it: "By touring around the world my compositions under his magic bow, Pablo de Sarasate has rendered me the most outstanding service and I am happy to be able to express here publicly, with the tribute of my admiration, that of my gratitude and of my friendship which follows him beyond the grave." (Saint-Saëns. Au Courant de la Vie. Pag 38. Paris 1914)

DECORATIONS AND HONOURS.

Sarasate had in total 41. We will mention here only the most prominent, by chronological order:
1)   Dec 8, 1857. Violin first prize from the Conservatoire de Paris*.
2)   April 12, 1861 Cross of Carlos III of Spain.
3)   Dec 3, 1876 Wendische Krone, Scheverin
4)   Sept 26, 1877 Zäringen Lowe, Baden

5) Jan 4, 1878 White Falcon Cross, Weimar
6) March 9, 1878 Crown of Prussia
7) Nov 7, 1878 Danebrook Cross, Denmark
8) Dec 15, 1878 Art and Science Medal of Dessau
9) Jan 26, 1879 Art and Science Cross of Russia
10) May 29, 1879 Honorary member of the National Academy of Music Stockholm
11) March 23, 1980 Comendador de número de la Real Orden de Isabel la Católica, Spain.
12) April 20, 1881 Encomienda de Isabel la Católica, Spain
13) June 15, 1881 Cross del Cristo, Portugal
14) NOV 19, 1882 Frederick Cross, Wurtemberg
15) June 25, 1883 Honorary Member of the London Phil. Society
16) March 20, 1886 Member of Club Bthvn, Rio do Janeiro
17) April 12,1886 Great Cross of Isabel la Católica, Spain. The Royal decree says: "*Willing to give a prove of My Royal esteem for Don Pablo Sarasate; I Resolve to bestow the Great Cross of the Royal Order of Isabel la Católica on him*" = *Given at the Royal Palace on the twelve of April of the year one thousand eight hundred and eighty six. MARIA CRISTINA.* On the decoration ceremony Sarasate was acclaimed with one of the most formidable and long-lasting standing ovations of his life, enhanced by enthusiastic hurrahs.
18) July 16, 1893 Chevalier de la Légion d'honneur*
19) May 26, 1893 Albregcht Cross, Saxony
20) March 1894 Benemerentis Cross, Rumania
21) August 1895 Leopold Cross, Belgium
22) April 1, 1898 Honorary Member of the quartet Society of Bologna (Italy)
23) Feb 10, 1900 Favourite son of Pamplona
24) Jan 25, 1902 Officier de la Légion d'honneur*
25) Feb 8, 1902 Grand Master of the Rumanian Crown
26) Oct 2, 1907 Great Cross of Alfonso XII, Spain

1845 AUER, LEOPOLD VON (b Veszprém, Hungary; d. Loschwitz, nr. Dresden 1930) THE LAST ROMANTIC. Musical. Hungarian violinist and TEACHER. School of Boehm.

When he was eight he began his studies at the Budapest conservatory with Ridley Kohne. He then entered the Vienna conservatory to study with Jacob Dont* (pupil of BOEHM) from 1857–58 After this he started a concert tour through several Austrian cities, and went to Hanover to complete his studies with Joachim from 1863 to 1864. There is not a clue that allows us to ascribe him to the Modern era, all on the contrary, his curriculum seems to indicate that he belongs fully to the Romantic, antivibrato, era. In 1864 he gave a successful concert in the Leipzig's Gewandhaus* that opened him the door to become leader* of the orchestra of Düsseldorf (1864-1866) and then of the orchestra of Hamburg, where he lead also a string quartet of deserved fame.

After having played in London a Bthvn trio with Piatti* (cello) and Anton Rubinstein* (Piano) in 1868, Rubinstein recommended him to replace Wieniawski as professor at the St. Petersburg conservatory, where he taught from 1868 to 1917. (Wieniawsky had left well printed there the Massart's vibrato during the 12 years he spent in this Conservatory as professor) It was in St Petersburg that Auer got acquainted with the new vibrato, which he never admitted, as we will presently see. He spent half a century as professor in Russia, during which time he exerted a decisive influence on the Russian violin school. But the teachings of Auer did not limit to St. Petersburg. He also taught in London, and Loschwitz (Dresden). Pretending that he was going on holiday, he left Russia for Norway, and from there to the USA in 1918, where he taught at the Julliard School in New York and the Curtis Institute in Philadelphia.

His technique was not perfect, and he declined the Tchaikovski's dedication of his vl conc. declaring it technically awkward. Tchaikovski rededicated it to Brodsky* who premiered it in 1881. But he nonetheless received works dedicated by Tchaikovski (Sérénade mélancolique, Violin concerto) Glazunov (String quartet 5; Violin concerto Op 82), Arensky and Taneyev.

Auer's style of teaching was virtuosity controlled by fine taste. Most of his pupils (Elman**, Zimbalist**, Polyakin*, Heifetz** Milstein** and many others) came to him as finished technicians so that he could develop their taste and interpretative powers. If he were, as everything seems to indicate, a teacher of the romantic school, he would be a typical example of disagreement on what the teacher thinks and what the pupils plays. Heifetz, Elman and all the others played with a most beautiful vibrato which was supposedly inconceivable for Auer. But the gramophone was stronger than all Auer's original ideas. Who would play without vibrato after hearing Ysaye and Kreisler play on the gramophone?

As pedagogue he wrote *Violin Playing as I teach it*, New York 1921; *Violin Masters and their Interpretation*, New York 1925 and *My Long Life in Music*, New York 1923.

When this book was about to go to print I received from London two recordings of Auer: Brahms/Joachim Hungarian dance 1 in G minor and Tchaikovski / Wilhelmj* Melodie Op 43-2, both recorded in C-17. (these recordings are simply a testimony, for he played them in 1920 when he was 75). They come to corroborate my suspicions that Auer ought to be a Romantic anti-vibrato teacher. In these recordings we can appreciate how his vibrato is conspicuous, used only in certain notes, whereas in others he plays without vibrato. His style resembles very much that of his teacher Joachim. These recordings confirm us in the idea that despite of his romantic antivibrato education, his pupils did not pay any attention to Auer's criticism against the vibrato, and the great majority continued to use it.

Abiding always by my principle not to relay on assumptions, but endeavour to find out facts and written evidence of everything I say in this book, and confronted with the patent paradox between Auer's antivibrato education and the majority of his pupils who used it, I had no choice but to go to London, to the British Library to read by myself Auer's published books. And not only have I found out what I was looking for, but killing two birds with the same stone, I found, as well, a precious evidence on Vieuxtepms' frontal opposition to the vibrato: In his book "Violin Playing as I Teach It" New York 1921, Auer observes with amazement that 90 out of every 100 violinists play with vibrato. And his amazement reaches its peak when he notices that even his own pupils play with it. Auer distinguishes two kinds of vibrato players:

1) Those who are under the impression that they are making their playing more effective.
2) Those who find the vibrato a very convenient device for hiding bad intonation, or bad tone production.

After some considerations on the different sorts of vibrato, and saying that many vibrato players have been mislead by unmusical (sic) teachers, he concludes that those who compulsorily make use of it are, in a way, the victims of an actual physical defect, whose existence, those who are cursed with it do not in most cases even suspect. And he traces the source of it to a group of sick or ailing nervous disease, hitherto undiscovered.!! The poor old man did not know what he was talking about. What would have been of the violin without the vibrato of Kreisler, Heifetz (his pupil) Francescatti, and all the rest of the 20th century violinists? Auer was the last Romantic, clinging stubbornly to his old-fashioned ideas up to his very last moment. Auer must have been in his last years very unhappy indeed, hearing all over the world the most famous violinists playing with what was for him the most abhorrent defect. He must have felt utterly alone and forsaken, living in a musical world he was unable to understand. Even worse, he had the most fortunate opportunity to hear, life, the best modern violinists of his time, without understanding and enjoying them. This chance, divine indeed, to be able to hear Wieniawski, Ysaye, Flesch, Kreisler, Thibaud, Enescu -Elman, , Milstein, Heifetz- (his own pupils)- and Francescatti, all at the peak of their fame, was completely wasted, through his lamentable distorted picture of reality, all he could see in them being violinists with an acute nervous ailing. As for me, I would give my kingdom for an audition of Wieniawski or of any good Romantic, Ernst, or Ole Bull, for example.

The precious evidence on Vieuxtemps is written in Auer's My Long Life in Music, New York 1923. He recalls an audition he was able to play for Vieuxtemps when he was fourteen, in 1869 during a tour in Styria, at Gratz. He was accompanied by a sceptic Madame Vieuxtemps at the piano. When he reached a cantabile phrase of the Fantasie Caprice he was playing, he performed it with oversentimental glissandos*, until, suddenly, Mme. Vieuxtemps leaped from the piano stool, and bending down to the ground looked everywhere under the furniture, the piano and the bureau in search of something she could not find despite all her efforts. Everybody was astonished, and Vieuxtemps asked her what she was looking for so anxiously. And she replied: "one or more cats must be hidden in this room miaowing in every key*" alluding to Auer's over-sentimental glissandos*. Auer left the room in tears, and he writes: "from that date on I hate all glissandos and vibratos, and to this very minute I can recall the anguish of my meeting with Vieuxtepms". (Vieuxtemps was then 49-years-old) <by the end of his life Vieuxtemps changed his mind and became favourable to glissandos* and vibratos, as becomes clear by his enthusiastic support of Marsick's (pupil of Massart) and Ysaye's interpretations of his own works>

If we come back now to book six, where we speak of Massart as founder of the Modern school, one of the reasons we relay on is the original designation of the vibrato; there we can see how Boyden*, speculating on the vibrato, relates Ysaye and Wieniawski to Vieuxtemps. This similitude is preposterous, and shows clearly that Boyden has not bothered to read Auer's book My Long Life in Music. Had he read it, he would have known that Vieuxtemps was a rabid enemy of the vibrato, making any similitude of him with Ysaye and Wieniawski, on this subject, absolutely inaccurate.

Auer's Strads:
-1690 Auer
-1691 Auer
-1694 Auer; Bang

-1700 Auer; Russian
-1711 Parke; Cho-Ming Sing
-1715 Auer; Rode
-1721 Auer; Macmillen

1848 MARSICK, MARTIN (b. Jupille-sur-Meuse, nr Liège; d. Paris 1924) Belgian composer, violinist and TEACHER. Modern. Musical. School of Massart.

At the age of eight he entered the Liège Conservatoire winning the first prize in a preparatory theory class in 1831. He then studied with Désiré Hynberg under whose teachings he won a medal in 1864. This allowed him to go the Brussels conservatory, where he studied with the famous teacher Léonard* from 1865 to 1867. Equipped with all these knowledge, Marsick made his dream come true, going to Paris to study with the famous teacher Lambert Massart, under whose teachings he won the PREMIER PRIX of the Paris Conservatoire* in 1869, after only one year of lessons. A scholarship of the Belgian government enabled him to go to Berlin in 1870 to study with Joachim.

To earn his living he played during his studies in the Opera orchestra. Marsick made his debut as soloist in Paris in 1873 at the Concerts Populaires, and started a carrier of touring soloist in 1877 going to many countries in Europe, including Russia, and to the USA. His playing was praised for its big sound and its facile bow technique and he was particularly well known for his interpretations of Wieniawski and Vieuxtemps, who supported him enthusiastically.

Saint-Saëns dedicated him his violin sonata 1.

In 1892 he replaced Eugene Sauzay* (pupil of Baillot, Romantic) as professor in the Paris Conservatoire*, reinforcing thus the growing monopoly of the modern school in it.

He founded a string quartet, and later a trio which had renown in the City of Light*.

When the gramophone appeared in 1910 Marsick was already 54, he had passed the fearful barrier of the 50s and he had the honesty not to record himself in the gramophone. In addition he had a mistress that was the scandal of the whole Paris, and he fled out in secret in her company, giving up all his musical engagements. (Liszt and the Comtesse d'Agoult* had to do the same thing in 1835) But playing all his pupils with vibrato, namely

Thibaud, Enescu and Flesch, we must conclude that he used the vibrato himself, all the more, being a direct pupil of Lambert Massart.

But his inclusion here is mainly as a teacher, for being the direct link between his teacher Massart and his two main pupils, ENESCU and FLESCH, becoming thus the connecting corridor through which the Massart's teachings passed onto these two great pedagogues who, in their turn, passed them to the main great violinists of the 20th century. Another illustrious pupil of Marsick was Thibaud, who is naturally included in this list.

He gave his name to his Strad: 1705 Marsick, owned also by Oistrakh.

1858 HUBAY and YSAYE

1858 HUBAY, JENÖ (b. Budapest. - d. Id. 1937) HALF ROMANTIC HALF MODERN. Hungarian violinist and TEACHER. Juggler + musical = virtuoso.

His real name was Jeno Hube, but at 21 he changed it to Hubay, a more Hungarian sonorous name. He began his violin studies with his father Karoly Hube (Romantic), better known as "Hube", professor of the violin at the Budapest Conservatory, and Kapellmeister* of the Hungarian National Opera. After having performed with great success a Viotti concerto in 1869, he was sent to the conservatory of Berlin to study with Joachim (Romantic) for five years. In 1878 he went to Paris, performing several times in the concerts Pasdeloup*. Here he made a close friendship with Vieuxtemps (Romantic), of whom he had the honour of editing his last works.

He was appointed professor of the Brussels conservatory in 1882, where he taught for four years, returning then to Budapest to replace his father's vacancy in the conservatory. He was knighted in 1907, and in 1913 he was made honorary doctor of the Koslovar University. In 1919 he was appointed director of the Budapest Academy.

Hubay curriculum, as we have seen was totally Romantic, but in his recordings he plays with vibrato.

If one reads what professor de Beriot has to say about the glissandos* (see his article in 1802), and next, one hears Kreisler playing his most elegant, sublime, divine ones, one is tempted to think that Beriot was a complete fool who had no idea on what violin playing is at all. But things are not quite that easy. The glissando* is a most dangerous ornament indeed, and it becomes a grave defect if not used with the most exquisite good taste. And it is because of his glissandos (and his vibrato, as well) that Hubay enters this list of superlative performers with a certain reserve. They are of a dubious taste, and give his music a tiring and repetitive monotony. (I have recorded a few pieces played by him to give an example) On the other hand, his pupil Szigeti improved them greatly, and under his hands they sound "comme il faut".

When the vibrato and the glissando* became, so to speak, readily available to Hubay's ears, around 1910 with Ysaye's recordings, he was already 52-years-old, and although he made his best to comply with, and to conform his play to, the new technique, his five years studies with Joachim plus the initial ones he had with his father, both Romantic, influenced his technique heavily, and prevented him to jump, all by himself, over the wall separating the Romantic from the new vibrato era. He is the true, recorded for ever, example of just what De Beriot had in mind when he forbade the vibrato and the glissando* in his *Méthode de violon en trois parties* (1858).

To play these two ornaments properly, one has to have the enormous musicality of their inventor, Massart, and that of his pupils, who were taught by him, in particular Kreisler.

Hubay, therefore, enters here, mainly, as a teacher, with pupils of great renown such as Szigeti, Telmanyi*, d'Aranyi*, Szekely* and Vegh*.

Hubay is a perfect example of long lasting faculties for violin playing. Our recordings were made when he was 70-years-old, and in some pieces, like his Hullamazo Ballaton, he surpasses his 16-years-old pupil Szigeti. (Both versions are included in our cas.) He is also an example of spontaneous embracing of the vibrato. His teacher, his father, has no direct link with none of the Massart school, and having studied with Joachim, it is clear that the vibrato came not through him.

Hubay had two valuable violins: an Amati and a 1726 Strad named Hubay.

1858 YSAYE, EUGENE (b. Liège - d. Brussels 1931) Belgian composer, conductor teacher and violinist. Modern. Massart school. Juggler + musical = virtuoso.

Ysaye was the first violinist in history to record with the Modern continuous vibrato, although not the first to play with it, for we know that Marsick, Wieniawski and the teacher of both Massart already used the vibrato. But they didn't live long enough to reach the gramophone era. Marsick could have actually recorded something, but due to personal problems he had to retire from the concert platform. He had a mistress and the very strict society of Paris did not consent this kind of scandal, so he had to leave Paris in company of his lover. (same thing happened with Liszt and his mistress the Comtesse d'Agoult*: they flew from Paris for a long journey to Switzerland and Italy. From this period are his ravishing piano pieces *Les années de pèlerinage* and his opened letters *Lettres d'un Bachelier ès musique*). Ysaye enters with full rights into the modern-vibrato era.

He was first taught by his father at the age of four. He entered then the Liège conservatory where he studied with Heynberg, under whom he won a second prize at the age of nine. He continued his studies with Heynberg for two more years, but a quarrel with his teacher made him leave the conservatory. He was re-admitted again in 1872 but, this time, into to the class of Rodolph Massart, (number "23 a" of the list of the Massart family) <do not mistake him with Lambert Massart> obtaining a first prize and a silver medal in 1873-4. He was transferred then to the Brussels Conservatoire with a scholarship to study with Wieniawski from 1874 to 1876. So it is when he was 16 that he learnt the vibrato through the Massart's pupil Wieniawski. In 1876 he moved to Paris to study with Vieuxtemps, who by that time must have fully accepted the vibrato, encouraging him to continue to play with it.

In 1879 he was offered the post of leader* of the Bilse orchestra in Berlin. Joachim, who was directing the Berlin conservatory, heard him and praised him enthusiastically. In 1879 he started a concert tour in company with Anton Rubinstein*, that took them to the main cities of Scandinavia. In 1883 they toured Russia with enormous success. Rubinstein influenced Ysaye greatly and he would always recognise him to be his "true master of interpretation". Later this same year he settled in Paris where he became close friend with the main musicians of the time such as Debussy, Fauré, Saint-Saëns and Franck, to name a few.

In 1886 he was appointed professor of the violin at the Brussels conservatory, a post he retained for the next 12 years. He combined his duties here with frequent tours to the main European cities, including several visits to the U. K.

He visited also the USA where he was greeted with enormous success, both as violinist and as conductor of the Cincinnati Symphonic Orchestra (1918-22)

Unequalled virtuoso, Ysaye achieved one of his greatest triumphs in Berlin in 1904, where he performed a wholly new version of the Brahms concerto, so far the monopoly of Joachim. He was also the great interpreter of the Mendelssohn concerto and of the works by Vieuxtemps. But above all he was the champion and ideal interpreter of the young French school: Franck, D'Indy, Chausson, Duparc, Ropartz, Lekeu, as well as Saint-Saëns, Debussy and Fauré. He is everywhere and always equal to himself as virtuoso, leader of the quartet Ysaye, conductor of the Ysaye concerts in Brussels (1917-23) and of the Cincinnati SO.

He was honoured with the dedication of many works, such as the Poème and concerto by Chausson, the sonata by Franck and the quartet by Debussy.

Ysaye started loosing faculties as usual at the age of 50 particularly troubled by the steadiness of his bow arm, which trembled on the strings. This was the main cause for him to devote to orchestra conducting. At the end of his life, his right foot had to be amputated, due to his diabetes.

His intense vibrato and powerful bowing made his tone unique. In the words of Carl Flesch, Ysaye was "the most outstanding and individual violinist I have heard in my life". This opinion was shared by a generation of violinists who idolised Ysaye: not least, Kreisler, Thibaud, Szigeti, and Enescu.

Only a little flaw: He was too obsessed with wizardry and speed. He sacrificed musicality in favour of pyrotechnics. In "C-17" I have recorded his finale of the Mendelssohn vl conc., which is allegro molto and not prestissimo, as he plays it. The speed he uses is unnecessary. Nevertheless he was very proud of this particular recording, which he considered to be his best. There are fashions, changing fashions, and the will-o'-the-wisp of the dazzling technique of Ernst and Wieniawski misled many a violinist, Ysaye being not an exception. For his series of recordings made at New York City in 1912, Ysaye was paid $ 33,000 plus a third of all profits; the money, he said, was for his grandchildren, but he lost the lot in the Wall Street crash.

Ysaye's recordings of 1912 were made in his full decline. Nevertheless one can appreciate the grandeur and quality of his play.

See index for his recordings.

Ysaye's favourite instruments:

-Strad Ysaye; Hercules of 1732

-Guarneri del Gesu "Ysaye" of 1740. Ysaye ordered to insert this label: "This violin is the most faithful companion of my life"

RECAPITULATION OF THE ROMANTIC ERA

If we were to believe the accounts made on the violinists of the Ancient and Romantic era we would be amazed to realize that almost everyone is, according to their assertions, equal or at least, second to Paganini. These reports must be considered against the background of the hyperbolic exaggerations proper of those days. It is impossible that the 90% of the fiddlers we have considered were equal to Paganini. We have to be most careful in our appreciation, and the reports of the time must be considered with extreme asepsis, as if we were in an operating theatre. We may say that the most reliable reporters of the time were Berlioz, Liszt, Baillot and Schumann. Well, according to them, we may say that <leaving apart Paganini, as it should be> the best was Viotti. Then, Joachim, Ernst, and Ole Bull can come in a second position. (Warning: Although Wieniawski, Ysaye and Kreisler were colossal fiddlers of the same epoch, they belong, as it has been said, to the Modern era, and they cannot be considered here)

We have seen how the Romantics had to coexist with the Moderns, and how little by little the Modern school had prevailed over the Romantic, so that after Sarasate, the last great Romantic player of the XIX century, all the following ones were Moderns. In the XX century we will only see Modern, vibrato players.

GRAPH OF THE ROMANTIC ERA

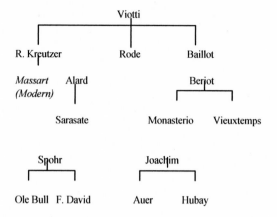

Viotti

R. Kreutzer   Rode   Baillot

Massart   Alard   Beriot
(Modern)

        Sarasate   Monasterio   Vieuxtemps

        Spohr   Joachim

Ole Bull   F. David   Auer   Hubay

THE VIENNA SCHOOL

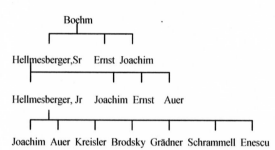

Boehm

Hellmesberger,Sr   Ernst Joachim

Hellmesberger, Jr   Joachim Ernst   Auer

Joachim Auer Kreisler Brodsky Grädner Schrammell Enescu

Kreisler and Enescu began as Romantics but became modern when they went to Paris to study with Massart and his pupil Marsick respectively.

BOOK EIGHT

THE GRAMOPHONE AND THE GLOBALISATION OF THE MODERN ERA

Although the possibility to record music, dates back to the acoustic, pre-electric period (1877-1925) the growth of a recorded repertory, and of a record industry, began in earnest at about the turn of the century (1910)

Ysaye inaugurated the gramophone era. This means that everyone could hear his recordings. No matter the particular ideas a teacher might have on the vibrato, pupils from all around the world could hear Ysaye's one, and if the teacher's idea did not coincide with what was heard on the gramophone, the pupil either changed of teacher or played his own way imitating Ysaye. And then came Kreisler, and then Heifetz and Francescatti. Who would follow a teacher with antiquated ideas on the evil of playing with vibrato, if it was really so beautiful? nobody. And there came high discrepancies between teachers and pupils.

No matter how great, the teacher is but a means to the end of training the violinist. Given the technical tradition obtainable in the early 20th century, the ultimate models for young violinists were the great players available through the gramophone, particularly Ysaye and Kreisler. The changes in style of violinistic interpretation engendered by the enhanced world-wide communications, with speedier travels, gramophone records and eventually radio and TV were to provide, resulted in the loose of teachers importance, and the once-distinctive German, Franco Belgian and Russian schools of playing being first to blur and eventually disintegrate.

We might as well have called the last era, the gramophone era, were it not by the fact of the enormous gap between the invention of the gramophone in 1910 and the date of birth of the founder of the school Lambert Massart in 1811 (almost a century).

What a great loss not to have him recorded. Notwithstanding Liszt had him well recorded in his mind and in his heart. Who could be Liszt in this as in so many other aspects! (particularly in the piano)

1873 FLESCH, CARL (b. Wieselburg, Moson, Hungary - d. Lucerne, Switzerland, 1944) Hungarian pedagogue, TEACHER and violinist. Massart school. Modern. Juggler + musical = virtuoso.

Flesch started his violin lessons at the age of five. From 1886 to 1890 he entered the Vienna conservatory to study under Grün (Romantic) and in 1891 he went to the Paris Conservatoire* where he studied under Martin Marsick, (pupil of Lambert Massart) who taught him the Massart's vibrato, leaving the Conservatoire in 1894 with a premier prix.

Besides his recordings, Flesch constitutes the direct link between Massart and all the rest of Modern players. Once his formative years had ended he made his debut in Vienna in 1895 playing in 1896 in Berlin for the first time. In 1897 he went to Bucharest to lead the Queen's String Quartet. In 1902 he moved to Amsterdam where he acquired a reputation as teacher and chamber music player during the five years he stood there. A milestone in his career was his series of five historical concerts he gave in Berlin, illustrating the development of violin music through the works of more that 50 composers from the 17th to the 20th century. This scheme was to be imitated by other violinists in the subsequent years.

He settled in Berlin in 1908, where he enjoyed international acclaim as solo virtuoso, as founder of one of the most renowned trios of the World (Flesch, Schnabel* and Becker*) and as teacher. From 1928 to 1934 he was professor of the Hochschule für Music leading also the violin department of the newly founded Curtis Institute in Philadelphia. He also gave private classes in Baden-Baden, that attracted pupils from all over the world (1926-34) In 1934 he settled in London, but the start of the World War made him go to Holland, where he was detained by the nazis. Finally he was permitted to return to his native Hungary.

From 1943 to his death he taught at the newly founded Conservatory of Luzern.

Flesch was praised mainly for his classical poise, his intellectual approach to music and his formidable technique. His great musicality is patent in his recordings of "C-17"

Flesch was one of the most formidable teachers of the 20th century, with pupils of such renown as Temianka*, Ida Haendel*, Goldberg*, Max Rostal*, Henryk Szeryng* Ginette NEVEU, Alma Moody and Joseph HASSID. As pedagogue he published several treatises, the most comprehensive of them being *Die Kunst des Violin-Spiels*. He also wrote a very concentrated one, the *Urstudien* which reduce technique to a few basic motions.

A Flesch medal was founded through the initiative of his pupil Max Rostal*. This competition became part of the Festival of the City of London in 1968, now called The City of London Competition for Violin and Viola. Held every two years, is presently one of the most important testing grounds for aspiring violinists.

Flesch is a living example of the discrepancies between the Modern-vibrato school (to which he pertained) and the Romantic orthodox theories. These theories were so deeply rooted in everybody, that despite his belonging to the Modern vibrato school through his teacher Marsick, he, nevertheless, continued to have some apprehension, and thus, in his *Kunst des Violin-Spiels* he wrote:

"From a purely theoretic standpoint the vibrato, as a means for securing a heightened urge for expression, should only be employed when it is musically justifiable".

But "C-17" shows us that he used it continuously, and the recordings of his pupils Neveu "C-13 and 17" and Hassid "C-17" show us that he taught it to them.

I have recorded:

- Handel: Prayer "C-17"
-    "   : March "C-17"
- Paganini: Caprice 20 "C-17"
- Fauré: Berceuse "C-17"
- Falla: Jota "C-17"
- Dobrowen: Hebrew melodie "C-17"

He played on the Strad Brancaccio of 1725

* * *

And so we arrive to the most salient, the most unique, the most remakable, violinist in history: the incomparable FRITZ KREISLER. In fact he was not the best, but he was the most singular of them all.

<u>1875 KREISLER, FRITZ</u> (b. Vienna 1875 - d. New York 1962) American composer and violinist of Austrian origin. <u>Modern</u>.

Pupil of Massart in Paris he was infected by the contagious tenderness, melancholy and poetry of his teacher. <u>Pure tenderness, melancholy, poetry and musicality</u>.

In this title we will deal with one of the most divine violinist in history, so we must take good care with what we say, and say it with extreme awe. Kreisler is KREISLER.

He began to learn the violin at the age of four with his father, a doctor and enthusiastic amateur violinist. He took some preparatory lessons with Jacques Auber (Romantic) after which he was admitted to the Vienna conservatory at the age of seven, the youngest child ever to enter. For three years he studied the violin under HELLMESBERGER Jr (Romantic) and theory with Anton Bruckner. Kreisler made his public debut in Vienna at the age of nine and won a gold medal when he was ten. An unprecedented distinction. So far his studies had been Romantic, and romantic would he have remained, were it not by fortune which made him go to Paris in 1886 where the most famous teacher in the world, Lambert Massart, was violin professor. Here he studied violin with Massart and harmony* with Leo Delibes. After only one year of classes with Massart, Kreisler left the Conservatoire with a premier prix. (<u>this means to say that he, in the incredibly short laps of one single year, was able to leave behind his Romantic training, built up during the long period of seven years, and acquire in the highest degree of perfection the modern vibrato</u>)

During the season 1889-90 Kreisler toured the USA as assisting artist to Moriz Rosenthal*, but with only moderate success. He returned to Vienna where he spent two years at the Gymnasium and two as a pre-medical student, followed by the military service. All this time, Kreisler barely touched his violin. However, once he decided on a musical career, he quickly regained his technique. To help him earn his life in 1896 he applied to join the Vienna Opera Orch. but failed, allegedly because of poor sight-reading. Two years later his revenge was sweet when he scored a staggering success as soloist with the Vienna Philharmonic, actually the same ensemble that had denied him a place. A year later his debut with the Berlin Philharmonic under Nikisch marked the beginnings of his international career. He reappeared in the USA during the 1900-01 season, then made his London debut at a Philharmonic concert under Richter in 1902. In 1904 he was presented with the Philharmonic Society's gold medal.

He was honoured with the dedication of Elgar's violin concerto, specially composed for him, that he premièred on the 10th of November, 1910 in Queen's Hall, with Elgar conducting. Among the raptured audience, there was a teenager with the script on his knees, pencil poised above the music, trying to seize the insaissable of Kreisler's eloquence: Joseph Szigeti**.

Other dedications include:

Ysaye: Sonata for violin solo Op 27-4
Martinu: Czech Rhapsody
Rachmaninof: Variation over a theme by Corelli.

At the outbreak of World War I Kreisler joined the Austrian army. He was medically discharged after being wounded, and moved to the USA (his wife's native country) in 1914. However, anti-German feelings ran so high that he had to leave the USA. In 1923 he toured Scandinavia, Japan, Korea, and China. In 1924 New Zealand, Australia, and Romania in 1928. From 1924 to 1934 he settled in Berlin. Upon the Austrian annexation by the Nazis he was offered the citizenship of France, but in 1939 he returned for good to the USA and became an American citizen in 1943.

I like to think of Kreisler as the mirror of his maestro Massart, with an unequalled vibrato, tender and melancholic. To hear Kreisler play and become instantaneously addict to the drug of his playing is, I suppose, as inevitable as death and taxes. It is what I describe as "Kreisleromania". His vibrato and his emotion are such that he can make his violin weep. Once you start listening to him you must continue hearing him uninterruptedly for months. Kreisler is Massart's "alter ego", his reincarnation, the branch that stems from Massart's tree.

When I uttered the words "the mirror of his maestro" it came to my mind that beautiful Shakespeare's sonnet: (sonnet 3):

> "Look in thy glass, and tell the face thou viewst
> Now is the time that face should form another;
> Whose fresh repair if now thou not renewst,
> Thou does beguile the world, unblessed some mother.
> For where is she so fair whose unear'd womb
> Disdains the tillage of thy husbandry?
> Or who is he so fond will the tomb
> Of his self-love, to stop posterity?

THOU ART THY MOTHER'S GLASS, and she in thee
Calls back the lovely April of her prime;
So thou through windows of thine age shalt see,
Despite of wrinkles, this thy golden time.
But if thou live rememb'red not to be,
Die single, and thine image dies with thee".

Kreisler knew very well who he was and who he was going to be, as stated in his following letter to Massart.

réponse à ma première lettre

Mon cher maître,

Il m'est impossible à
vous décrire la joie qui m'accablait en recevant votre charmante lettre qui me prouvait
si bien que je possède encore
l'amitié de mon cher maître
j'approuve parfaitement l'i-
dée que vous avez eu en vous
retirant à Nice afin d'y
mener une vie paisible sous
un ciel bleu, entouré par les
charmes d'une nature splendide

au bord d'une mer qui offre
des aspects éblouissants, enfin
une vie angélique. Quant à
moi, je me suis retiré à Vienne
afin d'y faire mes é-
tudes pour un examen, qui est
semblable au baccalauréat,
une espèce de volontariat, pour
le service militaire, qui exige
un savoir parfait des sciences.
L'hiver prochain, j'espère, je
ferai parler de moi, afin que
vous puissiez me nommer avec
fierté. Les succès que j'ai obtenus jusqu'à ce moment ne seront

que des nains à côté de ces
gigantesques que j'aurai.
A propos, cher Monsieur
Massart, je vous demanderai
à me faire savoir le resultat
du concours concours ayant
lieu au mois d'août de l'année
passée. J'en'ai pas eu de nouvelles qui m'auraient informées.
En vous assurant de mes
isentiments, toujours les mêmes
pour vous je
signe.

votre élève et ami

1891 ... Fritz Kreisler

TEXT OF KREISLER'S THIRD LETTER:

Vienne le 30/2 1891

Mon cher Maître,

Il m'est impossible à vous décrire la joie qui m'accablait en recevant votre charmante lettre qui me prouvait si bien que je possède encore l'amitié de mon cher Maître. J'approuve parfaitement l'idée que vous avez eu en vous retirant à Nice afin d'y mener une vie paissible sous un ciel bleu, entouré par les charmes d'une nature splendide, au bord d'une mer qui offre des aspects éblouissants, enfin une vie angélique. Quant à mois, je me suis retiré à Vienne à fin d'y faire mes études pour un examen, qui est semblable au baccaloréat, une espèce de volontariat, pour le service militaire, qui exige un savoir parfait des sciences. L'hiver prochain, j'espère, je ferai parler de moi, afin que vous puissiez me nommer avec fierté. Les succes que j'ai obtenus jusqu'à ce moment ne seront que des nains à côté de ces gigantesques que j'aurai. Â propos, cher Monsieur Massart, je vous demanderai de me fair savoir le resultat du concours ayant lieu au mois d'août de l'année passée. J'en'ai pas eu de nouvelles qui m'auraient informées.

En vous assurant de mes sentiments, toujours les mêmes pour vous je Signe Votre élève et amis Fritz Kreisler

1891(sic) <plutôt 1890> miss Schytte 1 prix
Kosman 1 prix
Mr Arfon 1 acst.
écrit par Massart
Quanté 2 prix

TRANSLATION OF KREISLER'S THIRD LETTER (The successes I have had so far are but dwarfs compared with the gigantic ones I shall have in the future)

Vienna, the 20/2 1891

My dear Maestro,

I cannot describe the joy that filled me upon receiving your charming letter that proved me that I still keep the friendship of my dear maestro. I fully agree with your idea to retire yourself to Nice to lead a peaceful life under a blue sky, surrounded by the charms of a splendid nature, by the side of a sea with dazzling aspects, in a word, an angelic life. As for me I have retired to Vienna to study for an examination similar to the General Certificate of Education, a sort of voluntary military service, that demands a perfect knowledge of sciences. Next winter, so I hope, I will make speak of me, so that you can name me with pride. The successes I have had so far are but dwarfs as compared with the gigantic ones I shall have in the future. Incidentally, dear Monsieur Massart, I would ask you to inform me of the results of last August competition; I did not have any news of it.

Assuring you that my high regard for you is as usual, I Sign Your pupil and friend   Fritz Kreisler

1891 (sic) <rather 1890> Miss Schytte 1st prize
Kosman 1st prize
M. Arfon 1st acst
Written by Massart
Quanté 2nd prize

* * * *

The poetry of his play, the elegance of his bowing, the intensity of his expression, enhanced by an unequalled vibrato, his shinning and warm tone, his "buon gusto", his spell, so characteristic of Vienna, his glissandos* (the most dangerous device on a violin) of the most beguiling beauty, his elegance and fine taste and his personal magnetism, have made of him a unique Artist, like the Spanish red wine Vega Sicilia.

To give the reader an idea of Kreisler's excellencies, we could say, without fear of exaggeration, that KREISLER IS TO THE VIOLIN WHAT CHOPIN IS TO THE PIANO.

His only little flaw: lack of technique. Kreisler was a complete lazybones and he had no scruples in acknowledging it. In one of his letters to Massart, jealously kept by that Belgian family I had the privilege to visit, he said:

KREISLER'S FOURTH LETTER
(Vous connnnaissez ma paresse, ma faineantise)

F Kreisler

Vienne le 1/9 1925

Mon cher Maître!

Aujourd'hui revenu de Carlsbad à Vienne, je me sens forcé de vous adresser ces lignes. Monsieur Massart, vous connaissez ma paresse, ma faineantise, surtout concernant le cas d'écrire des lettres, et moi je connais votre bonté paternelle donc je suis assuré que vous m'avez pardonné mon ingratitude semblante. Je joue au mois de Novembre à Berlin

mais je ne vous parlerai
point avant de vous pou-
voir prouver par des ac-
tions, par des journaux
mon succès. En même temps,
daignez accepter la demoiselle
qui vous présentera cette
lettre et qui ne désire
que de vous voir, de vous
jouer devant vous, et si
possible d'entrer dans
votre classe ou dans celle
de Mr Berthelier. Elle
est enthousiasmée de vous
et croit trouver son bon-
heur en travaillant sous
votre direction. Je vous
demande Mr Massart

comme signe du pardon,
que vous l'entendriez et
et lui diriez votre avis
aussi franchement que
je vous connais. Elle a
du talent et je crois
qu'elle vous plaira. En
vous présentant tous les
compliments possibles et
vous priant d'accepter
mes vœux pour vous
je suis
    élève et ami.

        Fritz Kreisler

TEXT OF KREISLER'S FOURTH LETTER
(Vous connaissez ma paresse, ma faineantise)

Vienne le 30/2 1891

Mon cher Maître!

Aujourd'hui revenu de Carlsbad à Vienne, je me sens forcé de vous adresser ces lignes: Monsieur Massart, vous connaissez ma paresse, ma faineantise, surtout concernant le cas d'écrire des lettres, et moi je connais votre bonté paternelle donc je suis assuré que vous m'avez pardonné mon ingratitude semblante. Je joue au mois de Novembre à Berlin mais je ne vous parlerai point avant de vous pouvoir prouver par des actions, par des journaux mon succès. En même temps dignez vous accepter la demoiselle qui vous présentera cette lettre et qui ne desire que de vous voir, de jouer devant vous, et si possible d'entrer dans votre classe ou dans celle de M. Berthelier. Ell est enthousiasmée de vous et crois trouver son bonheur en travaillant sous votre direction. Je vous demande, Monsieur Massart, comme signe de pardon, que vous l'entenderiez, luis disiez votre avis aussi franchement que je vous connais. Ell a du talent et je crois qu'elle vous plaira. En vous presentant tous les compliments possibles et vous priant d'accepter mes voeux pour vous je suis

Elève et amis   Fritz Kreisler

TRANSLATION OF KREISLER'S FOURTH LETTER

(you know well my laziness, my idleness)

Vienna, the 1/9 1890

My dear Maestro,

I have today returned from Carlsbad to Vienna, and I feel constrained to send you these lines: Monsieur Massart, you know well my laziness, my idleness, above all in what concerns writing letters, and I know your paternal kindness, therefore I am sure that you have forgiven my apparent ingratitude. I'll perform in November at Berlin but I will not tell you about it until I can prove you my successes with facts, through the papers. In the meantime I pray you to be so kind as to accept the young lady who will give you this letter, whose only desire is to meet you, and, if possible, to enter your class or that of M. Berthelier. She is very enthusiastic about you and her happiness will be to work under your guide. I pray you, Mr. Massart, as a sign of pardon, that you hear her play and let her know your impression, as frankly as I know you will do. She has talent and I think you would like her. With all my best wishes and compliments. I remain

Your pupil and friend, Fritz Kreisler

* * * *

He practised very little and he took pride in it: "*I need not practice,* he used to say, *just washing my hands with warm water is enough*"

But it was not enough. The great repertoire from Bthvn on, requires a great deal of technique, more as we advance in time, and he lacked that technique. His Bthvn vl concerto with Barbirolli, for example, is just passable, and he is unable to play his own *diabolic* cadenza* (the touch stone of all the Bthvn cadenzas*) with a minimum accuracy.[1] You may argue that he was too old (51) , but another version of 1926 with the Berlin State Opera Orch. under Leo Blech is also full of technical failures.

I have recorded almost his complete works; see index.

Kreisler's Strads:

1726 Kreisler; Greville
1732 Kreisler; Baillot
1733 Kreisler
1734 Kreisler; Amherst
-But his favourite instrument was the Guarneri del Gesu ex Kreisler of 1733.

The end of his musical career was astonishing: one day, overnight, in 1951 his interest in the violin waned; He sold his collection of instruments, and kept only a Vuillaume* of 1860.

Kreisler is the composer of the most accomplished, and most beautiful cadenza* for Bthvn's violin concerto, of many delightful small pieces and of dozens of pieces in the "olden style" which he ascribed to various 18th century composers such as Pugnani, Padre Martini*, Couperin, etc. When

---

[1] I say diabolic because a goddess of the violin of the calibre of Anne Sophie Mutter, in her recording with von Karajan in 1980 when she was 17, had real difficulties in playing it, which she overcame, very wisely, by slowing down the tempo. Be it as it were, the whole mankind is anxiously longing for another version of that concerto by a more mature "*Mutti*"

Kreisler admitted in 1935 that these pieces were a hoax, many critics were indignant, while others accepted it as a joke.

1880 THIBAUD, JACQUES (b Bordeaux; d Mont-Cement, nr Barcelonnet 1953) French violinist. Modern. Massart school. Musical.

He was first taught the violin by his father, and gave his first public concert in 1888 at Angers, performing the Bthvn's romance in F, and in Bordeaux the same year with a Wieniawski's concerto. Encouraged by Ysaye he went then to Paris to study with MARTIN MARSICK, pupil of Lambert Massart, and teacher of FLESCH and ENESCU, graduating with a PREMIER PRIX in 1896. Working at the "Rive Gauche's Café Rouge" in Paris he was heard and engaged by Eduard Colonne* for the Concerts Colonne*, at which he appeared some 54 times as soloist in the winter of 1898-9, thereby establishing the basis of his reputation, becoming famous overnight with his performance of Saint-Saëns's Le Déluge. His first tours in 1903 took him to Germany and America, making frequent appearances in Britain, all with immense success, marking the beginning of his glory. After two world wide tournées he formed with Pablo Casals*, and Alfred Cortot* his most famous trio, which has become legendary.

Like all the members of the Massart's school <and according to the maestro's motto that the violinist must not astonish but move> he was refined rather than robust. Sensuous and voluptuous, the art of Thibaud does not understand the rigor of tempo, or any other musical demand. He is pure sensuality, tenderness, seduction, sheer happiness, total freedom of enjoyment, erotic and luxurious. He was particularly praised by the silvery purity of his tone and the exquisite polish of his technique. He excelled in Mozart and in the Romantic composers.

In 1943 he founded with pianist Marguerite Long* the Marguerite Long - Jaques Thibaud Competition for piano and violin.

He lost his faculties much earlier than the usual barrier of 50 years of age. This is the reason why his recordings gather in this work 1922-27 do not quite show him as he was. Notwithstanding, his performance of Albeniz's Tango gives us a rather approximate idea of what might have been the style of his playing, and its musicality. Simply compare it with the same played by Zukerman and you will see the abysmal distance. But each one has his virtues. Give to God what is God's, and to Caesar what is Caesar's.

He never retired, continuing his performances until he was over 70, making a fool of himself. There is a CD with him (Philips 420859-2) recorded in 1950 when he was 70, of the Mozart's concerto 3 that is a total shame both for him and for mankind. Is it really so difficult to avoid ridiculousness and retire on time ?? It is hard to say which is worse, if the recording of Joachim or this one of Thibaud. Be it as it were it is very sad indeed.

He died in an air crash on his way to a concert tour in the Far East.

He played mainly on a Carlo Bergonzi, and gave his name to three Strads:

1709 Thibaud; Baillot, destroyed in his aeroplane crash.
1714 Thibaud; Berou
1716 Thibaud; Colossus

I send the reader to the index for his recordings.

1881 ENESCU, GEORGE (b. Liveny-Virnav, nr. Dorohoi - d. Paris 1955) Rumanian composer, pianist, conductor, TEACHER and violinist. Modern. Massart school. Most musical.

At the age of four he began to play the violin, and to compose the next year. He first studied with Caudella* before entering the Vienna conservatory (1888-1894) where he studied with Grün, Hellmesberger Jr. and Sigismund Bachrich, making his debut in Slanic, Moldavia in 1889. So far all his teachers were Romantic. From 1895 to 1899 he went to Paris to study with Martin Marsick, who taught him the Modern Massart school. In the French capital he found an artistic and intellectual milieu that stimulated his faculties. Princess Bibesco introduced him into the musical circles, where he made the acquaintance of Saint-Saëns and of Eduard Colonne* who had organised his series of Concerts Colonne*, where Enescu premiered his Poème Roumain in 1898. From now on Enescu will be divided between Paris and his native country, without abandoning his career of international concert tours, which began in 1923 by a triumphant tour of The USA.

PARIS. Besides the premier of his Poème Roumain already mentioned, he premiered accompanied by Cortot* his violin sonata n 1, in 1898, and accompanied Thibaud on the piano in the premier of his second sonata in 1900. In 1902 he created his trio with Fournier* and Casella*, and in 1904 the Enescu string quartet.

ROMANIA. Here he contributed decisively to the development of the musical life by conducting opera performances, creating examination committees for young talents, of which he was member of the jury, giving concerts, recitals, conducting, giving lectures, writing, etc. In particular he gave cycles of concertos and violin sonatas that covered the whole repertoire, he was member of the examination commission of the Bucharest conservatory, and honorary chairman of the Iasi Conservatory. In 1912 he founded the Enescu prize for Composition in Bucharest, founded the Enescu Symphony Orchestra in Iasi in 1917, and he inaugurated the Romanian Opera House of Bucharest, conducting Wagner's Lohengrin. He instituted, as well, the Romanian Composers' Society, being admitted to the Romanian Academy in 1932. Enescu was an accomplished musician in all respects. He had a prodigious memory; with an enormous repertoire covering from Bach to himself, which he played from memory. He was also a good pianist, and a superb conductor.

Enescu always wanted to be remembered as a composer, and he managed to become a first rank composer of Romania. Nevertheless, what interests us is how he played and to taught the violin.

a) Teacher: Most renowned all over the world, his best pupils were Ginette NEVEU, MENUHIN, Gitlis*, Ferras* and GRUMIAUX.

b) Violinist: The poetry and musicality of his play are indescribable, one has to listen to him to understand this.

I have recorded almost his complete works, I send the reader to the index.

Enescu is said to have played on an unnamed Strad., a Koll and a Guarneri del Gesu. None of these instruments are documented, however.

1887 PERSINGER, LOUIS (b. Rochester, Illinois; d. New York 1966) American pianist, violinist and TEACHER. Massart school. Modern.

His first studies were in Colorado USA. His rapid progress made him play in public at the age of 12. In 1900 he was sent to Leipzig to study with Becker* for four years. He then moved to Brussels to study with YSAYE and THIBAUD (both pupils of Massart) from 1905 to 1911.

In 1812 he returned to USA where he had a triumphant concert with Stokowski. After having toured the main cities of the USA he was appointed leader* of the Berlin Philharmonic Orch. and in 1915 he was made leader* of the San Francisco Orch.

He began his teaching career in San Francisco in 1916, remaining there till 1928. One of his first pupils was Menuhin.

He was at the same time an accomplished pianist, accompanying Menuhin on a tour in the USA from 1928 to 1929. On the occasion of his 75th anniversary, the Julliard School organised a recital where he played the first half on the violin and the second half on the piano.

He taught at the Cleveland Institute of Music (1929-30) and in 1930 he was the successor of Auer at the most renowned Julliard School. He is perhaps the most distinguished teacher in the USA, together with Galamian, having created a true American school.

Among his pupils are Camilla Wicks, MENUHIN, Guila Bustabo, Isaac STERN, and Ruggiero RICCI.

1890 ZIMBALIST, (Alexandrovich) EFREM (Rostrov-na-Donu, South West Russia, nr the mouth of River Don, on the sea of Azof; d. Reno, Nevada. 1985) American violinist, composer and teacher of Russian origin.

He first studied with his father, a professional violinist, conductor of the Rostov Opera. In 1901 he went to Auer** in S. Petersburg, graduating with Gold medal and the Rubinstein* Prize in 1907. That same year he made his successful debut in Berlin and London. Three years later, in 1910, he had a staggering success at his debut in the Gewandhaus* in Leipzig, playing the Tchaikovsky concerto under Nikisch. In 1911 he went to the USA where he played for the first time in America the Glazunov's concerto. In view of his many successes there he decided to settle in the USA.

Zimbalist married singer Alma Gluck* in 1914, with whom he played as accompanist, and soloist as well.

In 1928 he began teaching at the Curtis Institute in Philadelphia, being promoted to director from 1941 to 1968. During this period he married the founder of this Institute, Mary Louise Curtis.

Quiet and concentrated his performances are noble and poised. The quality of the sound and the tone he is able to extract from his Strads cannot be described in words, one has to hear him play, he is just divine. Together with Elman**, Polyakin* and Heifetz**, he is one of the best pupils of Auer**, although, as usual, he plays with vibrato, against Auer's teachings.

Imitating Flesch, he played a series of programs illustrating the history of violin music over four centuries.

As pedagogue he published *Solo Violin Music of the Earliest Period*. As a composer he wrote an opera, *Landara*; *Portrait of an Artist*, a symphonic poem; Chamber music and solo violin scores like *Carmen Fantasy* and *Sarasate's Ana*

He had four Strads:

1) the *Titian* of 1715, owned also by Grumiaux**.
2) the *Deurbroucq* of 1727.
3) the *Lamoureux* of 1735.
4) The *Swan* (*Chant du Cygne*) of 1737.

His discography is very scarce.

1891 DUSHKIN and ELMAN

1891 DUSHKIN, SAMUEL (b.Suwalki; d. New York 1976) He was born in the same town as Hassid. American violinist of Polish birth. Modern. Juggler.

Pupil of two direct pupils of L. Massart, RÉMY* and KREISLER, he is a grandson of him.

After being taken to the USA as a child, his talent was discovered at the Music School Settlement of New York, and he became a protégé of the American composer Blair Fairchild, who brought about his studies with RÉMY* (vl) <direct pupil of L. Massart, got premier prix in 1878, and was professor of the Paris Conservatoire* from 1896 to 1929> and Ganaye (composition) at the Paris Conservatoire and with Auer and KREISLER in New York.

Dushkin began to tour in Europe from 1918, and in the USA from 1924, when he first appeared with the New York SO. He became known as a persuasive advocate of contemporary music, a reputation enhanced by his close friendship with Stravinski who composed for him his vl concerto of 1931, and a duo concertante*.

Dushkin made also a certain number of transcriptions of other composers for his instrument, which he played with great success. I have recorded, played by him, the Stravinski's Russian dance (Petrushka) with Igor Stravinski at the piano in "C-17"

His Strads:

-1701 Dushkin
-1707 Dushkin; Bellarosa. It is today owned by Cho Liang Lin.
-1735 Dushkin (made by Omobono Stradivari)
Also a Guarneri del Gesu of 1739

1891 ELMAN, MISCHA (b. Talnoye, 200 Km S of Kiev, Ukraine; d. New York 1967) American violinist of Russian birth. Modern.

He studied in Odessa under A. Fiedmann (1897-1902) then he was discovered by Auer, who taught him at the St. Petersburg Conservatory (1903-4)

He began touring in Berlin in 1904, followed by sensational debuts in London (1905) and in New York (1908). His fame grew rapidly establishing himself as one of the great violinists of the world. He settled in The USA in 1911 and by 1923 he had acquired the American citizenship. In 1936, imitating Flesch, he gave at the Carnegie Hall a series of 15 concerts illustrating the development of violin literature.

Elman toured all over the world, and in 1926 he founded his own Elman string quartet. Martinu composed his concerto for Elman, who gave its first performance in 1944. Elman's popularity was enhanced by his more that 2 million gramophone records sold to the market.

Elman most glorious attribute was his rich, sensuous and infinitely expressive tone, which became legendary, enhanced by an intense vibrato. He was passionate and fiery, with strong vitality in his play.

He is an example of those pupils of Auer who played the Modern vibrato despite of Auer's Romantic anti vibrato ideas.

I have recorded, played by him, the Wieniawski's Souvenir de Moscou Op 6, in "C-17"

He had four Strads passing his name to two of them:

-1703 Shoofs
-1722 Elman, owned also by Joachim, and Napoleon.
-1727 Elman; Récamier, owned also by Napoleon.
- 1735 Samazeuil

1892 SZIGETI, JOSEPH (b. Budapest - d. Luzern 1973)

American violinist of Hungarian birth. Modern. Juggler + musical = virtuoso.

Born in the Carpathian village of Maramaros-Sziget, near Budapest, in Hungary, Szigeti began to study the violin with his father and an uncle, both professional musicians, at the age of three. In 1903 he entered the Franz Liszt Academy in Budapest where he studied with HUBAY. Two years later the young prodigy made his debut in Berlin. Here he had the opportunity to hear for the first time Ysaye, Kreisler and Elman, and in his own words he was "bowled over".

His debut in London was at the Bechstein (Wigmore) Hall in 1907, and here he settled until 1914. During this juvenile period Szigeti feverishly absorbed the City's rich musical and cultural life. He gave numerous concerts, premiering the concerto written for him by Hamilton Harty in 1909. He played also frequently with such renowned singers as Blanche Marchesi*, John McCormack* and Nellie Melba*. He played also sonatas accompanied by Myra Hess*, Lengyel, Wilhelm Backhaus and Busoni who exercised a strong influence on him; their friendship materialised in the revival by Szigeti of Busoni's neglected violin concerto throughout England and Europe in the 1912 season. An unforgettable experience was Kreisler's premier of Elgar violin concerto in 1910. Teenager Szigeti, who was among the raptured audience, sat with the script on his knees, pencil poised above the music, trying to seize the insaissable of Kreisler's eloquence, making notes.

Szigeti was extremely popular during the years preceding the first World War, and he began recording for HMV in 1908. The outbreak of the war and a tuberculosis that he contracted, made him retire from the concert platform, going to Davos (Switzerland) for his treatment. Here he gave master classes at the Geneva Conservatory. Once the war was over he resumed his concert tours, going to Russia more than ten times where he introduced the concerto 1 by Prokofief. During the season of 1925 he had a successful tour in the USA.

236

In 1930 he toured the Far East, South America, New Zealand and South Africa, and in 1938 he premiered the Blosch's concerto in Cleveland. In 1940 he settled in the USA, becoming citizen in 1951. After several international tours he settled in Switzerland in 1960. Having trespassed the barrier of the 50, he retired from his concert activities.

Szigeti matured very late, around 1930, being until then the prodigy child everybody knew. I have recorded the two periods of his career. In cas 20 we can hear the prodigious Szigeti in the beginning of side A of the tape, and the final track shows us the mature Szigeti in La Folia by Corelli in his full splendour. One must be very careful with his recordings, for after 1945, he is already in decline, as it is usual in almost all violinists. He played all sort of music, being a great advocate for the contemporary music. He had many dedications such as Bartok's Rhapsody n 1 and contrasts, concertos by Casella*, Frank Martin and Harty, the sonata by Rawsthorne and Bloch's La nuit exotique. He was a tireless performer of the music by Busoni, Milhaud, Berg, Stravinski, Ravel, Roussel and many contemporary composers.

Bartok dedicated him his rhapsodies No 1, and "contrasts".
Hamilton: Violin concerto
Casella*: violin concerto.
Prokofief: "Melody" Op 35-1
Rasthorne: Sonata for violin
Ysaye: sonata Op 27-1
Bloch: "La nuit exotique" and Violin concerto 1

He plays the Strad of 1724 Ludwig.

Also a Guarneri del Gesu ex Henri Petri.

BOOK NINE

THE XX CENTURY

And so we enter into the 20th century. From now on all fiddlers belong to the Modern-vibrato era, so it will not be necessary to state it at the beginning of each one. All of them are also juggler + musical = virtuoso, so I will omit this statement too. The typical and most abused assertion that the violinist in question has played with the best orchestras, under the most renowned conductors, will also be omitted, for it is a matter of course, by the mere fact of being included in this list.

THE MAIN ENTRANCE GATES

The Modern school enters the 20th century through three main gates:

1) Carl Flesch
2) Georges Enescu
3) Leopold Auer

The three great pedagogues of the 20th century. Flesch and Enescu are directly linked to Massart through Marsick. (or, as we said before, his grand sons)

Auer, the third great pedagogue of the beginnings of the century, on the contrary, was a frontal enemy of the vibrato, but as we have said under his article, despite of his prohibition, his pupils played with vibrato as the gramophone showed them the style of playing of the first great violinists of the century: Kreisler**, Ysaye**, Szigeti**, Francescatti**, and of the other two pedagogues Flesch** and Enescu**, whose style could be heard in the gramophone, as well. The gramophone was stronger than Auer's teachings.

THE VIOLINISTS

The 20th century breaks its fast with the birth of two idols of the violin:

1900 Jascha Heifetz
1902 Zino Francescatti

The 20th century has produced nothing less than seven divinities of the violin, five idols and two goddesses:

1) Heifetz.
2) Francescatti.
3) Oistrakh.
4) Stern.
5) Perlman.
6) Chung.
7) and Mutter.

1900 HEIFETZ, JASCHA (b. Vilna, Lithuania; d. Los Angeles 1987) American violinist of Russian origin.

Heifetz's precocious gifts for the violin were discovered very soon by his father Ruvim, a professional violinist, who started giving him lesson at the age of three. After these first familiar lessons Heifetz was sent to study with the prestigious teacher Ilya Malkin at the Vilna's Imperial School of Music; his progress was so fast that at the age of six he played the Mendelssohn violin concerto in Kovno. In 1910 he entered the conservatory of St. Petersburg, where he was taught first by the assistant to Auer, Nalbandyan, then by Auer himself. His first brilliant appearances were in St. Petersburg in 1911 and in Berlin 1912 playing the Tchaikovski concerto with Nikisch and the Berlin Philharmonic. This year he started touring Austria and Scandinavia. He profited of an invitation to tour the USA in 1917 to leave Russia for good. His debut at the Carnegie Hall in October of that year was a staggering success. Heifetz started touring the USA, and made debuts in London and Paris in 1920, Australia in 1921 and in 1922 Asia. Heifetz became an American citizen in 1925.

No less triumphant were his appearances in Palestine in 1926-1927. In 1934 he made an emotional return to Russia. At the end of World War II Heifetz reduced considerably his public performances, accepting the post of teacher at the University of Los Angeles.

Heifetz precocity was the subject of praises of all kinds, like Auer's' "I have never known such a precocity" or that of Kreisler "*we might as well take our fiddles and break them across our knees*!!" His name has been always considered as synonymous with violinistic perfection. Bernard Shaw, with his pungent sense of humour, wrote him the following telegram:

"13th June 1920
My dear Heifetz,

Your recital has filled me and my wife with anxiety. If you provoke a jealous God by playing with such superhuman perfection, you will die young. I earnestly advise you to play something badly every night before going to bed instead of saying your prayers. No one mortal should play as perfectly as that.

Sincerely G. Bernard Shaw"

In addition to his perfection he was most elegant.

He started recording very soon and since, contrary to Shaw's prediction, he lived long, he has bequeathed mankind with an enormous amount of recordings, which span from his first acoustic record made in Russia in 1911 to his last CD of 1972. All these have been recently gathered up in a very extensive collection of CDs.

I send the reader to the index for the recordings of Heifetz.

His Strads:
- 1714 Dolphin; Cho-Ming Sin
- 1715 Hochstein; owned also by Joachim.
- 1731 Heifetz; Piel
- But his favourite was a 1740 Guarneri del Gesu (ex F. David). It was this instrument the one F. David used for the premier of Mendelssohn's vl concerto in 1845.

He passed well unharmed the barrier of the 50s, playing to perfection until he was 72. Despite all his absolute playing perfection he lacks a certain musicality, his recordings being a little cool. They do not transmit emotions, or feelings in the sense Geminiani** wanted music to be performed. His total perfection does not allow the necessary musicality to bloom.

The majority of Heifetz's fans have a very particular feature that distinguish them from any other: they are not only his bigot fans, but they are as stubborn as a mule, and would not take heed to reason: Anything done by Heifetz is sheer perfection and that's all. No possible discussion or argument. In this sense my opinion on his musicality would seem to them just anathema. Sorry for that!

<u>1902 FRANCESCATTI, RENE [Called ZINO]</u> (b. Marseille - d. La Ciotat, [Bouches-du-Rhône department], half way Marseille–Toulon, along the coast of the Côte d'Azur, by the sea of the Golf du Lyon, Provence-Alpes-Côte d'Azur region, SE France. 1991) French violinist of Italian origin.

He learnt the beginnings of the violin from his father Zino, a renowned Italian teacher, and from his mother, violin teacher, as well. He started playing when he was five-years-old as a prodigy child, and played the Bthvn concerto at the age of ten at the Concert Classiques in Marseilles (two years younger than Joachim) He then played at the Garnier* Palace in Paris, but it is through records that he became famous by realising dozens of records for a subsidiary company of Pathe.

In 1924 he went to Paris where he made friends with Ravel, playing both in duo in a tour that took them to England, where they made Ravel's tzigane popular. To make his living Francescatti played for the Walter Straram Orch. where a beautiful violinist was playing. She later became his wife. She sacrificed her career at her husband's, becoming an indispensable wife. (A similar thing has done, exemplarily, Madame Galamian with her husband)

For three times he was invited to play in America, but he refused until in the end he accepted. (*a la tercera va la vencida* we say in Spain). According to Harrap's dictionary: "third time lucky". He went first to South America where his staggering success in the Teatro Colon in Buenos Aires is a prelude of what would happen in North America where he eventually settled in New York City.

He has been member of many international competition juries.

His virtuosity is dazzling, effortless and flawless. His vibrato most sensuous; his legato* unique. His only little flaw was that he was reluctant to abandon his legato, which harmed severely the incisive attack music sometimes require (for instance in Mozart). But, on the other hand, this very legato makes of him a unique interpreter of Bthvn. His concerto in D with Bruno Walter is simply superb, "C-9", and ranks among the best three in history, leaving aside prodigy Joachim's version, which will always remain legendary in our imagination, for we have not heard it, to be able to compare it with others. The dazzling Kreisler's cadenza*, is played absolutely flawless, and at an unbelievable speed. The whole concerto is really amazing. He played it after having passed the fearful barrier of the 50s, when he was 58 years old.

The Fracescattis were very close friends with the Galamians (see next article: 1903 Galamian) who never appreciated Francescatti in his full value. The very magnitude of Francescatti's tree, prevented them to see the wood.

I have recorded by him:

- Bthvn: sonata "Kreutzer" in A minor "C-05"
- Bthvn: vl conc. with Walter "C-09"
- Bach: vl conc. 2 in E Major BWV 1042 "C-16"

He played on a Strad of 1727 Hart to which he passed his name, and is called now Francescatti. This violin has a most particular oboe sound in certain notes.

Francescatti played to perfection until he was 73. Later he sold his Francescatti Strad to Salvatore Accardo, giving the product of his selling to his own "Foundation Zino Francescatti" to help the career of young virtuosi. His last performance, the Saint-Saëns concerto 3, played in New York City the 16 December 1975, at his 73-years-of-age, is another example of the absolute perfection with which he played all his life.

He made a very successful association with Casadesus* with whom he recorded the integral of Bthvn sonatas and many other works, touring over the main cities of the world.

DECORATIONS AND HONOURS. He was honour member of the Boston, Philadelphia and New York orchestras, and of the Société des Concerts du Conservatoire de Paris*; Commander of the Order of Knighthood, Commandeur de la Légion d'honneur*, Great Officer in the National Merit Order, Commander of Arts and Letters, Commander of the Order of Leopold of Belgium.

Francescatti's vibrato and tone are among the most sensuous, together with Perlman and Mutter.

1903 GALAMIAN, IVAN (b Tabriz NW extreme of Iran, the 4th largest city of the country. [Persia]; d New York City 1981) American TEACHER of Iranian birth.

Ivan Galamian was a superb performer, but he has been included here mainly as teacher, being one of the best teachers of the 20th century to judge by his pupils: PERLMAN, ZUKERMAN and CHUNG all three appearing in this book.

His ancestry was Armenian, and his father was a well-to-do merchant. When Ivan went to Moscow with his family he was two years of age. Little is known about his early years in Russia. They were times of revolution, social unrest and war, and he did not like to speak about this period of his life, not even with his wife.

Ivan began the study of the violin at an early age, and in 1916, when the nation was already caught up towards the revolution that occurred two years later, he was taken by professor Constantine Moistures in Moscow. His progress was fast and he graduated in 1919, being shortly afterwards admitted to the Bolshoi Theatre Orch.

After having been deprived of his entire family estate, and stripped of everything he had, Galamian was imprisoned. Although he was released later he decided to escape as soon as possible. The details of his escape are unknown, but by 1922 he was already in Paris.

There he took lessons from Capet* for two years before giving his first concert in 1924, which was followed by others in Holland, Germany and France. But soon he gave up performing and concentrated in teaching. He began his violin lesson at an early stage in Paris, very much helped by his teacher Capet*. He later became professor at the Russian Conservatory in Paris and the success of his young students spread his teaching fame as a "professor-magician". In 1934 a reviewer wrote: "Mr. Galamian showed us what a real master can do with talented pupils. We think that at the present time there is no any other teacher in Paris who can produce such a high standard of teachings". At the same time Galamian had started giving lesson in New York City, and for several years he taught in New York and in Paris six months in each, moving to New York permanently in 1937 when the unrest in Europe preluded the great World War.

In the northern region of New York State, in the vicinity of Elisabethtown, he founded the Meadowmount school, a boarding school for his violin students, where he taught till his death.

Galamian has revolutionised the technique of teaching the violin with enormous success. The main features of his method are described in his

"Principles of Violin Playing and Teaching" 1982 Prentice Hall inc. ISBN 0-13-710773-0

His theories lie in the conviction that putting a system into a book is a problematic undertaking because no printed work can ever replace the live teacher-student relationship. In his opinion the teaching must be individualised, there is no universal method but every student needs his own different approach.

Galamian's ideas centre on the building of an absolute technique the foundation of which lies in the correct RELATIONSHIP OF THE MIND TO THE MUSCLES, the smooth, quick and accurate functioning of the sequence in which the mental command elicits the desired muscular response. This mental-physical relationship is called CORRELATION. [The term correlation is perhaps not ideal inasmuch as it is most often used in connection with elements that are interdependent and on a more or less equal footing, whereas here we have to do with a relationship not between equals but between a superior (the mind) and subordinates (the muscles)] It is the improvement of this correlation which provides the key to technical mastery and technical control and not, as apparently is commonly believed and taught, the training and building of the muscles. What counts is not the strength of the muscles, but their responsiveness to the mental directive. The better the correlation, the greater facility, accuracy, and reliability of the technique. The question becomes, thus, on how to improve the correlation. The answer is that the player has to present the mind-muscle unit with problems to solve, problems that proceed from the simple to the ever more complex"

In his opinion it happens only too often with too many students that the mind wanders to different spheres while the fingers and hands are engaged in mechanical routine-functioning and endless repetitions. Practice of this kind, lacking both direction and control, is a waste of time. The student must keep his mind in constant mental alertness, by presenting to the mind, for transmission to the muscles, problems that progress from the simple to the ever more complicated. These are problems of timing, and co-ordination in the form of various patterns of rhythm, of bowing, of accentuation, and of the combination of all three of these factors.

In progressing from simpler to harder problems one very important principle has to be kept in mind: whenever one problem has been mastered, it is useless to repeat it over and over again. One should leave it alone and proceed to the next. By practising, as a routine, things that do not need any more practice, one is wasting time.

His ideas on intonation are also highly interesting:

The ear must control always the just intonation and the fingers must be ready to correct any lapse of intonation at the speed of dictation time. It is what he calls instant correction. For this end the performer must help himself with the aid of the vibrato. The performer must be capable to play in right intonation even with an untuned violin: "The artist must be extremely sensitive and should have the ability to make instantaneous adjustments in his intonation". (The best and easiest way to make such adjustments is by means of the vibrato)

...Advanced players, already in possession of a secure intonation, will find that their facility for quick adjustment can be improved by changing from time to time the instruments they use.<This practice is done by Perlman who changes from his Guarnerius to his Strad very often> It is also good advise not to interrupt the practice every few minutes to retune the violin. One should be able to play in tune on a violin out of tune" (Principles. Chapter two. Intonation. Page 22)

Galamian owned a Nicola Amati of 1680 the ex Walton.

1904 MILSTEIN, NATHAN (1904 Odessa, Ukraine, Russian Empire; d. London 1992) American violinist of Russian origin.

He started his violin studies at four years age, passing later to P. Stoliarski (1911-14) the teacher of D. Oistrakh. He played the Glazunov concert, under the author in 1914. But his true debut was in Odessa in 1920. His successes became ever more popular and played often with his fellow countryman Vladimir Horowitz. In 1925 both went out of Russia for a tour and left it for good. They played also in trio with Piatigorski*, an emegree as well.

Settled in Berlin in 1925 he played in Paris (1926) and the following year went to Brussels with the intention to study with Ysaye, but he refused in view of his mastery. Went to the USA in 1929 where he made his debut with the Philadelphia Orch. under Stokowski. He became naturalized in 1942. He returned many times to Europe to give recitals in Lucern, Berlin and Salzburg. As pedagogue he taught at the proficiency course in Muraltengut in Zurich and at the Julliard School of New York City. He passed amply the barrier of the 50s, playing to perfection until late in his life. His tone is round and pure, with a rigorous fidelity to the intentions of the author. He has an absolute command of both finger board and bow, and possesses a dazzling technique. He composed the cadenzas* for many Romantic concertos and a *Paganiniana* in homage to the father of all violinist, virtuosistic and difficult, but beautiful, which he premiered in New York in 1954.

He has been decorated Officier de la Légion d'honneur*.

-He played on the Strad. Goldman of 1716.
-Also on Strad. Dancla* of 1703
-Strad. Dancla* of 1710

1908 OISTRAKH, DAVID (b. Odessa - d. Amsterdam 1974) Soviet conductor, violist and violinist.

He first studied in his birthplace with Pyotr Stolyrsky from the age of five until his graduation (playing both viola and violin) from the Odessa Conservatory in 1926. It is here that he performs his first recital as leader* and soloist of the Odessa SO at the age of 16. In 1927 Glazunov invited him to play his concerto under him in Kiev. Oistrakh made his debut in Leningrad in 1928, and in Moscow the following year. In 1928 he had moved to Moscow, and there began a period of intense artistic growth. During the 1930s he won first prizes in the Ukrainian Contest (1930) and the All-Soviet Contest (1935); second prize, under Ginette Neveu, in the Wieniawski Contest (1935); and first prize in the Ysaye Concours in Brussels (1937). This was the beginning of his international career; during the war he played at the front, in besieged Leningrad, in hospitals and factories, and he celebrated peace with a performance of Bach double concerto in 1945 in Moscow with Menuhin (the first foreign artist to visit the Soviet Union after the war) in a magnificent concert. In 1946-47 he gave a cycle of programmes "the development of the violin concerto" which included the concertos by Sibelius, Elgar and Walton, as well as Khachaturian's, dedicated to him. At his N.Y. debut in 1955 he introduced Shostakovich's first concerto, written for him.

His technical mastery was complete, his tone powerful and warm at the same time, and his approach a perfect fusion of virtuosity and musicianship. His willingness to perform new music was notable and many Soviet composers dedicated works to him: Prokofief, Shostakovitz, Mayaskovsky, Khachaturian, Rakov, Vainberg.

In 1934 he was appointed professor at the Moscow Conservatory. He was named People's Artist of the USSR in 1954 and received the Lenin prize in 1960. He was also honoured by the Royal Academy of Music, London, and the Conservatorio di Sta. Cecilia, Rome. Among his pupils stands out Gidon Kremer**.

Another idol of the violin, he mastered to perfection all kinds of music, Ancient, classical, Romantic, Modern. He was terribly bold with his bow and left hand, making his, the Wieniawski's motto "il faut risquer" (one must take risks) although he missed very rarely. This was the main facet of his playing: his boldness, which gave his Strads a different particular tone due to the courage with which he played. His wizardry and musicality were most extraordinary.

His stance was totally still, and his countenance stern and immobile, giving an appearance of coolness and superficiality, at times appearing almost bored with his own play, standing at the opposite extreme end of Perlman and Monasterio, as far as facial expression is concerned. (Perlman shows a thousand and one different facial expressions that communicate to his public his own feelings while playing, and the same happened with Monasterio). But his music was feverishly passionate and musical.

I send the reader to the index for his recordings.

His Strads:

- 1702 Peterlongo; Hawley
- 1705 Marsick
- 1736 Youssopov, Oistrakh; Russian Government

He had also access to all the Strads. of the USSR government, having played in particular:
- 1699 Admiral Kasyerinov
- 1712 Ex Poliakyn
-He played also the Guarneri del Gesu Canon of Paganini of 1742.

He played to perfection well over his sixties.

1916 MENUHIN, YEHUDI, LORD (b. New York - d. Berlin 1999) American conductor, violist and violinist of Russian origin.

His parents, of Russian origin, met for the first time in Palestine, and later they met again in N.Y. where they got married. Jehudi showed very early amazing talents for music, particularly for the violin. The family having moved to San Francisco, little Jehudi was put under the care of Sigmund Anker, a professional violin teacher. After having listened with passion the fiddler Persinger** [1] he became his pupil when he was five. His progress was very fast and at seven he makes his debut with the San Francisco Orch. with the Symphony Espagnole by Lalo, and in New York City in 1926. But his father, who is not ignorant of the risks that waylay any prodigy child, renouncing to his own career embarks with the family to Europe. After a sensational debut in Paris in 1927, young Jehudi was put under the most eminent professors in Europe: Enescu** in Paris, Adolf Busch* in Bâle. While he was serving his apprenticeship, his public appearances were rare, but astounding; when he was twelve he started his tournées. His performance of the Bthvn concerto under Fritz Busch in 1927 in New York made him a celebrity. He then started touring the world with debuts in Berlin 1928 and London 1929. In 1928 he began making his first gramophone records, combining them with further lessons with Enescu and Adolf Bush*. The main characteristics of Menuhin playing before World War II were his technical command of the finger board, his deep understanding of the music he plaid, and a true sentiment expressed through remarkably beautiful, accurate sounds. The most sensational event of this young age period was his performance and later recording of Elgar's Violin concerto conducted by the author in 1932, aged then 75. During World War II Menuhin gave more than 500 concerts for the Allied troops. As soon as the War was over, he was the first to appear in the reopened Paris Opera*, the first foreign artist who went to play in Moscow (with Oistrakh), the first Jewish artist to play in Germany under Furtwängler.

After the War his playing diminished, both in technique and reliability.

In 1959 he settled in London. Menuhin has been one of the most active music promoters of the world, directing several musical festivals like the Bath Festival (1958-59) Windsor Festival (1969-72) and the Gstaadt Festival from 1956. He founded his own chamber orchestra, and conducted many leading orchestras. He also collaborated in the performance of Indian music in Western culture. He has founded also a school of young music students in Stoke d'Abernon, near London.

Menuhin has been involved in many other international fields, making of him one of the most salient figures of the 20th century.

---

[1] Persinger studied with Ysaye and Thibaud, both descendent pupils of Massart.

He has been honoured as Commandeur de la Légion d'honneur*, Knight of the Dutch Order of Orange Nassau, Nehru Award for International Understanding and Honourable Knight Commander of the Order of the British Empire.

A certain amount of works have been dedicated to him, viz. the sonata for solo violin by Bartok, duo for two violins by Milhaud, trio by Alexander Goehr. He is equally a virtuoso of the viola.

Pupil of Enescu** and Persinger** he inherits through them the Massart's vibrato; he played with enormous lyricism, sweetness and elegance.

With a great personal elegance, good looking, speaking fluently several languages, Menuhin became a sort of ambassador of the violin, the most "posh" violinist of the time, the one all snobs of every country should hear, the fiddler "a la mode". Nevertheless, he lacks that sort of passion, of fire, of sensuousness, voluptuousness, of absolute sensual gratification, sheer libidinous lust, that so much thrill me from the violin, and although I recognise all his outstanding merits, he is not "my cup of tea".

I have recorded:

- Viotti vl conc. 22 in A minor "C-5"
- Bthvn sonata Op 30-2 "C-10"

Menuhin's Strads:

-1714 Soil. Very recently sold to Perlman, is one of the most beautiful violins I ever saw, varnished in reddish colour. Just looking at it is a delight. As Charles Reade* put it "The very beau-ideal of the red Cremona violin...the ne plus ultra" (Four Letters on Cremona Violins, 1872, pg. 23,)

-1733 Khevenhueller, owned also by Joseph Böhm.

Menuhin owned also a Guarneri del Gesu of 1742, the *Lord Wilton*, which has been sold in November 1999 for an approximate amount of 4,800,000 dollars (four million, eight hundred thousand), the highest amount ever paid for a violin. It is now called the "ex Jehudi Menuhin".

1918 RICCI, RUGGIERO (b. San Francisco-USA) American violinist of Italian origin.

Critics have called Ruggiero Ricci "the most stupendous gift of the bow in our time" and a reincarnation of Paganini. His career is prodigious. In the following years since the ten-year-old prodigy child mesmerised his first audience, Ricci has played in more places, before more people, and recorded more music for violin than any violinist alive. Born in San Francisco in 1918, the third of seven children in a poor family, Ricci was given a violin and at the age of seven. He began to study with PERSINGER, the distinguished pedagogue, descendent pupil of Massart, who had recently launched the career of Yehudi Menuhin.

His debuts in San Francisco (1928) and Carnegie Hall, New York (1929) with the Mendelssohn concerto, left critics stunned. Further studies with Michel Piastro and Georg Kulenkampff* were followed by a tour of Europe in 1932, when he visited London, Paris, Berlin, Vienna, Rome and Scandinavia with distinct success. He studied next with Paul Stassevitch (1933-7) and with Persinger again, and made the transition from prodigy to mature virtuoso without apparent difficulty.

In the Army Air Force during World War II, "entertainment specialist", Ricci made music under a variety of unusual conditions, often without an accompanist; and necessity rekindled his interest in the solo possibilities of the instrument.

Since the war works for unaccompanied violin, especially Bach and bravura compositions of the virtuosi of the 19th century, have become a Ricci's trademark, yet he has enthusiastically explored almost every nook of the violin repertoire. Besides being the first to record all 24 Caprices of Paganini in their original version, he has premiered concerti by the contemporary composers Ginastera, Von Einem, Goehr, Joseph White, Joaquín Rodrigo, Benjamin Lees, and Gerard Schurmann. His own repertoire is the most varied of any violinist now performing, including a staggering 50 concerti alone. Ricci's discography lists more than 500 recordings and he has performed over 5,000 concerts in 65 countries.

For many years, Ricci exerted an important influence on violin students at the Julliard School of Music in New York City. Past teaching posts include Indiana University, and the University of Michigan, as well as annual master classes in Berlin and Rome. His book "left Hand Violin Technique" was recently published by G. Schirmer. Ricci teaches at the Mozarteum Conservatory in Salzburg, Austria.

Ricci's favourite instruments include: (After such a vast career, a staggering number of superb instruments have passed through his hands)

Amati of 1656
The Strad Tononi of 1683.
Strad "Spanish court"; *Ole Bull* of 1687 (decorated)
Strad "Ernst" of 1709
Strad Joachim of 1714
Strad Madrileño of 1720
Strad Monasterio of 1719
Strad Nestore; Rode of 1727
Strad "Lord Norton" of 1737
Guarneri del Gesu of 1734 Ex Hubermann, Cremona
Guarneri Plowden of 1735
Guarneri Gibson of 1734
Guarneri Lafont of 1735
Guarneri De Beriot of 1744
Carlo Bergonzi Constable of 1731

1919 NEVEU, GINETTE (b. Paris - d. San Miguel, Azores, aeroplane crash, 1949) French violinist.

She had the most opposite extremes: either very powerful, even harsh, or the sweetest tone with a butterfly bow touch, or as Anne Sophie Mutter puts it, in a happier phrase that mine: *She succeeds in uniting the strength of a tiger with very feminine sensitivity.*(it comes on her Web site in the internet. My ten favourite records. J. Brahms, Jean Sibelius.
http://www.anne-sophie-mutter.de/em_biographie.htm)

Her early years were the characteristic of the infant prodigy. A fascination for all things musical, and especially for the violin, was soon manifest, and her mother, who was a teacher of that instrument, presented the young child with a quarter-sized violin and started to give her lessons. Her progress was very fast and in 1924 she played for the first time in public the Schumann Chorale and Fugue*. By 1928 she played in the Salle Gaveau the concerto by Bruch in G minor. Her prizes came also very soon, winning the First Prize of the Ecole Superieur de Musique* and the Prix d'honneur of the City of Paris in 1928.

Her mother, well aware of the dangers that waylay any prodigy child, nurtured her first formative years with extreme zeal, choosing carefully her teachers and rejecting countless offers in order that the extraordinary gift would not be forced or stunted. To begin with she started by Enescu, a grand-son of Massart through Marsick. She then sent the girl to the Paris Conservatoire* in 1930, and after only 8 months she gained the first prize at the age of 11, a feat established by Wieniawski in the same Conservatoire fifty years earlier, and never equalled.

Her next step was to enter the Vienna International Competition in 1931, and although she won no prize, she was heard by Carl Flesch, the other great pedagogue of the 20th century. Flesch was so much impressed by her play that he asked, spontaneously, to be allowed to assume her teachings. Flesch's lessons took place from 1931 to 1935. It was at Flesch insistence (and with his financial help) that Neveu became a late entrant in what remains the most memorable of all international violin competitions, the WIENIAWSKI COMPETITION OF 1935. She had scarcely six weeks to prepare an unaccompanied Bach sonata, several Wieniawski's pieces, including the second vl conc. and, the work of her own choice, Ravel's Tzigane. In all there were 180 competitors, amongst the eldest being the out-and-out favourite, a Soviet competitor eleven years her senior called David Oistrakh. She won hands down the first prize ahead of a second Oistrakh. This skyrocketed her into universal fame. She started touring Germany and Poland in 1935, in 1936 she played in the main cities of the USSR, and in 1937 Canada and the USA. At the end of World War II she resumed her touring career, making her debut in London. She profited her stay there to tour all over Britain in 1946. In 1947 she played in South America, New York City and Boston. 1948 was the year of her tours in Australia and America again, and Europe, where von Karajan was amazed by her play. 1949 was going to be her last year, playing in Edinburgh with Cluytens, and a series of recitals playing the Bthvn concerto with Barbirolli in Britain. Her last appearance was in Paris the 20th October 1949 playing Bach's Chaconne and Ravel's Tzigane.

In her practising she was similar to Paganini, and the opposite of Kreisler. She practised as much as she could, and during the hour and a half interval between recording sessions, when any other soloist would have taken the opportunity to rest and relax, Neveu continued to practise in the artist's room, and in many cases her neck and chin were bleeding after such a lengthy and concentrated spell of playing.

She died in an aeroplane crash in the Azores going to the USA in 1949, at the age of 30. She was travelling in the same plane as Marcel Cerdan* who was going to the USA to recover the world boxing title that La Motta had taken away from him the previous year. Their flight was cancelled in the last minute in Azores due to a technical failure and the next flight was full. As both had extremely important tasks to fulfil in America that could not be postponed they implored, and finally obtained, two seats in that second flight, thanks to the kindness of two sympathetic passengers who, renouncing to their seats, allowed them to continue their journey. Shortly after take off the plane crashed into the ocean killing everybody on board. The two courteous persons escaped death and were born anew that day. Neveu's death was a terrible blow to such a meteoric career, but at least she had the consolation to be interred in the Paris cemetery Père Lachaise very near Chopin. Père Lachaise is, as Victor Hugo puts it, the most "posh" cemetery in the world. As he writes in Les Miserables "*to be interred in Père Lachaise is like having mahogany furniture. Elegance is recognisable there*" (Deuxième partie. Cossette. Livre huitième.- Les cimetières prennent ce qu'ont leur donnet. V.- Il ne suffit pas d'être ivrogne pour être immortel)

I have recorded:

- Brahms: vl conc. "C-13"
- Tartini: Variations on a theme by Corelli "C-17"

She was dedicated the sonata for vl, p. by Poulenc of 1942.

Neveu's Strad of 1730 was found totally damaged, and it is said that she had it clasped in her hands.

1920 STERN, ISAAC (b. Kremenets 1920) American violinist of Russian origin.

He started his piano studies at six, but two years later he changed to violin, at the San Francisco Conservatory. He studied with PERSINGER and with Blinder with whom he plays the double concerto by Bach at the age of 15. He played in 1935 the Brahms concerto with Pierre Monteux, and gives his first recital in N.Y. in 1937. But it is his first appearance at Carnegie Hall in 1943 that establishes the hallmark of his young glory.

After the World War interruption (when he performs for the troops even in the Pacific) he made his debut in Europe in 1948 at the Luzern Festival touring all Europe afterwards. In 1956 he toured the USSR. He also played in South America, Israel, Japan and Australia. In 1960 he founded his own trio with Rose* and Istomin*, playing mainly Bthvn and Brahms programmes in the USA, Paris and London.

He has recorded the complete Brahms piano quartets with Emanuel Ax, Jaime Laredo and Yo Yo Ma which won the Gramophone Award for "Best Chamber Recording of the Year" in 1991

He participates actively in the musical life of the USA as member of the Arts National Counsel, and as president of the Carnegie Hall, the demolition of which he has contributed to prevent.

Another idol of the violin his distinctive style reflects his vibrant passionate personality, total involvement in music and intense communication with his listeners. Perhaps his most distinguishing trait is the boldness of his play, which fears not the most intricate difficulties, resembling in this point to David Oistrakh and Wieniawski, whose motto was "il faut risquer" (one must take risks). His feeling of style is impeccable, finding always the right inflection to bring music alive. "To use the violin to make music, never to use music just to play the violin" is his principle.

"A sensu contrario" Stern is betraying here many of his colleagues who play anything, whatsoever, just to play the violin. This is a very characteristic feature of many a violinist: they play just to coax from their instrument beautiful and rightly tuned sounds, no matter what kind of music they play. (a good example is David Oistrakh) The goal is to produce beautiful sounds, (here lies the challenge) music is not that important.

He has been dedicated the concerto for vl, orch by Penderecki.

Stern's favourite instruments are:

-The "Vicomte de Panette", "Stern" , by Guarneri del Gesu of 1737
-The Ysaye by Guarneri del Gesu of 1740
-The Strad Kruse owned also by Kreutzer of 1721

I have recorded:

- Mozart: conc. 3 "C-12"
-Saint-Saëns: Introduction et rondo capriccioso Op 28 "C-15"

1921 GRUMIAUX, ARTHUR (BARON) (b. Villers-Pervin, nr Charleroi; d. Brussels 1986) Belgian violinist.

He showed special gifts for music from an early age, being encouraged by his maternal grandfather, a village band master, who sent him to study at the Charleroi Conservatoire. His progress was so fast that in 1933 he could go to Alfred Dubois, professor at the Brussels Conservatory, who had been pupil of Ysaye, for high degree teachings. In 1939 he won the Vieuxtemps and François Prume prizes; the next year he became the first winner of the prix de virtuosité, newly instituted by the Belgian government. His training was completed with a period of study with ENESCU in Paris.

No sooner had he made his debut with Münch playing Mendelssohn concerto when the invasion of Belgium put a stop to his career. During the War he made no public performances, but played with a private quartet, the Pro Arte Quartet. At the end of the War he started again his public career, making his British debut in 1945 with the BBC SO. His fame grew rapidly and he toured the main cities of Europe and the USA in triumph. When his old teacher died in 1949 he was offered his post as professor in the Brussels Conservatory.

He is perhaps a little too worried with intonation, which damages his interpretations that appear too cold, lacking emotion. In one of his photographs, one can see him staring anxiously at the fingerboard, with great concentration, so as to stop* the strings in the exact place. This attitude hinders the spontaneity of the fluent phrasing a musical performance requires, which should be led by the ear, never by the eye.

<Professor Galamian describes it very well: "The building of good intonation rests mainly on the sense of touch in combination with the guidance of the ear. The fingers are like blind people who guide themselves through a sightless existence by touching objects which mark their paths from place to place. The analogy is pertinent to the training of the fingers on the violin. The hand learns gradually to orient itself, to find its proper location by the feel of the neck (and the body of the instrument in upper positions*) From the hand position* thus secured, the fingers in their turn learn to acquire, through the sense of touch, the feeling for correct placement and for proper stretch. In this they are continually helped, guided, and controlled by the ear" Principles of Violin Playing and Teaching. Second edition, 1985, 1962. Prentice-Hall Inc. A Simon & Schuster Company. Englewood, New Yersey 07632. Printed in the United states of America. Chapter two: The left hand. Intonation. Page 19. ISBN 0-13-710773-0>

Indeed this is the proper way to play music, and if the player is too worried about his fingering positions, it only damages the interpretation, which is, perhaps, more precise, technically speaking, but to the disadvantage of musicality. So, for example, Liszt never looked at the keyboard, all his paintings show him playing gazing in the distance, either towards the ceiling or the public. This explains the enormous liking he had to play in darkness, which in the concert hall made an enormous impression on the public. Remember, also, the evening he spent with Berlioz in

Legouvé's* house (see it under Paganini) where he played the adagio* of the Bthvn's sonata in C sharp* minor (Moonshine) submerged in an absolute darkness, which was about to kill Berlioz from emotional suffocation. In this sense we may derive that technique, just by itself, is contrary to musicianship, and it is only a means to the goal of playing a piece musically. This, I understand it well, is very difficult to digest, for after studying pure technique during the long years of hard work a musical career demands, and having become a pure machine of "mechanical" drills, the virtuoso must react against himself, and making a Copernican turn of 180 degrees, he has to become again a human being, abandoning all his mechanism, to reappear spiritual, passionate, tender, or whatever, but in short, a "human" performer, anything except mechanical, with certainly some failures, but his playing stemming directly from his soul.

This departure from the drilling mechanical technique applies also to the score, which must not be played to the letter. (those who play the score to the letter are the pianola and the modern computer) In this respect, let me remember you what Liszt said:

"The virtuoso is not a bricklayer who, hammer in hand, painfully and consciously cuts the stone according to the design of an architect... he creates just as the composer created".

He was made Baron in 1973.

For concerts he used mainly a Guarneri del Gesu of 1714, the "Ex-Hemmel"

His Strads:
- The 1704 Remenyi*
- The 1715 Titian
- The 1727 Ex General Dupont
I have recorded the Mendelssohn's vl conc. played by him in "C-08"

He is considered the head of the Belgian school.

1923 HASSID, JOSEPH (b. Suwalki Poland - d. London 1950) Polish violinist.

Very little is known of this superb violinist, whom I discovered by sheer chance on a programme of the BBC in which they said that the appearance of a violinist of such calibre occurs only every 50 years.

256

His tragic career, extremely short, as if a jealous God would like to wipe him out of the world, left mankind little room to appreciate it. It was like a divine meteor brightly shining through the sky for the very brief seconds of its fall to earth.

Joseph Chasyd, known professionally as Joseph Hassid, (a change of name made already by numerous artists like Gayarre*, Sarasate, Arrieta*) was born on 28 December 1923 in the Polish border town of Suwalki. (same town as Dushkin) Like the immense majority of musical genius, he showed his gifts for the violin from an early age. His father, aware of this aptitudes, nurtured him with as much musical knowledge as he could. In 1933 he was sent to the Chopin School of Music in Warsaw, and after only one year of studies he became one of the youngest competitors of the very first International Wieniawski Competition of 1935, which has been up to the present day the most prestigious for the quality of its competitors, viz.: Oistrakh, Neveu, and Hassid. As we already know it was won by Neveu ahead a second prize Oistrakh. Hassid performance was besmirched by a lapse of memory that did not mislead the members of the jury as for the immense quality of this superbly gifted child.

Hassid went on to study with CARL FLESCH who, it appears, had so little to do in the way of teaching the boy's technical skills that he focused upon Hassid's musical and interpretative development. Flesch intense teachings went on from 1927 to 1930. He then proudly invited the greatest musicians and violinists to hear his prodigy child, not least Kreisler, Szigeti, Thibaud.

Hassid made his debut in London during the Spring of 1940, playing both at Queens Hall and Wigmore Hall. After a few concerts in which Hassid had another lapse of memory, he started recording. He made only eight 78 rpm of them, that constitute the irrefutable proof that he was one of the most phenomenal talents in violin playing. But by the end of that year Hassid became seriously ill, with further bouts of memory and reacting aggressively against his violin and his own father. An acute schizophrenia was diagnosed, and he had to be hospitalised remaining there for the rest of his days. After his father's death in 1949 the doctors who looked after him made the drastic decision to take an attempt to cure him via brain surgery, but it did not succeed, and he died a few days later on November 7th 1950. He was not yet 27 years old. All we have from Hassid are the 8 recordings when he was sixteen in 1940. But they are more than enough to appreciate in them a prodigious musicality. His style is secure and clear, sweet and pure, virile and beguiling. In a word, he was one of the most formidable violinists in history.

I have recorded the complete works by him. I send the reader to the index.

  1929 SUK, JOSEF (b. Prague) Czech violinist, grand son of Josef Suk, the famous composer and violinist, and great-grand son of Dvorak.

He began his studies very soon with Kocian*, whose pupil he remained until Kocian's death in 1951. He also studied at the Prague Conservatory and later with Plocek and Hlounova at the Prague Academy (1951-53). His public debut was in 1940 and he took part in exchange concerts in Brussels and Paris during the period of 1948-49. But it would take some more years for him to earn his reputation as soloist, when he appeared in 1959 with the Czech PO on a tour of three continents. He made his British debut at the Promenade Concerts in 1964 playing Dvorak and Mozart, and that same year he appeared for the firth time in the USA with the Cleveland orch.

Suk showed a great interest for chamber music founding a duo with Zuzana Ruzickova* in 1963 and a trio with Starker* and Julius Katchen* from 1967 till Katchen's death in 1969. He is also founder of his own Suk Chamber Orch. since 1974.

He has been honoured with the Grand Prix du Disque several years, State Prize in 1964; in 1970 he was named Artist of Merit. He has won the Edison Prize in 1972, the Wiener Floteuhr in 1974, and the National Prize in 1977.
He is praised for his tone of silk, great perception of style, deep feelings and true expression of the author's message.

Suk's Strads:

-1683 Suk; owned also by Dvorak
-1710 Suk; Duke de Camposelice; Vieuxtemps
-1729 Suk; Libon; Stuart, owned also by Viotti
-He plays also a Guarneri del Gesu "Prince of Orange" of 1744
- and a Giovanni Guadagnini* ex Vieuxtemps of 1758

From Suk I have recorded:

- Haydn vl con Hob VII-4 in "C-12"

  1941 ACCARDO, SALVATORE (b. Turin, Italy) Italian conductor and violinist.

Son of Vicenzo, a passionate violin amateur, he began his studies at the age of six. When he was eight he put under the tuition of Luigi D'Ambrosio at Naples Conservatory, obtaining his diploma in 1956; then he studied with Ivonne Astruc at the Accademia Chigiana, Siena, where he got a postgraduate diploma. In 1945 Accardo aged 13 gave his first recital with Paganini's capriccios.

He won the International Competition at Vercelli (1955) and Geneva (1956) and in 1958 both the Italian Trofeo Primavera della RAI-TV and the Paganini International Violin Prize at Genoa.

Accardo has toured in triumph the main cities of Europe and North and South America. His repertoire is very wide going from Bach and the baroque music to the most contemporary one, passing through the romantics and classics. He is particularly fine in the music by Paganini, of whom he has recorded the 24 caprices and the six concertos. With a formidable technique and a very sensuous vibrato he communicates to his audience his passion and good taste for music.

He has developed also a great interest for chamber music, founding the Orchestra da Camera Italiana of Turin in 1968 and organising every year the Ensemble Music Week at Naples. From 1968 to 1971 he was first violin* of the ensemble I Musici. In 1992 he founded the Accardo Quartet.

He teaches at the Accademia Chigiana, Siena and has created a school for string instruments at Cremona: the Academia Walter Stauffer. As pedagogue he has published :L'Arte del Violino, Milano 1987.

He has been dedicated several works: *Dikhtas* by Iannis Xenakis, *Fantasia for violin and orch.* by Walter Piston and *Argot for solo violin* by Franco Donatoni.

Accardo has been awarded with the highest decoration in Italy: Gran Croce di Cavaliere dal Presidente della Republica Pertini in 1982.

Accardo's Strads:

- 1717 Ex Reiffenberg
- 1718 Fierbird, Ex Saint Exupéry
- 1719 Zahn
- 1727 Francescatti; Hart
- 1727 Reynier

He has had the honour of playing Paganini's Guarneri del Gesu "Canon" of 1742.

He has also a Montagnana of 1742

I have recorded:

- Paganini: vl conc. 2 "la campanella "C-18"
- Paganini: vl conc. 6: Adagio* and rondo "C-06"

1945 PERLMAN, ITZHAK (b. Tel Aviv, Israel)

Another idol of the violin. The son of a barber, he was victim of poliomyelitis at the age of four, which deprived him of the use of his legs. (a misfortune that might have been providential for his devoting to violin playing). [1] He began violin lessons shortly afterwards at the Shulamit High School in Tel Aviv with Rivka Goldgart, and by the age of ten he had given numerous public recitals and broadcast concerts with the Israeli Broadcast Orch. In 1958 he participated in a competition to appear on the American TV, the Ed Sullivan Show, claiming the first prize; this allowed him to obtain several scholarships to study in the USA with professor GALAMIAN at the Julliard School. He made his professional debut in Carnegie Hall in 1963, and the following year he won the Leventritt Memorial Competition, which brought him immediate engagements with the major American orchestras including the New York P.O.

In 1965 he made a sensational return to Israel, and in 1968 he made his debut in Britain with the London SO at the Festival Hall.

He has developed a great interest in chamber music, and it was he who organised the chamber concerts in the London South Bank Summer Music series of the season 1968-69. (In a video tape entitled Remembering Jaqueline du Pré you can see him playing a quartet with the following cast: du Pré, violin; Perlman, cello; Zukerman, viola; Baremboim, piano)

In 1970 he initiated his own master class at Meadowbrooks Festival USA.

---

[1] It is my deep feeling that, were it not for this tragic illness, apparently so cruel and devastating, Mr. Perlman would have been today a vulgar basketball player in the Israel team, instead of being the best violinist alive.

As a general rule, you need not see the performer, to listen to music; quite on the contrary, many people prefer to close their eyes to concentrate better in sound. This would be a fatal error with Perlman. If you don't see him play, you loose half of it.

His tone is superb, most powerful and extremely beautiful. He is most sensuous and daring, making his the Wieniawski's motto "il faut risquer" (one must take risks), though he misses very rarely. But this is only half of his art. The other half is the passion, the joy, the sensuality, the happiness, the enormous pleasure he feels playing his beloved violin; all these and many other sensations being transmitted to the audience through his thousand and one different facial expressions. In this manner his own, personal enjoyment is visually transmitted to the public, and this is extremely important, for there is no musician in the world who enjoys better his own music than Perlman. In addition, he is in love with his violin, with whom he ardently dances cheek to cheek, caressing it in innumerable different ways with his chin and cheek, all those faces of delight being a source of constant musical delight for the listener. We have seen the same attitude in Monasterio when we spoke of him.

I earnestly advise the reader to go to the concert to hear him carrying opera-binoculars, to be able to see him at close range (they are indispensable for the full enjoyment of his performance) Or else buy one of his many video films. If you don't see him play you will only have half of his art.

He is the living example of Nietzsche's article at the beginning of this work.

In 1982 he was named Honorary Music Director of the University of South Carolina, and in 1986 he was honoured with the Medal of Liberty by President Reagan, in appreciation of his outstanding contribution to American life and achievements.

As the Larousse de la Music rightly says, Perlman *has the ability to transform the most insignificant piece of music into a masterpiece, thanks to a phrasing of great pureness and a radiant sound.*

Mr. Perlman is, everybody knows, "the" best violinist alive.

I send the reader to the index to see his recordings.

Perlman's favourites instruments are:

-He started with a Carlo Bergonzi.
-Later he played on the Strad. General Kyd, Sinsheimer, of 1714 with wich you can see him play the Bthvn conc. in a video with Carlo Maria Giulini. He sold it in 1980.
-A Guarneri del Gesu "Ex Sauret*" of 1740 of an unbelievably beautiful orange colour. And
-The 1714 Strad Soil, recently bought from Menuhin.

He bought the "ex Sauret*" and the "Soil" on the same year of 1986!!

1945 KANTOROW, JEAN JACQUES (b. Cannes, France) French violinist.

He made his first studies of the violin at the Conservatoire of Nice, to change later to the Paris Conservatoire*, where he won first prizes in violin (1960) and chamber music (1963).

He won a gold medal in the London Carl Flesch Contest in 1962, prize Queen Elisabeth of Belgium, prize Sibelius in Helsinki, Paganini prize at the International Contest of Genoa, prize of Montreal, and prize of Geneva in 1965.

He then started a career of international performer, and devoted as well to teaching at Strasbourg and Holland.

With a wide ranging repertoire spanning from Bach to our contemporary music his tone is elegant and at the same time poised and brilliant. He was leader of the Chamber Dutch Orch, until its dissolution, when he accepted the direction of the Regional Orch. of Auvernia at Clermont-Ferrand, France.

Nothing special to say of this superb violinist.

I have recorded:

- Chausson: poème "C-12"

1947 KREMER, GIDON (b. Riga, Latvia). [The capital of Latvia, belonged to the Soviet union until it regained its independence in 1991].

Kremer showed gifts for music, in particular for the violin, from a very early age. He was sent to study the violin at the Moscow Conservatory under David Oistrakh. In 1963 he won the First Prize of the Latvian Republic and in 1970 he was winner of the Tchaikovski International Competition, Moscow 1970.

Kremer has toured all the main cities of the world, and his abundant recordings bear testimony of his excellent quality as a performer.

I have recorded:

- Leopold Mozart: Vl duos "C-02"
-Schumann: vl conc. "C-14"
-Ernst variations on *O mamma, mamma cara*, "C-19" based on a set of variations by Paganini that were the delight of Berlioz, (see 1814 Ernst)
-Vieuxtemp's Fantasia Appassionata, Op 35 for violin and orchestra superbly played. (on Ernst variations on *O mamma cara* Kremer is beyond his depth, committing various lapses of all kinds. Ernst was too much a violinist to be emulated)

His favourite instruments:

A Guadagnini*
Guarneri del Gesu Ex F. David 1730
Strad. ex Baron von Feilitzsch, Hermann of 1734

1948 CHUNG, KYUNG-WHA (b. Seoul, South Korea)

She is one of the two goddesses of the 20th century. After having showed extraordinary gifts for the violin at an early age she was encouraged by her parents to study it, and her progress was so fast that by the age of nine she gave a sensational recital in Seoul playing Mendelssohn violin concerto. She was then sent to the USA to study with the miraculous teacher Galamian at the Julliard School in New York City from 1960 to 1967 under whose guide she built up her fabulous technique. It was in the year 1976 that she won together with Pinchas Zukerman the Leventritt Award. This feat gave her international fame, making her sensational debut in New York City in 1968. Her first European appearance was with the London SO under Previn at the Festival Hall of 1970.

Her many recordings witness her splendid capacity to coax from her violin the most sweet and musical tones. Her phrasing and accurate understanding of the music she plays is also astonishing. Her recording of

Bthvn's concerto with the Concertgebouw under Klaus Tennstedt stands among the 4 best of the 20th century (with Francescatti, David Oistrakh and Perlman). To make justice to this recording we must say that Klaus Tennstedt conducts it superbly, as well. (In the front cover we see Kyung–Wha Chung proudly showing off her Stradivarius, once owned by Corelli, the Harrisson of 1693).

An excellent fiddler, with only one little flaw: she swings too much her body. A fiddler must remain as straight as a ramrod and although what counts is tone and music, good manners are important, as well. I do not share the famous Praetorius' "boutade" (Syntagma Musicum ii, 1618) when talking about fingering he says: "...many think it is a matter of great importance, and despise such organists that do not use this or that particular fingering, but this, in my opinion, is not worth talking about: let the player run up and down the keyboard with his first, middle or third finger or even with his nose, if that will help him, provided that everything is done clearly, correctly and gracefully"

No Sir, there are forms one should submit to. A graceful posture is fundamental for fiddlers, and pianists, as well. Moving while playing is somewhat vulgar, proper only of the oriental serpent tamers, or also of the wind players of a symphony orchestra. But the stance of a solo violin player must be almost immobile.

But she is not to be blamed. The culprit is her teacher Galamian, who says: "Posture. How to stand or to sit should not be the object of exact prescriptions other than that the player should feel at ease".(Principles. Chapter two. Body and instrument. Pag. 12) But immediately afterwards he says: "WHAT SHOULD BE AVOIDED ARE EXAGERATTED BODILY MOTIONS WHILE PLAYING. THEY ARE NOT ONLY UNPLEASANT TO SEE, BUT..."

(An astonished anonymous press writer who was present at a recording session of Jascha Heifetz on October 27, 1917 said he saw "a young man of dignified aristocratic gentlemanly bearing, without a mannerism or swaying of the body like a chained elephant...")

Be it as it were, being Chung one of the THREE best violinists alive (with Perlman and Mutter, they form the "HOLY TRINITY" of the violin heaven), it is unquestionable that we can indulge in the luxury of "spoiling" her and ignore this minute, venial little sin.

She owns the Strad Harrison of 1693, owned at the very beginning of this history by Corelli [and later by Giardini**]. The British say: "life goes round in circles"; the violin circle has just closed with her, ending what I describe as the super-motorway of the violin, straight from Corelli to her, without brake, link by link, from teacher to pupil, as follows: Corelli - Somis -Pugnani - Viotti - Kreutzer - Lambert Massart - Martin Marsick - Flesch (who teaches Neveu, Szeryng* and Hassid) - Enescu who teaches (Neveu, Menuhin, Ferras*, and Grumiaux) - and them to the gramophone - and finally Kyung-Wha Chung, who plays on the same Strad as Corelli. The circle is closed!. Corelli's super-highway has been completed to our day.

A last minute change: Ms. Chung has divested herself of the Strad Harrison which is now at the:

America's Shrine to Music Museum
The University of South Dakota
414 East Clark Street
Vermillion, SD 57069, USA
E-mail: smm@usd.edu

She plays currently a Guarneri del Gesu of 1735.

She has been awarded the highest honour of the Government of South Korea: the medal of Civil Merit.

I have recorded:
- Elgar: Salut d'amour "C-13"
- Bruch: Scottish fantasy "C-14"

1948 ZUKERMAN, PINCHAS (b. Tel Aviv. Israel) Israeli violist, conductor, pedagogue, chamber musician and violinist of Polish descent.

His father, a violinist as well, encouraged his childhood instinct for music, and sent him to the Tel Aviv Academy of Music on 1956, where he studied with Ilona Feher, a pupil of Hubay. A decisive milestone in his career was the opportunity he had to be heard by Casals* and Isaac Stern** in 1961, who amazed by his gifts, recommended him and obtained some scholarships, the America-Israel and Helena Rubinstein Foundations, that allowed him to enter the Julliard School N.Y., acting Stern as his legal guardian. There Zukerman studied with Galamian and extended his interest to the viola.

His first successful public appearance was at the Spoleto Festival in Italy in 1966. Encouraged by this triumph he entered in 1967 at the Leventritt Memorial Competition, in which he obtained the first prize together with Kyung Wha Chung. This was the beginning of his international career touring extensively North America, to which he added the many times he had to deputise Stern whose health was weakening. He made his debut in the USA at the Lincoln Centre in New York City in 1969. He went then to Europe where he made his debut in Britain at the 1969 Brighton Festival. His first gramophone record was in 1968. He is much involved also in chamber music where he plays indistinctly the viola or the violin, and has been Artistic Director of the South Bank Summer Music from 1978 to 1980, and music director of the St. Paul Chamber Orch. from 1980 to 1986. He holds an honorary doctorate from Brown University and an Achievement Award from the International Centre in New York. He has been presented with the King Solomon award by the America-Israel Cultural Foundation and the Medal of Arts by President Reagan in 1983.

He plays on a Guarneri del Gesu.

I send the reader to the index for his recordings.

1960 LIN, CHO LIANG (b. Taiwan, China) Chinese-American violinist.

His remarkable talents for music were soon discovered by his parents who gave him a violin education from the age of five. From 1972 to 1975 he studied at the Sidney Conservatory. In view of his excellent progress he was sent to New York City where he entered the Julliard School to study with Dorothy De Lay from 1975 to 1978. His first public appearances were in the USA with the Philadelphia Orch. and in London with the London Symphony Orch. in 1976. He tours all over the world in concert and his recordings are excellent.

As chamber musician he maintains his association with the Chamber Music Society of Lincoln Centre in New York, and has founded the Taipei Chamber Music in 1997.

I have recorded:

- Sarasate: Intruducción y tarantella Op 3 "C-13"
- Haydn: Vl conc. 1 in C major Hob VIIa "C-15"

-Currently he plays on a Guarneri of 1734 "The Duke of Camposelice"

1963 MUTTER, ANNE-SOPHIE (b. Rheinfeldin, Germany)

Mutter's exceptional talent for the violin was shown very early. In 1968 the five-years-old Mutter was sent to study with a pupil of Carl Flesch: Erna Honigberger, a half Jewish teacher who had fled the nazi Berlin to take refuge in the "Schwarzwald" (the Black Forest) in the 1940s. So Mutter is a direct descendant of Massart, his great-great-grand-daughter, to be more precise. As Mutter recalls, Erna had a wonderful way of teaching small children, interrupting their work with some games from time to time. After one year of tuition Mutter won the highest prize at the Jugend Musiziert (Germany's national competition for young musicians) Her lessons with Honigberger lasted until 1973 when she died. After having been heard by Henryk Szeryng* he recommended her to another pupil of Flesch: Aide Stucki with whom she studied in Switzerland until 1977. In 1976 she was a competitor at the Lucerne Festival in 1976. Karajan, who was present, was greatly impressed by her play, and proclaimed the 14-year-old Mutter "the greatest musical prodigy since the young Menuhin". She embarked on her career as soloist in 1977 at the Salzburg Whitsun Concerts under Karajan direction. As a protégée of the omnipotent Karajan, Mutter was skyrocketed into fame, recording and concertizing with her mentor and other leading conductors and orchestras. She has toured all the main cities of the world, and her many recordings show her immense talent, formidable technique and prodigious musicality.

The moment Mutter puts bow to string she beguiles the ear with her captivating and uniquely individual sound. Her tone is sensual, vibrant and indescribably pure and sweet. It is as if her great beauty would be transmitted to her Strad Lord Dun Raven, plunging her audience into a sublime atmosphere. She is the seventh and youngest divinity of the 20th century.

Although she is widely considered as a hero, she still lacks her definitive consecration, the "accolade" to the Parnassum, what the ALTERNATIVA is for *bull-fighters,* i.e. a ceremony through which they are promoted from apprentice matador, to full-matador with all its rights and duties, too. What is this "alternativa" for the violin?

Ever since the12-year-old prodigy Joachim played in London with a staggering success the Bthvn concerto, under the baton of Mendelssohn in 1843, the concerto in D has become the touch stone for every violinist. It is not extremely demanding in technique, nor a concerto for virtuoso show off, but it requires the maximum amount of musicality. More than one super-stars of the violin have totally crashed against this hurdle. It is true that she has recorded one with Karajan, but it is not very satisfying, or is it?.

It is essential that she records another that could be measured up to her, one which she will proudly show to posterity as the masterpiece she deserves, one that would astound, as we are all sure it will, her listeners *"from here to eternity"*. (on her web page of 16 Dec 2000, it is announced that she is going to play it in September 2001 in London under Maestro Masur, and again in New York City, at Carnegie Hall, shortly afterwards). The expectations are running high at the top of excitement. Will she measure up with herself? All her devoted admirers, in the ranks of whom I brag to be, believe she will. Her golden opportunity is there. (I will certainly be there to witness that crucial event. Revenge, sweet revenge, how these thoughts must have been haunting her mind since that disgraceful version with Karajan in 1980, at her 16 years of age!)

I send the reader to the index for her recordings.

Honours and awards:

For her numerous recording she has been awarded the Record Academie Prize, the Deutscher Shallplattenpreis, the Grand Prix du Disque, the Ediso Award, and the Internationaler Shallplattenpreis. Her recording of Penderecki's 2nd violin concerto, under the composer, dedicated to her won the Grammy Best Instrumental Soloist Performance with Orchestra. On February 2000 she obtained the Grammy Award for Chamber Music Performance, with her complete Bthvn violin sonatas.

She has been dedicated works by:
Penderecki: Sonata for vl p 2.
Penderecki: "Metamorphosen" 1992-5. Concerto for vl and orch.
Moret: "en Rève" vl concerto with chamber orch. 1988
Lutoslawski: Partita* for vl and orch.
Rihm: "time Chant" Music for vl and orch.
Rihm: "Panthom und Eskapade". Fantasy for vl and orch.
Courrier: "Aftersong"

She has been honoured with the Bavarian Order of Merit, the Medal of Merit of the Land of Baden-Württemberg, The German Order of Merit (first class) and the Austrian Cross of Honour for Science and Art.

In 1987 she founded the Rudolf-Eberle-Stifung, which encourages young players in Europe.

Her Strads are:

-The Lord Dun Raven of 1710
-The Emiliani of 1703

1974 VENGEROV, MAXIM (Novosibirsk, capital of Western Siberia.) Russian violinist. Juggler.

This book will be ended, God willing, around the Summer of 2001. But in the mean time I had the opportunity of seeing and hearing Vengerov.

At his 26 years of age he has gone all the way down the road of virtuosism, in the sense of jugglery. His exceptional command of the fingerboard and of the bow, and the speed with which he can play are absolutely astonishing, and there is nothing else he can learn in this avenue. In addition, his attitude on the stage provokes the blind admiration of all his fans, not necessarily music connoisseurs, but who are absolutely overpowered by his gestures and histrionic movements, taking them for genuine deep musical feelings. He gesticulates more than a chimpanzee, and swings his body in all imaginable, exaggerated, directions, like a chained elephant. (What a difference with his compatriot David Oistrakh, who remained as straight as a ramrod!).

But this is precisely the secret of his glory. All this ridiculous paraphernalia dazzles his young fans, who, lacking any musical background, take him as the *non plus ultra* of the violin. In this respect we are witnessing a kind of "renaissance" of the hippie movement of the 1960s, and an increasing number of youngsters, perhaps a little fed up with "hard rock", are emerging with force, and crowd his concert halls, all with abundant crops of untidy hair, very much in the style of the hippies of the good old times. His fame grows by the day, and his earnings too.

This is not a reason to ignore his true merits: in 1984 he won the Wieniawski Violin Prize for Young Students in Poland and in 1990 he got first prize at the Carl Flesch International Competition. He has been awarded with numerous record prizes.

The big question mark, now, is: will he complement his dazzling virtuosity with the necessary musicality to become a true virtuoso in the sense we have given to this word all along this book, i.e. Juggler + musical = virtuoso? I personally think he will not. It would run against his own interests. The style he has adopted so far provides him with 1) world-wide fame. 2) enthusiastic storms of applause from his unconditional fans, and 3) money, the three main *golden calves** of the 21st century...

> *Who can ask for anything more? ...*
> *who can ask for anything more?*

(*I Got Rhythm*, Gershwin, from the film *An American in Paris*)

He plays on the Strad Ex Kiesewetter of 1723, lent to him by Clement Arrison through the Stradivari Society of Chicago.

Confronted with his exceptional virtuosity, all I can do is to cite Charles Reade*: *It* (the violin) *can be prostituted to the performance of difficulties, and often is; but that is not its fault.*

Or I can also, reversing the order, write in the end the epitaph which Berlioz puts in the introduction of his Memoires:

Life's but a walking shadow, a poor player,
That struts and frets his hour upon the stage,
And then is heard no more; it is a tale
Told by an idiot, full of sound and fury,
Signifying nothing.   (Shakespeare. Macbeth, act V, scene V)

GRAPH THE MODERN SCHOOL

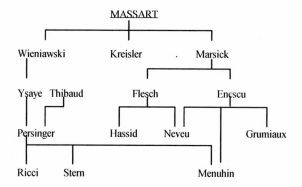

Auer (Romantic, but his pupils use the vibrato against his prohibition)

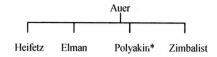

ACKNOWLEDGEMENTS

The drafting of this book would have been simply impossible without the consultation of the following books, encyclopaedias, dictionaries, journals and periodical publications. It has been also vital the invaluable help of the following institutions, and eminent personalities that have kindly helped me in the search of all the information I needed to complete this work, and without their assistance this book would not have achieved its final form.

Charles Burney*, in the conclusion of his monumental *General History of Music*, complains bitterly of his long lasting efforts to complete his work, in the following terms: "*I have at length arrived at the end of a work that has been thirty years in meditation, and more than twenty in writing and printing.*" (Vole II. Book IV. Pag 1024) I, on the contrary, have spent eleven years since I embarked on the present work, that have been the most exciting and interesting in my life; my travels have taken me to Pamplona, Paris, London, and Belgium in pursuit of authentic material connected with the violinists studied herein, and in particular with Lambert Massart, Sarasate and Leopold Auer.

I owe a specific debt of gratitude to the Belgian musicologist Jose Quintin, to the Trésorier de la Société Liégeoise de Musicologie, M. Philippe Gilson, to all the staff of the Bibliothèque National de France, in particular M. Gilles Devincre, de la Direction de l'imprimé et de l'audiovisuel, Departement de la phonothèque; also Mmes. Fougerais, Chantale & Vivianne Billard of the Centre de Documentation et des Archives of the Paris Conservatoire*.

Last but first, I am grateful beyond measure to three persons who helped me with particular care in the search for documentation of the Belgian and, in particular, the Liège School of Violin during my stay in Belgium: JOSEPH PHILIPPE, on the one side, and on the other THE POSSESSORS OF THE MORE THAN ONE THOUSAND MANUSCRIPT LETTERS ADDRESSED TO MASSART, whose anonymity I will preserve for ever, a charming and delightful married couple who allowed me to enter into their own house to peruse for many a day all those letters that they and their ancestors have kept and filed with meticulous care and devotion, granting me a princely hospitality, or rather, making me feel at home as if I were another member of the family. I wish to extend my warmest personal regards to their whole family.

F I N I S.

SOURCES CONSULTED

-Altadill: Memorias de Sarasate. Pamplona 1909.

-Archives Comunales de Liège.

-Archives Générales de la ville de Liège.

-Arteche, Miguel: Carlos Gardel*. Tango que me Hiciste Bien. Editorial Andrés Bello. Santiago de Chile. 1985.

-Association du Bureau des Etudiants du Conservatoire National Superieur de Musique et de Danse de Paris. Le Conservatoire de Paris*: regards sur une institution et son histoire. Paris 1995.

-Auer, Leopold: My Long Life in Music. New York 1923.

-Auer, Leopold: Violin Playing as I Teach It. New York 1921.

-Ayuntamiento de Pamplona: Sarasate en el Recuerdo. Pamplona 1994.

-Baillot: L'Art du violon. Nouvelle méthode. Paris 1834.

-Baker & Slonimsky: Dictionnaire biografique des musiciens. Paris, Laffont, 1995.

-Beriot: Méthode du violon 1858.

-Berlioz : Beethoven. Espasa Calpe. Colección Austral. N 992.

-Berlioz: Correspondance Generale. Flammarion, Paris, 1972.

-Berlioz: Journales des Debats.

-Berlioz: Mémoires. Flammarion, Paris 1991.

-Biblioteca Nacional de España, Madrid, Spain.

-Bibliothèque Nationale de France, Paris.

-Bollioud de Mermet*, Louis: De la corruption du goust dans la musique françoise. Lyons, 1746.

-Boyden*, David : History of Violin Playing from its Origins to 1761. Oxford University. 1965.

-British Library. London.

-Burney*, Charles: A General History of Music. London 1776.

-Burney*, Charles: The Present State of Music in France and Italy: or, the journal of a tour through those Countries, undertaken to collect materials for a general history of music. London 1771.

-Burney*, Charles: The Present State of Music in Germany, The Netherlands and United Provinces, or The Journal of a tour through those Countries undertaken to collect materials for a general history of music. London 1773.

-Cardus, Conrado: Estructura y Sonoridad de los Instrumentos de Arco. Real Musical. Madrid 1996.

-Centre d'accueil et des recherche des Archives nationales (CARAN) Paris.

-Conservatoire national supérieur de musique et de danse de Paris.

-Conservatoire Royal de Music de Liège.

274

-Conservatorio Profesional de Música, Madrid, Spain.

-Conservatorio Superior de Música "Pablo Sarasate" Pamplona, Spain.

-Dictionnaire Biographique des Musiciens. J. Baker & N. Slonimsky. Paris. Laffont, 1995.

-Donington, Robert: La música y sus instrumentos. Alianza Editorial, Madrid, 1986.

-Ehrlich: Berühmte Geiger der Vergangeheit u. Gegenwart. Lpiz. 1893.

-Einstein, Alfred: A Short History of Music. Third American Edition. 1986 Dorset Press, New York, ISBN 0-88029-097-8.

-Espasa Calpe: Berlioz: Beethoven. Colección Austral. Madrid 1979.

-Exposition "Deux siècles d'Enseignement du violon au Conservatoire" Paris Avril 1997.

-Fayolle*, François: Notice sur Corelli, Tartini, Gaviniès, Pugnani et Viotti (Paris 1810).

-Fetis*: Biographie universelle des musiciens. Paris 1870.

-Fetis*: Supplément à la Biographie universelle des musiciens. Paris 1878.

-Flesch: Die Kunst des Violin-Spiels. Berlin 1923.

-Galamian, Ivan: Principles of Violin Playing & Teaching. New Jersey. USA 1962.

-García* Jr, Manuel: Traité complet de l'art de chant. Paris 1878.

-Goodkind, Herbert K. Violin Iconography of Antonio Stradivarius. Larchmont, New York, 1972. Library of Congress catalogue card n. 73-169961.

-Green, A. H. Elisabeth: Miraculous Teacher, Ivan Galamian and the Meadowmount Experience.

-Gregoire: les artistes musiciens belges. Brussels 1887.

-Guhr, Karl: L'art de Jouer du Violon de Paganini. Departement de la Musique de la Bibliothèque Nationale de France Cote UM8 c 63.

-Hallé*, Sir Charles: The Life and Letters of Sir Charles Hallé: being an autobiography. C. E. and Marie Hallé. London 1896.

-Hawkins*, Sir John: A General History of the Science and Practice of Music, London 1776.

-Hondré, Emmanuel. Listes des professeurs du Conservatoire (Paris) des origines à nos jours.

-Huarte Mayers, Alberto: Nuestro Amigo y Paisano Pablo Sarasate. 1996, Pamplona, Spain.

-Huarte Myers, Alberto: Nuestro Amigo y Paisano Pablo Sarasate. Pamplona 1996.

-International Who's Who in Music & Musicians Directory. Cambridge, England, 1992.

-L'Abbé le fils: Principes du violon pour apprendre le doigté de cet instrument, et les differens agrémens dont il est susceptible. Paris 1761.

-La Mara: ed. Franz Liszt Briefe. 8 vols. Leipzig 1893 – 1905.

-Lahee: Famous Violinists of Today and Yesterday. London 1902.

-Larousse de la Musique.

-Laurencie*, Lionel de la: L'école française de violon de Lully a Viotti. 3 vol. Editions Minkoff. Paris. 1991.

-Le Blanc*, Hubert: Défense de la basse de viole contre les entreprises du violon et les prétentions du violocel. Amsterdam, chez Pierre Mortier. 1740.

-Legouvé*, Erneste: Soixante ans de souvenirs. Paris, 1886.

-Library of Congress. Washington. USA.

-Liszt: Lettres d'un Bachelier ès Musique. Le Castor Astral. 1991.

-Manuscript letters addressed to Massart and his wife by the most eminent musicians of the time, kindly showed to me by a collateral descendant of Massart.

-Martiny: Histoire du Théâtre de Liège. Lüttich 1887.

-Massin, Brigitte: Franz Schubert. Fayard 1977.

-Massin, Jean et Brigitte: Ludwig van Beethoven. Ediciones Turner, S. A. 1987.

-Massin, Jean et Brigitte: W. A. Mozart. Fayard 1970.

-Ministerio de Asuntos Exteriores - Dción. Gral. Protocolo, Cancillería y Ordenes. Madrid.

-National Geographic Atlas of the World.

-New Grove Dictionary of Music and Musicians.

-Nietzsche: Menschliges, Allzumensliches. Ein Büch für frei Geister. Human All-Too Human. Dresden 1878.

-Nuovo Dizionario Ricordi della Musica e dei Musicisti.

-Ollivier, M. Daniel: Correspondance de Liszt et de la comtesse d'Agoult*, Editions Bernard Grasset. Paris 1933.

-Pasquali - R. Prince: Il Violino (El Violín) Ricordi Americana. Buenos Aires, 1952. ISBN 950-22-0185-X.

-Perez Ollo: Temas de cultura Popular. Sarasate.

-Philippe, Joseph: Sur un évantail de Marie-Antoinette et des musiciens liégeois de Paris. Extrait de "Si Liège m'était conté". Liège n. 8 (1963).

-Pierre, Constant: Bernard Sarrette* et les origines du Conservatoire nationale de musique et de déclamation. Paris 1895.

-Pierre, Constant: Biographie de L. Massart. Conservatoire de Paris 1900.

-Pierre, Constant: Histoire du Concert spirituel* 1725-1790. Paris 1900.

-Pierre, Constant: Le Conservatoire National de musique et de déclamation. Ducuments historiques et administratives recueillis ou reconstitués, Paris, Imprimerie Nationale, 1900.

-Pougin*, Arthur: "Le violon: les violonistes et la musique de violon du XVI au XVIII siècle". Paris, 1924.

-Quintin, José: Importance et rôle international de l'École liégeoise de violon. Société liégeoise de musicologie. Bulletin trimestriel. N. 31. October 1980. Pag 1-25.

-Quintin, José: several private letters to me.

-Reade, Charles: Cremona Violins. Four Letters Descriptive of Those Exhibited in 1873 at the South Kensington Museum. Alexander Broude, Inc. New York. N.Y. 1873.

-Régistre des bâthemes de l'Eglise Saint Denis à Liège. De 1811 à 1819. Pag 10, 23 July.

-Registre des professeurs du Conservatoire. Archives et documentation, Conservatoire National supérieur de musique et de danse de Paris (CNSMDP).

-Registres des Palmarès de fin d'année et cahier des classes (Service et documentation) Conservatoire Nationale supérieur de musique et de danse de Paris. CNSMDP.

-Saint-Saëns: Au courant de la vie. To the Happy Few. Paris 1914.

-Sala-Museo de Pablo Sarasate, Pamplona, Spain.

-Salazar*, Adolfo: Conceptos Fundamentales en la historia de la Música, Revista de Occidente. Madrid, 1965.

-Salazar*, Adolfo: Historia de la música. Revista de Occidente. Madrid, 1965.

-Salazar*, Adolfo: Juan Sebastian Bach. Alianza Música 1985.

-Schering*, Arnold: Zur Gesichte der Solosonate in der ersten Halfte des 17 Jahrhunderts.

-Shakespeare: The Complete Works. Tudor Edition. Collins, London, 1951.

-Société Liégeoise de Musicologie.

-Sopeña, Federico: Historia de la Música. 2ª edición, Ediciones y Publicaciones Españolas.

-Spitta*, Philipp: J. S. Bach. (2 vols 1873-1880).

-Spohr: violinschule 1832.

-Straeten, E. van der: The History of the Violin. London 1968.

-Verlaine*: Oeuvres poétiques complètes. Gallimard. France 1989. pag. 68.

-Vier, Jacques: Franz List. L'artiste–Le clerc. Collections Jules Lemaitre. Editions du Cèdre. Paris.

-Vilier J. :Franz Liszt, Paris 1950.

-Wagner: Mi Vida. Turner. Madrid 1989.

-Walker, Alan: Franz Liszt. Faber and Faber. London-Boston. 3 vol. 1988, 1989, 1997.

-Zamacois, Joaquín: Teoría de la Música. Editorial Labor. Madrid, Barcelona,1984.

It also helped me a great deal hearing the musical examples referred to in the cassette's contents

CASSETTES' CONTENTS

(Being the cassettes for my exclusive and personal use they are not available to the reader)

"C-01"
Side A:
00:00 MONTEVERDI: Orfeo (fragments) Scene 1 act 2; Scene 3 act 3: The English Baroque Soloists: Elliot Gardiner
14:30 LULLY: Suite orch. Amadis de Gaula: Collegium Aureum Dir.: R. Peters.
37:12 TORELLI: Conc. a quatro in forma di pastorale per il Santo Natale in G minor Op 8-6: Capella* Savaria Dir.: Pal Nemeth.
Side B:
00:00 TORELLI: Concerto grosso* in F Major Op 6-6: The Brandenburg Consort: Roy Goodman
13:45 WIENIAWSKI: Vl conc. 2 in D minor Op 22: Heifetz vl. London P.O.: John Barbirolli
32:25 WIENIAWSKI: Scherzo tarantella Op 16: Heifetz
36-52 VIVALDI: Sonata Op 2-2 RV 31: Heifetz
43:00 PONCE*: Estrellita: Heifetz

"C-02"
Side A:
00:00 TORELLI: Sonata Op 5-5: Chiara Banchini vl
03:05 CORELLI: "La Folia" sonata Op 5-12 (arr David): Enescu
12:30 BIBER: Mystery Sonatas. Joyful mysteries: Musica Antiqua Köln: Reinhard Goebel*
Side B:
00:00 LECLAIR: Sonata Op 9-3: D. Oistrakh vl
11:55 LECLAIR: Conc vl, strings and continuo* in D Major Op 7-2: F. J. Maier* vl and conduct. Collegium Aureum
MOZART, LEOPOLD: Duets for two vls.: Kremer, Grindenko vls.

"C-03"
Side A:
00:00 VIVALDI: The four seasons Op 8. Winter and storm at sea: I Musici. Federico Agostini vl
18:48 MANFREDINI: Concerto grosso* in C Major Op 3-12: Collegium Aureum.
29:20 J. S. BACH: sonata 1 BWV 1001 adagio* Anne Sophie Mutter

00:00 J. S. BACH: Partita* n 1 in B minor BWV 1002: Viktoria Mullova vl.

28:52 GEMINIANI: Concerto grosso* Op 2-5. La Petite Bande: vl & conductor S. Kuigken

37:40 GEMINIANI: Sonata in A major: N. Milstein** vl

"C-04"
Side A:
00:00 TARTINI: Sonata in G minor "The Devil's trill*": Mutter. vl.

16:23 LOCATELLI: Sonata Op 8-10 for vl, cello & continuo*: Introduzione Op 4-6 Freiburger Barockorchester: T. Hengelbrock

32-40 GLUCK: la corona: sinfonia*

38:15 GLUCK: la danza: sinfonia*

Orchester der Warschauer Kammeroper. Dir.: Bugaj
Side B:
00:00 GLUCK: Orfeo ed Euridice. Act 4 "J'ai perdu mon Euridice" Callas. Orq. Nal. Radiodif. Française: Georges Prêtre.

04:25 GLUCK: Obertura Ifigenia in Aulide. Czech PO Cond: Karil Sejna.

17:00 STAMITZ: Sinfonia* in D Op 7-6: Praha Camera Orch.

28:50 STAMITZ: Vl conc. in C Camerata of Bern. vl & cond. T. Füri

"C-05"
Side A:
00:00 NARDINI: vl conc. in D flat*. Eduard Melkus vl. Capella* Acad. Vienna: A. Wenzinger.

22:30 VIOTTI: vl conc. 22 in A minor: Y. Menuhin vl & cond. Menuhin Festival Orch.
Side B:
00:00 KREUTZER: Bthvn: Sonata in A minor "Kreutzer" Op. 49: Francescatti vl; Casadesus* (p)

31:25 "Nel cor piu non mi sento" opera La Molinara by Paisiello. Johan Sutherland, soprano

33:05 PAGANINI: Variations on "nel cor piu non mi sento" Viktoria Mullova

"C-06"
Side A:
00:00 RODE: Bthvn: vl sonata 10 Op 96 in G: Perlman

28:20 PAGANINI: Vl conc. 6 in E minor, Op Post: adagio* & rondo polonaise: Accardo vl. London PO. Dutoit.
Side B:

00:00 PAGANINI Capriccios 1 to 12: Perlman vl

"C-07"
Side A:
00:00 PAGANINI: Capriccios 13 to 24: Perlman
35:00 PAGANINI: Selection of several movements of guitar sonatas MS 84: Zigante (guit)
Side B:
00:00 PUGNANI: Obertura n 3 in B flat* Major: Ensemble L'Astrée.
19:00 KREUTZER: Duo for two vls: J. Michal & M. Carfi
28:35 SPOHR: vl conc. n 8 Op 47 "in modo d'una scena cantante" in A minor: Heifetz. RCA Victor SO. Cond: Izler Solomon (1954)

"C-08"
Side A:
00:00 LIPINSKI: vl conc. 2 in D "militaire" Op 21: Igor Ivanof vl. Warsaw National SO: S. Wislocki.
26:55 VIEUXTEMPS: vl conc. 5 in A minor Op 37. Viktoria Mullova The Ac. of St Martin in the Fields. Sir Neville Marriner.
Side B:
00:00 DAVID: Mendelssohn: vl conc. in E minor Op 64:A. Grumiaux. Royal Concertgebouw. B. Haitink
25:45 JOACHIM PLAYS THE VIOLIN:
Bach: Partita* in B minor (bourrée)
Joachim: Romance in C
Brahms: Hungarian dance 1 in G minor
34:40: Esta noche me emborracho (Carlos Gardel*)

"C-09"
Side A:
00:00 JOACHIM: Bthvn: vl conc. in D "in memoriam" Francescatti. Columbia SO. Walter. (recorded when he was 59)
43:15 PERLMAN: Fiocco (Arr Fuessi): Allegro
Side B:
00:00 ERNST: Variations on "the last rose of summer". Midori vl
10:00 WIENIAWSKI:
Mazurka "Obertas" in G Op 19-1 Ysaye vl
Mazurka "dudziais" in D Op 19-2 Ysaye vl
15:10 WIENIAWSKI: Legende in G minor Op 17. Mutter. Wiener Phil. James Levine.

23:00 SARASATE PLAYS THE VIOLIN:
Sarasate: Capricho vasco

Sarasate: Tarantella
Sarasate: Miramar (Zortzico)
Sarasate: Habanera
Sarasate: Zapateado (all composed by him)
Bach: Partita* in E (Prelude) (Recorded in 1904)

"C- 10"
Side A:
00:00 AUER: "in memoriam" Tchaikovski: vl conc.: D. Oistrakh. The Philadelphia Orch. Ormandy.
35:00 YSAYE PLAYS THE VIOLIN:
Chabrier: Scherzo-valse (pieces pittoresques 10)
Fauré: Berceuse
Brahms: Hungarian dance 5 in G minor (arr Joachim)
Side B:
00:00 MENUHIN: Bthvn: Sonata 7 in C minor Op 30-2 Kempff* (p)
29:00 KREISLER PLAYS THE VIOLIN
Kreisler: Caprice viennois Op 2
Kreisler: Schön Rosmarin
Kreisler. Liebslied
Kreisler: Polichinelle
Kreisler: Gavotte (arr partita* n 3 BWV 1006 Bach)
Kreisler: Sérénade espagnole (Arr Glazunov Op 20-2)

"C- 11"
Side A:
00:00 KREISLER ON THE VIOLIN
Libesfreud (Kreisler)
Rondino on a theme by Bthvn (Kreisler)
La precieuse (Kreisler)
The Londonderry air (Trad. /Kreisler)
The old refrain (Brandle/Kreisler)
Poupée valsante (Poldini/Kreisler)
Humoresque Op 101-7 (Dvorak/Kreisler)
Larghetto (Sonata vl 1 Weber/Kreisler)
Midnight bells <Der Opernball> (Heuberger/Kreisler)
Chanson Hindou ("Sadko" R. Korsakof/Kreisler)
Danza Española vida breve (Falla/Kreisler)
37:25 HEIFETZ: Bthvn. Romance 2 in F Op 50 RCA Victor Orch. William Steinberg.

Side B:
00:00 ENESCU ON THE VIOLIN:

281

Enescu: Sonata 3 in A minor Op 25. Lipatti* (p)
23:00 HEIFETZ: Sarasate: Aires Gitanos Op 20
31:12 HEIFETZ: Bthvn Romance 1 in G Op 40 RCA Victor Orch.
William Steinberg

"C-12"
Side A:
00:00 STERN. vl.: Mozart: vl conc. 3 in G K 216. Columbia Chamber
Orch: vl & cond Stern
24:00 SUK vl: Haydn: vl conc. 4 Hob VII-4 Suk Chamber Orch. Cond.
Joseph Vlach.
Side B:
00:00 KANTOROW. vl. Chausson: Poème Op 25. New Japan
Philharmonic. Cond: Michi Inoue
16:30 ZUKERMAN vl:
Falla. Danza española (Vida breve)
Ravel: Piece en forme d'havanera
Albeniz: Tango
Brahms: Hungarian dance 1
Paradis: Siciliana
33:30 ZUKERMAN vl: Mozart: Adagio* for vl & orch. in E K 261
Minnesota Saint Paul Chamber Orch. vl & cond. Zukerman

"C-13"
Side A:
00:00 PERLMAN vl: Saint-Saëns: vl conc. 3 in B minor Op 61 Orch
de Paris. Baremboim
28:50 ZUKERMAN vl: Elgar: la capricieuse Op 17
34:05 OISTRAKH vl: Mozart: Rondo in C K 373
40:25 OISTRAKH vl: Mozart: Rondo in B flat* K 261a
Side B:
00:00 LIN vl: Sarasate: Introducción y tarantella Op 3
04:57 NEVEU vl: Brahms: vl conc. in D Op 77. Philharmonic Orch.
Issay Debrowen.
43:10 CHUNG vl: Elgar: Salut d'amour Op 12

"C-14"
Side A:
00:00 CHUNG vl: Bruch: Scottish Fantasy Royal PO. Rudolf Kempe
28:45 MUTTER vl:
Ravel: Tzigane
Massenet: Meditation. Wiener Philharmoniker. James Levine
Side B:

00:00 MUTTER vl: Sarasate: Fantasia de concierto sobre motivos de Carmen de Bizet. Wiener Philharmoniker. Levin

2:30 KREMER vl: Schumann: vl conc. in D minor (work without Op Nr). Europe Chamber Orch: Nicolaus Harnoncourt.

"C-15"
Side A:
00:00 OISTRAKH vl: Sibelius: vl conc. in D minor Op 47. Philadelphia Orch. Eugene Ormandy

31:00 STERN vl: Saint-Saëns: Introducción y rondo capriccioso Op 28. Philadelphia Orch. Ormandy.

40:05 PERLMAN vl: Sarasate: Jota navarra

44:55 PERLMAN vl: R. Korsamof: Flight of the bumble-bee (Arr Kreisler)

Side B:
00:00 SARASATE PLAYS THE VIOLIN

Chopin: nocturne in E flat* Op 9-2

04:25 LIN vl: Haydn: vl conc. 1 in C Hob VIIa. Minnesota orch: Sir Neville Marriner.

24:40 PERLMAN vl: Falla: suite* popular española:

El paño moruno

Nana

Canción

Polo

Asturiana

Jota

38:20 PERLMAN vl:

Grasse: Wellenspiel

Mendelssohn: Sweet remembrance (Lieder* ohne Worte) Op 19-1 (Arr Heifetz)

Alex de Taeye: Humoresque

"C-16"
Side A:
00:00 BACH: vl conc. 1 in A minor BWV 1041 Wiener Simphoniker vl & cond D. Oistrakh

15:45 BACH: vl conc. 2 in E BWV 1042: Francescatti vl. Luzern Festival Strings. Baumgartner.(Rec. 1972)

35:01 HANDEL: sonata vl in E Op 1-15: Heifetz vl.

Side B:
00:00 HANDEL: Sonata in D minor Op 1-13: Enescu vl.(Rec. 1929)

13:50 HANDEL: Pasacaglia for vl & cello: Heifetz vl – Piatigorski*

20:05 PUGNANI: Largo espressivo: Enescu vl

24:00 ENESCU PLAYS THE VIOLIN: Bthvn: Derviches choir
25:55 Wagner: Albumblat in E flat*.
29:20 D'Ambrosio: Serenade
32:20 Kreisler (composer): Aubade provençale "in the style of Couperin"
39:20 RODE : Minuet-caprice: Thibaud vl
40:50 THIBAUD vl: R. Korsakof: Hymn to the sun (arr Kreisler)

"C-17"
Side A:
00:00 CHOPIN: Souvenir de Paganini: Fou T'song* (piano)
04:09 TO BE SUNG TO BAILLOT: SMOKE GETS IN YOUR EYES (Dinah Washington)
07:40 HASSID vl: Elgar: La capricieuse
11:10   " : Tchaikovski: Melodie
14:25   " : Massenet: Meditation.
18:25   " : Dvorak: Humoresque
22:00   " : Sarasate: Playera
26:12   " : Sarasate: Zapateado
29:45   " : Achron: Hebrew melodie
34:30   " : Kreisler (composer): Caprice viennois
38:20   " : Elgar: La capricieuse
42:10 NEVEU vl: Tartini: Variations on a theme by Corelli
Side B:
00.00 YSAYE vl: Mendelssohn: vl conc. (Finale)
05:10 FLESCH vl.: Handel: Prayer
08:45 Handel: March
12:00 Paganini: Caprice 20
15:50 Fauré: Berceuse
18:55 Falla: Jota
22:00 Dobrowen : Hebrew melodie
26:20 AUER vl.: Brahms: hung dance 1
28:55 Tchaikovski: Melody
32:45 ELMAN vl: Wieniawski: Souvenir de Moscow
37:35 DUSHKIN vl: Stravinski: Russian dance.
40:20 YSAYE vl.: Vieuxtemps: Rondine
45:15 KREISLER vl: Bthvn: vl conc. (fragment)

"C-18"
Side A:
00:00 THIBAUD vl: Albeniz: Tango
02:45 Debussy: La fille aux cheveux de lin
04:50   "   : En bateau

08:20 Rameau: Tambourin
10:00 Wieniawski: Caprice in A minor
11:40 Vieuxtemps: Sérénité
14:30 Dvorak: Slavonic dance
18:02 Granados: Danza española in E minor
22:40 " : Danza española in D
26:25 Saint-Saëns: Le deluge
29:55 " " : The swan
32:15 Simonetti: Madrigale
Side B:
00:00 PAGANINI: vl conch 2 "la campanella" : Accardo vl. London
PO: Dutoit
30:45 CHUNG vl: Saint-Saëns: vl conch 1: orch. Symph. Montreal:
Dutoit

"C-19"
Side A
00:00. VIEUXTEMPS: Fantasia Appassionata Op. 35. Kremer vl.
15:50. ERNST: Variations on Carnaval de Venise Op. 18. (after
Paganini) Kremer vl.
22:25. BACH: sonata 2 BWV 1003. Perlman vl
Side B
00:00. BACH: Bourrée (partita* 1 BWV 1002) Perlman. (Joachim C-8)
03:30. BACH: Preludio partita* 3 BWV 1006 Perlman. (Sarasate C-9)
07:05 BACH: partita* 2 BWV 1004 Perlman vl.

"C-20"
Side A
SZIGETI vl.
00:00 Handel (arr. Hubay) Larghetto from sonata N° 9 (1913)
03:49 Mozart: (arr. Burmester) Minuet divertimento N° 17 in D (1908)
06:33 Schubert, Franz: The Bee. (1908)
07:48 Rubinstein*, Anton: (arr. Wilhelmj*) Romance (1908)
11:10 Sibelius: (arr. Hermann) Valse triste (1912)
15:85 Arnold: Nocturne (1911)
18:10 Hubay: Zephyr (1913)
21:35 Laszlo: Ungarische Weisen (1909)
24:50 Corelli: La Folia (1940)
Side B
RICCI, RUGGIERO vl.
00:00 Bruch: vl conc. In G minor Op. 26 (1958)
23:23 Saint-Saëns: Havanaise Op 83 (1960)

"C-21"

<u>Side A</u>

HUBAY vl

<u>Hubay</u>: Hullamazo Ballaton

   " : Intermezzo

   " : Berceuse

   " : Pici Tubicam

<u>Bach</u>: Suite* 3

<u>Handel</u>: Larghetto

SALGAN-DE LIO (tangos)

-Bahia Blanca

-Desvelos

-Organito de la tarde

-Hotel Victoria

INDEX TO CASSETTES

(Being the cassettes for the exclusive and personal use of the author, they are not available)

ACCARDO vl
Paganini:
vl conc 2 " la campanella" "C-18"
vl Conc 6 Op post in E minor adagio* and rondo "C-06"

ACHR0N, JOSEPF:
Hebrew melody Op 33: Hassid vl. "C-17"

AGOSTINI vl
Vivaldi: The four seasons Op 8: Winter and storm at sea:
I Musici "C-03"

ALBENIZ
Tango: Thibaud vl "C-18"
Tango: Zukerman vl "C-12"

ARNOLD
Nocturne. Szigeti vl (1911) "C-20"

AUER vl.
Brahms/Joachim:- Hungarian dance 1 in G minor:
Auer vl "C-17"
-Melodie (souvenir d'un lieu chèr) Op 42-3
(arr Wilhelmj*): Auer vl "C-17"
Tchaikovski:
-vl Conc: Oistrakh vl "C-10"

BACH
Bourrée (partita* 1. BWV 1002. Perlman vl "C-19"
Partita* 1 in B minor BWV 1002: Joachim vl. "C-08"
Partita 1 in B minor BWV 1002: Mullova vl "C-03"
Partita 2 BWV 1004 Perlman vl "C-19"
Partita in E Major (prelude) Sarasate vl "C-09"
Prelude partita 3. BWV 1006. Perlman vl. "C-19"
Sonata* 1 BWV 1001 (Adagio*) Mutter vl "C-03"
Sonata* 2 BWV 1003 Perlman vl. "C-19"
vl conc 1 BWV 1041: vl-conductor Oistrakh "C-16"
vl Conc 2 en E BWV 1042: Francescatti vl "C-16"
BANCHINI, CHIARA vl

287

Torelli: Sonata Op. 5-5: Ensemble 415 "C-02"

BEETHOVEN
Chorus of Dervishes: Enescu vl "C-16"
Romanza vl-orch. 2 in F Major Op 50: Heifetz vl "C-11"
Romanza vl-orch. 1 in G Major Op 40: Heifetz vl "C-11"
Sonata 7 in C minor. Menuhin vl – Kempff* p "C-10"
Sonata in A minor "Kreutzer" Op 47: Francescatti vl "C-05"
Sonata vl 10 Op 96 in G Major (under Rode):
          Perlman vl - Ashkenazy p "C-06"
vl conc.(under Joachim): Francescatti vl "C-09"

BIBER
 Mystery sonatas: Joyful mysteries 1,2,3,4,5:
     Reinhard Goebel* vl "C-02"

BRAHMS
Hungarian dance 1 in G minor (arr. Joachim)
     "   "   1   "   "   : Auer vl "C-17"
     "   "   1   "   "   : Joachim vl "C-08"
     "   "   1   "   "   : Zukerman vl "C-12"
Hungarian dance 5   G minor (arr. Joachim)
     "   "   5   "   "   : Joachim vl "C-10"
     "   "   5   "   "   : Ysaye vl "C-10"
vl Conc. en D Major Op 77: Neveu vl "C-13"

BRUCH
Scottish fantasy: Kyung Wha Chung vl "C-14"
vl concerto in G minor Op. 26 Ricci vl-P. Gamba (1958) "C-20"

CHABRIER
Scherzo-valse (pieces pittoresques 10): Ysaye vl "C-10"

CHAUSSON
Poème vl-orch: Kantorow vl "C-12"

CHOPIN
Nocturne in E flat* Major Op 9-2: Sarasate vl "C-15"
Souvenir de Paganini: Fou T'song* (piano) "C-17"

CHUNG, KYUNG WHA vl
Bruch: Scottish fantasy "C-14"

288

Elgar: Salut d'amour Op 12 "C-13"
Saint-Saëns: Vl conc 1 in A Major Op 20. Dutoit "C-18"

CORELLI
Concerto grosso* in F Major Op 6-6 "C-01"
La Folia sonata Op 5-12 (Arr. David): Enescu vl "C-02"
La Folia   "   Op 5-12   "   : Szigeti vl (1940) "C-20"

D'AMBROSIO
Serenade: Enescu vl "C-16"

DAVID, FERDINAND
David: Arr of Corelli's "La Folia": Enescu vl "C-02"
Mendelssohn: vl conc Op 64 Grumiaux vl "C-08"

DEBUSSY
En bateau: Thibaud vl "C-18"
La fille aux cheveux de lin: Thibaud vl "C-18"

DUSHKIN vl
Stravinsky: Russian dance (Petrushka) I Stravinsky p "C-17"

DVORAK
Humoresque Op 101-7: Hassid vl "C-17"
Slavonic dance: Thibaud vl "C-18"

ELGAR
La capricieuse Op. 17: Hassid vl "C-17"
La capricieuse Op 17: Zukerman vl "C-13"
Salut d'amour Op 12: Kyung Wha Chung vl "C-13"

ELMAN vl
Wieniawski: Souvenir de Moscou Op 6 "C-17"

ENESCU vl.
Bthvn: Chorus of Dervishes "C-16"
Corelli: Sonata "La Folia" (arr. David) "C-02"
D'Ambrosio: Serenade "C-16"
Enescu: Sonata vl-p. Op 25-3 Lipatti* (p) "C-11"
Handel: Sonata in D Major Op 1-13 "C-16"
Kreisler: Aubade provençale Style de Couperin "C-16"
Kreisler: Tempo di menuetto Style de Pugnani "C-16"
Pugnani: Largo espressivo "C-16"

Wagner: Albumblat en E flat* Major "C-16"

ERNST
Variations on Carnaval de Venise, Op. 18. Kremer vl. "C-19"
Variations on the "last rose of summer": Midori vl "C-09"

FALLA
Danza española (la vida breve): Zukerman vl "C-12"
Suite* popular española:
-Asturiana......... Perlman vl "C-15"
-Canción .... Perlman vl "C-15"
-El paño moruno: Perlman vl "C-15"
-Jota................. Perlman vl "C-15"
-Nana............... Perlman vl "C-15"
-Polo................ Perlman vl "C-15"

FAURÉ
Berceuse Op 16: Ysaye vl "C-10"

FIOCCO
Allegro (Arr. Fuessi): Perlman vl "C-09"

FLESCH, CARL vl
Dobrowen: Hebrew melodie "C-17"
Falla: Jota "C-17"
Fauré: Berceuse "C-17"
Handel:
-March "C-17"
-Prayer "C-17"
Paganini: Capriccio 20 (arr Kreisler) "C-17"

FRANCESCATTI vl
Bach: vl conc 2 en E Major BWV 1042
Luzern Festival Strings: R. Baumgartner "C-16"
Bthvn: Sonata Kreutzer (under Kreutzer) "C-05"
Bthvn: vl conc. (under Joachim) "C-09"

GEMINIANI
Conc grosso* Op 2-5: Petite Bande: vl-cond Kuigken "C-03"
Sonata vl-p in A Major: Nathan Milstein** vl "C-03"

GLUCK
Ifigenia in Aulide: obertura. Czech PO. Sejna "C-04"

La Corona: sinfonia* "C-04"
La Danza: sinfonia* "C-04"
Orfeo et Euridice Act 4 "J'ai perdu mon Euridice": Callas.
Orq. Nal. Radiodif. Française. Cond George Prêtre "C-04"

GRANADOS
Danza española in E minor: Thibaud vl "C-18"
Danza española in D Major : Thibaud vl "C-18"

GOEBEL* vl
Biber: Mystery sonatas; Joyful mysteries 1-2-3-4-5: "C-02"

GRASSE
Wellenspiel: Perlman vl "C-15"

GRUMIAUX vl
Mendelssohn: vl. conc. in E minor Op 54 "C-08"

HANDEL
Sonata Op. 1-9. Larghetto Arr Hubay. Szigeti vl (1913) "C-20"
Sonata vl-p. Op 1-13: Heifetz vl "C-16"
Sonata vl-p. Op. 15: Heifetz vl "C-16"
Pasacaglia vl-cello: Heifetz vl "C-16"

HASSID, JOSEPH vl
The complete recordings: all in "C-17"
Achron, Joseph: Hebrew Melody Op 33
Dvorak: (arr. Kreisler) Humoresque Op 101-7
Elgar: La capricieuse Op 17
Elgar: La capricieuse Op 17
Kreisler: Caprice viennois Op 2
Massenet: Meditation
Sarasate: Playera   Op 13-1
Sarasate: Zapateado Op 23-2
Tchaikovski: Melodie Op 42-3   all in "C-17"

HAYDN
vl conc in C Major hob VIIa : Cho Liang Lin vl "C-15"
vl conc 4 Hob VII-4 : Suk vl "C-12"

HEIFETZ vl
Bthvn Romanza vl. y orq. 1 in G Major Op 40 "C-11"
Bthvn: Romanza vl. y orq. 2 in F Major Op 50 "C-11"

Handel: Pasacaglia vl. y cello "C-16"
Handel: Sonata Op. 1-13 "C-16"
Handel: Sonata Op. 1-15 "C-16"
Ponce*, Manuel: Estrellita "C-01"
Sarasate: Aires gitanos Op 20 "C-11"
Spohr: vl. conc. 8 in A minor Op 47 "C-07"
Vivaldi: Sonata Op. 2-2 RV 31 "C-01"
Wieniawski: Scherzo-tarantella Op 16 "C-01"
Wieniawski: vl. conc 2 Op 22 en D minor "C-01"

HEIFETZ ARRANGEMENTS
Rimski-Korsakof: flight of the bumble-bee: Perlman vl "C-15"
Mendelssohn: (Lieder* ohne Worte Op 19-1): Perlman vl "C-15"

HUBAY
Berceuse. Hubay vl "C-21"
Hullamazo Ballaton. Hubay vl "C-21"
Intermezzo. Hubay vl "C-21"
Pici Tubicam. Hubay vl "C-21"
Zephyr Szigeti vl (1913) "C-20"

HUBAY PLAYS THE VIOLIN
Hubay: Hullamazo "C-21"
  "   : Intermezzo "C-21"
  "   : Berceuse "C-21"
  "   : Pici Tubicam "C-21"
Bach: Suite 3 "C-21"
Handel: Larghetto "C-21"

JOACHIM PLAYS THE VIOLIN
Bach: Partita* en B minor (bourrée) "C-08"
Brahms: Hungarian dance 1 en G minor "C-08"
Joachim: Romanza en C Major "C-08"

JOACHIM, COMPOSER
Cadenza* to Bthvn vl conc: J. Szigeti vl "C-08"
Romanza en C Major: Joachim vl "C-08"

JOACHIM, ARRANGEMENTS
Brahms: Hungarian dance 1 in G minor: Auer vl "C-17"
Brahms: Hungarian dance 1 in G minor: Joachim vl "C-08"
Brahms: Hungarian dance 1 in G minor: Zukerman vl "C-12"
Brahms: Hungarian dance 5 in G minor: Ysaye vl "C-10"

KANTOROW vl
Chausson: poème vl-orch "C-12"

KERN, JEROME
Smoke gets in your eyes
(to be sung to Baillot) Dinah Washington "C-17"

KREISLER COMPOSER

ARRANGEMENTS
Capriccio 20 (Paganini) Flesch vl "C-17"
Chanson Hindu (R. Korsakov) Kreisler vl "C-11"
Danza española (vida breve-Falla) Kreisler vl "C-11"
Humoresque Op. 101-7 (Dvorak) Kreisler vl "C-11"
Humoresque Op. 101-7 (Dvorak) Hassid vl "C-17"
Larghetto vl sonata 1 (Weber) Kreisler vl "C-11"
Midnight Bells (Heuberger) Kreisler vl "C-11"
Poupée valsante (Poldini) Kreisler vl "C-11"
The Londonderry air (trad) Kreisler vl "C-11"
The old refrain (Brandel) Kreisler vl "C-11"
Variations on theme by Corelli (Tartini) Neveu vl "C-17"

COMPOSITIONS:
Aubade provençale style Couperin: Enescu vl "C-16"
Cadenza* to the Bthvn vl conc: Francescatti vl "C-09"
Caprice Viennois Op 2: Hassid vl "C-17"
Caprice Viennois Op. 2: Kreisler vl "C-10"
La precieuse Style Couperin: Kreisler vl "C-11"
Liebesfreude: Kreisler vl "C-11"
Liebeslied: Kreisler vl "C-10"
Rondino Bthvn's theme: Kreisler vl "C-11"
Schön Rosmarin: Kreisler vl "C-10"
Tempo di menuetto style Pugnani: Enescu vl "C-16"

KREMER vl
Ernst: Variations on Carnaval de Venise Op. 18 "C-19"
Leopold Mozart: duetto for 2 vl "C-02"
Schumann: vl conc in D minor (without Op number) "C-14"
Vieuxtemps: Fantasia Appassionata. "C-19"

KREUTZER

Bthvn: Sonata "Kreutzer": Francescatti vl-Casadesus*. P "C-05"
Kreutzer: Duo for 2 vls: Michel-Carfi vls "C-07"

LASZLO
Ungarische Weisen. Szigeti vl "C-20"

LECLAIR, JEAN MARIE
Sonata vl-p Op 9-3: David Oistrakh vl "C-02"
vl conc in D Major Op 7-2: Franz Joseph Maier* vl "C-02"

LIN, CHO-LIANG vl
Haydn: vl conc 1 in C Major Hob VIIa "C-15"
Sarasate: Introduccion y tarantella Op 3 "C-13"

LIPINSKI
vl conc 2 in D Major "Militaire" Op 21: Ivanof vl "C-08"

LOCATELLI
Sonata Op 8-10 vl, cello, continuo* "C-04"
Introduzione Op 4-6 "C-04"

LULLY
Suite orchestral Amadis de Gaula "C-01"

MAIER*, JOSEPH vl
Leclair: vl con in D Major Op 7-2 "C-02"

MANFREDINI
Conc grosso* in C Major Op 3-12: Collegium Aureum "C-03"

MASSENET
Meditation (from Thaïs, act 2): Josef Hassid vl "C-17"

MELKUS vl
Nardini: vl conc in E flat* Major "C-05"

MENDELSSOHN
Sweet remembrance (Lieder* ohne Worte) Op 19-1
(arr Heifetz):Perlman vl "C-15"
vl conc (under F. David): Grumiaux vl "C-08"

MENUHIN vl
Bthvn: Sonata vl-p in C minor Op 30-2 Kempff* (p) "C-10"

294

Viotti: vl conc in A minor "C-05"

MILSTEIN** vl
Geminiani: Sonata vl y p in A "C-3"

MONTEVERDI
Orfeo: (Fragments) "C-01"

MOZART
Adagio* for vl and orch K 261: Zukerman vl "C-12"
Divertimento 17-Minuet. Arr Burmester Szigeti vl (1908) "C-20"
Rondo concertante* vl orch K 261a: Oistrakh vl "C-13"
Rondo vl orch in C Major K 373: Oistrakh vl "C-13"
vl conc 3 in G Major K 216: vl and conductor Stern "C-12"

MOZART, LEOPOLD
duetto for 2 vls: Kremer-Grindenko vls "C-02"

MULLOVA vl
Bach: Partita* 1 in B minor BWV 1002 "C-03"
Paganini: "nel cor piu" variations "C-05"
Vieuxtemps: vl conc 5 in A minor Op 37 "C-08"

MUTTER vl
Bach: Sonata 1 BWV 1001 (adagio*) "C-03"
Ravel: Tzigane "C-14"
Sarasate: Fantasia sobre motivos de Carmen "C-14"
Tartini: "Devil's trill*" sonata in G minor "C-04"
Wieniawski: Legende in G minor Op 17 "C-09"

NARDINI
vl conc in E flat* Major: Eduard Melkus vl "C-05"

NEVEU, GINETTE vl
Brahms: vl conc in D Major Op 77 "C-13"
Tartini: Variations on a theme by Corelli (arr Kreisler) "C-17"

OISTRAKH vl
Bach: vl conc 1 BWV 1041: vl-conductor Oistrakh "C-16"
Leclair: sonata vl-p Op 9-3 "C-02"
Mozart: Rondo concertante* vl-orch K 261ª "C-13"
Mozart: Rondo for vl-orch in C Major K 373 "C-13"
Sibelius: vl conc in D minor Op 47 "C-15"

Tchaikovski: vl concerto "C-10"

PAGANINI
Capriccios 01-12: Perlman vl "C-06"
Capriccios 13-24: Perlman vl "C-07"
Selection of movmts. guitar sonatas: Zigante (Guit) "C-07"
Variations on "nel cor piu": Mullova vl "C-05"
vl conc 2 "la campanella" Accardo vl "C-18"
vl conc 6 E minor Op post; adagio*-rondo: Accardo vl "C-06"

PARADIS
Siciliana: Zukerman vl "C-12"

PERLMAN vl
Alex de Taeye: Humoresque Op 61 "C-15"
Bach: Bourrée (partita* 1 BWV 1002) "C-19"
   "   :Partita* 2 BWV 1004 "C-19"
   "   :Preludio partita 3 BWV 1006 "C-19"
   "   : Sonata 2 BWV 1003 "C-19"
Bthvn: Sonata vl-p 10 Op 96 "C-06"
Falla: Suite* popular española: all in "C-15"
            "   "   "   :-Asturiana
            "   "   "   :-Canción
            "   "   "   :-El paño moruno
            "   "   "   :-Jota
            "   "   "   :-Nana
            "   "   "   :-Polo. all in "C-15"
Fiocco: (Arr Fuessi) Allegro "C-09"
Grasse: Wellenspiel "C-15"
Mendelssohn: Sweet remembrance
(Lieder* ohne Worte Op 19-1) arr. Heifetz "C-15"
Paganini: Capriccios Op 1 (01 - 12) "C-06"
Paganini: Capriccios Op 1 (13 - 24) "C-07"
R. Korsakof: Flight the bumble-bee (arr Heifetz) "C-15"
Saint-Saëns: Vl conc 3 in B minor Op 61 "C-13"
Sarasate: Jota navarra (danzas españolas Op 22-2) "C-15"

PONCE*
Estrellita: Heifetz vl "C-01"

PUGNANI
Largo espressivo: Enescu vl "C-16"
Obertura 3 B flat* Major: Ensemble L'Astrée "C-07"

RAMEAU
Tambourin: Thibaud vl "C-18"

RAVEL
Pieza en forma de habanera: Zukerman vl "C-12"
Tzigane: Mutter vl "C-14"

RICCI, RUGGIERO vl
00.00 Bruch: Violin Conc in G minor Op. 26 -P. Gamba. "C-20"
23:25 Saint-Saëns: Havanaise Op. 83-P. Gamba "C-20"

RIMSKI-KORSAKOF
Flight of the Bumble-bee (arr Heifetz): Perlman vl "C-15"
Hymn to the sun: Thibaud vl "C-16"

RODE
Sonata vl-p 10 in G Major Op 96: Perlman vl "C-16"
Minuet-caprice: Thibaud vl "C-16"

RUBINSTEIN*, ANTON
Romance arr Wilhelmj*. Szigeti vl (1908) "C-20"

SAINT-SAËNS
Havanaise Op. 83 Ricci vl (1960) "C-20"
Introduction et rondo Op 28: Stern vl "C-15"
Le Deluge: Thibaud vl "C-18"
The swam: Thibaud vl "C-18"
vl conc 1 in A Major Op 20: Chung vl "C-18"
vl conc 3 in B minor Op 61: Perlman vl "C-13"

SALGAN (piano)– DE LIO (guitar) <tangos>
Bahia Blanca "C-21"
Desvelos "C-21"
Hotel Victoria "C-21"
Organito de la tarde "C-21"

SARASATE COMPOSER
Aires gitanos Op 20: Heifetz vl "C-11"
Capricho vasco Sarasate vl "C-09"
Fantasia sobre motivos de Carmen: Mutter vl "C-14"
Habanera Sarasate vl "C-09"
Introducción y tarantella Op 3: Sarasate vl. "C-09"

Introducción y tarantella Op 3: Lin vl "C-13"
Jota navarra (danzas españolas Op 22-2): Perlman vl "C-15"
Miramar (zortzico) Sarasate vl "C-09"
Playera: Hassid vl "C-17"
Zapateado Sarasate vl "C-09"
Zapateado: Hassid vl "C-17"

SARASATE ON THE VIOLIN
Bach: Partita* in E Major (prelude) "C-09"
Chopin: Nocturne op 9-2 "C-15"
Sarasate: Capricho vasco "C-09"
Sarasate: Habanera "C-09"
Sarasate: Miramar "C-09"
Sarasate: Tarantella "C-09"
Sarasate: Zapateado "C-09"

SCHUBERT, FRANZ
The Bee. Szigeti vl (1908) "C-20"

SCHUMANN
vl conc in D minor (without Op number): Kremer vl "C-14"

SIBELIUS
Valse Triste arr Hermann: Szigeti vl (1912) "C-20"
vl conc in D minor Op 47: Oistrakh vl "C-15"

SIMONETTI
Madrigale: Thibaud vl "C-15"

SMOKE GETS IN YOUR EYES (To be sung to Baillot)
Jerome Kern. Featuring Dinah Washington "C-17"

SPOHR
vl. conc. 8 in A minor: Heifetz vl "C-07"

STAMITZ
Symphony in D Major Op 7-6 "C-04"
vl conc in C Major: Füri vl "C-04"

STERN vl
Mozart: vl conc 3 in G Major K 216: vl-cond Stern "C-12"
Saint-Saëns: Introduction et rondo capriccioso Op 28 "C-15"

STRAVINSKY
Russian Dance (Petrushka): Dushkin vl-I. Stravinsky (p) "C-17"

SUK vl
Haydn: vl conc. 4 Hob VII-4 "C-12"

TAEYE, ALEX DE
Humoresque: Perlman vl "C-15"

SZIGETI vl
Arnold: Nocturne (1919) "C-20"
Corelli: La Folia (1940) "C-20"
Handel: Sonata 9-Larghetto. Arr Hubay (1913) "C-20"
Hubay: Zephyr (1913) "C-20"
Laszlo: Ungarische Weisen (1909) "C-20"
Mozart: Divertimento 17-Minuet. Arr Burmester (1908) "C-20"
Rubinstein*, Anton: Romance Arr Wilhelmj* (1908) "C-20"
Shubert, François: The Bee (1908) "C-20"
Sibelius: valse Triste Arr Hermann (1912) "C-20"

TARTINI
Sonata in G minor "The Devil's trill*": Mutter vl "C-04"
Variation on a theme by Corelli: (arr Kreisler) Neveu vl "C-17"

TCHAIKOVSKI
Melodie (souvenir d'un lieu chèr) Op 42-3: Auer vl "C-17"
Melodie (souvenir d'un lieu chèr) Op 42-3: Hassid vl "C-17"
vl conc (under Auer): Oistrakh vl "C-10"

THIBAUD vl
Albeniz: Tango "C-18"
Debussy: En bateau "C-18"
Debussy: La fille aux cheveux de lin "C-18"
Dvorak: Slavonic dance "C-18"
Granados: Danza española in D major "C-18"
Granados: Danza española in E minor "C-18"
Rameau: Tambourin "C-18"
Rimski-Korsakof: Hymn to the sun "C-16"
Rode: Menuet-caprice "C-16"
Saint-Saëns: Le Deluge "C-18"
Saint-Saëns: the swam "C-18"
Simonetti: Madrigale "C-18"

Vieuxtemps: Sérénité "C-18"
Wieniawski: Caprice in A minor "C-18"

TORELLI
Concerto a quatro in forma di pastorale Op 8-6 "C-01"
Sonata Op 5-5: Chiara Banchini vl "C-02"

T'SONG*, FOU (piano)
Chopin: Souvenir de Paganini "C-17"

VIEUXTEMPS
Fantasia appassionata Op. 35. Kremer vl "C-19"
Sérénité: Thibaud vl "C-18"
vl conc 5 in A minor Op 37: Mullova vl "C-08"

VIOTTI
vl conc 22 in A minor: Menuhin vl "C-05"

VIVALDI
Four seasons Op 8: Winter and storm at sea: Agostini vl "C-03"
Sonata Op 2-2 RV 31: Heifetz vl "C-01"

WAGNER
Albumblat in E flat* Major: Enescu vl "C-16"

WIENIAWSKI
Caprice in A minor: Thibaud vl "C-18"
Legende in G minor Op 17: Mutter vl "C-09"
Mazurka "Dudziais" in D Major Op 19-2: Ysaye vl "C-09"
Mazurka "Obertas" in G Major Op 19-1: Ysaye vl "C-09"
Scherzo-tarantella op 16: Heifetz vl "C-01"
Souvenir de Moscou Op 6: Elman vl "C-17"
vl conc 2 Op 22 in D minor: Heifetz vl "C-01"

YSAYE PLAYS THE VIOLIN
Brahms: Hungarian dance 5 (arr Joachim) "C-10"
Chabrier: Scherzo-valse (Pieces pittoresques 10) "C-10"
Fauré: Berceuse Op 16 "C-10"
Mendelssohn: vl conc (Finale) "C-17"
Wieniawski: Mazurka "Dudziais" Op 19-2 "C-09"
Wieniawski: Mazurka "Obertas" Op 19-1 "C-09"
ZIGANTE (GUITAR)
Paganini: Several movmts. of guitar sonatas "C-07"

ZUKERMAN
Albeniz: Tango "C-12"
Brahms: Hungarian dance 1 (arr Joachim) "C-12"
Elgar: La capricieuse Op 17 "C-13"
Falla: Danza española (vida breve) "C-12"
Mozart: Adagio* vl-orch. K 261 in E Major "C-12"
Paradis: Siciliana "C-12"
Ravel: Pieza en forma de habanera "C-12"

DATE OF BIRTH INDEX

-1632 Lully
-1644 Biber
-1650 Walther
-1653 Corelli
-1658 Torelli
-1678 Vivaldi
-1684 Manfredini
-1685 Handel, Bach and Domenico Scarlatti
-1686 Somis
-1687 Geminiani and Pisendel
-1690 Veracini
-1692 Tartini
-1695 Locatelli
-1697 Leclair
-1709 Benda, (founder of the German school)
-1714 Gluck
-1716 Bini and Giardini
-1717 Stamitz
-1719 Mozart, Leopold
-1722 Nardini
-1725 Lolli
-1727 L'Abbé le Fils
-1728 Gavinies
-1731 Pugnani
-1731 Cannabich, Christian (German school)
-1739 Dittersdorf, Carl Ditters von (German school)
-1751 Campagnoli
-1751 Haack, Karl (German school)
-1755 Viotti
-1766 Kreutzer
-1767 Eck, Friederich J. (German school)
-1771 Baillot
-1771 Cannabich, Carl (German school)
-1774 Rode
-1774 Eck, Franz (German school)
-1774 Möser, Karl (German school)
-1789 Maurer, Ludwig (German school)
-1801 Kalliwoda, Johann Wenzel (German school)
-1782 PAGANINI, the virtuoso par excellence.

-1784 Spohr (The brightest star of the German school)
-1790 Lipinski
-1795 Boehm
-1800 Hellmesberger Sr
-1802 Beriot
-1810 Bull and David
-1811 Massart
-1814 Ernst (Romantic)
-1815 Alard (Romantic)
-1820 Vieuxtemps (Romantic)
-1828 Hellmesberger Jr. (Romantic)
-1831 Joachim (Romantic)
-1835 Wieniawski (Modern)
-1836 Monasterio (Romantic)
-1844 Sarasate (Romantic)
-1845 Auer (Romantic)
-1848 Marsick (Modern)
-1858 Hubay (50/50 Romantic, Modern)
-1858 Ysaye (Modern)
-1873 Flesch
-1875 Kreisler
-1880 Thibaud
-1881 Enescu
-1887 Persinger
-1890 Zimbalist
-1891 Dushkin and Elman
-1892 Szigeti
-1900 Heifetz
-1902 Francescatti.
-1903 Galamian
-1904 Milstein
-1908 Oistrakh
-1916 Menuhin
-1918 Ricci
-1919 Neveu
-1920 Stern
-1921 Grumiaux
-1923 Hassid
-1929 Suk
-1941 Accardo
-1945 Perlman and Kantorow
-1947 Kremer
-1948 Chung and Zukerman

-1960 Lin
-1963 Mutter
-1974 Vengerov

INDEX TO VIOLINISTS WITH THEIR DATE OF BIRTH

-Kremer 1947
-Kreutzer 1766
-L'Abbé le Fils 1727
-Leclair 1697
-Lin 1960
-Lipinski 1790
-Locatelli 1695
-Lolli 1725
-Lully 1632
-Manfredini 1684
-Marini 1587
-Marsick 1848
-Massart, Lambert 1811
-Maurer (German school) 1789
-Menuhin 1916
-Monasterio 1836
-Monteverdi 1567
-Möser, Karl (German school) 1774
-Mozart, Leopold 1719
-Mutter 1963
-Nardini 1722
-Neveu 1919
-Oistrakh 1908
-Paganini 1782
-Perlman 1945
-Persinger 1887
-Pisendel 1687
-Pugnani 1731
-Quantz 1697
-Ricci 1918
-Rode 1774
-Sarasate 1844
-Somis 1686
-Spohr 1784 (The highest figure of the German school)
-Stamitz, Johann 1717
-Stern 1920
-Suk 1929
-Szigeti 1892
-Tartini 1692
-Thibaud 1880
-Torelli 1658
-Vengerov 1974
-Veracini 1690

-Vieuxtemps 1820
-Viotti 1755
-Vivaldi 1678
-Walther 1650
-Wieniawski 1835
-Ysaye 1858
-Zanetti* 1626
-Zimbalist 1890
-Zukerman 1948

ENCYCLOPAEDIA

-ABEL, CARL FRIEDERICH (1723 Cöthen; d. London 1787) German composer and viola da gamba player of the first magnitude. Son of Christian Ferdinand Abel, father of Leopold August, and consequently his brother. Great friend of Bach they established the Bach Abel concert series in London.

-ABEL, LEOPOLD AUGUST (1718 Cöthen, midway Leipzig-Magdeburg, [Saxony-Anhalt Land]; d. Ludwigslust, midway Hamburg-Berlin, Mecklenburg Land. 1794) Member of a distinguished family of German musicians. Eldest son of Christian Ferdinand Abel (1683-1737), viola da gamba and violinist, he was composer and violinist. Pupil of Benda** in Dresden in 1735, he played for the orchestras of Brunswick 1745 and Sonderhausen 1757-65. Konzertmeister* in Brandemburg-Schwedt, he shared his post with Benda in Berlin. He ended as first violin* in the Kapelle* of prince Mecklenburg-Schwering in Ludwigslust. (Konzertmeister).

-ACADÉMIE ROYALE DE MUSIQUE: (The Paris opera) (known also as Académie d'opéra). Created by Louis XIV in 1669 on the advise of Colbert*, who had been convinced by Perrin*, exploiting his chauvinism, that France should have a French opera of its own, where everything should be French, words and music, as had the Italians. On June 1669 Perrin* received a 12 year privilege to establish "académies d'opéra for the performance of operas in French music and verses similar to those of Italy". The "Académie d'opéra" had as main goal to spread French operas with public performances not only in Paris, where it should have its head office, but in the rest of the French cities as well. It had no governmental subsidies, and ought to live out of its box-office only. To this end it was granted the sole privilege within France to stage operas, this monopoly thought to be enough to make it run. Consequently it was forbidden to anyone, no matter how important his condition might be, to attend the shows without paying their ticket. Unfortunately this monopoly was insufficient, and the Académie had innumerable difficulties and bankruptcies, starting by Perrin* himself. He inaugurated the Académie in 1671 at the Salle de Jeu de Paume de la Bouteille with a most successful pastorale, *Pomone*, (libretto by him, music by Cambert*, which they boasted to be the first opera in French) that run for 146 performances, but his business managers kept for themselves the receipts, and Perrin* was put behind bars for debts. The Académie d'opéra was forced to close in 1672. Lully**, seeing Perrin* in these difficulties, bought from him the privilege at a very low price, by paying his release and assuring him a small life pension. Lully, the favourite musician of the Sun King*, was named director of the new Académie, called Académie Royale de Music (1672) receiving from the king lavishing help, which allowed him to directed it without problems during his life time. Later, two other operatic giants dominated the opera's production: Rameau (1733-63) and Gluck (1733-79). The adverse economic vicissitudes and several fires that ravaged its buildings made the Opéra move its premises more than 7 times, change name more that 5 times and have countless directors. The building we know now is a masterpiece of the Second Empire style, designed by Charles Garnier* in 1875, called Palais Garnier*, or Théâtre National de l'Opéra. On the 13 July, 1998 a new building was erected by order of François Miterrand and designed by the Canadian-Uruguayan architect Carlos Ott: the Opera-Bastille, located at the place de la Bastille in Paris. The ensemble Palais Garnier*-Opera-Bastille is known as Opéra national de Paris. (O.N.P.)

-ACCIDENTAL: A sign placed to the left of a note, which alters its established, conventional pitch, by one or two semitones, either raising or lowering it. It may be: sharp*, flat* or natural. To raise a note one semitone we add to it the sign *sharp** (#), which sharpens the note by a semitone; the double sharp (x) raises the note two semitones. Sign (*b*) "flat*", lowers the note one semitone, and the double flat (*bb*) lowers it two semitones. Notes that are altered by an accidental can become natural if we add to them the *natural* accidental. This sign annuls the previous alteration that the note had. By using these accidentals we can make two notes of different names to have the same pitch. For example B sharp* (#) = C = D double flat* (bb); *la* double sharp* (x) = *si* = *do* flat (b). Two notes with different names and the same pitch are called *enharmonics**.

-ADAGIO: 1) (Italian: slowly) A tempo instruction put at the beginning of a musical piece that indicates that it should be played slowly. 2) Any piece of music played at a slow pace.

-AGOULT, MARIE DE FLAVIGNY, COMTESS D'. (1806 Frankfurt am Main, 35 Km NE of Mainz, upon River Main, Germany; d. Paris 1876) Her father, the Comte of Flavigny, had emigrated to Germany. She married Colonel Charles d'Agoult, but the moment she saw Liszt she fell in love with him at first sight. Both lovers fled Paris in 1834. She was the mother of all the "legitimate" sons of Liszt, viz, Blandine (1835), Cosima, [secon wife of Wagner] (1837) and Daniel (1839). [Liszt, being a well known womaniser, is supposed to have had many other children]. They separated in 1839 and after bitter dispute Liszt was awarded the care of his offsprings. Marie returned to Paris and began her career as a novelist with her pseudonym DANIEL STERN with an autobiographical novel, Nelida, complaining bitterly of her relations with Liszt. Among her writings we must mention *Lettres républicaines, Jeanne d'Arc, Mes souvenirs, Dante and Goethe*, and *Mémoires*.

-ALBERGHI, PAOLO TOMMASO (1716 Faenza, half way between Bologna and San Marino; d. id 1785) Italian violinist and composer. Pupil of Tartini**, he first played at the Faenza orchestra as third violin under the direction of his brother Francesco, becoming first violin* in 1755. On his brother's death he became maestro di capella*. He was most praised for his virtuosity; his violin composition are full of extravagant difficulties, in the manner of Tartini. he was an excellent teacher as well, having among his pupils Bernardo Campagnoli** and Cristoforo Babbi.

-ALLGEMEINE MUSIKALISCHE ZEITUNG. The most prominent music periodical in Germany (Leipzig 1798-1848) it was also the most comprehensive of them all, containing essays, reviews, biographical information, description of instruments, news, letters, and miscellaneous, with an extensive panel of the most illustrious collaborators (more than 130) that were the base of its international reputation.

-ANET, JEAN-BAPTISTE. Called Baptiste (1661 ?; d. Luneville, 20 Km S E of Nancy, 1755) French violinist and composer. One of the best pupils of Corelli**, made his debut in the milieu de Saint-André-des-Arcs in Paris. He inaugurated the Concert spirituel* by playing a sort of contest with Guignon*. It was him who first showed the elegance of the violin in the French school. He was a great composer and one of the best violinists of his time, with a most musical style, that avoided any kind of jugglery.

-ARIA: The aria in opera is a song sang by one of the singers, in which the author puts all his talent to make it attractive and melodious and where the singer can show off all his abilities. There are independent arias for each and every singer of the opera, and some are to be sang by two or more of them at a time.

-ARIETTA: Italian: little or small aria. The aria in opera is a song sang by one of the singers, in which the author puts all his talent to make it attractive and melodious and where the singer can show off all his abilities. There are independent arias for each and every singer of the opera, and some are to be sang by two or more of them at a time.

-ARPEGGIO. Italian "arpeggiare", to play the harp. To play the notes of a chord* one after the other instead of simultaneously. Its name derives from the usual way to play the harp, often in arpeggios.

-ARRIETA, EMILIO [PASCUAL] (1832 Puente la Reina, 23 Km S-W of Pamplona; d. Madrid 1894) Famous Spanish composer. Studied in the conservatory of Milan with Vaccai, obtaining first prize at the end of his career. Among his works we can name *El Sarao, La Conquista de Madrid, El Grumete* and his most famous opera *Marina*.

-ARTÔT, ALEXANDRE JOSEPH MONTAGNEY (1815 Brussels; d. Ville d'Avrais, nr Paris 1845) Belgian violinist. Know as "Le bel Artôt" (*Artôt the handsome*). He was the son of Maurice Artôt, (1772-1829) first horn at the Théâtre de la Monnai and teacher of the Brussels conservatory, and Theresa Eva Ries, cousin of Ferdinand Ries*, a superb pianist, pupil of Bthvn. Alexander began to study the violin with his father at the age of five, and in 18 months played a Viotti** concerto at the Theatre de la Monnai. Continued his studies with Snel, first violin* of the same theatre, who sent him to Paris. Here he worked under Rodolph** and August Kreutzer*, but his last three years of studies were conducted by Massart**, due to frequent indispositions of August. Artôt got his premier prix in 1828. Soon after, he started a tour through Brussels, London, Belgium, Italy, Germany and other European countries. He also toured the USA with the soprano Cinti-Damoreau. His playing was delicate, most elegant and precise. Berlioz wrote for him Rêverie et caprice op. 8 (1839). In his most brilliant career he collected five Strads: *Artôt* of 1709; *Artôt, Cessole* of 1716; *Artôt* of 1722; *Artôt, Alard* of 1728; and the *Artôt, Godowski* of 1728. Sir Charles Hallé* refers spitefully how once he accompanied Artôt in Bthvn's sonata "Kreutzer" in the presence of Ernst, at a dinner party. No sooner Artôt had gone, *Ernst sprang up and said: "Come, Hallé, let us play the Kreutzer"... He played it magnificently*. This utterly bad taste remark, of which, unfortunately, is replete his Autobiography, only reveals his envious character, as well as it shows an evident fact. i.e. that Ernst was far and away "the" best violinist alive in his time, which is something everybody knows. Comparisons are odious!!

-ARTÔT, DÉSIRÉE (MONTAGNEY): (1838 Paris; d. Berlin 1907) Belgian mezzo-soprano. Studied with Paulina Viardot*. Made her debut in Paris and in London before Queen Victoria in 1875. Much praised by many critics including Berlioz. Entered the Paris Opera* in 1858 on Meyerbeer's recommendation, but several intrigues made her resign the following year. Sang in Italy, Belgium, Germany and Russia, where Tchaikovsky proposed her marriage. She married instead the Spanish baritone Mariano Padilla, with whom she sang in Italy, Austria, Germany and Russia. She belonged to the family of the first premier prix of Massart, Alexandre Artôt*.

-AUBER, DANIEL-FRANÇOIS-ESPRIT (1782 Caen; d. 1871 Paris). The foremost representative of the opéra comique* in France. His successes in this genre (*Fra diavolo, Le maçon, La fiancée, Le domino noir, Haydée, Le premier jour du bonheur*) led him and his librettist Scribe to be commissioned another opera genre, the French grande opera, generally of historical theme, with spectacular mise en scène. Their first one was *La Muette de Portici* 1828, that was the prelude of Rossini's *William Tell* and Meyerbeer's *Robert le Diable*. Charles X honoured him with the Légion d'honneur*; Louis-Philippe appointed him director of the Paris conservatoire* succeeding Cherubini, and Napoleon III named him musical director of the Chapelle* Imperial. He had the historical honour (for us) of having ordered the admission of Lambert Massart as violin professor in the conservatoire de Paris*. His street in Paris, rue Auber, between place de l'Opéra and boulevard Haussmann, is one of the most representative of the City of Light*.

-BALTZAR, THOMAS (c1630 Lübeck, the largest Baltic harbour of Germany at the Land of Schleswig-Holstein; d. London 1663) German violinist and composer. Studied with Franz Tunder and Gregor Zuber. Had a high salary at the court of queen Christina of Sweden. He moved later to London where he amazed his private audiences with his absolute command of the fingerboard and virtuosity, being the first great virtuoso to play in England. He was much praised by John Evelyn and Anthony Wood, who in his diary recorded having seen Baltzar running up and down his fingers along the finger-board *"insensibly, and all with alacrity, and in very good tune"*. Carl Stiehl calls him the Paganini of his time. (Ein Paganini seiner Zeit). He died, the victim of alcohol abuse, in his early thirties, and is interred in Westminster Abbey.

-BASSO (BASSO CONTINUO): see continuo

-BAUDRON, ANTOINE LAURENT (1742 Amiens; d. Paris 1834) French violinist, and composer. Pupil of Gavinies**, he joined the orch. of the Comédie Française in 1763, becoming its leader* 1766. He collaborated with Beaumarchais and is said to have composed the aria* "Io son Lindor" from Il Barbiere di Siviglia.

-BECKER, HUGO (1863 Strasbourg; d. Geiselgasteig, nr Munich, 1941) German cellist. Studied under Piatti*. Solo cellist of the Frankfurt Opera (1884-6), was teacher at the conservatory there. Teacher of the Berlin Hochschule für Musik (1909-29) Played with Flesch**, Ysaye** and Busoni. He published with Sago Rynar the *Mechanic und Ästhetik des Violoncellospiels*. Had two Strads: the "Cristiani" of 1700 and another of 1719 called now "Becker". (he is one of the very few players of the 20th century to transmit their name to the Strad. they play on).

-BERGONZI, CARLO (? Cremona; d. id 1747) Famous Italian luthier*, only overshadowed by Stradivarius and the Guarneri family. Said to have studied with Giuseppe Guarneri "filius Andrae", his violins characterized by a remakable delicacy in form and detail.

-BERRY, DUKE OF, [CHARLES DE BOURBON] (1778 Versailles; d. Paris 1820) French member of the royal family and high ranking military man. Second son of the Count of Artois (Charles X) he escaped with his parents fighting with the allied army in the siege of Thionville (1792) and of the Condé, till 1797. Louis XVIII named him colonel of the army. On the return of Napoleon he was made general but had to escape. After the battle of Waterloo he returned to Paris but did not mix again in politics. On the night of February 13, 1820, he was assassinated by a fanatic buonapartist at the entrance of the Opera in Paris. This incident brought about Viotti's** resignation as director of the Opera.

-BERTEAU, MARTIN (c 1700, ?; d. Angers 1771) French cellist, considered the father of the French school of cello playing. Played with immense success at the Concert spirituel* in Paris. La Borde* said he was the professor that contributed most to the improvement of this instrument.

-BERTHEAUME, ISIDORE (1752 Paris; d. St Petersburg 1802) French violinist. Prodigy child he appeared in triumph on many occasions at the Concert spirituel* and the Concert d'Emulation. Pupil of Gavinies**. Conductor and co-director of the Concert spirituel*, 1789-91, he became Konzertmeister* of the duke's Oldenburg court in Eutin. Superb virtuoso, he rivalled with Viotti**, although, of course, he had not the same calibre. Several of his sonatas have a scordatura* in the style of Lolli**.

-BLANCHARD, HENRI-LOUIS (1791 Bordeaux; d. Paris 1858) French dramatist, critic, composer and violinist. He studied first in Bordeaux with Beck, and later in the Paris conservatoire*: violin with Kreutzer, and with Mehul and Reicha* composition. Composed a large number of vaudeville* airs, some very popular like *Guernadier, que tu ne m'affliges* and *Tra, la la*. Conductor of the orchestra of the Théâtre des Variétées (1818-29). Director of the Théâtre Molière from 1830 he staged there several plays of him, some very successful like *Camille Desmoulins*. His opera *Diane Vernon* was performed at the Théâtre des Nouvautées. Composed chamber music, concertinos (Italian: little concert) and songs. As a critic he wrote for *La Pandore, L'Europe Litéraire, Le foyer* and *Le Monde*. But his principal work was as contributory editor of the *Révue* and *Gazette Musical*.

-BLAVET, MICHEL (Besançon 1700; d. Paris 1768) French flautist and composer. Autodidact, he mastered the bassoon and the flute. In 1726 he made his debut at the Concert spirituel*, which marked the beginning of his brilliant career. Blavet appeared at the Concert spirituel more that any other musician, and he was unanimously praised for the purity of his singing tone, dazzling technique and just intonation. Frederick the Great, while still Prince, offered him a place at his Prussian court, but he declined. In 1738 he was appointed first flute of the Musique du roi*, and in 1740 of the Paris Opera*. Blavet attracted the admiration of Voltaire, Telemann, Hubert le Blanc* and last, but certainly not least, QUANTZ**.

-BOCCACCINO, BOCCACCIO (1467 Ferrara; d. Cremona 1525) Italian painter, refined and sensitive, he had a strong influence from the painters of Venice, mainly the Bellini brothers and Cima de Conegliano. His influence extended to the Cremonese, Lombardian, Ferrarese and Venetian schools. His works have always the Ferrarese style, but his Venetian inspiration is patent in his "Sposalizio di S. Caterina", his masterpiece and in the altar of the church of S. Giuliano in Venice, "La Zingarella" "Santa Caterina" and "Annunciazione".

-BODINUS, JOHANN AUGUST (1725 Rudolstadt, 30 Km S. of Erfurt [Thuringia]; d. id 1800) German violinist and composer. Studied with Benda** in Gotha, and returned to his natal town to play at the court's orchestra. In 1770 he was appointed Konzertmeister* and director of chamber music. After a paralysis which prevented him to play the violin, he became orchestral director.

-BOLLIOUD DE MERMET, LOUIS (1709 Lyon; d. id. 1794) French academicist and musician. Member of the Académie des Beaux Arts de Lyon in 1736, and of the Académie des Sciences et Belles Lettres de Lyon in 1739, he was elected Secrétaire Perpétuel in 1758 when both merged. His only work *De la Corruption du Goust dans la Musique Françoise*, Académie des Beaux Arts, Lyons, 1746, is dedicated to prove that good taste lies on following the steps of (if not imitating) the great composers of the past, particularly Lalande and Lully, and also in the adaptation of music to the *rules of nature*, that is, melodies that sound agreable to the ear and conform to what nature demands from music: harmony*, gratification of the senses and mind, poise, enhancement of verses in opera, etc. Notwithstanding, he comes across enormous difficulties on trying to define what is beauty in accordance with nature, (using absolutely childish arguments). His exaggerated dependence on the past, make of him a reactionary, impermeable to innovation, having little sound arguments on what he says. All this is only natural, if we consider the difficulties Plato encountered in defining (which he never achieved) what was beauty in his dialogue Hippias the Major or about Beauty.

-BONONCINI, GIOVANNI MARIA (1642 Montecorone, nr. Modena; d. Modena 1678) Italian composer and theorist. Pupil of Uccellini*, he was maestro di capella* of the cathedral of Modena, and member of the academia Filarmonica in Bologna. He is the most salient representative of the instrumental school of Modena, avoiding any instrumental virtuosity. He was the last stage leading to Corelli's** Op 2.

-BONPORTI, FRANCESCO ANTONIO: (1672 Trento; d. Padua 1749) Italian violinist pupil of Corelli** he excelled as a composer. He is said to have influenced J. S. Bach in some of his works i. e. the movement "ecco" of his invention Op 10. His contribution to the violin sonata is very important.

-BORGHI, LUIGI (1745 Bologna; d. London c1806) Italian violinist pupil of Pugnani**. Very active in London, was leader of the second violins at the Handel commemoration in 1784. Member of the quartet Cramer.

-BOYDEN, DAVID (1910 Westport, at the mouth of River Saugatuck, Long Island Sound, midway New York City and Hartford, S-W Conn. USA) First magnitude American musicologist. Bachelor of Arts, *Magna cum Laude,* from the university of Harvard (1932), he received his Master in Arts from Harvard in (1938). He taught at

313

the university of California at Berkeley from 1938-75. He has been twice vice-president of the American Musicologist Society (1954-56) (1960-62) a Fullbright Fellow at Oxford and three times the recipient of the Guggenheim Fellowship (1954, 67 and 70) He has published three textbooks for students, included his famous *Introduction to Music*, and has dedicated the bulk of his studies to the history of string instruments, and string playing, standing out his *History of Violin Playing from its Origins to 1761*.

-BRAMANTINO, BARTOLOMEO SUARDI, called IL. (c1455 Milan; d. id 1536) Italian architect and painter disciple of Donato Bramante. During his youth in Milan he painted mainly "St. Martin" the "Madonna" and the "Adoration of the Shepherds". Other mature works include a "Madonna with Saints" and "Flight into Egypt". He was court painter and architect of Francesco Sforza.

-BRETÓN, TOMÁS (1850 Salamanca; d. Madrid 1923) Spanish composer and conductor. He studied at the Escuela de Nobles y Bellas Artes, and at the Conservatorio de Madrid. At 11 he already earned his life playing in small orchestras. With the scholarships of the Royal Academy of San Fernando and of King Alfonso XII, he travelled to Milan, Rome, Vienna, and Paris for further studies. Founder of the Unión Artistico Musical, he taught at Madrid's Conservatory and conducted the Sociedad de Conciertos. Among his compositions we must mention *Los Amantes de Teruel* (1889), *La Dolores* (1895), with its most popular jota *Aragón*, and his masterpiece *La Verbena de la Paloma* (1894), a zarzuela* wich has remained legendary ever since. It is said that on the première's day he was terrified and thought it would be a complete fiasco; but it is just enough to hear its overture or the "nocturne" to realize that it is a masterpiece. He was decorated with the cross of Carlos III, and that of Alfonso XII.

-BRODSKY, ADOLPH (1851 Taganrog, Seaport in the northern of Taganrog Gulf, sea of Azof, Rostov province, S-W Russia; d. Manchester 1929) Russian-Jewish violinist. Studied with Hellmesberger, Jr** in Vienna. Became senior professor in Leipzig in 1880. He led the Walter Damrosch's New York Orch. (1890-94). In 1895 he went to Manchester as leader* of the Hallé's* orch. and senior violin professor of the newly created Royal Manchester College of Music. He will be remembered for having premiered the Tchaikovski concerto, declared unplayable by Auer**. He owned the Strad Halir, owned also by Mendelssohn of 1694, and the Strad Brodsky of 1702.

-BROKEN CHORD: To play the notes of a chord* successively instead of simultaneously.

-BROSSES, CHARLES DE, called President Brosses: (1709 Dijon; d. id 1777) Learned jurisconsult, philologist, antique dealer, First President of the Parliament of Bourgogne (in those days the Parliament was actually the High Court). Friend of Buffon and Diderot, and bigot dilettante, he undertook, in company of some friends and replete of enthusiasm, a journey to Italy in the style of Burney*, to see and hear by himself the best of it all, including music, writing a series of letters that he later published under the title of *Lettres écrittes d'Italie*. He was also the author of *La Mécanique des langues*.

-BROWN, ABRAM: Little have I been able to gather from this performer, except for a concise reference of Burney* in his Gene2ral History of Music: "(Festing*)

314

was succeeded by Mr Abram Brown, a performer who had a clear, sprightly, and loud tone, with a strong hand; but though he had travelled through Italy, he was ignorant of Music, and the pieces he played consisted of *notes, et rien que des notes*: for he had no soul or sense of expression. He brought over a favourite solo of Tartini (the second in the second set, published by Walsh), with which alone he figured at all concerts, for at least six or seven years, without entering into Tartini's true style of playing it, or that of any performer of his school. Mr. Brown, however, had not the mortification either to feel or know his defects; but, on the contrary, was conforted with a full conviction of his superiority." (General History of Music. Vol. 2. Book IV. Pag. 1012) Such was the ridiculous competence Giardini faced in England, which amounted to none.

-BRUNI, ANTONIO BARTOLOMEO (1757 Cuneo, half way between Monaco and Torino in the Piedmont; d. id 1821) Italian violist and violinist resident in Paris. Pupil of Pugnani**, made his debut at the Concert spirituel* the Corpus Chriti of 1780, in competition with R. Kreutzer, playing a concerto of his own composition and appeared there four more times with considerable success. First violin* at the orch. of the Théâtre de Monsieur in 1795, director of the orch. of the Opéra Comique and of the Théâtre des Bouffons. He owned the viola Strad Bruni, De Boulogne of 1710

-BURNEY, CHARLES: (1726 Shrewsbury; d. London 1814) English composer and first magnitude writer on music. His capital work *General History of Music*, (4 Books. 1776-1789) is a valuable source of understanding of the music of his time, having known and heard many musician during his many travels for this purpose. Burney*'s history was contemporary with Hawkins'* General history.

-BUSCH, ADOLF (1891 Siegen, 65 Km east of Bonn; d. Guilford, Vermont, bordering New Hampshire, 10 Km north of Massachusetts, USA 1952) German composer and violinist. He was taught the violin by his father at the age of three. At 11 he entered the Conservatory of Cologne. Leader* of the orchestra of the Koncertverein in Vienna in 1912, violin teacher of the Berlin Hochschule für Musik. Founded his own Busch quartet, which got international fame. Played in trio with Rudolf Serkin*. In 1939 he moved to the USA where he founded the Marlboro School of Music in Vermont. Greatly admired as a soloist, with deep sense of music, excluding any virtuoso showmanship. Among his pupils stands out conspicuously Menuhin. He played on the Strads Busch of 1716 and the Wiener, Busch of 1732.

-CADENZA. A part of a concerto where the orchestra keeps silent, specially designed so that the soloist can play all alone to show off his virtuoso abilities on the instrument.

-CALENDAR, FRENCH REVOLUTION: The anti-religious fever of the Revolution attacked even the Gregorian calendar (the usual in the majority of world countries), making a new, laic, revolutionary calendar, exclusively for the French Revolution. Its author was Gilbert Romme, and month's names were given by the poet Fabre d'Églantine; It was instituted by the decree of the Convention October 24, 1793. Year numbers would start from its adoption, "an I" (year I) beginning on the 22 December 1792. The 12 months were: The first three AUTUMN moths were: *vendémiaire* (vintage) *brumaire* (misty) *frimaire* (foggy). WINTER: *nivôse* (snowy) *pluviôse* (rainy) *ventôse* (windy) SPRING: *germinal* (germinating) *floréal* (flowery) *prairial* (prairies) SUMMER: *messidor* (harvest gift) *thermidor* (heat gift) *fructidor* (fruits gift) Napoleon abolished it on January 1, 1806, restoring the Gregorian calendar, i.e. the universal one.

-CAMBERT, ROBERT: (c1627 Paris; d. 1677 London) French composer and singer. He studied harpsichord in Paris with Chambonnières. In 1652 he entered as organist at the church of St. Honoré, attracting the attention of queen mother, Anna of Austria, who named him maître et compositeur de la musique of the queen. In collaboration with the librettist Perrin* he was the first to stage a complete opera in French,: the pastorale Pomone which run for 146 performances. With Pomone he inaugurated the Académie Royale de Musique*, (Académie de l'Opéra) in 1671.

-CAMPRA, ANDRÉ (1660 Aix-en-Provence, département Bouches-du-Rôhne, région Provence-Alpes-Côte-d'Azur, 25 Km North of Marseilles; d. Versailles 1744) French composer. One of the best representatives of French opera. After having a good musical tuition in his home town, he became Maître de Chapelle* in Notre-Dame de Paris. He had the privilege to see in his lifetime his works *l'Europe galante, Hesione, Tancrède, Fêtes venetiennes* be replayed several times. He has left sacred music, (motets, masses, Requiem, Te Deum) and Opera-ballet (*l'Europe galante, le Carnaval de Venise, la Sérénade vénittienne, Les Muses*) and tragédie lyriques (*Hesione, Tancrède, Idoménée*)

-CANZONA. The canzona (Italian "song") is distinguished by two main features: a) It is a four-four time vocal composition, with its typical rhythm: a minim followed by two crotchets, or its variant: minim, two quavers, and two crotchets. b) It is arranged in fugal* imitations*. These fugues* were basically assigned to two or more treble choirs, supported by one or more basso continuo* choirs. When these canzonas were transformed into violin sonatas the fugue* was assigned to two violins which dialogued among themselves, supported by a basso continuo* (organ or harpsichord).

-CAPELLA, Italian: See Chapel*

-CAPET, LUCIEN (Paris 1873; d. id 1928) French violinist and composer. Studied at the Paris Conservatoire* with Maurin*, disciple of Baillot** and Habeneck*. Won first prize in 1893 by unanimous decision. Had a brilliant career as soloist and quartet leader. His several chamber ensembles were admired for their unanimity of style, purity of interpretation and perfect blending of their members who, renouncing to their individual virtuosity, played in favour of the group's amalgamation. In 1924 he became director of the Institut de Violon de Paris. As teacher he wrote *La Téchnique supérieure de l'archet*, Paris 1916.

-CAPILLA, Spanish: See Chapel

-CAPRON, NICOLAS (c1740 Paris?; d. id 1784) French violinist and composer. Pupil of Gavinies**, appeared more that 100 times in the Concert spirituel* with considerable success. Leader* of the orch. of the Concert spirituel in 1762, and then conductor in 1762. He was an excellent teacher most appreciated in Paris.

-CARTIER, JEAN BAPTISTE (1765 Avignon; d. Paris 1841) French violinist and pedagogue. Pupil of Viotti**, he entered the service of Queen Marie Antoinette. From 1791 to 1821 was assistant director of the Paris Opera and later member of the orchestras of the Napoleon and Bourbon regimes. One of his sonatas "in the style of Lolli" uses the first violin with the typical scordatura* of Lolli** (see his article). As pedagogue he published *L'Art du violon*, Paris 1798 and an *Essai historique du violon*. He played on the Strad. Cathedral 1707, and the Sasserno of 1717 .

-CASADESUS, ROBERT (1899 Paris; d. Id 1972) French pianist and composer. Won first prize in the Paris conservatoire* when he was 14, and shortly afterwards first prize in harmony* and the Grand Prix Diémer. Played in duo with Francescatti and founded a piano duo with his wife, Gaby Cassadessus, née L'Hôte. At 22 he was piano teacher at the American Conservatory in Fontainebleau, which he later directed. Among his many records, his complete piano works by Ravel won an international prize. Honours: Brahms Medal of Germany, Commandeur of the Légion d'honneur*, and Commander of the Order of Léopold in Belgium.

-CASALS, PABLO (1876 Vendrell, midway Tarragona-Barcelona; d. San Juan de Puerto Rico 1973) Spanish cellist, composer and conductor. He studied first the cello in Barcelona with José García, then went to Madrid to study chamber music with Don Jesús de Monasterio** and counterpoint* with Tomás Bretón*. Solo cello of the orchestra of the Opéra de Paris (1895-989) he taught the cello at the Barcelona conservatory from 1897. His fame grew up so fast that he soon devoted to an international concertist career. A fan of chamber music he founded with Cortot* and Thibaud** a trio wich has remained legendary. He founded and conducted the orchestra Pablo Casals in Barcelona (1919), and created in Prades, Pyrénées-Orientales, France, a Festival in 1950. He became a legend during his life time, very much like Andrés Segovia with his guitar, and it was he who introduced the Bach works into the international repertoire. Full of fire and ardently passionate, his performances are bold, unrestrained, and audacious. His abundant discography attest to it. His decorations include the Légion d'honneur*, the United Nations Peace Prize, and the Royal Philharmonic Society's gold medal. He was the dedicatee of Moor second concerto, Schoenberg's arrangement of a harpsichord concerto by M. G. Monn, Faure's Serenade, and the Tovey concerto of which he gave the première in 1934 at Edinburgh. Casals played on two valuable cellos: a Vuillaume* 1840-50?; and another marked Bergonzi* which, since Bergonzi never made a cello, is supposed to be of one of his disciples.

-CASELLA, ALFREDO (1883 Turin; d. Rome 1947) Italian composer, conductor, pianist and organiser. The most influential musical figure between the two World Wars. Studied in the Paris conservatoire* with Fauré and Leroux, made friends with Debussy and Ravel; he was very active in the musical life of Paris and was assistant to Cortot* in his piano chair at the Conservatoire. In 1915 he returned to Italy, where he intensely promoted the renaissance of the Italian composers of the XVII and XVIII centuries, being at the same time musicologist, critic, pedagogue and pianist. Heading the new neo-classical movement with Pizetti and Malpiero his music has an absolute personality, remaining as far from Romanticism as from Impressionism. He made concerts for soloist instruments like the cello, violin and piano, chamber and symphonic music, and for the stage as well: *La Giara*, (1924), *La donna Serpente* (1932), *La Favola d'Orfeo* (1932), *Il Deserto Tentato* (1937) and made also ballets like *Il Convento Veneziano* (1925) *La Camera dei disegni* (1940), *La Rosa del Sogno* (1943).

-CASINI, GIOVANNI MARIA (1652 Florence – id 1719) Italian church musician, organist and composer. First organist at the Florence cathedral 1676 and organist to the Prince Ferdinando de Medici and Cosimo III of Tuscany he was reputed the best organist in Italy. Teacher of composition of Francesco Feroci* and Francesco Maria Veracini**. His statement on Antonio* and Francesco M. Veracini is most relevant: "the heart, rather than cleverness, guided and accompanied the fingers and bow of these virtuosi"

-CASTIL-BLAZE, FRANÇOIS HENRI JOSEPH (1784 Cavaillon, 50 Kms E of Nîmes; d. Paris 1857) French first magnitude writter on music, librettist and composer. Wrote in the *Journal des Débats, Le Constitutionel, Le Menestrel, Revue and Gazette Musical de Paris*. Put into French the main operas of the moment, by Rossini, Mozart, Weber, that were staged with success. One of the leading critics of the Restoration (1815-20) and Louis-Philippe (1830-48). He favoured the traditional music of France and Rossini, very much in the taste of his compatriots, more inclined to like Meyerbeer that Berlioz. The French people did not understand the symphonic or romantic German works. Bthvn, for instance, was only discovered by a minority of them (Berlioz, Habeneck*) as late as 1828. This situation was due, to a large extent, to the sort of criticism fostered by Castil-Blaze. He translated, adapted, and modified the plots and music of operas by Mozart, Bthvn, Weber, Rossini, Paer* and Cimarosa, adding some fragments of his own composition, but at least he made this operas known in France. This kind of pastiches were called "castilblazades".

-CASTRATO: A man who has been castrated (removal of his testicles) in his childhood to preserve his soprano voice, and to avoid the natural changes in male pitch in puberty. This habit dates back to the second half or the 16th century, when women were banned from church choirs and the stage by the Roman Catholic Church. The first known one was Jacomo Spagnoletto, a Spaniard. They were the most famous and best paid of all musicians, being considered in the world of opera almost as gods. The use of castratos started from the very beginning of the opera, with Peri's *Euridice* (1600), Monteverdi's *Orfeo* (1607) and Vitali*'s *Aretusa* (1620). The miraculous advantage of the castrato was that he kept the beautiful soprano voice of a child, but with the much more strong emission of an adult. The peak of their popularity was between 1650 and 1750. The Sistine Chapel* of the Pope had several of them in its choir. The last castrato known was Alessandro Moreschi, who has made some recordings. A bad singer with a worse voice it is really pitiful and shocking to hear a man with a total female voice. They were formally forbidden by Pope Pius X in 1903.

-CASTRUCCI, PIETRO: (1679 Roma; d. 1752 Dublin) Italian violinist pupil of Corelli**. When still young he went to London where he received the patronage of Lord Burlington, Handel's protector. Great virtuoso and juggler, he led Handel's opera orchestra for over 20 years. In 1750 he retired to Dublin, where he died in poverty.

-CAUDELLA, EDUARD (1841 Iasi; d. Id 1924) Romanian composer, violinist and teacher. Studied first with his father, the cellist Francisc Caudella, then in Germany and Paris with Ries, Vieuxtemps and Alard. Toured in concert Paris, Berlin and Frankfurt (1855-61) Teacher at the conservatory of Iasi and conductor of its orchestra. Founded a course in musical aesthetics in Iasi's University.

-CAZZATI, MAURIZIO (c1620 Lucera, 65 Km East of Campobasso, 130 Km North West of Bari; d. Mantua 1677) Italian composer and instrumentalist. Maestro di capella* in S. Andrea, Mantua; of the duke of Sabbionetta in Bozzolo; in the Academia della Morte, Ferrara; and Sta Maria Maggiore, Bergamo. From 1657 to 1673 he was in Bologna as an important member of the musical life there. He is notable for his contribution to the development of the violin sonata. His sacred music is abundant.

-CERDAN, MARCEL (1916 Sidi Bel Abbes, 80 Km south of Oran, 400 Km west of Algiers, Algeria; d. 1949 aeroplane accident in the Azores) Although born in Algeria, he was one of the most cherished boxers in France. Nicknamed "The Moroccan bombardier" he became Europe's welter champion defeating the Italian Turiello in 1939. He became world middleweight champion defeating Tony Zale in 1948 in Jersey City, USA. Acclaimed as a national hero on his return to France, he went back to the USA to defend his title, loosing against La Motta in 1949 in Detroit, but none of them took this defeat very seriously, Cerdan having been injured in his shoulder from the second round. In any case a revenge fight was arranged between them in 1949 in the USA. It was while he was travelling to the USA to recover his world title that he was killed in an aeroplane crash in Azores in 1949. In the same plane was travelling Ginette Neveu** who was killed like everyone on board. The story is that their plane was grounded for technical reasons, and the next one with same destination was already full. In view of the highly important appointments both had in America that could not be delayed, they implored, and obtained, two seats thanks to two kind persons who renouncing to fly, gave them their seats. Soon after take-off the plane crashed into the ocean, and the two kind persons were born anew. He was the lover of the mythical French singer Edith Piaf*.

-CHABRAN (Chiabrano, Chabrano), CARLO FRANCESCO (1723 Turin, d. London ?) Italian composer and violinist. He studied with his uncle Somis** in Turin. In 1737 he entered as violinist in the orch of Turin's royal chapel*. He played 20 times at the Concert spirituel* in 1751 with great success, *"which became a sort of enthusiasm justified by the most brilliant and easy execution, wit and stunning agility, just intonation and precision; also, the pleasant music which he played, of which he was the author, added charme to his play".* (Mercure*)

-CHAPEL: Germ.: Kapelle*; Italian: Capella*; French: Chapelle; Spanish: Capilla*. Chapel has had, along history, many different meanings, mainly: a place of worship, and the group of priests who officiate in it, mainly; but in the sense we have used it in this book it means the salaried group of musicians who serve an ecclesiastical institution or the court or household of a monarch or a high ranking prelate, prince, or nobleman.

-CHAPELLE: (French) See Chapel

-CHORD: Two or more notes that are to be played simultaneously.

-CHROMATIC: Based on a scale* of 12 semitones per octave*, (called also dodecaphonic*: Dodeca, Greek: twelve). Normally applied to notes marked with *accidentals** other than those the established in the *key** in which the passage is written. One of the most complicated musical systems, see: a) R. Bullivant: The Nature of Chromatism. The Music Revue, ed. G. Sharp (Cambridge, GB) xxiv

319

(1963) 97-129. b) W. J. Mitchell: The Study of Chromatism. Journal of Music Theory. Yale University School of Music. (New Haven, USA) vi (1962) 2-31. A sequence is chromatic when it proceeds by semitones.

-CIAMPI, VINCENZO (1719 Piacenza; d. Venice 1762) Italian composer. His first years were in Italy, but in 1748 he went to London to stay till 1756, when he returned to Venice. Author of opera comique* (*Bertoldo, Bertoldino e Cacasenno, La favola de' tre gobbi*) opera seria (*Didone*, his best, *Antigona*) oratorios and sacred and secular music.

-CITY OF LIGHT: (Ville Lumière) Paris. Its sobriquet. In the Paris Great Exhibition of 1867 Napoleon III introduced, as a great novelty, the street lightning, that at night turned Paris into a wonder-land, the "City of Light", as it became known.

-CITY OF THE SEVEN HILLS: Rome is surrounded by seven hills, namely: The Aventine, Caelian, Capitoline, Esquiline, Palatine, Quirinal, and Viminal.

-CLEMENT, FRANZ (1780 Vienna; d. 1842 Vienna) Austrian virtuoso violinist, composer and conductor. Clement is most famous today for the Bthvn dedication of his violin concerto: *Concerto par Clemenza pour Clement, primo violino e direttore al theatro a Vienna dal L. van Bthvn, 1806,* (Concerto by Clemency for Clement, first violin and director of the theatre in Vienna, from L. van Bthvn) that was premiered by him. He played from the age of four. He was very much acclaimed in England. From 1802-1811 he was director of the newly founded Theater an der Wien. He travelled through Russia, Germany and Prague. Very gifted musician, he marvelled Spohr**, and Bthvn, as well.

-COLBERT, JEAN-BAPTISTE: (1619 Reims, France; d. 1683 Paris) French Controlleur General de Finance and Secretary of State for the navy, he became personal assistant to Cardinal Mazarin*, who strongly recommended him to Louis XIV. The Sun King* gave him his confidence, becoming one of the most important of his counsellors, both in his private affairs and in the administration of France. He reconstructed the whole economy of the kingdom, reforming public finances, the chaotic system of taxation, reorganising the industry and commerce. He also gave a strong impulse to foreign trade, making of France a great power at sea, both in its merchant and fighting fleet, reforming ports, and creating a professional naval force. Great promoter of arts, he founded, among others, the Académie Royale de Musique*, (The Paris opera*)

-COLONNA, GIOVANNI PAOLO (1637 Bologna; d. id 1695) Italian composer, teacher and organist. Son of a well known organ builder studied the organ from an early age. First organist in the orch of S. Petronio, he was maestro di capella* when Cazzatti* moved. He was also maestro di capella* at the church of the Madonna della Galliera and San Giovanni in Monte. Founder of the Accademia dei Filarmonici, was elected its principal in 1672. Important composer of oratorios, masses, motets and secular dramatic works.

-COLONNE, CONCERTS: Series of concerts given under the leadership of Eduard Colonne*. Very popular in Paris, they started by an association with music publisher Hartmann in the Théâtre de l'Odéon in Paris as *Concert National* in 1873. Taking advantage of the ardent nationalism that ensued the Franco Prussian* war of 1870, the institution was a total success. They moved to the Théâtre du Châtelet in

1873. Colonne broke up with Hartman for economic reasons and founded a new society, the Association Artistique, which later became the Concerts Colonne. In constant rivalry with the famous Concerts Populaires of Pasdeloup*, he based his successes on the popularisation of works by Berlioz, which he definitively imposed in the repertoire, and of other relevant French composers, such as Saint-Saëns, Lalo, Gounod, Bizet, Debussy, Charpentier and Chausson. He promoted also the music of Wagner. A warm and passionate conductor, he overcame Pasdeloup* for his sheer musicianship.

-COLONNE, EDUARD (1838 Bordeaux; d. Paris 1910) French violinist and conductor. Studied at the Paris Conservatoire*, winning first prize in harmony* under Elwart (1858), and in violin under Sauzay* (1863) First violin* at the orchestra of Pasdeloup* and of the Opéra, he created and directed his own Concerts Colonne*. He toured USA, Portugal, Spain, England, Russia and Germany. A passionate and vibrant conductor he was praised for his intense Romanticism.

-COLTELLINI, CELESTE (1760 Livorno; d. Capodimonti, Naples 1829) Italian mezzo-soprano. Studied with Manzuoli in Florence and Mancini in Vienna. She made her debut in la Scala, Milan, appearing later in Venice and Naples. In Vienna she premiered Cimarosa's La Contadina in Spirito. Mozart wrote for her the trio *Mandina Amabile* (k480) and the quartet *Dite almeno* (k479), and Paisiello wrote for her *Nina, o sia la pazza per amore*. She was famous for her expressiveness, excellent deportment on the stage and musical refinement.

-COLLET, RICHARD: The only data I could find of him come from Burney*: "At this time (1745) [he] played the first violin [at Vauxhall Gardens]. His tone was full, clear, and smooth, and his hand strong; but having neither taste nor knowledge of Music, he always remained an inelegant player." (G. History. Vol. 2. Pag 1011)

-COMMUNE DE PARIS (March 18 to May 28, 1871) Insurrection of the people of Paris against the provisional government created to negotiate peace with the Prussians at the end of the Franco Prussian* war in 1870-71. When the siege of Paris by the Prussians ended, a great disorder spread over the French capital. To restore order, the provisional government entered into several street battles with the insurgents, but not wishing to crush the people of Paris, the head of the executive, Thiers, ordered his troops to leave the capital and retire to Versailles. The people of Paris organised spontaneously the Commune de Paris, a most extraordinary kind of communist regime, made by everybody, without any leading party, its power actually and effectively coming from the popular masses. A Central Committee was organised, which decided to convoke general elections among the people of Paris to select their representatives to a new government: the commune de Paris. It consisted of representatives of workers, socialists, old republicans, federalists, who wanted France to be a federal state of communes (municipalities) of all provinces, radicals and anarchists. They called for very advanced measures, such as the total abolition of the capital profit in favour to the workers, free, integral, secular tuition, suppression of work by night for bakers, end of church support, police and press regulation exclusively by the people and 10-hour workday among others. It was crushed in a bath of blood in what was called the *bloody week*. The Commune scheme was later taken by Marx, Mao, Fidel Castro and Lenin, with the only remark that what they brought was the dictatorship of the leading party, supposedly in the name of the people, whereas here the true source of government was actually the people itself.

-CONCERT SPIRITUEL: The Concerts spirituel were the shrine where a great number of our fiddlers and many other prominent artists of the time were consecrated. Consequently we will indulge in them lavishly. They were a series of sacred concerts founded by Anne Danican Philidor in 1725 to provide musical entertainment on days when, following Christian law, the Académie royale de musique* (the Opéra) had to be closed. ["Holy- Days"] At first these concerts were devoted to church, sacred, music (hence the "spirituel") but soon secular music was accepted. During their short existence they became the centre of the musical life in Paris, without diminishing, of course, the paramount merits of the Opera. The absolute and exclusive command over music in France granted by the Sun King* to Lully** in the Académie royale de musique*, like all monopolies, was hideous, and many different ways to bypass it were put in place, defying high fines and other punishments that threatened all who did not comply with it. In particular, elegant private concerts were organised at the "chic" houses of high personalities in Paris, like Mollier, the duke of Aumont, Mlle. Maes, Monseigneur Clérambault, the duke of Noailles, the prince of Condé, the count of Clermont (who hired the services of no one less than Pagin*), Le Riche de la Pouplinière* and Louis François de Bourbon, prince of Conti, where friends and people of their entourage could enjoy what amounted to be public, though very much restrained, concerts. (There is a famous painting at the Louvre in Paris of a concert at the home of prince of Conti, with Mozart at the harpsichord). The need to satisfy the ever increasing demand of music, other than that of the Opera, without the written permission of Lully and his successors, was met by the brilliant idea of Anne Danican Philidor, to organise a series of concerts which would not run counter the privileges of the Royal academy, nor diminish their incomes, viz: the Concerts spirituel. These concerts would be doubly spiritual: for the *days* on which they took place and for the *kind of music* performed: A) For the *days* of performance: the concerts would take place precisely on days in which the Opera was closed: on religious festivities or "holy days", so that they could not claim they were making competence against them. These holy days included: Purification day, February, 2 (it celebrates the purification of the Virgin Mary, when she, in obedience to Jewish law, went to the Temple in Jerusalem both to be purified and to present Jesus to God as her firstborn, 40 days after she gave birth to the Son of God.) // Easter fortnight: (The two weeks preceding Easter). // Good Friday: (Commemorates the Crucifixion of Christ). // Easter: (commemorates the Resurrection of Jesus-Christ three days after his Crucifixion and his triumph over death) // Ascension: (Commemorates the miraculous ascension of Christ to Heaven; it takes place 40 days after Easter). // Pentecost: (also named Whitesunday, commemorates the descent of the Holy Ghost on the disciples, infusing them with divine gifts, in particular the "gift of tongues", the ability to speak in other tongues. It is held 50 days after Easter). // Corpus Christi: (Feast in glorification of the real presence of the body (corpus) of Jesus in the Eucharist (the Holy Wafer) when The Host is carried in procession in a monstrance. Observed on the Thursday after Trinity Sunday). // Assumption:

(feast celebrating the dogma that Virgin Mary was taken [from Latin: assumpta] in body and soul to Heaven. Observed on the 15th, August.) // Nativity [of Virgin Mary] (Celebrated August ,8). // All Saints' Day, (the 1st of November. Commemorates all the Saints of the Church, known and unknown. [as a curiosity, in Spain it is customary to stage Don Juan Tenorio, by Zorrilla.]) // Christmas Day: (commemorates the birth of Jesus the 25th December.) B) For the *kind of music* performed: To make their music as different as possible from that of the Opera, they would consist only on sacred music. Sacred or religious music, played on sacred or religious festivities, i.e. the Concerts spirituel. Only on these conditions, and provided an annual fee to be paid to the Académie royale* in compensation, could Philidor start his Concerts spirituel. By the time Philidor forged his scheme Lully had already died, so all the negotiations were made with his successor M. Francine. In the end they took the form of a royal privilege granted to Philidor to run these concerts in the city of Paris, for a three-years term. A notary act is preserved in the Archives Nationales. M.C. CXVI, 245. Of the staggering success of its first performance, gives us an idea this highly praising review of the Mercure* : *Having the king authorised M. Philidor to perform spiritual concerts at the hall of the Cent suisses in his chateau of the Tuileries*, that include motets with large choirs, and French and Italian sinfonias* of the best authors…it would be very difficult to find anywhere else a better ensemble of voices and instrumentalist, for the best players of the Musique du roi*, Académie royal de musique* and other excellent masters, in number of sixty, compose this excellent band, whose admirable performance, that attracts so many people, is totally due to M. Philidor.* (March 1725, p 614) Non spiritual music, (profane or normal) was gradually slipped unnoticed, first by playing instrumental music (sinfonias*, symphonies, concertos, sonatas* etc), and then adding operatic music, as the rigid control relaxed over time. The total chaos of the French Revolution in 1789 put and end to these concerts.

-CONCERTANTE: In a concerto manner, i.e. a dialogue between a solo instrument with the orchestra.

-CONCERTINO: It has two meanings: a)The beautiful title with which is honoured the leader* of the orchestra, or, [to add a little confusion] b) concertino is also the small group of instruments (normally two violins and a basso continuo*) that plays in a concertante* (dialoguing) basis with the rest of the orchestra, called "ripieno" in the concerto grosso*. This concertino is called also "coro favorito". The whole ensemble of concertino plus the ripieno is the tutti or concerto grosso.

-CONCERTO GROSSO: A musical genre of the XVIII century in which a small group of solo instruments (usually two violins and a basso continuo*) selected within the orchestra play in concertante* style i.e. in dialogue, with the whole orchestra. The selected group is called "coro favorito" (favourite) or concertino* <notice that *concertino** is also the title of the first violin* in the orchestra>. The remaining members of the orchestra were the "ripieno". The ensemble concertino* + ripieno formed the "tutti" or "concerto grosso*". The individualistic spirit of Romanticism reduced this group to a single instrument in the soloist concerto. In the few cases where there were more that one soloist instrument (Bthvn, Brahms) we speak of double or triple concerto.

-CONCERTS COLONNE: Series of concerts given under the leadership of Eduard Colonne*. Very popular in Paris, they started by an association with the music publisher Hartmann in the Théâtre de l'Odéon in Paris as *Concert National* in 1873. Taking advantage of the ardent nationalism that ensued the Franco Prussian* war of 1870, the institution was a total success. They moved to the Théâtre du Châtelet in 1873. Colonne broke up with Hartman for economic reasons and founded a new society, the Association Artistique, which later became the Concerts Colonne. In constant rivalry with the famous Concerts Populaires of Pasdeloup*, he based his successes on the popularisation of works by Berlioz, which he definitively imposed in the repertoire, and of other relevant French composers, such as Saint-Saëns, Lalo, Gounod, Bizet, Debussy, Charpentier and Chausson. He promoted also the music of Wagner. A warm and passionate conductor, he overcame Pasdeloup* for his sheer musicianship.

-CONSERVATOIRE DE PARIS (see Paris conservatory)

-CONTINUO (BASSO CONTINUO): It refers both to a certain kind of polyphonic* voice or part i.e. the accompanying harmonies; and to the instruments that play this continuo. Any instrument with polyphonic capacity to play the bass or accompanying harmonies of a musical piece is a continuo. It has much to do with the idea of polyphony*, being the continuo the instrument that plays the bass (low) or lower part of the polyphonic* work. Several of these instruments: keyboard [organ, clavicembalo, harpsichord] – string: [lute, guitar, harp,] having the possibility to play both the low and the treble part of the composition, were the most adequate for this purpose. The basso* is that part of a musical piece upon which the melody is constructed, the basis and the foundation upon which the whole polyphony* is interwoven, where the melody is embroidered with its bass complement. The continuo* has normally an accompaniment character, but it has its own personality too, constituting another voice, as independent as the treble, with its character of principal part as well.

-CORTOT, ALFRED (1877 Nyon, bordering the lake of Geneva, midway Geneva and Lausanne; d. Lausanne 1962) French pianist, conductor and pedagogue. A mythical figure of the 20th century music, he was neither a giant pianist, nor a supreme conductor, but he was an ardent promoter of music in all senses, particularly as a pedagogue. His ideas, preferring always musicality to virtuosity, were revered by his contemporaries. He studied the piano at the Paris Conservatoire* with Decombes, a pupil of Chopin, winning first prize in 1896, and was lucky enough to hear Clara Schumann*. A fervent wagnerian he conducted for the first time in France Tristan und Isolde, Götterdämmerung, and Parsifal, Brahms's Requiem, Bthvn's Missa Solemnis, and many unpublished works by Roussel, Magnard, Dindy, Ladmirault and Chausson. Professor at the Paris Conservatoire* (1907-17), he founded in 1919 the Ecole Normale de Music in Paris, his own teaching school of which he was director. In 1905 he founded with Thibaud** and Casals* his mythical trio. Cortot was also a very daring and individual juror with the highest sense of justice: when Dinu Lipatti* was awarded a ridiculous second prize at the Vienna International Competition of 1933, behind a first Ladislav Kohn, Polish pianist, unworthy of it, he resigned from the jury in protest for such an unjust decision. And when Michelangeli was awarded the first prize at the Geneva International Piano

Competition of 1939, he, who was among the juries, had no scruples in dedicating him one of his photographs with the inscription: *"with all my devoted admiration"* How many members of a jury have done this with one of the contenders?. Spiritual, delicate, lyrical and dreamy he was soundly called *"the poet of the piano"*.

-COSTA, LORENZO (c 1460 Ferrara; d.Mantua 1535) Italian painter one of the most famous of the Ferrarese school, he excelled in his atmospheric style. He worked at Bologna with the painter Francia, the most important of the Bolognese school. He succeeded Andrea Mantegna* in the court of Mantua, where he left many works of relevance. His masterpieces are in the altars of several churches in Bologna.

-COUNTERPOINT: A compositional technique consisting in making several voices to be heard simultaneously according to a system of rules. It is the basis of all the polyphonic* music and also of the fugue, the most complicated of all counterpoints*. At the very beginning there were only two voices, that had the same number of notes each. Notes were called then punctus, thus the name *punctus contra punctum.*(note against note). But the number of voices increased and their relations became more and more complicated, being interwoven by complex relations of different number of notes for each voice, divers rhythms, modes and tonalities.

-CRESCENDO: To increase gradually the sound volume.

-CUI, CESAR: (1835 Vilnius, capital of Lithuania; d. Petrograd, now St. Petersburg 1918) Russian composer and music critic of French origin. Besides his studies in music, he was a military engineer, of which he became professor. His expert writings on fortifications were deservedly famous. In S. Petersburg he met Balakiriev who was a decisive influence on him. He composed several, too long, unsuccessful operas, with a deficient, clumsy orchestration; also choral, orchestral and chamber music, songs and solo compositions. As critic he contributed to many journals, like *Nedelya*, *Novoye Vremya* and *Gazette musical* de Paris, among many others. Among his writings on music we must single out La Musique en Russie, 1880.

-CUZZONI, FRANCESCA (c1700 Parma; d. Bologna 1770) Italian soprano, possibly the best of her time. Her first important appearance was at Venice in 1718 in Pollarolo's Ariodante. In 1723 she arrived in London where she settled for an uninterrupted long period of most successful performances, singing numerous operas by Handel and Bononcini*. Here she competed successfully against the monopoly of the castratos*, specially Carestini and Farinelli. She also toured the main cities of Europe. She was the marvel of many important music connoisseur, not least Quantz, having a tessitura* of three octaves*, reaching the C 5. She sang like a nightingale, with a natural warble, perfect shake (trill*), most sweet cantabiles, and perfect intonation. She was plane and small, but conquered her audiences with her voice. She had a fierce rivalry with soprano Bordoni. Her voice was highly flexible and pathetic, with a ravishing trill*. The New Grove Dictionary devotes her 2 full pages!!

-CZERNY, KARL (1791 Vienna; d. id 1857) Austrian composer, pianist and teacher. Studied piano first with his father, later with Bthvn. At 3 he played the piano, and at 10 he played from memory all the main repertoire. One of the most highly reputed piano teachers in the world, his most salient pupils were Thalberg and Liszt. As pedagogue he wrote an enormous amount of massive works: Die Schule der Geläüfigkeit (School of virtuosity); Die Schule des Virtuosen (School of the virtuoso); Die Kunst der Fingerfertigkeit (Art of loosing fingers). A prolific composer he wrote more than one thousand mediocre works.

-DALL'OGLIO, DOMENICO (c 1700 Padua; d. Narva, Estonia, along Narva River, 15 Km short of its outfall into the Gulf of Finland, 130 Km W of S. Petersburg, 1764) Italian violinist and composer. Pupil of Tartini**, he started as violinist of the orchestra of S. Antonio in Padua. In 1735 he went with his brother Guises, a cellist, to the Russian court, where they remained for 29 years. He was much appreciated there as a virtuoso and composer, as well. His violin compositions are filled with virtuoso difficulties.

-DAMPER: A devise that stops the strings of the piano making them silent as soon as the finger releases the key it has depressed to produce the sound. In the piano the string sounds as long as the finger keeps depressing its corresponding key, all the rest of them remaining silent unless you depress another one. But the damper pedal*, also called "sustaining pedal", raises the dampers from all the strings, allowing them to vibrate freely in sympathy with the key depressed (Sympathy: in physics, a relation or harmony* between bodies of such nature that vibrations in one causes sympathetic vibrations in the other or others. Webster) The use of the (sustaining) pedal has been always seen with extreme apprehension, both by teachers and concertists. We may say that until the 1960s its use was very restricted indeed, as is patent from the recordings of such gigantic virtuosos like Walter Gieseking, Busoni, Schnabel* or Wilhelm Kempff*. In particular Gieseking was much praised for his legatos* without pedal, a sort of "miracle" that he only could achieve, particularly in Mozart. This apprehension was due to customary uses from the Renaissance and the Baroque to the Classical periods. Bthvn, as in so many other fields, was the first to introduce massively the legato* in his works, by using freely the pedal, for which he was accused of mixing confusedly the sounds at the piano. But after the 1960s the use of the pedal has been generalised, reaching the *just milieu*, where wisdom is, in the crystal clear play of Radu Lupu, and the apotheosis of the pedal* in Michelangeli, who kept always complaining that the piano was too much percussive, which he counterbalanced with his magic use of the pedal, to the point that in some of his recordings (Bach's Chaconne and Chopin, for example), he is closer to an "organ" that to the piano. The result is a strength and a deepness in his sound that no one else has achieved. He really submerges you in sound, which surpassing the stereophonic, becomes quadraphonic. You are really enveloped by his sounds from all sides. On the other hand, a magician of the absence of pedal is Glenn Gould in his Bach performances.

-DANCLA, CHARLES (1817 Bagnères de Bigorre, Hautes Pyrénnées nr Tarbes; d. Tunis 1907) French composer, teacher and violinist, the most celebrated member of a French family of musicians, Charles studied first with Dussert in his home town, and he was able to play for Rode**, who had retired to Bordeaux, at the age of nine. Rode gave him recommendation letters for Cherubini, director of the Paris conservatoire*, Baillot** and Kreutzer**. He studied in the Paris conservatory* with Guérin and Baillot and won first prize in 1833. He played at the orch of various theatres in Paris, being leader* of the Opéra Comique and first violin* of the Société des Concerts du Conservatoire* under Habeneck*. His idol was Vieuxtemps**. He did not tour, so his fame spread mainly in France. He formed a string chamber music ensemble with the members of his family, which was very appreciated in Paris. He was teacher at the conservatoire de Paris* and as a pedagogue wrote *20 Études brillantes et caracteristiques* Op 73, and *Ecole du méchanisme* Op 74. He had the following Strads: Dancla, De Villares of 1691; Dancla of 1703, owned also by Milstein; Dancla of 1708; Dancla of 1710, owned also by Milstein; and the Guarneri del Gesu "Dancla" of 1726?

-D'ARANYI, JELLY (1895 Budapest; d. Florence 1966) British violinist of Hungarian origin. A great-niece of Joachim she studied with her sister Adila Fachiri (née D'Aranyi) and her teachers Grundfield and Hubay in Budapest. Joachim wanted to give her classes but by the time she was old enough he had died. So at 14 she had no more tuition. A formidable easiness for the violin made her famous. She played frequently with her sister Adila Fachiri, in trio with another sister, pianist Hortense, "Titi", and had a memorable 20 years partnership with the formidable pianist Dame Myra Hess*. Her play was full of fire, and she marvelled Ravel with her Hungarian folk pieces which inspired him to compose the Tzigane, dedicated to her. With the help of some friends, she bought the 1710 Strad. Lord Dun Raven, owned now by Mutter**, and for which she had to give a valuable Bergonzi she owned. Works dedicated: Bartok: sonatas 1 and 2 for vl, p; Ravel: Tzigane; Somervell: Konzertstück; Williams: Concerto accademico. Holst dedicated his double concerto to both sisters Jelly and Adila.

-D'AUVERGNE, ANTOINE (1713 Moulins, capital of the department of Allier, Auvergne region [hence his name]; d. 1797 Lyon) French composer and violinist. Son of a violinist, he went to Paris to study with Leclair** in 1739. Became violinist of the orchestra of the opera in Paris in 1744, and leader* in 1751. His career was impressive: Compositeur du roy in 1755, director of the Concert spirituel* in 1762, co-director of the Opera in 1769. He retired voluntarily and went to Lyon where he died poor and forgotten. He gave a decisive impulse to the opéra comique.

-DÉTACHÉ: (French détacher: to detach) To play each note well detached from one another. It has several patterns: Simple détaché: To detach one note from the other, a different bow is taken for each note, but without break between them, so each bow has to be continued until the next takes over. All notes are even and smooth. This détaché is almost slurred*, and the detachment between notes is scarcely perceptible. Accented détaché: each note starts with a sudden articulation produced by increasing the pressure and speed of the note. Détaché porté: this stroke has a slight swelling at the start followed by a gradual lightening of the sound. Détaché lancé: a short quick stroke characterised by a great initial speed in the bow which subsequently slows down in the end of each note.

-DIATONIC: A composition is diatonic when it conforms to the very strict rules of the scale* based on a principal note: the tonic*, and on the inflexible relationship of all the eight notes of its octave*.

-DIMINUENDO: (Also *decrescendo*)To decrease gradually the sound volume.

-DITTERSDORF, CARL DITTERS VON (1739 Vienna; d. Château de Rothlhotta, Bohemia, 1799) Austrian composer and violinist. His father had enough money to procure him a good education on the violin, French and religion. He entered the renowned orchestra of Prince Sachsen-Hildburghausen in Vienna in 1751. He undertook a journey with Gluck to Bologna. He succeeded Michael Haydn as Kapellmeister* to the court of bishop Grosswardein in Hungary. He frequented Haydn and Mozart in Vienna. He has left a prolific number of works, instrumental, vocal and operatic, of which *Doctor und Apotheker* has survived to our days. He died in extreme poverty.

-DODECAPHONIC: see chromatic.

-DONT, JACOB (1815 Vienna; d. id. 1888) Austrian composer and violinist. Studied with Hellmesberger Sr, and Boehm at Vienna coserv. Played at the orch. of the Hofburg 1831-34. Professor at the seminar of Sacta Anna, where he had as pupil Auer, and at the academia of Music. From 1873 he taught at the Vienna coserv.

-DORAT, JEAN: [Also spelled DAURAT, his true name was Jean Dinemandi] (1508 Le Dorat nr. Limoges [hence his byname]; d. Paris 1588) French humanist, superb Hellenist and founder and mentor of the poets' group "The Pléiade". Born to a noble family, he made solid studies of ancient languages at Paris. He taught Jean Antoine de Baïf, whose father he replaced as director of the College de Coqueret. Here he formed with his pupils Pierre Ronsard, Pontus de Tyard, Rémy Belleau, Baïf and Joachim du Bellay, and the dramatist Etienne Jodelle a renowned group of poets named La Pléiade, after the seven Greek poets of Alexandria. He composed more than 15,000 poems in Greek and Latin, and was professor of Greek at the College Royal from 1556 to 1567. His influence extended to Germany, Italy and England.

-DOSSI, DOSSO. Original name GIOVANNI LUTERO called (1480 Mantua; d. Ferrara 1542) First magnitude Italian painter, leader of the Ferrarese school of the 16th century. He is famous for his landscapes and the worm atmosphere created in them, with an unearthly light. He was influenced by Titian. To be mentioned are the "Nymph and Satyr" and "The Sorceress Cire" his most famous works. Ariosto in his Orlando il Furioso places him among the best painters of his age.

-DUBOURG, MATTHEW: (1703 London, d. Id. 1767) English violinist and conductor. Pupil of Geminiani**, he soon became famous in Ireland and London. He played several times with Handel, and was a show off virtuoso. Master and Composer of State Music in Ireland (1728), Leader* of the King's Band in London (1752) and Master of Her Majesty's Band of Music in London (1761).

-DUPONT, GUILLAUME-PIERRE (1718 Paris; d. id 1778) French violinist. He studied with Leclair** and the Mercure* in 1738 defines him as a young violinist who promises much and causes astonishment. He made his debut at the Concert spirituel* in 1739, playing three pieces of his teacher Leclair, returning several times to those concerts until 1755 as soloist. In 1745 he entered the orchestras of the Concert spirituel* and the Académie Royale de Musique*, until he retired in 1773.

-DUPONT, JEAN-BAPTISTE (Very active in Dunkirk and Paris between 1773-83) French violinist. He made his debut at the Concert spirituel* in 1746, on the Ascension Day, playing with L'Abbé le Fils**. By 1774 he was first violin* of the Dunkirk Orchestra. He played often at the Concert spirituel*, both alone and in duo with Gavinies**.

-ECK, FRANZ (1744 Mannheim, Baden-Wurttemberg Land, SW Germany, by the Rhine River at the mouth of the canalized River Neckar, halfway Mainz-Stuttgart; d.

Strasbourg 1804) German violinist. Violinist at the court of Munich, he started travelling in concert from 1801. In 1802 he met Spohr** and made him his pupil, travelling together through Germany and Russia. In S. Petersburg he became solo virtuoso to the court. He developed madness and the tsar had him taken to his brother in Nancy. He died probably in an asylum in Strasbourg. His violin playing was powerful and precise, always pleasing, and with an exceptional technique for ornamentation and "irresistible charm" in the words of Spohr**. Owned the Strad Eck of 1717.

-ECOLE ROYALE DE CHANT ET DE DECLAMATION Until the French Revolution, the musical knowledge was taught in the "maîtrises" i.e. choirs and music schools, looked after by the clerical chapters of the different local churches. Upon their closing by the Revolution, another system had to be put in place to substitute them. This reform took two ways, that of the *École royale de chant**, and that of the *Ecole supérieure de la garde nationale**. i) The *École royale de chant* et de déclamation* was founded as part of the Académie Royale de Musique* (Paris Opera) in 1784, thanks to the efforts of the French musician François-Joseph Gossec* (b. Vergnies, Hainaut 1734; d. Passy, annexed to Paris: XVI arrondissement. 1829) who was its first director. Its aim, as its name implies, was the training of opera singers and theatre declamation, to which the teachings of string and keyboard instruments were added. It had to follow the example of the conservatory of Naples. Other subjects taught in the school were declamation, dance and fencing, all importante for the good appearance on the stage. Gossec* was its first director, and Piccini* the first singing teacher. Became under the Revolution Ecole Public de Chant, it was suppressed by the decree of the Convention of 16 thermidor an III* (see calendar* French Revolution) that created the Paris Conservatoire*. All its teachers passed to the Conservatoire.

-ECOLE SUPÉRIEUR DE MUSIQUE DE LA GARDE NATIONALE. The task to replace the old church schools by secular ones was entrusted to the formidable musical administrator Bernard Sarrette*, who became the head of the Ecole Superieur de music de la garde nationale, and later, the first director of the Paris conservatoire*. His nation-wide plan included the creation of 30 [first degree] musical schools, 15 [second degree] ones, in replacement of the maîtrises, and a few [third degree] others, that will provide refreshment courses, plus an Ecole supérieur in Paris. All of them should provide free tuition. None of them were created with the exception of that of Paris: the Ecole supérieur de music de la garde nationale*. One day prior to the demolition of the Bastille by the populace, the 13th July 1789, Bernard Sarrette* was named captain of the National Guard, entrusted with the responsibility to organise a band within the regiment, which he did by creating the Ecole Superieur de music de la garde nationale, with the double task to give open air concerts in patriotic and civic festivities, and to train the musicians of the Garde nationale. This new body of the Garde nationale took part in many public, patriotic events, as well as in the main civic festivities, not least, the transference of Voltair's ashes to the Paris Panteon in 1791. In order to produce new recruits for the band, and increase its size, Sarrette* drew up a plan for a school of military music, which was accepted in 1792, founding the Ecole gratuite de la garde national, where 120 pupils, sons of soldiers of the Garde nationale, were given free tuition, establishing the first school for wind instruments in France. In order to increase the size of the Ecole Superieur de music de la garde nationale, to reaffirm its goals, and redefine its statutes, Sarrette* obtained a decree (1793) transforming it into the Institut national de musique*. Sarrette*, wishing to extend the teachings of the Institut to singing, and string and keyboard instruments, took-over the existing École royale de chant* et de déclamation, incorporating it to the Institut, in 1794. The following year this enlarged Institut national de musique* became the Conservatoire de Paris*. The Ecole supérieure de musique de la garde nationale passed successively by several denominations which make its identification very confusing: Ecole gratuite de la garde nationale (1792), Institut national de musique* (1793), Conservatoire national de musique et de déclamation (1795). Under the Restoration it changed to Ecole royale de musique, then it became again Conservatoire de musique et de déclamation (1822), until it took its definitive name: Conservatoire nationale supérieur de musique et de danse de Paris, located in the Cité de la musique, 209, avenue Jean-Jaurès, 75019 Paris.

-ENHARMONIC: Two notes are said to be enharmonic when their names are different but due to the alteration of one or both of them with one or two accidentals*, they amount to one and the same pitch. B sharp = C; F flat = E; Fa = Sol double flat*; Mi sharp* = Fa; Re double sharp = Mi; Si sharp = Re double flat. To make them enharmonic it is sufficient to alter the lower note by one or two increasing accidentals* (Sharp* #) or lowering the higher by one or two Flat* accidentals* (Flat*, b) depending on the distance between them, until they reach the same pitch. So, G and A are separated by an interval* of second (two semitones). If we increase G with two sharps* (on the staff* it is marked by an x, meaning double sharp) the resulting pitch will be A. On the contrary, if we decrease by two Flats* (bb) the A it will result in pitch G. We can arrive at the same result if we divide their interval* distance between the two (two semitones) half and half each, i.e. Increase G by one sharp* (#), and decrease A by one flat* (b). G # sharp = A b flat. If the intervening distance is an interval of one semitone only, we can do the same operation by adding or decreasing a sharp or a flat accidental* to one of the notes. E and F are distant only a semitone. Correspondingly E sharp = F, and viceversa F flat = E.

-ESLAVA, HILARION (1807 Pamplona; d. Madrid 1878) Maestro de capilla* at Burgo de Osma, Seville and the Royal Chapel* in Madrid. Founder of the España Musical, a group whose aim was to foster opera in Spain. Composed operas like Il solitario del monte selvaggio, Pedro el cruel, sacred music and pedagogical writings: Método completo de solfeo, Escuela de harmonía, and a vast Lira sacro-hispana, an anthology of Spanish sacred music. He composed for Gayarre* the florid Misere Grande.

-ETERNAL CITY: Rome. So called because it is the religious and spiritual centre of the Roman Catholic Church.

-EUSTACHE, SAINT: see Saint Eustache.

-FARINA, CARLO (c1600 Mantua; d. c1640 Massa, 10 Km S. of Carrara, 40 Km N of Pisa, Toscana) Italian composer and violinist. Remarkable performer he was Kapellmeister* in Dresden 1625-32, returning then to Mantua. One of the first great composers of sonatas, he exploited all the technical possibilities of the violin in an endless, fertile display of the descriptive possibilities of his instrument, filled with innovatory effects such as "col legno" (striking the strings with the stick), sul ponticello*, multiple stopping* and glissandos* that imitated the sound of cats, cocks, dogs, soldiers, and all sort of musical instruments. All his compositions date from his stay in Dresden. His influence in Germany was colossal, and we can trace it to Walther**. His most renowned piece is the *Capriccio Stravagante.*

-FAYOLLE, FRANÇOIS (1774 Paris; d. Id 1852) French writer on music. Having studied mathematics and with a basic notion of music, his main writings are devoted to music: *Dictionnaire des Musiciens.* (Dictionnaire historique des musiciens, artistes, amateurs, morts ou vivants. Paris 1810-11). *Notice sur Corelli, Tartini, Gavinies, Pugnani et Viotti.* Paris 1810; *Paganini and Beriot.* Paris, 1831.

-FEL, MARIE (1713 Bordeaux; d. 1794 Chaillot) French singer. One of the most famous singers of the Académie Royale de Music*. She studied in Paris with Madame Van Loo*, née Anna-Maria-Critina Somis, a celebrated Italian teacher and singer, daughter of Somis**. In her brilliant career, besides performing over a hundred operas, she appeared 284 times at the Concert spirituel*, where she sang with violinists Mondonville* and Gavinies**. For over 35 years she reigned unimpaired at the Académie royale de musique* and the Concert spirituel*. (1733-1769). She was most celebrated for her flexibility, expressiveness and clear articulation, with a natural voice of total equality in all her notes, from the lowest to the highest, along two and a half octaves*, having all the same loudness and round sound, as if they were the pearls of a precious collar. [in keyboard instruments a perfectly performed scale* is said to be "pearled"] (Those who are familiar with the art of singing, or "bel canto", know well that it is precisely the equalisation of the notes of a singer throughout all his tessitura* what matters most to a singing maestro) This equality and evenness, was possessed by her as a natural gift, without any effort or study. This was her most salient characteristic, and made the writer Grim to say in the Mercure*: "What she has by nature, nature denies to others, who must make up for the lack of this gift with hard work". J. J. Rousseau dedicated his "Salve Regina" to her.

-FEROCI, FRANCESCO (1673 S Giovanni Valdarno, 30 Km S-E of Firenze; d. Florence 1750) Italian composer and church musician. Great organist, pupil of Casini*, he replaced him as organist at the Florence cathedral. He was teacher of composition of F. M. Veracini**.

-FERRARI, DOMENICO (1722 Piacenza; d. Paris 1780) Italian composer and violinist. One of the best pupils of Tartini** he made his debut in Vienna in 1749 with great success. In 1753 he entered the Wurtenberg court of Stuttgart, playing as soloist with Nardini**. He later moved to Paris where he had triumphant performances at the Concert spirituel*. No sooner had the Parisian connoisseurs declared that they knew not any fiddler superior to Pugnani, after his performance in the Concert spirituel on March 25, 1754, than on March 31 they heard Ferrari*, and they considered him the absolute perfection. *He distinguished himself by the use of harmonic* sounds, and perfect octave* passages. He had infinite grace, was learned, and had a good taste that placed him beyond any praise.* (Mercure*,

March 1754. Pags. 193, 183). Owned the Strad Peterlongo, Hawley, owned later by Oistrakh, of 1702.

-FERRARI, GAUDENZIO (1470 Valduggia, <Piemonte>; d. Milan 1546) Italian architect and painter. Influenced by Il Bramantino* (frescoes in the Madonna delle Grazie in Varallo and "Padre Eterno" and "Sta Anna e S. Gioacchino" of the Pianacoteca di Torino). The influence of Il Perugino* is seen in the reredos of Sta Maria di Arona. He was also influenced by Leonardo. Of special mention are his works in the Sacromonte di Varallo, Cathedral of Como, S. Gaudenzio in Novara, S. Cristoforo in Vercelli, the cupola of Sta Maria dei Miracoli in Saronno, and the Madonna di Torino.

-FERRARI, GIACOMO GOTIFREDO (1763 Rovereto, 20 Km S of Trento, on River Leno; d. London 1842) He studied singing and harpsichord from an early age and at 20 he was able to play the flute, violin, double bass and oboe. He went to Paris in 1787 being maestro al cembalo to the new Théâtre de Monsieur and singing teacher. Composed two operas and two ballets, some piano sonatas and several song collections. His writings include methods of singing and music theories, but his main work was the *Anedotti piacevoli e interessanti occorsi nella vita di Giacomo G. Ferrari*. London 1830. These anecdotes, contrary to what happens in similar works, are interesting and reliable.

-FERRAS, CHRISTIAN (1933 Le Touquet, Pas-de-Calais, on the English channel on the mouth of River Canche, 30 Km south of Boulogne) French violinist. Studied in the conservatories of Nice and Paris with Calvet. Made his debut at 13. Won the Scheveningen International Competition and the Prix Long*-Thibaud**. Numerous tours around the world. His many recordings show him as a good interpreter of classics, romantics and moderns, specially the French. Has two Strads: a) The President of 1721, and b) the "Minaloto" of 1728.

-FESTING, MICHAEL CHRISTIAN (b ?; d. London 1752) English composer and violinist, was a pupil of Geminiani**. Master of the King's Music in 1735, director of the orch of the Italian Opera House 1737. Directed the subscription concerts in Hickford's Room from 1739, founder of the Society of Musicians, where Handel was a member. Director of the Pleasure and Ranelagh Gardens. His influence was strong until the arrival of Giardini,** with his happy, gay style, full of embellishments. Burney* says: Festing, whose health and favour began to decline in the year 1750 (the year of Giardini's arrival to England) died about 1752, after mortifications of many kinds, the least of which were not those arising from the rapid success and universal applause of Giardini." (General History of Music. Vol. II. Book IV. Music in England during the XVIII century. Pag. 1012.)

-FETIS, FRANÇOIS-JOSEPH (1784 Mons; d. Brussels 1871) Belgian musicologist and composer. Professor of counterpoint* and fugue* at the Paris conservatory* and head of its library, he was also director of the Brussels conservatory. His monumental work *Biographie universelle des musiciens* is an indispensable source of consultation. Fetis owned two valuable Strads: the Boissier, Sarasate of 1713, kept now at the Conservatorio de Madrid, and the Muntz, Salabue, of 1736, one of the jewels of luthier Tarisio*.

-FIORILLO, FEDERIGO (1755 Brunswick; d. London 1822) Italian composer and violinist. Son of the opera composer Ignacio Fiorillo, he started, like Paganini, with the mandolin, to turn later to the violin. After having travelled through Poland and S. Petersburg, he became leader* of the orchestra at Riga 1782-84. In 1875 he played at the Concert spirituel* in Paris where he remained three years. He then moved to London playing regularly from 1788 to 1794. He was also a virtuoso of the viola playing it in the Salomon string quartet. His last concert was in 1794, a very premature victim of the 50s at only 39 years of age. As pedagogue his *36 caprices* are among the indispensable learning works for students.

-FIRST VIOLIN: Called also the leader* of the orchestra and the concertino*. He is the head of the group of first violins of an orchestra. The violins are divided into first and second violins, each with a head, director or principal violin. The first violin is also the head of the whole orchestra, which he represents. He has the title of *Concertino**. For more details see leader*.

-FLAT: An accidental* sign put to the left of a note on the stave* which decreases its conventional pitch by one semitone. If we decrease it by a double flat, it will be decreased by two semitones, or one tone. A single flat is marked *b* on the staff*, and the double flat *bb*. The notion of tones and semitones is so basic that we take it for granted that the reader knows it, or will easily learn it. The normal diatonic* scale*, in major* mode*, is do, re, mi, fa, sol, la, si, do. Each note is separated from the other by one full tone (two semitones) except for the intervals* mi-fa, and si-do, that are apart only one semitone.

-FLETA, MIGUEL [MIGUEL BURRO FLETA] (1897 Albalate de Cinca, Huesca, 40 Km N-W of Lérida; d. La Coruña 1938) Spanish tenor of the first magnitude. His name "Burro" meaning donkey, he altered the order of his names, putting in first place Fleta. He started as a shepherd in his home village. A famous "jota" singer, Miguel Asso, marvelled by his voice, sent him to a jota competition in Villanueva de Gállego (Zaragoza), but the unimpressed members of the jury found on him nothing to write home about. This utter failure was a dreadful blow for Miguel, but his father, endowed with a dauntless temperament and determination sent him to Barcelona's conservatory. With the natural scepticism they received Miguel as an insignificant provincial shepherd, and magnanimously granted him a routine audition without any possible consequence, for all posts were already allocated. Fleta's voice reached the upper floor, where a maestra of singing, Luisa Pierrik, was giving her lesson. She leaped from the piano stool, and run down to see who was singing. From then on she became his teacher and his wife, as well. Fleta started his lyrical career with Francesca da Rimini in Trieste in 1919, but his international triumph came in Vienna with Aida in 1920. From then on he sings in all the main cities of Europe and North and South America with immense success. On his debut in Madrid in 1922, Fleta is carried on shoulders by a group of admires from the Teatro Real to his hotel, like a triumphant bull fighter. And similar triumphs will accompany him until he parted with his teacher Pierrik in 1926. Without guide and her continuous training, he became intoxicated with his own successes. He used to sing beyond measure, even in the cold open, prolonging his recitals until late at night in the streets and in bull fight rings, too, to allow more people to hear him. In two years he just ruined his voice. His own success had killed him. Fleta's reign had lasted only six short years. the voice is one of the most delicate and fragile instrument of the human being, and it must be taken with extreme care. Fleta is one of the tenors that had transmitted more emotions in history, together with Tito Schipa, McCormack*, Aureliano Pertile and Caruso. His abundant discography bears testimony to it.

-FLOOD, GRATTAN (1859 Lismor, Waterford, midway between Cork and Clonmel, South of Ireland; d. Enniscorthy, 25 Km N of Wexford, 1928) Irish music historian, composer and organist. Honorary Doctor of Music for the National University of Ireland, awarded the Papal Cross Pro Ecclesia et Pontifice and elevated to the Order of S. Gregory, he wrote important accounts on music history, and biographical studies.

-FODOR, JOSEPHUS ANDREAS (1751 Venlo, midway between Eindhoven and Düsseldorf, by the frontier with Germany; d. St Petersburg 1828) Dutch violinist and composer, pupil of Benda**. He toured extensively as virtuoso through Europe. In 1787 he settled in Paris and in 1792 in St Petersburg.

-FONTANA, GIOVANNI BATISTA (15? Brescia; d. c1630 Padua) Italian composer and violinist. Very little is known about him except that another Brescian, Cerasio Gussago dedicated a sonata to him. Together with Marini*, he is one of the first important composers of sonatas for violin. His works derive from the vocal "canzona*", and are mostly for three parts, the continuo* being another part rather than an accompaniment.

-FORTE: (From Italian forte: loud) In music a loud sound as opposed to soft (*Piano**). It is marked with an *f* in the score. Like the "Piano*" it has three degrees of intensity: (1) standard loud is Forte, *f.* (2) Louder is *ff* and (3) very loud *fff* (*Fortissimo*).

-FOURNIER, PIERRE (1906 Paris) French cellist. Began to study the piano, but after an attack of polio he turned to the cello. Teacher of the Paris conservatoire* 1941-49. Has played as soloist and in many chamber music ensembles, taking Casals's* place at the mythical trio with Thibaud** and Cortot*; he played also with Szigeti**, Primrose* and Schnabel*; and with Szeryng* and Kempff*. Officier de la Légion d'honneur he plays on a Goffriller* of 1722.

-FOURTH STRING: The G string of the violin, i.e. the lowest in pitch. On the violin, strings are named in a descending order, from the highest to the lowest. The highest is the first string (E), the second is the (A), the third is the (D) and the fourth the (G). Baillot and, above all, Paganini, played ravishing pieces on this string only.

-FRANCO PRUSSIAN WAR (19 July 1870 - 10 May 1871) One of the main politics of Louis Napoleon III, emperor of the French second empire, was to rally the French people behind him by means of an international belligerent policy, entering in numerous wars in Europe and America with the aim to have a foreign common enemy that will unite the French against the adversary. The last of these wars was against the Prussians, headed by Bismark. The French suffered a humiliating defeat in the battle of Sedan, where Napoleon III was taken prisoner. He was deposed and the third republic was proclaimed. The Prussians, then, sieged Paris, which defended fiercely for some time, but finally they capitulated. After several street battles with the insurrected people of Paris, who were suspicious that the new government would restore the monarchy, the provisional executive government left Paris and retired to Versailles. Immediately after the *commune de Paris** was spontaneously created.

FRÄNZL, FERDINAND (1767 Schwetzingen10 Km W of Heidelberg, 20 Km SE of Mannheim; d. Mannheim Baden-Wurttemberg Land, SW Germany, by the Rhine River at the mouth of the canalized River Neckar, halfway Mainz-Stuttgart. 1833) German composer and violinist, son of Ignaz. Studied with his father. Made numerous tours as a virtuoso. Leader* of the orch. of Framkfurt am Main in 1792. In 1820 he toured again through Poland, Vienna and Russia, where he enjoyed the exceptional favour of the tsar. Replaced Carl Cannabich as musical director of the orch. of Munich court. He was the most oustanding violinist of the Spohr** generation, influencing even him through his pupil Franz Eck. He was also a splendid conductor.

FRÄNZL, IGNAZ (1736 Mannheim Baden-Wurttemberg Land, SW Germany, by the Rhine River at the mouth of the canalized River Neckar, halfway Mainz-Stuttgart; d. id. 1811) Grew under the influence of Johann Stamitz. He got one of the higest salaries of the orch. of the Palatinate. Applauded at the Concert spirituel* in 1768. Music director of the Nationaltheater in Munich. Organised the Academie-Konzerte, a private orchestra that was the center of musical life in Mannheim.

-FRASI, GIULIA (Fl 1740-70) Italian soprano. Studied in Milan with Brivio, and in London with Burney*. Sang for many years in The King's Theatre in many operas, sometimes taking the role of man, and in other salient theatres in London. Handel dedicated her, wonderful series of parts. He engaged her for his oratorio season of 1749, remaining his prima donna until his death. She had a "sweet and clear voice, though cold and unimpassioned" (Burney*).

-FRENCH REVOLUTION CALENDAR: See calendar* French Revolution

-FRIEMAN, GUSTAW (1842 Lublin; d. Odessa 1902) Polish violinist of Swedish descent. He first studied with Serwaczynski* in Lublin. From 1862 to 1864 he studied in Paris with Massart**, winning the Grand Prix and Amati Award in 1865. He then started a concert career that took him to the main cities in Europe, specially in Russia. He was professor of the violin at the Music Institute in Warsaw and taught also for many years at the Odessa Conservatory, becoming its director in 1889. He is, together with Wieniawski**, the introductor of Massart's vibrato in Russia.

-FRONDE, THE: (In French, *La Fronde*) Several civil wars in France (1648-1653) rebelling against the growing power of king Louis XIV. The rebellion was unsuccessful, and produced the backlash to increase those powers, paving the way for the most despotic absolutism of the Sun King*. The frond was a reaction against revenue measures approved by the government and against anything foreign, especially queen Anna of Austria, mother of Louis XIV, and the Italian born cardinal Mazarin*, first minister.

-FRONDISTS: see Fronde.

-FUGUE: It is at the basis of all the science of harmony*, being the most complicated of all compositional techniques. As in everything else it reached its ultimate summit in Bach. Great genius such as Mozart and Bthvn had real difficulties in handling it. Generally speaking we can say that it consists in the application of imitation* to the various voices of the fugue, that are to be heard simultaneously, which, by the effect of the gap of their beginning, they give the impression that they are chasing one another, by repeating three main different themes, at a delayed starting point for each. Fugue derives from the Latin *fuga*, meaning "run away". Thus the first theme seems to flee constantly ahead from the following imitative voices that try to catch it, but will never do it, due to the delay of their start. It is a composition that seems endless, a vicious circle without stop, or as I like to put it "an open tap". The fugue* involves also the art of counterpoint*, to the "point" that professors of harmony* are called also counterpoint teachers. The three main themes of the fugue are the *theses* or main theme, also called "exposition", the *answer,* and the *counter-subject.*

-FURETIÈRE, ANTOINE (1619 Paris; d. 1688 Paris) French lexicographer, novelist and satirist. Initiated at the legal profession, he soon abdicated, and took the holy orders that would provide him with the necessary incomes with which to pursue his literary vocation. He entered the Académie Française in 1662, but his mordant and extravagant character provoked many envies within the institution. When in 1684 he was allowed to publish a *Dictionnaire Universel*, he was unjustly accused of having copied the dictionary that the Académie was preparing, and was expelled from this institution. His Dictionnaire was not published until after his death, in The Hague in 1690.

-FUX, JOHANN-JOSEPH (1660 Hirtenfeld, Styria; d. Vienna 1741) Austrian first magnitude pedagogue, and sacred music composer. He was prolific too on instrumental music both for keyboard and violin. He is considered a follower of the traditional heritage of Palestrina, and the most eminent founder of the Austrian music of the XVIII century. As pedagogue his main work was the *Gradus ad Parnassum*, the most remarkable counterpoint* treatise ever to be written. Under the form of a dialogue between the master, Palestrina and the pupil, himself, it became a must for every musician, not least Haydn and Bthvn. Of special interest are the existing copies with hand written notation by Padre Martini*, Haydn, and Leopold. Mozart.

-GARCÍA, MANUEL Jr. [MANUEL PATRICIO GARCÍA SITCHES] (1805 Madrid; d.1906 London) Spanish baritone and maestro of singing. There are two Manuel García, father and son, and both were the best singing teachers of their time, which make things very confusing, for they only used their first name García. Manuel Patricio García Sitges, Jr. was a son of Manuel (del Popolo Vicente) García* Sr., and brother of the most famous prima donnas María García (Malibran*) and Paulina García (Viardot*). Both took their artistic names from their husband's. He studied singing with his father Manuel [del Popolo] García* Sr. and harmony* with Fetis* in Paris. His father Manuel García* (del Popolo), was a superb tenor and one of the best singing teachers of his time, to judge by his daughters Paulina Viardot* and Maria Malibran*, both his pupils. Manuel Patricio became, in his turn, the best teacher of his time, with such excellent pupils as Jenny Lind*, Julius Stockhausen*, Mathilde Marchesi* and Sir Charles Santley*. He taught at the Paris Conservatoire* 1847-50, and at the Royal Academy of Music, London, from 1848 to 1895. As pedagogue he wrote *Traité complet de l'art du chant, Mémoire sur la voix humaine, Observations on the human voice, Observations psycologiques sur la voix humaine.* His invention of the *laryngoscope* (1855) brought him world fame.

-GARCÍA, MANUEL Sr. [del Popolo Vicente]: (1775 Seville; d. Paris 1832) Spanish tenor, composer and maestro di canto. García was not his own name but his stepfather's. He never knew his true father. Educated at the choir of the cathedral of Seville, he studied with Antonio Riba. He first appeared as a singer and a composer of *tonadillas* in 1789, and became rapidly famous in both. His operetta *El Seductor Arrepentido* and the opera *El Poeta Calculista* were very successful. His international successes began in Paris, and then in Italy where he created the part of Almaviva (Il Barbiere di Seviglia, Rossini) in 1816, specially written for him. From then on he became the principal singer of the music by Rossini in the world, premiering Il Barbiere in London, Paris and New York City. His strong personality clashed frontally with his daughter María (Malibran*) becoming particularly cruel with her. Is there anything better on earth for a singing teacher than to have in his daughter, taught by him, the best soprano in the world? There are some gut, satanic reactions on certain fathers against their own sons that are inexplicable, which the generational gap cannot account for. They are much more perverse and abhorrent than that, a refinement of cruelty. As a teacher, besides his two daughters Maria Malibran* and Pauline Viardot* and his son Manuel García Jr.* (Sitches) he had pupils of the calibre of Mme Méric-Lalande*, and Adolphe Nourrit*.

-GARCIN, JULES AUGUSTE, Called SALOMON (1830 Bourges; d. 1896 Paris) French violinist, teacher and conductor. Garcin was one of the most illustrious violinists in France. Having won the first prize of the Paris Conservatoire* in 1853 as pupil of Alard**, he was admitted to the opera orchestra in 1856. Here he soon became solo violinist, then third conductor in 1871 and chief conductor in 1885. His association with the Société des Concert du Conservatoire* started in 1860, becoming soon solo violinist, and in 1885 principal conductor. In this post he promoted with energy German music. He premiered also Cesar Franck's symphony at the conservatoire in 1889. His long teaching career at the Conservatoire began in 1875 leading the preparatory classes until 1890, when he was promoted to violin teacher, to substitute Massart**. He was also a founder member of the Société Nationale de Musique in 1871. He was decorated Chevalier de la Légion d'honneur* in 1889. Had three Strads: De Barreau of 1715, owned also by Joachim and Mendelssohn; the Defauw, Arbos of 1729; and the Baker, Garcin of 1731.

-GARDEL, CARLOS [CHARLES ROMUALDE GARDES] (1890 Toulouse, France; d. Medellín, Colombia. Aeroplane crash, 1935) Gardel was born in Toulouse, 76 rue Récluanne, the 11 December 1890. French singer settled in Argentina. He never got the Argentinean naturalisation, remaining always French, but it is thanks to him that the Argentinean tango got a universal esteem, being its foremost mythical advocator. The best baritone tango singer in history, Gardel is the quintessence of tango. The illegitimate son of Berthè Gardes, his natural father did not recognise him, and she was expelled from home as a revolting prostitute that had dishonoured the family's good repute. In 1893 Berthè and her baby stowedaway on a steamship to Buenos Aires, to start a new life far from her family, renting a small humble lodging in calle Uruguay 160. Later they moved to the famous calle Corrientes. To earn her living she worked as house cleaner. Gardel remained all his life particularly grateful to his mother upon whom he lavished his most tender cares. When Gardel became universally famous and very rich, being witty, good-looking, with a most winning appearance, and elegant, he was harassed by all the women of the world, but he would not marry, preferring to be free to smother his "mother" with attentions. Forty years after Gardel's birth his natural father, driven by greed of his money, went to Buenos Aires to propose Berthè marriage, but she bluntly rejected, and Gardel did not even speak to him. Besides his abundant discography he made several motion pictures, such as *Espérame* (1933), *Melodía de Arrabal* (1933) *La Casa Seria* (1933) *El Tango en Broadway* (1934), *El Día que me Quieras* (1935), and *Cazadores de Estrellas* (1935) (He was also a consummate song composer, with immortal songs as *El Día que me Quieras*, a remarkable whistler and a superb recitor). His singing style was warm, sweet and pathetic, and was enhanced by the most beguiling *portamento* di voce* which inevitably reminds us of Kreisler, to the point that we may say that Gardel is the Kreisler of tango, a compliment well deserved indeed.

-GARNIER, CHARLES (1825 Paris; d. 1898 id) French architect famous for the creation of the Opera of Paris (Palais Garnier). Other buildings include the casinos of Montecarlo, Bath and Vittel, and the villas at Bordighera, specially his own one.

-GARNIER, PALAIS GARNIER (Opera de Paris, the building)

-GAROFALO, BENVENUTO TISI (called "IL GAROFOLO" (1481 Ferrara; d. ? 1559) Italian painter. His first apprenticeship was under Domenico Panetti, but his first great influence came from Boccaccio Boccaccino* and Lorenzo Costa*. Under their influence his style became fresh and graceful, with gentle, delicate forms and vivid colours. (fresco in the Palazzo di Ludovico il Moro, Ferrara) He was an ardent lover of the minute forms, decorating numerous tables and other furniture, with special mention of the "Arpa estense" Modena. Galleria Estense. He fall also under the influence of Raphael and Michelangelo, the "Madonna e Santi" in the Galleria Estense and "The Baptiste Taking Leave of His Father" in Salvatore, Bologna, being superior examples. He worked also with Dosso Dossi* whose influence we can see in his "San Sebastian" at the Museo nazionale, Naples. Also remarkable is the splendid ceiling in the Palazzo di Ludovico il Moro in Ferrara. The influence of Mantegna* is patent in the ceilings of the Seminario at Ferrara. He was the most prolific Italian painter of the Ferrarese school.

-GARRICK, DAVID (1717 Hereford; d. London 1779) English most famous actor, impresario and director of French Huguenot origin. After his debut in 1741 he became soon the leading Shakespearean actor of the country. His ability to sustain dramatic illusion was notorious, rejecting the pompous declamatory style in vogue. As stage director he suppressed the incidental diversions, concentrating on the drama itself, and took from Paris his advanced lightning technique. Among his pupils stands out Guadagni*, an Italian castrato* for whom Gluck created the role of Orpheus.

-GASPARINI, FRANCESCO: (1668 Camaiore nr. Lucca; d. Roma 1727) Pupil of Corelli** and Pasquini, he excelled as a composer. He started as choir master of the Ospedale della Pieta in Venise. In 1725 he moved to Rome where he was maestro di capella* di San Giovanni di Latran. An excellent teacher he had as pupils Domenico Scarlatti, Quantz**, and Benedetto Marcello. He was a composer, writer and jurist of deserved fame.

-GAYARRE, JULIAN (1843 Valle del Roncal, Navarra; d. Madrid 1890) Legendary Spanish tenor, one of the greatest singers of all times. Born into a humble family, he started working in a foundry in Pamplona, and it was by sheer chance that he turned to singing. In the summer of 1865 the famous maestro Eslava*, sojourned for a few days in Pamplona. He was told that there was a small choir in a smelting works that he should hear. The good-natured composer accepted to hear them and was bowled over by Gayarre's voice that excelled over all. He immediately took him to Madrid to study at the Conservatory. Later he was sent to Milan where he soon acquired fame, making his debut with L'Elisir d'Amore. His triumphs took him to S Petersburg, London, Vienna and the main cities of Europe. He excelled by the sweetness of his voice, both in the treble and in the lows, its wide range, his breath control, and an unmatchable faculty to sustain notes.

-GEVAERT, FRAÇOIS AUGUSTE, BARON DE (1828 Hyusse, nr Oudenaarde; d. Brussels 1908) Belgian composer and musicologist. Studied with Jan Mengal in Ghent. At the age of 15 he became piano teacher at the Ghent conservatory. Won the Belgian prix de Rome with his cantata Le roi Lehar in 1847. He travelled to Spain, Germany and Italy, publishing important studies on the state of music in those countries. He settled in Paris in 1851, where he staged several operas with great success. At the outbreak of the Franco Prussian* war in 1870 he returned to Brussels, succeeding Fetis* as director of the conservatory. During the 37 years he was running it with remarkable energy, he made it grow to be one of the most important centres of musical teaching in the world. He cultivated operas, cantatas and sacred music. But his main works are related with musicology: *Nouveau traité d'instrumentation*, translated to Russian by Tchaikovsky, and to German, English and Portuguese, declared "Monument of universal knowledge". *Cours métodique d'orchestation, Traité d'harmonie théorique et pratique.* He was made baron for composing the national anthem of Congo, on demand of king Leopold II of Belgium.

-GEWANDHAUS: The most important orchestra in Leipzig, it was founded in 1781. Under the enthusiastic zeal of Mendelssohn as its Konzertmeister*, it became one of the best ensembles in Germany. Ferdinand David. Furtwängler and Bruno Walter were its most renowned regular conductors having guest conductors of the calibre of Wagner, Richard Strauss, Brahms, Grieg and Tchaikovski.

-GINGOLD, JOSEF (1909 Brest-Litovsk (Belarus), by the border with Poland, 200 Km E of Warsaw, on the right bank of western Bug River; 330 Km SW of Minsk; d. Bloomington, Indiana USA 1995) American violinist and teacher of Russian origin. After having studied in the USA with Graffman in New York City (1922-27), he went to Europe to study with Ysaye** in Brussels. Leader* in the NBC Toscanini's orch., Detroit SO, and Cleveland SO, he played at the Primrose* String Quartet and the NBC String Quartet. He taught at the Western Reserve University, Indiana University. He was invited to give master classes at the Paris Conservatoire* 1970-74, which he considered to be his greatest honour, and was guest teacher at the Toho Music School in Tokyo. Member of the international juries of Queen Elisabeth, Brussels, and Wieniawski, Poland. He plays the Martinelli Strad of 1683.

-GITLIS, IVRY (1922 Haifa) Israeli violinist. Studied at the Conservatoire de Paris*, claiming first prize in 1935. Later he studied with Enescu, Flesch and Thibaud. First prize in the Thibaud contest. Plays the Strad. Sancy, Kubelik of 1713.

-GLISSANDO: (Italian: to slide) In string instruments the effect of sliding the finger over a string while it is vibrating, so that the sound go from one pitch to another without releasing the string, making the sound "slide" in continuous increase or decrease without detaching any of the intervening pitches. By its own nature the glissando is made very legato*. In voice it is called *portamento*. The most dangerous ornament on all instruments, (slide trombone, string and voice) it becomes horrendous if not used with the maximum good taste, to the point that the French call it *degeulando* (vomiting disgusting). The maximum examples of divine glissandos are Kreisler, on the violin, Gardel, (singing) Segovia (guitar) and Anton Karas (on his zither in the legendary film "The Third Man")

-GLUCK, ALMA [Née Rebe Fiersohn] (1884 Bucharest; d. New York 1938) American soprano of Romanian origin. She went to the USA when very young and married Bernard Gluck under whose name she is known. She made her debut with the Metropolitan Opera Co. in 1909 as Sophie in *Werther* with great success. She devoted mainly to singing recitals, both in her public appearances and in her records. Her style and voice is one of the purest one can hear. She married a second time with the violinist Efrem Zimbalist** , who accompanies her on the violin in many of her performances.

-GOEBEL, REINHARD (1952 Siegen, Westphalia, Germany, 75 Km east of Köln) German violinist. Studied in Cologne and Amsterdam with Maier*, Leonhard and Gawriloff. Founder of Musica Antiqua Köln, they play mainly ancient music. Has toured all the main cities of the world and has an abundant discography, mainly of Bach, Telemann and Biber** .

-GOFFRILER, MATTEO (c1659 Bressanone, at the confluence of Rivers Rienza and Isarco, Trentino, (Alto Adigio) N. Italy; d. Venice 1742) Italian luthier*, started his craft in Venice, under Martin Kaiser. He was the first important maker of the Venetian school.

-GOLDBERG, SZYMON (1909 Wloclawek, midway between Bydgoszcz and Warsaw; d. Toyama, Japan 1993) American conductor and violinist of Polish birth. Studied with Flesch. Leader* of the Dresden PO 1925-28. Furtwängler chose him as leader* of the Berlin PO 1929-34. Played chamber music with Hindemith, Primrose* and sonatas with Lili Kraus and Radu Lupu. Plays a Guarneri of 1734, the "Baron Vitta". Has an abundant discography.

-GOLDEN CALF: Idol worshipped by the Hebrews during the period of the Exodus from Egypt. According to Exodus 32, during the long absence of their leader Moses to Mount Sinai, they asked his brother Aaron, to design a golden calf to worship. When Moses returned with the tables of the Law, given directly to him by God Himself, and saw his people worshipping an idol, he broke the tables (symbolizing the break of the covenant relationship with God) and ordered the golden calf to be melted. The golden calf has symbolized, ever since, the supreme act of apostasy.

-GOLDSCHMIDT, OTTO (1829 Hamburg; d. London 1907) German pianist, composer and conductor. Studied mainly at the conservatory of Leipzig under Mendelssohn, and von Bülow. Played and taught in Hamburg (1846-48) He went to London where he heard Jenny Lind*, "the Swedish nightingale" and accompanied her in Hamburg and on a tour in USA. They got married in 1852. They toured Europe before settling in England in 1858. Taught the piano at the Royal Academy of Music from 1863 becoming vice-principal in 1866. He organised music at the Rugby School (1864-9) In 1875 he founded the London Bach Choir, giving the first complete performance in England of Bach's B minor Mass (St James Hall 1879). Goldschmidt was providential in the life of Sarasate**: after having met him by sheer chance in a railway travel to Frankfurt in 1877, he decided to take care of all Sarasate's main expenditures and earnings, becoming his artistic agent fostering his incomes considerably. An ugly press campaign accused him of spending heedlessly his wife's fortune, calling him a dull pianist and "the Prince Consort of Song", accusing him of squandering her fortune. But she staunchly defended her husband and sued them for libel, winning the case in her favour.

-GOSSEC, FRANÇOIS JOSEPH GOSSE, called GOSSEC (1734 Vergnies, Hainaut, Austrian Netherlands, now Belgium; d. 1829 Passy, annexed to Paris: XVI arrondissement.) One of the most fertile French composers of the XVIII century, he succeeded Rameau as director of the orchestra of the wealthy La Pouplinière*, where he met Johann Stamitz. From 1762 he worked for the princes of Condé and Conti. He wrote operas, symphonies, chamber music, and a lot of patriotic music for the Republique. He directed with Leduc* and Gavinies** the Concert spirituel*, was sous-directeur of the Académie Royale de Music*, director of the newly founded Ecole Royale de Chant* et de Déclamation, member of the Directing Committee of the Opéra, and founding professor of composition of the Paris Conservatoire* . Napoleon named him member of the examining body of the Opéra, and he was one of the first to be distinguished with the Légion d'honneur*. He was an innovator of choral and orchestral writing, adding horns and clarinets and experimenting with novel combinations of instruments and voices that preluded Lesueur* and Berlioz.

-GOUBAUX, PROSPÈRE (1795 Paris; d. id 1859) French writter and innovator, of a very humble origin. As writer we must mention *Les mystères de Paris, Trent ans ou la vie d'un jouer; Le Prétandant* with Eugène Sue*; *Richard d'Arlington* in collaboration with Alexandre Dumas; *Clarisse Harlowe* in collaboration with Legouvé*. He reorganised the whole public teachings in France, and his private school Pension Saint-Victor, later Chaptal became one of the most famous in Paris.

-GOULD, GLENN (1932 Toronto; d. id. 1982) Canadian pianist. After studying in the conservatory of Toronto and a staggering beginning he soon, at the beginning of the 60s, renounced to public appearances, devoting to Hi-Fi recordings. His extreme stravagance is notoriuos in his video recordings. His preferred authors are Schönberg and above all Bach, of whom he has made the best ever recordings. For him there is nothing but Bach in music, the rest of composers being just vulgar, and to stress his view, he has recorded some, distorted on pourpose, works by Bthvn and Brahms, for example, ridiculising them. His version of Liszt transcription for piano of Bthvn's sixth symphony, is a travesty of the original. But in Bach he is "the" supreme interpreter: just what Arnold Schering* was looking for. (see him in the encyplopaedia).

-GRÄDNER, HERMANN (1844 Kiel; d. 1929 Vienna) German violinist, conductor and composer. He studied music with his father, then with Hellmesberger Jr.*. Teacher of the Conservatory of the Gesellshaft der Musikfreunde, conducted also the Singakademie and was professor of the university of Vienna.

-GRAUN, CARL HENRICH (1704 Wahrenbrück; d. Berlin 1759) German composer and Kapellmeister* of the Berlin opera under Frederick the Great. One of the best composers of his time, he wrote 20 operas, numerous cantatas and the passion Der Tod Jesu, his masterpiece. Graun was always at the mercy of Frederick the Great's taste. Anything he did not like was immediately struck out. So he had little choice to express himself freely.

-GUADAGNI, GAETANO (1725 Lodi; d. Padua 1792) Italian castrato*. He started singing in Venice, and in 1748 went to London to sing at the Haymarket theatre. Handel, highly impressed by him, gave him the parts of his Messiah and Samson, previously sung by Susana Cibber. In Vienna his most famous role was Orpheus, specially created for him by Gluck. Friederick the Great presented him with a gold snuff-box set with diamonds. His successes took him to the main cities of Europe. As an actor he was taught by Garrick*, who "took great pleasure in forming him". Burney* describes him as having an *uncommon elegant and noble figure; his countenance replete with beauty, intelligence and dignity; and his attitudes and gestures full of grace and property..."*

-GUADAGNINI: Italian family of luthiers*. The most important of them is Giovanni Baptista. (c1711 Piacenza; d. 1786) He worked in Piacenza, Milan , Cremona, Parma and Turin. His violins are the most valuable of the second half of the XVIII century.

-GUASTAROBBA: Mentioned in the New Grove Dictionary under Campagnoli** to have been his teacher, and defined as a noted pupil of Tartini**.

-GUÉNIN, MARIE ALEXANDRE (1744 Maubeuge (France), midway between Reims (Fr.) and Gent (Belgium), by the frontier with Belgium; d. Estampes 1835) French violinist and composer. Pupil of Capron* and Gavinies**. Played in duo with Capron*, Stamitz** and Paisible* in the Concert spirituel*. Played in the orch, of the Concert spirituel*, Musique du Chambre du roi, and the Opera.

-GUIGNON, JEAN-PIERRE [Giovanni Pietro Ghignone] (1702 Turin; d. Versailles 1774) Italian violinist, naturalized French. One of the best pupils of Somis**, he made his debut in Paris at the newly founded Concert spirituel* playing a sort of contest with Anet*. In 1733 he was named Ordinaire de la musique du roi*. Leclair**, who was also first violin* of this ensemble, unable to bear his exasperating competition, just resigned from his post out of shear jealousy. Naturalized French in 1741 he was honoured that same year as *Roy et maître des ménétriers et joueurs d'instruments*, which accorded him the right to inspect musical and dancing institutions all over the country. Guignon, in company of Mondonville*, made several triumphant tournes in France. A very active violinist, he was among the most brilliant virtuosos of his era, matching and even surpassing the playing of great performers such as Anet*, Guillemain*, Gavinies**, Mondonville* and Leclair**. After 1750 Guignon did not perform in public. (Another victim of the 50s)

-GUILLEMAIN, LOUIS GABRIEL 1705 Paris; d. 1770 Chaville) French composer and violinist. Pupil of Somis** he became in 1737 Ordinair de la chapelle* et de la chambre du roi, entering to the service of the queen in 1759. He was, after Leclair**, the best violinist in France.

-GUILLOTINE: Attributed to the French physician Joseph-Ignace Guillotin (1738 Saintes Charente-Maritime Department, along Charente River 90 Km N of Bordeaux; 60 Km W of Angoulême, in the centre of the *cognac* region(France); d. ? 1810) of whom it derives its name. This machine for capital punishment was already in use in Genoa in the XVI century. M. Guillotin was elected to the National Assembly in 1789, and it was at his instigation that a law was passed requiring all death sentences to be carried out by means of this machine, that would make the execution as painless as possible. At the same time it would abolish the privilege of death by decapitation confined so far to nobles. But it was not him who actually designed the guillotine, but another physician, Dr. Louis, in 1792. Under the Terror* Guillotin was imprisoned, but luckily he had not to experiment his own machine, being acquitted the 9 Thermidor (see calendar* of French Revolution). He died twenty years later of natural death.

-HAACK, KARL (1751Potsdam; d. id 1819) German violinist and composer. Direct pupil of Benda**, joined the orch. of the prince of Prussia in Potsdam and in 1796 became leader of the royal chamber ensemble. He was very appreciated in Berlin and Potsdam, perpetuating Benda's school through his pupils, mainly Möser* and Maurer*.

-HABENECK, FRANÇOIS ANTOINE (1781 Méziers, 40 Km west of Paris, by River Seine; d. 1849 Paris) French conductor, composer, violinist and teacher. Son of a musician from Mannheim he was pupil of Baillot**. First prize of the Paris conservatoire* in 1804. Violinist of the Opéra and the Opéra-Comique, he conducted the Concerts français, and later those of the Société des concerts du Conservatoire* de Paris, which he inaugurated with Bthvn's heroic symphony (3rd). He then premiered in Paris the rest of Bthvn symphonies, being the great propagator of his music in France. Professor at the Paris conservatoire (1825-48). He wrote a violin method. Owned the Strad Foutaine, Habeneck of 1736.

-HAENDEL, IDA 1924 (b 1924 Chelm, 70 Km east of Lublin, Poland) British violinist of Polish birth. Won the Warsaw conservatory gold medal in 1933 and the first Huberman Prize. Later she took lessons with Enescu and Flesch. During World War II she played for the red cross. Has toured America, Russia and Canada. An emotional reserve she appears rather cool. Has written "Woman with Violin: an Autobiography, London 1970. Valuable instruments: A Guarneri and a Strad of 1696.

-HALLÉ, SIR CHARLES: (1819 Hagen, Westphalia, d. Manchester 1895) English pianist and conductor of German origin. Studied first with his father practising the piano and chamber music within a cozy family childhood. He replaced his ailing father to conduct the Zauberflöte and der Freyschütz with only 12 years. After some studies of harmony* at Darmstad with Johann Christian Rinck, he went to Paris with the idea to take piano lessons from Kalkbrenner*, but having no time to spare he directed him to his pupil Osborne* with whom he had a few lesson, but he was virtually self-taught. Here he became friend of Cherubini, (to whom he discovered, to his great pleasure, the Bthvn sonatas, with which he was not at all familiar), of Chopin, Liszt, Berlioz and Wagner, settling later in England. In 1857 he founded the Hallé orchestra in Manchester. As from 1893 he was director of the Royal

Manchester College of Music. He was the first pianist ever to play the complete Bthvn sonatas in Paris and London.

-HARMONIC SOUND OR HARMONICS: Scientifically, every sound, such as we hear it, is the result of making vibrate a column of air or a string. This vibration of the whole string is primarily the pure sound, but it has a series of concomitant vibrations, that derive from the fact that the string vibrates not only as a whole but also in all its subdivisions. The principal sound is called "fundamental sound". The other subdivisions are called harmonic sounds, and result of the division of the string in two halves, three thirds, four fourths, etc. All the harmonics and the fundamental sounds vibrate simultaneously. Every harmonic is therefore named after the division in nth times the length of the string. The 2nd harmonic, the division of the string by two, results in a frequency double of the fundamental; the 3rd multiplies it by three, and so on. These harmonics constitute the timbre of every instrument and of the human voice, and mark their intensity. The harmonic sounds were discovered first by father Marin Mersenne*. The first to study them in depth in relation with the violin were Mondonville* and L'Abbé le Fils**. In string instruments, guitar, violin, the harmonics can be singled out and make them sound independently by fingering slightly at a certain point (node) of the string. They have a very high frequency sound, like the crystal sound of the Harmonica* (musical glasses) with which they bear a remarkable resemblance. As for the simultaneity of the fundamental with its harmonics*, Berlioz, who was gifted with perfect pitch, was able to recognize in the Weimar bells many harmonics that sounded together with the fundamental pitch, and in particular he heard one of them play at the same time the seventh minor and the octave* [fundamental sound in F, a resonance in F octave*, and the seventh E flat*]. (Berlioz: Opened letter to List published in the *Feuilleton des Debats* August 28th, 1843).

-HARMONICA (Musical glasses) An instrument made of crystal glasses graded by size, that are rubbed with a humid finger producing all the musical semitones of the scale*. They can be tuned more precisely by adding water to raise their natural pitch. Gluck, Berlioz and Mozart (quintet for harmonica, flute, viola, oboe and cello K. 617) were fascinated with it. Benjamin Franklin made substantial improvements in it.

-HARMONY: The basic science of music, that deals, in general, with the harmonious relations between all sounds in music, more specifically the different voices of a polyphonic* work, and the sounds of a chord*.

-HASSE, JOHANN ADOLF (1699 Bergedorf, 15 Km S E of Hamburg – Venice 1783) German composer of the first magnitude. Although his name may not be as familiar as Scarlatti or J. C. Bach, he was the most widely admired composer of italian opera-seria in Germany and Italy. In close collaboration with Metastasio*, the best poet and librettist of his time, his operas, masses, vocal and instrumental music are among the finest in history.

-HAUPTMANN, MORITZ (1792 Dresden; d. 1868 Leipzig) German theorist and composer. Studied violin with Spohr**. Member of the Royal chapel* in Dresden (1812) Music teacher to prince Repnine in Russia, and violinist at the orch of the court of Cassel under Spohr (1822-42) Kantor* of the Tomasschule in Leipzig (1842) and professor of harmony* and composition at the conservatory of this city from 1843. That same year he became editor of the Allgemeine musikalische Zeitung* and in 1850 he founded with Schumann the Bach Gesellshaft. As theorist his main works are *Erläuterungen zu J S Bach Kunst der Fugue**, and *Die Nature der Harmonik und Metric*, where he discussed the harmonic* system based upon a Hegelian dialectic relation between thesis, antithesis and synthesis, as follows: the tonic* is the thesis, the antithesis is the fifth (dominant), or the stronger opposing factor, resulting in the interval* of 5th which is neither consonant nor dissonant, and which is completed by a mediating note the major third (synthesis) Thesis, antithesis and synthesis conform the major triad, which is the smallest intelligible musical unit. The key* system is based on a triad of triads. Hauptmann's theory is based on the harmonic* dualism of major* and minor* modes*. Hauptmann owned a valuable Strad, the Bott, Cambridge, of 1725, owned also by McCormack and Spohr.

-HAUTETERRE, ELISABETH [also know as Halteterre, Hoteterre] (flourish 1735-65) Pupil of Leclair** she dedicated to him her first book of sonatas for violin solo and continuo*. She appeared at a Concert spirituel* in April 1737, where the Mercure* says *she played with all the intelligence, vivacity and precision imaginable*. A section in her first book devoted to bow strokes for novices, indicates that she devoted also to teaching.

-HAWKINS, SIR JOHN (1719 London; d. id 1789) English attorney and music historian. Contemporary of Burney*, he published, at the same time as him, also a monumental work: *A General History of Science and Practice of Music*, rather anarchical in its presentation and showing a great disconformity with the music of his time, particularly the instrumental, "noise without harmony*".

-HEINE, HEINRICH (1797 Düsseldorf; d. Paris 1856) First magnitude German poet, journalist and writter, highly controversial, particularly in his own country. Of Jewish parents, he was the author of the most popular lieders* in Germany, and of many poems, sweet and sour. In his journey histories he combines poetry, social criticism, and autobiography. His sarcastic, satirical writing caused him grave difficulties with the German authorities, who tried to silence him through censorship. But he went to Paris, and from there he went on with his aggressive satires. Here he became the painter of Paris for the Germans and the correspondent in Paris for the German journals. During Hitler's reign his name was forbidden as a damned poet, but his works continued to be printed under the signature "unknown writer". Involuntary homage to him, for everybody knew who it was.

-HERRANDO, JOSÉ (? c1700 – c1750 Madrid) Spanish violinist, composer and pedagogue. Pupil of Corelli**, he performed for the court of the duke of Alba. Between 1732-1762 he was first violin* of the Capilla* Real del Convento de la Encarnación in Madrid. His main contribution to the art of violin is his treatise *Arte y Puntual Explicación del Modo de Tocar el Violín* (Paris, 1756) the first Spanish publication on violin playing.

-HERTEL, JOHANN WILLHELM (1727 Eisenach, 50 Km W of Erfurt, Thuringia, at the confluence of Hörsel and Nesse Rivers; d. Schwering, 1789) German violinist, keyboard player and composer. Member of a distinguished family of musicians, he was taught by the most eminent teachers of his time: C. P. E. Bach, C. H. Graun* and Benda**. He was court composer in Schwering, and private secretary to princess Ulrike in the same town. In his youth he was considered one of the best virtuosi of the violin. He was an outstanding composer in instrumental music, but his notoriety was in his vocal works, that placed him among the most tasteful composers of the late 18th century.

-HESS, MYRA, Dame. (1890 London; d. id 1965) English pianist. One of the most formidable pianists of the XX century, her astonishing, energetic touch is one of the most powerful I ever heard; it is just awesome, and it surpasses many of our modern pianists, with a much more advanced technique, be them men or women. (she owes it to the relaxation technique of her teacher Matthay* [similar to that of Liszt]) All this technique is mastered by a staggering musicality and delicacy. First studied at the Guildhall School of Music, then at the Royal Academy of Music with Tobias Matthay*, a major influence on her career. In 1907 she started a career of international concertist that took her in triumph to Europe, and the USA. During World War II she gave daily concerts at the National Gallery in London, mostly without fee. With a wide range of repertory, she excelled in Bthvn, Mozart, and the romantics, without forgetting Bach. For her achievement as a public benefactor she was made Dame Commander of the Order of the British Empire. Honorary doctorates of several universities, Cambridge, Reading, London, St Andrews, Manchester, Durham. Her very scarce discography, that shows her in her full magnificence is an absolute must.

-HESS, WILLY (1859 Mannheim, Baden-Wurttemberg Land, SW Germany, by the Rhine River at the mouth of the canalized River Neckar, halfway Mainz-Stuttgart; d. Berlin 1939) German violinist. Studied with his father, a pupil of Spohr**, and later with Joachim** in Berlin. Leader* of the opera and museum concert orchs. at Frankfurt am Main. Teacher at the conservatory of Rotterdam 1886, conservatory of Cologne (1895-1903), and at the Royal Academy of Music in London (1903-4) .In 1910 he settled in Berlin to teach at the Hochschule. Also a remarkable quartet player. Highly influenced by Joachim, he played on a G. B. Guadagnini*.

-HILLER, JOHANN ADAM (1728 Webdisch-Ossig, nr Görlitz; d. Leipzig 1804) Composer, music critic and pedagogue. His role in the development of musical life in Leipzig was capital: Director of the Grosses Koncert (1763-71); founder of a school of singing in 1771 and director of the Gewandhaus* from 178; Kantor* at the Tomasschule (1789-1801). Founder and editor of the Wöchentliche Nachrichten, forerunner of the Allgemeine musikalische Zeitung*; Composer of many delightful songs and practically the founder of the Singspiel* in Germany. He wrote also several sacred and secular vocal works.

-HOFKAPELLE German: High chapel*

-HÜTTENBRENNER, ANSELM (1794 Graz; d. Ober-Andritz nr. Graz 1868) Austrian composer. Son of a wealthy landowner he studied law and the piano in Graz, going later to Vienna to study with Salieri. He became friendly with Bthvn and Schubert. Kapellmeister* of the Steirmärkischer Musikverein in Vienna in 1825. Wrote several operas, symphonies, secular and church music, songs and piano pieces. His memoires are interesting, and reveal importante facets of the life of Schubert.

-IMBAULT, JEAN-JERÔME. (1753 Paris; d. id 1832) French violinist. The favourite pupil of Gavinies**, he gave a highly promising concert in 1770. But his glory was ephemeral, and by 1880 his natural shyness was remarked by the

346

Mercure*. He participated in many French orchestras, sometimes as leader* and soloist. He made a considerable fortune as music publisher.

-IMITATION: We found it in the origins of western harmony*, being also its first manifestation. The *Rota of Reading* of 1250 *Summer is icumen in* is made in imitation. It consists in the repetition of a tune by another voice in the same composition, but with a certain gap between them and generally at a different pitch. It reminds the echo effect. Imitation is also at the base of the fugue*.

-INGRES, JEAN-AUGUSTE DOMINIQUE (1780 Montauban; d. Paris 1867) One of the most salient French painters of the XIX century. Leader of the French tradition of the Neo-classical school, he is distinguished by his crystal lighted atmosphere, cool design and a special care of contour lines. His eternal idol was Raphael. His best paintings: *La Vierge à l'Hostie* (1854, musée d'Orsay), *Le Bain Turque* (1862 Louvre) *La Venus Anadyomène* (1848 musée Chantilly). He exerted an enormous influence in his time, forming a great number of distinguished disciples. Ingres also went into history for his remarkable talent in violin playing. He played, when still a child, at the orchestra of the chapelle* of the bishop of Montauban. He later entered the second violins of the orchestra of the theatre Capitole of Toulouse, where he played as soloist a concerto by Viotti with immense success. In Paris he took lessons from Baillot** in 1813 and later with Sauzay*. Having won the painting Prix de Rome he went as *pensionnaire* to the city of the seven hills*. It was here that he met Paganini, at the house of the Austrian Ambassador in Rome, prince Wenzel von Kaunitz-Rietberg, in 1819, a great music lover. It was here that Paganini played all the quatuors of Bthvn, requesting Ingres to play the second violin. When he returned to Paris in 1824 he played frequently at the quatuor of Baillot, and in company of Sauzay, as well. Liszt, in a letter to Massart** from Rome March 1, 1839 says: *I see very often M. Ingres who is very kind with me. We play a lot of music together. Did you know he plays very charmingly the violin? We have the project to play together all the music by Mozart and Bthvn.*(Franz Liszt. L'Artiste, le Clerc. Letter VII. J. Vier. Editions du Cèdre. Paris 1950) He played with Liszt the Bthvn's sonata "Kreutzer", provoking Liszt's enthusiasm, described in one of the Lettres d'un bachelier es musique, and fully transcribed in book four, Paganini). He also played frequently with the great French opera composer Ambroise Thomas*. In French *le violon d'Ingres** means one's favourite hobby. The great appreciation he drew from all these masters contrasted sharply with the opinions of other important musicians like Hallé and Gounod who despised him scornfully. Gounod in his Mémoires d'un Artiste, Paris 1886, p. 87, says: *"M. Ingres played the violin. He was not a professional, even less a virtuoso, but he had played, in his youth, at the orchestra of the theatre of his native city, Montauban."* And Hallé, in his Autobiography, says: *[Ingres] Great artist as he was, with an immense reputation, he thought less of his paintings than of his violin playing, which, to say the least of it, was vile.* (of course Ingres was not a virtuoso, but as he himself said: "I have no the dexterity nor the skill of the true violinists, but I stop at the right note", alluding to his perfect intonation. *Lumière des Cimes. – La France – Trésor des Cités – Montauban. Revue de synthèse du vivant, n° 30 [hiver 1985-86].)* Who are right, Liszt, Baillot, Sauzay, Thomas and Paganini, who played with him happily, non feeling dishonoured to accompany him, or Gounod and Hallé? I rather incline for Paganini, Liszt and the others.

-INSTITUT NATIONAL DE MUSIQUE: Having been abolished the École supérieur de la garde nationale* by the *Commune de Paris**, Sarrette*, once the Commune was over, profited of the occasion to increase its size, reaffirming its goals, and redefining its statutes, obtaining a decree (1793) that transformed it into the Institut national de musique*. See École supérieur de musique de la garde nationale*.

-INTERVAL is the distance between two notes of different names, including both, expressed in tones and semitones, or in semitones only, depending on what kind of scale* they belong to: a) if it is to the diatonic* scale*, which includes tone and semitone intervals, the distance will be expressed in tones and semitones; or b) if it is to the chromatic* or dodecaphonic* scale based on semitones only, which comprises twelve semitones (from Latin dodeca= twelve) the distance will be expressed in semitones only. The interval, for instance, between *do* and *fa* is (do,re,mi,fa=4) and between *do* and *mi* (do, re, mi=3). The names of intervals are the result of dividing the total distance between the two pitches by the intervening notes in equal parts: following our example, the interval between *do* and *fa* is a "4th of two tones and one semitone", and that between *do* and *mi* is a "3rd of two tones". There is only one exception to this rule: two notes of different names (*spelling*) can amount to the same pitch, despite their different names. Since what counts is really the pitch, both are the same and single note, call it one or the other name, and therefore there is no interval between them: it may happen between two notes separated by one or two semitones. It is enough to increase or decrease one of them by that semitone, adding to it an accidental*, a sharp* notation #, which increases it a semitone, or a flat* signature *b*, to make them one and the same pitch. For example *do # (sharp*)* and *re b* (flat*) are the same note, either of them: do sharp or re flat, doesn't matter which. There is no interval between C sharp and D flat. It is what in harmony* is known as "enharmony*". Mi is the same as Fa *b*, flat , both are enharmonic*. Or said in English spelling B # = C = D *bb*. D must be lowered two semitones to be equal to C because it has an interval of a whole tone with C, therefore it has two flat signatures. A bit complicated, I'm afraid!

-ISTOMIN, EUGENE (1925 New York) American pianist. Studied with Rudolf Serkin* at the Curtis Institute, Philadelphia. Won the Leventritt Award in 1943. Active touring around the world. Plays mainly XIX century works.

-JACOBI, GEORG (1840 Berlin; d. London 1906) German composer, conductor and violinist. After having studied in Berlin with Eduard and Leopold Ganz, he moved to Brussels in 1849 to study with Beriot**. When Beriot ceased his lessons he went to Paris to study with Massart**, claiming first prize in 1861. He played at the orch of L'Opera Comique, and won the competitive examination for the post of first violin* at the Opéra. He formed his own string orch of 16 members playing concerts at the Société Nationale des Beaux Arts. In 1869 he conducted the Bouffes-Parisiennes, staging many Offenbach performances. When the Franco Prussian* war started he went to London where he remained till his death. Here he conducted the Alhambra Theatre and the Crystal Palace orch. He taught at the Royal College of Music from 1896.

-JACOBINS: Club des Jacobins. (Jacobeans) The most famous political group of the French Revolution, representing the far left. They led the revolutionary government with their extreme equalitarism and violence from mid 1793 to mid 1794. They originated at Versailles (nr Paris) in April 1789, moving to Paris in October of the same year, where they held their sessions in a former convent of Dominican fathers, known as the Jacobins. Highly organised, they had their affiliated local clubs in every important provincial city of the country, through which they disseminated their countersigns and orders, being, at the same time, perfectly informed of what went on everywhere. They became the main instrument of the Reign of Terror*. Their great leader was Robespierre*.

-JAMBE-DE-FER, PHILIBERT (c1515 Champelite; d. c1566 Lyon) French composer. He flourished in Lyons where he composed numerous psalms, a set of them dedicated to king Charles IX for his entry in Lyons. He also wrote a treatise for amateurs: *Epitome musical des tons, sons et accordz, es voix humaine, fleutes d'Alleman, fleutes à neuve trous, violes & violons.* Lyons 1556. A capital source of information of the music of that time, he explains the rudiments of music, such as scales*, notation, solmization, keys*, etc. He then studies the tuning and playing technique of the flute, viola da gamba, and the violin, the first important treatise to study our instrument.

-JANIN, JULES: (1804 Saint-Etienne; d. Paris 1874) French literary reviewer at the Journal des Débats (1830-74). Illustrious journalist and novelist, he was one of the main pillars of the *Journal des Debats.* Garrulous, and opportunist, he abused of the powers of the press for his own benefit and to the detriment of his enemies. Very well paid, he was popular among the followers of the monarchy of Louis-Philippe. His writings seem today vacuous and nonsense, but at the time he enjoyed a reputation of a brilliant and witty writter. But his notoriety in history derives mainly from having provoked the fury of Baudelaire, who wrote a "Letter to J. Janin" in which his attacks are contrasted with the capital aspirations of the new Romanticism: *"Death!... Melancholic sky of modern poetry. First magnitude stars".* Janin wrote the words for Berlioz's *Chants des Chemins de Fer.*

-JESUITS. Most renowned in Germany for their schools, which were similar to conservatories, where they taught, among other subjects, music, in particular, to sing and to play upon instruments. They were free institutions, mainly devoted to the poor, similar to the old conservatories in Italy. Many musicians have been brought here, not least Leopold Mozart.

-JETÉ: (French "jeter": to throw). Also called "ricochet" (French "ricocher": to bounce) and getatto (Italian "getare": to throw) This bowing is based entirely on the natural bounce of the stick. Similar to the staccato*, several notes, clearly separated, and well detached from one another, are played in one bow direction, either up or down, but instead of provoking every bounce, like in the *flying staccato** there is only one single impulse, that which occurs when the bow is "thrown" onto the string for the first note. After this the bow is allowed to jump by itself, following the initial impulse, as would do a rubber ball.

-JOMELLI, NICCOLO (1714 Aversa, 10 Km N of Naples; d. Naples 1774) First magnitude Italian composer. He was the real reformer of the opera seria far before Gluck. He was most prolific both in opera and in religious music, with an imposing repertoire of opera seria, comic operas, intermezzos, pastorales, oratorios, passions, sacred cantatas, and instrumental music.

-JULLIEN, LOUIS: Had 36 names. Viz. [1) Louis, 2) Cesar, 3) Julio, 4) Jules-Bazin, 5) Georges, 6) Maurice,7) Roch, 8) Antonio, 9) Jean, 10) Eugène, 11) Josué, 12) Jules-dela-Plane, 13) Thomas-Thomas, 14) Pierre, 15) Thomas, 16) Michel, 17) Thomas, 18) Luc, 19) Dieudonné, 20) Vincent, 21) Emanuel, 22) Abel, 23) Adolphe, 24) Albert, 25) Noé, 26) Bertrand, 27) Lucien, 28) Barthélemi, 29) Daniel, 30) Artus, 31) Pierre-Manuel, 32) Alphonse, 33) Joseph-le-Brun, 34) Joseph-Barème, 35) Alexandre, 36) Arbon] (1812 Sisteron, 25 km NW of Digne; d. Paris 1860) French composer and conductor. Everything in Jullien's life has something of a craziness and extravagance, beginning with his 36 first names, going through his most extravagant life, and ending in a lunatic asylum where he met his unhappy end. The son of the bandmaster of Sisteron, he had 36 godfathers, namely all the members of the Sisteron Philharmonic from whom he derives his 36 Christian names. Studied in the Paris Conservatory*. From 1836 to 39 he lead the entertainment and dances at the Jardin Turc, with great popularity. In 1938 he went to London and gave numerous concerts there and all around the British Isles with enormous success, his aim being to popularise classical music by giving his tickets very cheap, and mixing sublime music with much lighter music that would attract as much public as possible. (the one shilling public) He invited also the most renowned soloists (among them Monasterio**) He gave a most extravagant cult to his conducting, with a jewelled baton and dandy dresses, endowing all his concerts with a sumptuous flamboyance. He established the early "Promenade Concerts" which were to be so popular ever since. He was interned in an asylum at the end of his days in Paris.

-KALKBRENER, FRÉDÉRIC [FRIEDERICH WILHELM]: (1785 ? near Kassel; d. Enghien-les-bains, northern outer suburb of Paris, 10 Km W of Le Bourget airport. 1849) French pianist, teacher and composer of German origin. Studied first with his father, then at the Paris conservatoire, winning first prize in piano and harmony* in 1801. In 1815 he moved to England, where he won his great reputation, touring Ireland and Scotland. From 1825 to 1835 he was the foremost pianist and teacher in Paris. His play was crystal clear, neat and distinct, with a special ability for melodious legato passages. His technique was based on the total independence of hand and fingers from the arm, playing from wrists instead of arms. the opposite extreme of Liszt, who relied on the whole elbow, arm and hand weight. He invented an adjustable horizontal rail, parallel to the keyboard on which the forearms ought to rest, with the aim of developing the total independence of hands and fingers. Those familiar with the piano need not much imagination to figure out that he must have played similarly to Horowitz: if you see him play at close range his forearms seem actually to be resting on this devise, such is the total relaxation of his hands and fingers. His most famous pupil was George Osborne*.

KAMMEL, ANTONIN (1730 Belec, Bohemia; d. London 1787) Czech Composer and violinist. His first education was at the Patres Piares College, Slany, where he received a thorough musical education. Studied philosophy and law in Prague 1751-54. Later he went to Italy to study with Tartini. Excelled in his adagios. Wrote only instrumental music. A bit too sweet at some places, he was very successful in his life time.

-KANTOR: German: singer. The principal, solo singer. In Germany he was also the director of music of any educational establishment connected with the church. It was one of the most highly esteemed jobs in Germany. Bach was Kantor of the Tomasschule in Leipzig from 1723 until his death. The Kantor had among his duties to compose, to train the choir and to direct, and teach music.

-KAPELLE: German: Chapel*.

-KAPELLMEISTER: German: musician, managing director of the orchestra of the Chapel*. He is the main responsible of all the affairs concerning the Chapel*, and generally, also, its conductor.

-KATCHEN, JULIUS 1926 Long Branch, N. J. USA, port city 50 Km S. of New York City; d. Paris 1969) One of the most formidable pianists of all times, besides his complete command of classical music he had the added virtue of having in his blood the sheer sense of "rhythm", like a good black jazz pianist. This gave him the possibility to play Gershwin and the moderns to the manner born. He was totally at home with all the romantics, particularly Brahms, and with Bthvn as well, but he could also play a galant, sweet Mozart. He combined all this with a superb academic tuition, having graduated in Philosophy from the Haverford College at 19. All these ingredients make of him the ideal interpreter of the Bthvn's sonata nr 32, Op 111, where at the end of the "Arietta*" comes a syncopated, very fast, rhythmic section, marked "l'istesso tempo", that he plays with an amazing jazz rhythm that makes you think it is being played by the very Fats Waller* himself.

-KELZ, MATTHIAS (c1635 Schongau, 60 Km S-W of Munich, Upper Bavaria; d. 1695 Augsburg, 55 Km N-W of Munich) German composer and government official. Made his music studies at the Jesuit* Gymnasium in Augsburg. His violin sonatas, very demanding for the player, remind those of Biagio Marini*.

-KEMPFF, WILHELM (1895 Jüterbog, midway Leipzig-Berlin; d. Positano 25 Km S. of Napoli) German pianist. Studied at the Berlin Hochschule für Musik. Started his international career in 1916. Acclaimed as a distinguished pianist, his many recordings attest to it. Perhaps a little dry with the pedal*, he only followed the current of his times, that demanded a very restricted use of it, as is patent in Walter Gieseking. Charles Hallé, also, reports (autobiography) how he found at the start of one of the piano concertos he played that the pedal was not working, so he had to play it all without it. Next day a press critic praised his wise, "restricted" use of the pedal. An eminent teacher, as well, he was director of the Stuttgart Musikhochschule and gave master classes at the Marmorpalais in Potsdam.

-KERLL, JOHANN KASPAR (1627 Adorf, Vogtland, 60 Km S. of Gera, by the frontier with the Czech Rep.; d. Munich 1693) German composer and organist. He studied in Rome with Carissimi and Frescobaldi. Went to Brussels where he was organist of the chapel* of Léopold Wilhelm. In 1656 he was Kapellmeister* to the Bavarian Elector in Munich. In 1673 he settled his residence in Vienna till his death. All his operas were staged during his life. He composed also instrumental music.

-KEY: called also tonality*; see scale and octave.

-KOCIAN, JAROSLAV (1883 Usti nad Orlici, 135 Km E of Prague; d. Prague 1950) Czech violinist, teacher and composer. First studied with his father a violin teacher, then at Prague conservatory 1896-1901. He gained immediate prestige as international soloist touring Europe and America. Professor in Odessas's conservatory (1907-9) leader of the Odessa Czech quartet. Professor and rector at the Masters' School of the Prague Conservatory. Among his pupils stands out Suk**.

-KONZERTMEISTER German: Leader* of the orchestra.

-KREUTZER, AUGUST (1788 Versailles; d. Paris 1832) French composer and violinist, brother of Rodolphe Kreutzer**. He studied at the Paris conservatoire* with his brother Rodolphe, winning first prize in 1801. He worked at the orchestras of the Théâtre Favart, of the Opera (1801) and of the Imperial Chapel* in 1804. He replaced his brother Rodolphe at his death as teacher at the Paris Conservatory.

-KREUTZER, LEON (1817 Paris; d. Vichy 1864) French composer, pianist and writer of music. Son of August Kreutzer*, who was the brother of Rodolphe**. He wrote for *L'Union, Révue Contemporaine, Révue et Gazette musicale de Paris, L'Opinion Publique*, and *Le Théâtre*. He collaborated in the articles *L'Opéra* and *L'Opéra Comique* of the *Enciclopédie du XIX siècle*. It was him who wrote to Massart: *You make your Stradivarius tremble!*.

-KULENKAMPFF, GEORG (1898 Bremen; d. Schaffhaussen 1948) German violinist. Studied with Willy Hess* in Berlin, where he himself taught 1923-26. Succeeded Flesch at the conservatory of Lucerne. Very cherished in Germany. Had the Strad Kuhlenkampff, Nadaud of 1734.

-LA BORDE, JEAN-BENJAMIN (1734 Paris; d. Id. 1794) French composer, violinist and writer on music. Born to an aristocratic family his life was full of vicissitudes, with an irresponsible youth, he was ruined more than once, and had many intrigues in court. Confident of king Louis XV, and very influential with Marie-Antoinette. Friend of Beaumarchais and Voltaire, during the revolution he escaped Paris to live quietly in Rouen and Val St. Germain. But he was caught in Rouen, arrested and guillotined*. His publications include *Essai sur la musique ancienne et moderne*, Paris 1780 and *Mémoires sur les proportions musicales*, Paris 1781. He wrote opera comiques* such as *Gilles, garçon peintre*; *Le dormeur éveillé* and *Le revenant*.

-LAFONT, CHARLES PHLIPPE (1781 Paris; d. Tarbes 1839) French violinist and composer. He first studied with his mother, sister of violinist Bertheaume*, and later with his uncle Bertheaume. He then studied two years with Rodolphe Kreutzer** and some time with Rode**. His first success was at the Concert Français in Paris (1802). When Rode left for Russia, freed of competition, he soon became one of the leading violinist in France. He replaced Rode in St. Petersburg as solo violinist to the Tsar remaining there six years. In 1815 he was named solo violinist to Louis XVIII. He had a memorable encounter in Milan with Paganini playing both in a sort of contest at La Scala. Although Paganini stated in a letter, magnanimously in all respects, that *he had greater beauty of tone than him*, it is, nevertheless, a tall tale hard to swallow, indeed. Notwithstanding, Lafont represented for a long period the culmination of the French school of Viotti**, Kreutzer and Rode. Spohr** ranked him first among French violinists, praising his "beauty of tone, greatest purity, power and grace", but lacking deepness of feelings. (It is shocking to see how everybody seemed to be the best violinist in France for Spohr, giving an appearance of great fickleness in his musical admirations: 1) He considers the Kreutzers as the most cultivated in Paris. 2) Rode particularly captivated him. 3) And the same story for Lafont. Who of the four? Make up your mind Mr. Spohr!! His valuable instruments include: Guarneri del Gesu Lafont of 1735. Strad Lafont, Haff of 1699; Strad Lafont, Lady Tennant of 1699; and Strad La Font, Laurie of 1708.

-LAHOUSSAYE, PIERRE NICOLAS (1727 Chalone sur Saône, 55 Km S. of Dijon, in the Burgundy region.; d. 1801 Regensburg, called also Ratisbona, on the right bank of River Danube, 90 Km N. of Munich) French composer and violinist. Pupil of Tartini**. Prodigy child. Tartini valued him to the point of declaring that he would become the "terror of violinists". In sharp contrast to these predictions he embraced the important, though much more obscure, job of conductor of the orchestras of the opera in London, the Concert spirituel*, Comédie Italienne and Théâtre de Monsieur. Teacher of the conservatory of Paris. Sacked from it for economic reasons he devoted to private teaching, until he went deaf. His last years were spent in poverty and oblivion.

-LALANDE, JOSEPH-JÉRÔME LEFRANÇAIS DE. (1732 Bourg en Bresse [France]; d. Paris 1807) Famous French astronomer. Studied first law in Paris and became interested in astronomy when he met the noted astronomer J. N. Delile in the hotel Cluny in Paris. In co-ordination with the work of Nicolas L. Lacaille in Cape of Good Hope, he went to Berlin in 1751 to make lunar observations, which led to the calculation of the Moon's distance to Earth. This feat granted him admission to the Academy of Berlin, and the post of adjunct astronomer of the Academy of France. He organised international co-ordination to observe Venus, which culminated in an accurate calculation of the distance Sun-Earth. In 1762 he was appointed professor of astronomy in the College of France, Paris. He instituted the Prize Lalande, awarded yearly to the main astronomical contribution of each year. His tables of planetary positions were the best available until the beginning of the 19th century. Among his works we must cite *Bibliographie astronomique*, *Traité d'astronomie* and *Histoire céléste Française*. Also his voluminous *Voyage d'un Français en Italie*, where he relates the dream of Tartini on his Devil's Trill* Sonata.

-LAMBERT, MICHEL: (1610 Champigny-sur-Veude, nr. Loudun, 70 Km SW of Tours, France; d. 1696 Paris) French composer, singer and singing teacher. A choirboy at Champigny, he was admitted as page in the chapel* of Gaston of Orleans in Paris, the elder brother of Louis XIII. He then was violinist and singer in Mlle. De Montpensier's* six violins ensemble. In 1661 he was appointed *Maître de Musique de la Chambre du Roy*. Lully** married his daughter Madeleine, with great pomp, at St Eustache*, in the presence of Louis XIV and his queen Marie-Thérèse of Austria. For the next three years he collaborated with Lully on the music of several ballets. He was reputed to be the best singing teacher in Paris.

-LASSEN, EDUARD (1830 Copenhagen; d. Weimar 1904) Belgian composer of Danish origin. Studied at Brussels conservatory winning prizes for piano (1844) and composition (1847) and the Belgian Prix de Rome, which enabled him to tour Germany and Rome. Liszt helped him greatly. He succeeded him as court music director in Weimar. A good friend of Don Jesus de Monasterio** (from the Brussels conservatory) there is a moving anecdote with him. (See 1836 Monasterio).

-LAURENCIE, LIONEL DE LA (1861 Nantes; d. Paris 1933) French musicologist. Graduated in Law and Sciences. Began to study the violin with a first prize pupil of Massart**, Leon Reynier (see Massart's list of laureates in book six, year 1848), and music and counterpoint* at the Paris conservatoire* with Bourgault-Ducoudray. Lecturer on music history and aesthetics, he was archivist, librarian and vice-president of the Paris section of the International Music Society. Author of very interesting music books like *l'École française de violon* (by far his best), *Orphée*, which views Gluck's opera from every angle, a fascinating metaphysical study: *Le goût musical*, and *Les créateurs de l'Opéra française*.

-LAURENTI, (a) BARTOLOMEO GIROLAMO (1644 Bologna; d. ? 1726) Father of Laurenti (1) Pupil of E. Gaibara, Burney* identifies him as teacher of Corelli**. He was one of the first members of the Accademia Filarmonica founded in 1666. First violin* of San Petronio's orchestra he shared his post with Torelli**. He toured numerous cities as virtuoso. In 1706 he retired from the orchestra of S. Petronio on full pay, a clear sign of his importance within the orchestra.

-LAURENTI, (b) GIROLAMO NICOLO (b ?; d. Bologna 1751) Son of Laurenti Bartolomeo (a). Composer and violinist. Pupil of his father and of Torelli**, he replaced his father in the S. Petronio orchestra. Admitted to the Accademia Filarmonica in 1698. He was named director of the S. Petronio orchestra by Perti in 1734.

-LE BLANC, HUBERT. (Flourished early 18th century). French jurist, churchman and music writter. A visionary of the viol, he considered it "the" gift of God to the music of the French. He fancied to create a sort of paradise of the viol (*Empire de la viole*). Kind of a "freak", his accounts on Parisian cultural and musical life are, nevertheless, interesting. His main work is *Defense de la basse de viole contre les entreprises du violon et les prétentions du violoncel* (sic). *Amsterdam, 1740*.

-LEADER: (of an orchestra) The leader is the first violin* or concertino*, the head of the first violins, he who represents the orchestra and leads it. Do not mistake with the conductor, who is the director of a performance, although at the beginnings the leader was also the conductor. In those days the conductor directed the orchestra from the place of the first violin*, having both capacities, i.e. that of first violin and that of conductor. Today the leader is the head of the orchestra, the main figure within it and its representative, taking care of the homogeneous play of all the violins under him (first violins), just as the head of the cellos takes care of the cellos, and so on. The conductor, on his side, is the one who takes care of the unanimity of the execution and interpretation of the whole orchestra, by means of his visible gestures: the movements of his baton, hands, his head or even a slight glance. Even today a soloist (pianist, violinist) can also conduct the orchestra, the first from his stool, the other standing in front of the orchestra. Another duty of the leader is to direct the tuning of all the instruments of the orchestra, taking as reference the "A" pitch given by the first oboe. The subsequent noisy confusion produced by the sound of all the instruments tuning at the same time was one of the things that most vividly attracted the imagination of the young Wagner, making of him a hopeless addict to music, as he himself confesses, in his book "My Life".

-LEDUC, SIMON (c1748 Paris; d. id 1777) French violinist and composer, Pupil of Gavinies** played at the orchestra of the Concert spirituel* as second, and then, first violin*. He also played as soloist his own works. Together with Gossec* and Gavinies** he was co-director of that institution. He merited an entry in Leopold Mozart's diary: *"he plays well"*. He played on a Guarneri del Gesu Leduc of 1745.

-LEGATO: (See also *slur**) Means that the notes under this notation must be played smoothly connected with each other, without any interruption of sound.

-LÉGION D'HONNEUR: The highest decoration in France, it was founded by Napoleon by law of 29 Floral, year X [see calendar*, French Revolution] (19 of May, 1802). Its has three degrees: Chevalier, Officier, Commandeur. And two dignities: Grand Officier and Grand Croix (cross). Its sovereign and Grand Maître is the head of state of France.

-LEGOUVÉ, ERNEST (1807 Paris; d. id 1903) Famous French writter. He excelled in poetry, novel and theatre, particularly in the latter. He made his debut with the play *La découverte de l'imprimérie* which secured him a prize from the Académie Française. In 1847 he gave a series of lectures on the *Histoire morale des femmes*, which enshrined him as one of the most salient lecturers in France. Commander of the Légion d'honneur* in 1887, he published among many others: poems: *La mort d'Ophélie* (put in music by Saint-Saëns and Berlioz) *Les morts bizarres, Les viellards*; plays: *Guerrero ou la trahison, Adrienne Lecouvreur, Bataille de Dames, Contes de la reine de Navarre, Medée, Les deux reines* with music by Gounod, etc ; other writings: *Edith de Falsen, La femme en France au XIX siècle, L'art de la lecture* a delightful didactic work on how to read in public, with many examples and anecdotes, translated to all the European languages, *Nos filles et nos fils*. Special mention deserves his *Soixante ans de souvenirs*, plagued with touching anecdotes of his time. Intimate friend of Berlioz, he lent him the right amount in the right moment (1838) for which Berlioz was eternally grateful. Their dialogue went on like this: //-*How is advancing your work on the opera Benvenuto Cellini?* – I haven't yet finished the first act. I can't find enough time to write it – *But what if you had that time?* – Oh my God, I'll write from dawn till dusk – *What would you need to feel free?* – Two thousand francs which I haven't – *And what if anyone... if somebody ... if there... for Heaven's sake, help me!* - What? What do you mean? – *Well, if one of your friends would lend them to you....* – To which friend could I ask such a fortune? – *You would not need to ask for it..., it..., it is me who is offering you...* // < Hector Berlioz. Mémoires. Flamarion. Paris 1991. XLVIII. Pag. 290> The overture of Benvenuto Cellini was dedicated to Legouvé.

-LEITMOTIF: Germ: "leading motif" A musical theme clearly recognisable that symbolizes a person or an idea. This theme is recurrent and returns as often as that idea or person comes back to action. Although we can find it as soon as in Grétry *Richard, Coeur de lion*, 1784, and Mehul's (*Ariodante*, 1799) it was Berlioz *Symphonie fantastique* with its *"idée fixe"* (an obsessive theme representing his beloved Harriett Smithson), followed by Liszt, *Symphonic Poems*, who were its true inciters. Wagner developed it to the highest state of perfection.

-LÉONARD, HUBERT (1819 Bellair, nr Liège; d. Paris 1890) Belgian violinist, teacher and composer. Made his debut in Liège in 1832. Entered the Brussels conservatory in 1832. He went then to the Paris Conservatoire* where he studied with Habeneck* 1836-39. Played in the Théâtre des Variétés, Opéra-Comique and Académie Royale de Musique* (Opera). He made a good friendship with Vieuxtemps**. Toured Europe in concert from 1845 to 1852. Succeeded Beriot** at the Brussels conservatory in 1853 and remained till 1866. Excellent chamber music player, he was an outstanding teacher, and as his pupil Ovid Musin said: *"...he was one of the greatest pedagogues of all times, whose method was designed to develop equally and with uniformity the bowing thecnique, style, musical knowledge and comprehension necessary to make a complete artist"*

-LESCHETIZKY, THEODOR (1830 Lancut, 20 Km E of Rzeszow, Poland; d. Dresden 1915) Polish pianist and teacher. Together with Liszt, he was the most influential teacher of piano of his time. He studied first with his father Jozef, musical director of the Potocki family. In 1840 his family moved to Vienna where he studied with Czerny* (one of the best piano pupils of Bthvn and teacher of Liszt and Thalberg among others). Great friend of Anton Rubinstein*, at his request he became piano teacher at the conservatory of S. Petersburg. Made several tours as pianist but his fame was, above all, as teacher. He settled in Vienna where a monument for him was raised in his life time. He was also a remarkable conductor. On his activities as such he had declared: *"conducting is not difficult. It is harder to play six bars well on the piano than conducting the whole of Bthvn 9th symphony"* .

-LESUEUR, JEAN-FRANÇOIS (1760 Drucat-Plessiel, by the mouth of River Somme, nr Abbeville; d. Paris 1837) French composer. In 1786 he was named maître de chapelle* de Notre Dame* de Paris. He devoted many of his compositions to the praise of the Republic. He wrote many famous operas (*La Caverne, Ossian ou les Bardes, Le Triomphe de Trajan*) Professor of composition at the Paris conservatory* he influenced very much Gounod, and specially Berlioz, who took from him the liking for sumptuous instrumentation.

-LIEDER: German word meaning "song". Lieder has remained in the general vocabulary of music in its German spelling. It has generally the connotation of a song sang in an intimate surrounding, excelling in this genre Schubert, Schumann, Bthvn, Brahms.

-LIGHT, CITY OF: See City of light.

-LIND, JENNY: (1820 Stockholm; d. Wynds Point, Herefordshire, 1887) Famous Swiss chocolates... Oh! no! rather, famous Swedish soprano; sorry for that. She was nicknamed "the Swedish nightingale". She started as a prodigy at 10. Her true operatic debut was in 1838 with Schubert's *Der Freischütz*. For the next five years she sang all the major operas of the moment, but in 1841 her middle voice started giving signs of fatigue. She then had recourse to Manuel García Jr* in Paris, the miraculous Spanish maestro of singing, who built anew her voice, extending her treble range to g'''. With her improved voice she continued her career in Vienna, Berlin, Hanover and Hamburg, returning to Stockholm in 1845. She sang several times under Mendelssohn. She went to London in 1847 and had a staggering success before Queen Victoria. The whole London fell at her feet. She was also a superb lieder* singer. Her voice only lasted five years, but she was magic. Chopin in a letter of May 4, 1848 said: " She sings with amazing purity and certainty, and her Piano* is so steady and smooth and even as a thread of hair". And a connoisseur of the calibre of Sir Charles Hallé* in his Autobiography said: *"Never have I been moved by any singer as by her, and never again shall be, I feel certain"*. Lind married the pianist Otto Goldschmidt*, he who took in charge all the financial matters of Sarasate**, (contracts, hotel reservations, tickets for his tours, expenses, etc), what we call today an artistic agent. She staunchly defended her husband against adverse critics who called him a dull pianist and "the Prince Consort of Song" accusing him of squandering her fortune. She sued them for libel and won the case.

-LIPATTI, DINU (1917 Bucharest; d. Geneva 1950) Romanian pianist and composer. Born to a cultivated musical family his father had studied the violin with Sarasate and Flesch, his mother was a good pianist, and Enescu was his godfather. He was awarded a ridiculous second prize at the Vienna International Competition of 1933, behind a first Ladislav Kohn, Polish pianist, unworthy of it, who has remained totally unknown ever since. He must have had a very strong recommendations indeed. Cortot*, who had nominated Lipatti for the first prize, resigned from the jury in protest for such an unjust decision. [Cortot has always been a very daring and individual juror with the highest sense of justice. When Michelangeli was awarded the first prize at the Geneva International Piano Competition of 1939, he, who was among the juries, had no scruples in dedicating him one of his photographs with the inscription: *"with all my devoted admiration"* How many members of a jury have done this with one of the contenders?] Cortot* invited Lipatti to study privately with him in Paris. He established his reputation as pianist of the first order after the second World War. He was not only a superb virtuoso but, above all, a musician of the rarest delicacy and sensibility, very suitable for Chopin and Mozart. His records attest to it.

-LISZTOMANIA: Liszt had always something of superhuman, and he enjoyed to provoke hysteria among his admirers, particularly on ladies. To this end he habitually wore a whole array of medals to his concerts, which would become the much coveted trophies when his followers irrupted into the platform under a storm of applause, to congratulate him. The kind of hysteria he provoked on his lady admirers was equal to that induced by Elvis Presley or the Beatles. If the reader "reads" Alan Walker's book Franz Liszt, he will find countless anecdotes of this kind. (Franz Liszt. Faber & Faber. 1989 UK). Even when he was a priest, late in his life, he continued to give a supernatural appearance to all he did: the way he walked, the way he played the piano, the elegance of his deportment, the luxury of his parties. The Comtess d'Agoult*, his mistress, and the mother of his "legitimate" children, writes that *she fell in love with him at first site, from the very moment she saw him floating into the drawing room, walking as if he were weightless, handsome and thin, like a ghost*. We can find a very accurate plastic depicture of Liszt's awesome, phantasmagoric appearance, in one of his finest portraits: *Liszt at the door of the monastery of Santa Francesca Romana*, an oil painting by George Healy, 1869, that hangs in Craigie House, the former residence of the Longfellow family in Cambridge, Massachusetts. There is an illustration of it in Alan Walker's, Franz Liszt, volume 3, The final years, pag. 167. Liszt is seen here with his long, grey hair, penetrating black eyes, and his tall, slim figure shrouded in pitch-black priestly vestments, holding a candlestick aloft, emerging from total darkness, that produces a most impressive awe, as if it were the Transfiguration of Christ. When Sir Charles Hallé* met him for the first time in Paris he said: *"Liszt is the most original being in existence. When I entered I found an assembly of thirty or forty persons, among them many of the first artists of Paris, and even several ladies, who had come to pay him homage"*.

-LOMBARDINI, MADDALENA, Mme SIRMEN (1735 Venice; d. ? after 1785) Italian composer and violinist. She started her studies at the Mendicanti in Venice and later studied with Tartini** in Padua. In 1760 she returned to Venice but continued her studies with Tartini by correspondence. The first of these letters, dated March the 5th 1760 became universally famous, for it contained the résumé of Tartini's pedagogical principles (*Letter to Maddalena Lombardini*). It was translated into English by Burney*, and later into German and French. After finishing her studies with Tartini she embarked on a concert tour in Italy, during which she met and married Ludovico Sirmen, composer, violinist and maestro di capella* of S Maria Maggiore in Bergamo. The couple went on to Paris in 1768 and had great success at the Concert spirituel*, particularly she. In 1771 she went to London where she had even better successes that those of Paris. She continued in triumph throughout the UK until 1772, when she abruptly gave up the violin and decided to embark on a singer career, making a fool of herself, accepting secondary roles, with no success whatsoever. After 13 years of ridiculous attempts to sing, she tried to return to the violin at the Concert spirituel* in Paris, but it was a complete failure. The violin is so difficult that it demands constant attention. There has been only one person who had been able to leave it completely for a long period, and return to it without any loss, whatsoever, of his faculties: Viotti. She was one of Tartini's favourite pupils.

-LONG, MARGUERITE (1874 Nimes; d. Paris 1966) French pianist. First prize of the conservatoire de Paris*, she was professor there (1906-40) In 1920 she founded her own school of piano, and in 1946 she established with Jaques Thibaud an international piano and violin competition. Great friend and interpreter of Ravel, Debussy and Fauré. Ravel's piano concerto in G is inscribed to her, and she has recorded it under the baton of the author.

-LOTTO, IZYDOR (1840 Warsaw; d. id 1936) Polish violinist. Pupil of Massart**. Won first prize in 1853. From 1852 he played as soloist in many important cities of Europe. If we believe professor Josef Gingold* he had a technique similar to Wieniawski's, but he got extremely nervous in front of his audience and never became the superb virtuoso he could have been. He devoted instead to teaching becoming professor of the Music Institute of Warsaw. In 1880 he was appointed leader* of the opera orchestra. He bought himself his master's Strad Kreutzer of 1731.

-LUTHIER: (French) Violin maker. As its name implies, they originated as lute makers. French "luth".

-MAESTRO DI CAPELLA: See Kapellmeister.

-MAIER, FRANZ JOSEPH (1925 Memmingen, Germany, midway between Augsburg and the lake of Konstanz, border with Switzerland.) German violinist and conductor. Studied at the Munich academy of Music and the Music Gymnasium in Frankfurt. In 1943 studied at Saarbrücken and, after the war, in the Hochschule fur Music,

Cologne. Professor and leader of the violin master classes in the Cologne Musikhochschule. Co-founder of the Collegium Aureum. His abundant discography places him among the finest baroque players, with original instruments.

-MAJOR (MODE) A mode is major when in the scale* of its tonality* or key* the two semitone intervals* are between notes (3 and 4) and (7 and 8) of the diatonic* octave* scale*. Major mode tends to have a triumphant, happy character, whereas minor is usually sad and melancholic.

-MALIBRAN, MARIA [née MARIA GARCÍA] (1808 Paris; d. Manchester 1836) Elder daughter of the Spanish maestro of singing Manuel García* Sr., and sister of Pauline Viardot*. One of the best mezzo-sopranos of her age, she studied with her father, who was particularly harsh with her. Maria's marriage to Eugene Malibran was decided as a means to escape from her father's harsh cruelty against her, but became a total failure and they soon broke. She later married de Beriot**. She made her début in London as Rossina in Il Barbiere di Seviglia in 1825. Between 1825 and 1830 she was acclaimed in New York, Paris, Rome, Milan and Naples. She died as consequence of a horse ride accident in 1836 at 28, in the peak of her universal glory. Alfred de Musset's poem *Stances* was dedicated to her, two weeks later, and Robert Russell Bennett composed in 1935 the opera Maria Malibran based on her life. She was extraordinarily beautiful and elegant, as shown in her portrait by Luiggi Petrazzi in the Museo Teatrale alla Scala, Milan (1834).

-MANTEGNA, ANDREA (c 1431 Vicenza nr Venice; d. Mantua 1506) First magnitude Italian painter, the most eminent of the Vicenza school. His extraordinary gifts showed very early. Master in creating illusions of space and magnificence, by painting in a perspective from bellow to above (*di sotto in su*) The main example is the "Camera degli Sposi" at the Palazzo Ducale in Mantua. Also to be mentioned are two "St Sebastians", "The Crucifixion" "The Death of the Virgin" and "the Triumph of Caesar" among many other master pieces.

-MARCHESI, BLANCHE (1863 Paris; d. London 1940) French soprano. The daughter of the formidable singing maestra Mathilde Marchesi*, she studied with her. Her debut was in London in 1896. Her first opera was *Die Walküre* in Prague in 1900. She specialised in Wagner operas.

-MARCHESI, MATHILDE née GRAUMANN(1821 Frankfurt am Main, 35 Km NE of Mainz, by River Main, Germany; d. London 1913) One of the most salient professors of singing of her time. After her first studies in Frankfurt and Vienna with Nicolai, she went to Paris in 1845 to study with the formidable Spanish maestro of singing Manuel García, Sr*. She only sang once as Rossina in Il Barbiere at Bremen in 1853. She became professor of singing at the Vienna Conservatory in 1854 and lasted seven years. In 1861 she moved to Paris where she gave private lessons. Returned to the Vienna Conservatory teaching from 1868 to 1878, continuing with private lessons until 1881. She returned then to Paris where she opened her own school of singing. Among her many famous pupils we can name at random Nellie Melba*, Emma Calve, Eames, D'Angeri, Papier, etc. She published her singing method in Paris in 1886.

-MARINI, BIAGIO (1587 Brescia; d. 1663 Venise) Italian composer and violinist. Together with Fontana* he is one of the first to compose sonatas and sinfonias* for violin, filled with difficulties, namely multiple stopping*, scordaturas*, a continuous triple stop* in the *Capriccio in modo di una lira,* and many other difficulties in the echo sonata for three violins. He was the first to introduce the tremolo* and slurs*. In 1615 he was appointed violinist in St Mark, in Venise, under Monteverdi. In 1620 he was back in Brescia where he worked at the Accademia degli Erranti. In 1621 he was at the court of the Farnese in Padua. From 1623-49 he was Kapellmeister* at the court of Neuburg am Donau. In 1649 he was maestro di capella* of Sta Maria della Scala in Milan, and in 1652 director of the Accademia della Morte, Ferrara. The end of his life was shared between Venise and Brescia.

-MARPURG, FRIEDERICH WILHELM (1718 Seehof, nr Wendemark, Brandenburg; d. Berlin 1795) German journalist, critic, composer, theorist, musicologist and civil servant. Born to a well-to-do family he received a thorough and extensive education. He spent all his fortune in his early travels. From 1749 he is in Berlin where he participates very actively in the musical life, publishing three periodicals: *Der Kritische Musicus an der Spree* (1749-50); *Historisch-Kritische Beyträge zur Aufnahme der Musik* (1754-62), and *Kritische Briefe uber die Tonkunst* (1760-64) .A fervent admirer of Bach, he writes the *Abhandlung von der Fuge,* one of the first comprehensive studies on the fugue* in the Baroque period. As composer he has left various keyboard and vocal pieces, and as pedagogue we must mention *Anfangsgründe der Theoretischen Musik* (1757) and *Kritische Enleitung in die Geschichte und Lehsätze der alten und neuen Musik* (1758)

-MARTEAU, HENRI (1874 Reims; d. Lichtenberg, a district of the city of Berlin 1934) Swedish composer, violinist and conductor of French origin. His father was an amateur violinist, and his mother, German, a pupil of Clara Schumann*; his first studies were with the famous Belgian teacher Léonard*. In 1891 he entered the classes of Garcin* at the Paris conservatory* winning first prize the following year. He toured Russia, and the USA in concert and was teacher of the Geneva Conservatory from 1900 to 1907. In 1908 he succeeded Joachim** at the Berlin Hochschule für Musik. In his early years he was considered one of the greatest performers of the violin, particularly in Mozart, Bach and his contemporaries. His best instruments: a Guarneri del Gesu Marteau of 1731, and two Strads: Marteau, Vidoudez of 1709; and the cello Marteau, Delphino of 1709.

-MARTINI, PADRE See Padre Martini.

-MASCITTI, MICHELE (Sta. Maria, 35 Km N. of Napoli; d. Paris 1760) Another salient pupil of Corelli**. After a few years spent in Naples, he travelled through Italy, Germany and the Netherlands, settling finally in Paris. He soon attracted the attention of the duke of Orleans, and through him he was heard by the king and his entourage. He enjoyed a great popularity in Paris. After having served for the duke of Orleans, he entered the service of the affluent family Crozat. He was naturalized French in 1739.

-MATTEIS, NICOLA (b Naples; d. ?London c1707) Italian-English violinist and composer, resident in England. As a performer he impressed Burney*, and other chroniclers of the time. Composer of many interesting and virtuosistic sonatas* and suites* for violin solo, where he was influenced by Biber** and Walther**, he was a precursor of Bach's solo sonatas.

-MATTHAY, TOBIAS (1858 London; d. High Marley, nr Haslemere 1945) English piano teacher, pianist and composer. Of German parents, he entered the

Royal Academy of Music in 1871, becoming teacher from 1880 to 1925. His theories were exposed in *The Art of Touch* (1903), a pioneering work that gives a full scale analysis of the physical aspects of piano playing, dividing the vertical movements of the fingers into categories, with special emphasis on muscular relaxation, the result of which is a most strong, peerless, touch, by thrusting the whole weight of the shoulder, arm, hand and finger upon the keys, with a more robust strength that by hammering them with the fingers only. The swing of fingers hammering the keys, no matter how fast, can never be as strong as the whole loose weight of shoulder, arm, hand and finger, as if you would allow an elephant to walk over the keys. Total relaxation, and weight technique with loose shoulders, this is the secret already used by Liszt. The most renowned of his pupils was Dame Myra Hess*.

-MAURER, LUDWIG (1789 Potsdam; d. St. Petersburg 1878) German violinist and composer. He studied with Friederich the Great's Konzertmeister*, Carl Haack* a direct pupil of Benda**. He was admitted to the royal chapel* in 1803. He travelled through Germany, Russia, and Paris. Met Rode** in Mitau, and Baillot** in Moscow. He was director of the opera in Hanover from 1824 to 1832. He had a great command of the violin technique, and a surprising dexterity as virtuoso.

-MAURIN, JEAN-PIERRE (1822-1894) French violinist, professor of the Paris conservatory* (1875-1894) Pupil of Habeneck* won the first prize from the Conservatoire de Paris* in 1843. He had been previously pupil of Baillot**, whose teachings he continued. His pedagogical faculties were notorious. Wrote the 24 Etudes Artistiques, addressed to initiated pupils, aimed at the mastery of the bow both in technique and style. They are presented in an old fashion style remembering Bach's sonatas* and partitas*. He played on four valuable Strads: Maurin, Boucher of 1718; Maurin, Kruse of 1721, owned also by Kreutzer and I. Stern; the Maurin, de Chaponay of 1722, owned also by Wilhelmj; and the Maurin, Rubinoff of 1731.

-MAYSEDER, JOSEPH (1789 Vienna; d. id 1863) Austrian violinist and composer. After two triumphant appearances in Vienna in 1800, he played for Empress Marie Therese in 1802. Excellent quartet player, particularly in Bthvn, Haydn and Mozart, he was leader* of the theatre orch. Vienna (1810), Soloist at the Hofkapelle* and to the emperor, and musical director of the Hofkapelle (1836) Honours: Salvator medal, Freedom of Vienna, Order of Franz Joseph.

-MAZARIN, JULES, (CARDINAL): (1602 Pescina, Abruzzi, Kingdom of Naples, 100 Km E of Rome / 135 Km N of Napoli; d. 1661 Vincennes, Residential suburb E. of Paris. France) Papal diplomat in his youth, he became first minister of France under Louis XIV.

-McCORMACK, JOHN (1884 Athlone, right in the very centre of Ireland, county of Westmeath, along River Shannon, by the frontier with county Roscommon, south of Lough (lake) Ree, 115 Km E. of Dublin.; d. Dublin 1945) Irish tenor, naturalised American. Almost without studies he won a medal at the National Irish Festival in Dublin in 1903. His best teacher was Vicenzo Sabatini in Milan 1904-06. He sang all kind of operas, mainly Italian, and Mozart and Handel. Being a bad actor he left opera and changed to recitals, which gave him very successful evenings. His musical good taste and his superb style made of him one of the best tenors of all times. In his many recordings we can appreciate the sweetness and technique of his voice in his prime, particularly in Mozart's "il mio tesoro". These recordings are the mirror where all tenors should look in. His voice is a perfect blending of Caruso and Tito Schippa. This tenor transmits emotions like very few do. He really gives you the creeps. He bought himself three valuable Strads: the Healy of 1711; the McCormack, Edler of 1723; and the Bott, Cambridge of 1725, owned also by Hauptmann and Spohr.

-MEDICIS, VILLA: see Villa Medicis

-MELBA, NELLIE Dame. [Hellen Porter Mitchell] (1861 Richmond, Melbourne; d. Sydney 1931) Australian soprano of Scottish descent. After her first years of study in Melbourne (the source of her stage name) she went to Paris to study with the formidable Mathilde Marchesi*. Within a few years of her debut in Brussels, the world was at her feet. She has appeared in every main operatic city of the world, with Covent Garden as her artistic home. She made more that 150 records, some in duo with Caruso.

-MERCURE: One of the first periodicals of France, highly reputed all over the country, called at the beginning *Mercure galant*, that began in 1672. It started to be published every two months and consisted of more that 200 pages each. It became Mercure de France in 1724, and lasted until 1832.

-MÉRIC-LALANDE, HENRIETTE (1798 Dunkirk; d. Chantilly, residential town 30 Km N. of Paris 1867) French soprano. Pupil of Manuel (del Popolo) García* Sr., she premiered *Il Crociato in Egitto* by Meyerbeer in Venice (1824) and sang with success in Munich, Milan, Vienna and Naples. In 1827 she premiered Bellini's *Il Pirata* but she had already lost her voice, which trembled. Bellini noticed that she was "incapable of delicate sentiment". At her best she was a brilliant dramatic soprano, with good presence in the stage and a solid technique.

-MERSENNE, PÈRE MARIN (1588 La Soultière, Maine; d. Paris 1648) French philosopher, mathematician, theologian and music theorist of the first magnitude. Studied at the Jesuit college in La Flèche, then he continued in Paris. His most important contribution to music is his monumental *Harmonie universelle* Paris 1636. He considers many aspects of music such as singing, acoustics, modes and consonances and dissonances. An extensive part is devoted to instruments, with well selected musical examples of the past and contemporary. He was the discoverer of the harmonic* sounds.

-METASTASIO, PIETRO [Trapassi, Antonio Domenico] (1698 Rome; d. Vienna 1782) The most important librettist of his time, his librettos were set to music by the most famous composers of the epoch such as Vinci, Albinoni, Porpora, Hasse*, Fiorillo, Galuppi, Jommelli*, Paisiello, Traetta*, Piccinni*, Mercadante, Vivaldi, Handel, J. C. Bach, Gluck, Scarlatti, Caldara, Sachinni, Cimarosa, Cherubini, Graun* and, last but first, Mozart.

-MINGOTTI, REGINA, née VALENTIN (1722 Naples; d. Neuburg an der Donau, upon the Danube River, 65 Km N of Munich, 1808) Austrian opera singer of Italian origin. She joined the Mingotti opera troup in Graz, and married Pietro Mingotti. After a great success in Dresden, she was engaged at that court, where she took decisive lessons from Porpora. Sang successfully in Naples, Madrid and Prague. Went to London in 1754 with a staggering success at the King's Theatre. In association with Giardini she took the management of this Theatre, but it was a catastrophic failure. Perfect mistress of her voice, although "her greatest admirers allowed that her voice and manner would have been still more irresistible, if she had had a little more female grace and softness." (Burney*)

-MINOR (MODE) A scale* or tonality* is minor when its two semitone intervals* are between notes (2 and 3) and (5 and 6) in the diatonic* octave* scale*. Major mode tends to have a triumphant, happy character, whereas minor is usually sad and melancholic.

-MODE: See major*, minor* (mode)

-MODULATION: A series of chords* that the science of harmony* proposes for the change from a certain key* (or tonality*) to another, in a musical composition. i. e. if the piece is being played in C major*, (Its tonic* or diatonic* key* is C major) and you want to change to E minor, instead of changing all of a sudden, harmony* has a series of chords* that make the change smooth and harmonious. Of course the genius of the composer has a lot to add to these basic propositions.

-MONDONVILLE, JEAN JOSEPH CASSANÉA DE (1711 Narbonne; d. Belleville nr Paris 1772) French violinist and composer. He was taught by his father, an organist. He played first at the Concert spirituel* in 1734. His play at the Concert spirituel on Passion Sunday of 1739 was reported as "admirable and singular" by the Mercure*. Singular because of the harmonic* sounds that he produced in the sonatas Op 4 he had played, the first time ever to produce such particular sounds on the violin. Mondonville was the first to study these harmonics* in depth, and to play them in public, although their discoverer was Mersenne*. He played frequently at the Concert spirituel* with the flautist Blavet*, with Guignon* and Marie Fel*. His operas, motets and instrumental music, had deserved fame.

-MONTPENSIER, ANNE MARIE LOUISE D'0RLEANS, DUCHESS OF. Known as Mademoiselle de Montpensier because her father, uncle of Louis XIV, had the designation of "Monsieur". She inherited an immense fortune from her mother and was prominent during the minority of Louis XIV, and the war of the Fronde*, which forced Louis XIV to leave Paris. On his return in 1652 he exiled her until 1657.

-MORDENTE: An ornamentation of a specified note which consists in playing a trill* half a tone below or half a tone above the main note (that which is embellished) ending in the main note.

-MORIGI, ANGELO (1725 Rimini; d. Parma 1801) Italian composer and violinist. Pupil of Tartini,** he appeared in London in 1750 obtaining great successes. In 1758 he entered at the service of the duke of Parma becoming first violin* in 1766, and director of music in 1773.

-MOSCHELES, IGNAZ (1794 Prague; d. Leipzig 1870) German pianist, composer and conductor. He was taught in Vienna by Salieri. He met Bthvn who entrusted him with the transcription for piano of Fidelio. He met Mendelssohn in Berlin, and went to London where he stayed (1826-46) having an important role as teacher and concert organiser. Bthvn's last letter in thanks for an economic aid from the London Philharmonic Society was addressed to him. One of the most salient pianist of his time, Schumann regarded him as one of the best contemporary composers.

-MÖSER, ANDREAS (1859 Semling, nr Belgrade: d. Berlin 1925) German violinist, pedagogue and theorist. Having studied for engineer and architect, he turned to music in 1878 studying violin with Joachim**. A premature accident forced him to interrupt his violin carrier in 1883 becoming teacher of the Berlin Musikhochschule in 1900. As pedagogue he wrote Methodik des Violinspiels 1923, Technik des Violinspiel 1923, and his best, Violinschule 1905.

-MÖSER, KARL (1774 Berlin; d. id 1851) German composer and violinist. Pupil of his father, and Karl Haack*, he played in Friederich Wilhelm II private chamber ensemble. He toured to London and met Rode** and Viotti**. The effect was so shocking that he retired to perfect his technique. In 1807-11 he settled in S Petersburg. Back in Berlin he was promoted to Konzertmeister* of the Hofkapelle*. He was a reputable conductor.

-MOSSI, GIOVANNI (b. End 17th century, Rome; d. mid 18th century, Rome.) Italian violinist and composer. An outstanding pupil of Corelli**, his fame as a player remained mostly local. He had close relations with the Ottoboni family, the patrons of Corelli. He served also to Princess Vittoria Altieri-Pallavicini.

-MULTIPLE STOPS (doble, triple, quadruple stops) On the violin to stop a string is to press it firmly against the fingerboard, so as to make it vibrate only from the finger to the bridge, as opposed to an *open* string which vibrates freely all along its length. Consequently multiple stops are those that stop simultaneously more than one string to play them at the same time as in a chord*. Due to the positioning of the strings in the violin, some triple and quadruple stops must be arpeggiated. (see arpeggio)

-MUSIQUE DU ROI: It relates to the orchestras of the kings of France. They were three: Musique de la Chambre, Musique de la Grand Écurie, and Musique de la chapelle* royale. A) Musique de la Chambre: comprising 1) a small group of very selected musicians. 2) Les 24 violons du Roi. 3) Les Petits Violons, a group of 21 violins that the king deemed indispensable. B) Musique de la Grande Ecurie: They provided music for the great political events of the court. C) Musique de la chapelle* Royale: specialized in opera and sacred music, it was an enormous ensemble of 9 sopranos, 24 tenors, 27 baritones, 13 basses and 18 hautes-contres, and a good orchestra. The genre most cultivated was the motet. Lalande directed it for a long period.

-NAUMANN, JOHAN GOTTLIEB (1741 Blasewitz, nr. Dresden; d. id. 1801) German composer, conductor and violinist. Pupil of Tartini, Hasse* and Padre Martini*, he excelled as composer. Among his works we must cite Chora och Alonzo, Gustaf Wasa, Orpheus og Eurydyke, La Clemenza di Tito and La Dama Soldato.

-NOTRE DAME DE PARIS: The Paris cathedral, in Gothic style, built between 1163-1350.

-NOURRIT, ADOLPHE (1802 Montpellier; d. Naples 1839) French tenor. Pupil of M. García, Sr., he made his debut in the Paris Opera* in Gluck's Iphigenie in Tauride in 1821. He replaced his father as the Opera's principal tenor from 1827-37. He sang in every important city of Europe, premiering a great number of operas. He was appointed Professor of lyrical declamation of the Paris conservatoire* in 1827. A very intelligent and cultural person to a degree not usual for a singer, he contributed with success to the conception of many new operas that he sang. He threw himself from the top of the hotel where he was lodging, and lost his life.

-OCTAVE: It is the basis of all musical systems, oriental or occidental, tonal or atonal. If we take a certain pitch, let us say C on an instrument and we increase it towards the treble we will arrive to a moment in which the original pitch is repeated but with double sound frequency, that is C'. The margin between this two equal pitches is called octave* in the diatonic* system because there are eight pitches, or notes, in it: C – D – E – F – G – A – B – C' again. Or if you wish, do, re, mi, fa, sol, la, si, do'. They form the interval* of octave. In the atonal, dodecaphonic* or serial music the interval* of octave continues to be the same, i.e. the pitch repeats itself with double frequency, but now the interval between the repeated notes consists of twelve, (not eight) semitones which replace the eight notes of the diatonic* scale*. The octave is also the basic notion of a scale*, i.e. the notes that by degrees go up as if climbing a stair, step by step, from the lower pitch to its equal of double frequency. The diatonic scale has eight notes, 5 have an interval* between them of a whole tone: (C and D; D and E; F and G; G and A; A and B) <the white keys of a piano separated by a black> and two are apart one semitone: E and F; and B and C. On the diatonic* scale* the relationship of all its intervening notes is most rigorous in its hierarchy, and it conforms the rules of harmony*. The octave is divided into eight grades designated with Roman numbers: Grade I is the tonic*, the most important and that which gives the name and rules of all the diatonic* octave* scale*, in our case (C); the II is the supertonic (D), for it occupies the immediate superior place from the tonic*; the III is the modal (E), for its interval* with the tonic* will determine whether the scale* is in minor* or major* mode*: If it has a major (complete) interval* of third with the tonic (two tones) the scale* will be major*, and if its interval* is a third diminished by a semitone, the E becoming E flat* the mode* will be minor*. In the major* mode the semitone interval* is between E and F. But in the minor case, by flattening* the E we make the semitone interval to be between notes D and E flat. The IV is the subdominant (F), for it lies prior to the dominant. The V is the dominant (G); VI is the superdominant (A); VII is the sensitive (B) thus called because it has a keen attraction to the tonic*; and the VIII is the octave (C). The most important of them is the tonic, followed by the dominant, at an interval* of 5th from the tonic, and then the subdominant at an interval of 4th from the tonic.

-OPERA COMIQUE: In France a kind of light opera that alternates singing with spoken words, similar to its analogous *Singspiel** (Germany) and *Zarzuela** (Spain). It started at the beginning of the 18th century, consisting in ridiculing the fashionable operas of the day. As the monopoly of opera in France was granted to the Académie royale de musique* (Paris opera) they had to invent another kind of opera in which there were spoken dialogues. It evolved rapidly, and their subject was not limited to comic subjects, but were of all kind like Cherubini's *Médée* which was a drama. At the beginning it evolved from the Vaudeville*. Among its most salient composers and librettists we must mention: First the librettist Favart who staged an impressive number of them both in Paris and Vienna. (*Le coq du village*; *Les vendages de Tempé*; *Les amour de Bastien et Bastienne*; *Les moissoneurs*; *Les rêveries renouvellées des Grecs*) And then, J.J. Rousseau: *Le devin du village* – Grétry: *Le huron*; *La Lucile*; *Zémir et Azor*; *Richard coeur de Lion*; *Les deux avares*; *La fausse magie* – Adam: *Pierre et Catherine*; *Le chalet* (more that 1000 performaces); *Le sourd ou l'auberge plein*; *Le postillon*; *Le* *toreador ou l'accord parfait* – Auber*: *Le maçon*; *Lestocq*; *La sirene*; *Fiorella*; *Fra diavolo* – Boieldieu: *La dot de Suzette*; *Ma tante Aurore*; *Le calif de Bagdad*; *Nouveau seigneur du village*; *Jean de Paris*; *La dame blanche* – Philidor: *Blaise le savatier*; *Le sorcier*; *Tome Jones* – Monsigny: *Les aveux indiscrets*; *On ne s'avise jamais du tout*; *Le roi et le Fermier*; *Felix*; *La belle Arsenne*; *Rose et Colas* – Thomas: *Le songe d'une nuit d'été*; *Le caïd*; *Psyche*; *Le carnaval de Venise*; *Mignon* – Hérold: *Marie*; *Le pré au clercs*; *Zampa*.

-OPERA DE PARIS (See Académie royale de musique) The Paris opera, in full Théâtre National de l'Opéra. Its building, (also known as Palais Garnier*) was designed by the architect Charles Garnier* and was opened in 1875. It is a masterpiece of the second empire style.

-OSBORNE, GEORGE ALEXANDER (1806 Limerick, Port and main town of County Limerick, at the head of the estuary of River Shannon, SW Ireland; d. London 1893) Irish pianist and composer. Autodidact, he had some decisive refresher courses with Kalkbrenner*. Very fashionable both in England and Paris, as pianist and teacher. Among his pupils stands out Sir Charles Hallé*.

-OSTINATO: (Italian: obstinate) A musical pattern, which is repeated with obstinacy. Chopin's la Goute d'eau, and Berceuse are ostinatos, as well as Ravel's Bolero and Bthvn's adagio* of the Moonshine sonata, for example.

-PACINI, GIOVANNI (1796 Catania, eastern Sicily; d. Pescia, on the line Pisa, Bologna, 30 Km NE of Pisa and 90 SW of Bologna, 1867) Italian opera composer. After having studied singing and composition with padre Mattei, he had his first success with *Annetta e Lucindo* when he was seventeen. He collaborated with Rossini several times and reached his summit with *Furio Camillo* 1839 and *Saffo*, his masterpiece. One of the most glorious composers of Italy he made successful competition to Bellini, Rossini and Donizetti.

-PADEREWSKI, IGNACY JAN (1860 Kurylowka, Podolia; d. New York 1941) Polish composer, pianist, Prime Minister and politician. He first studied the piano and music at the Conservatory of Warsaw. In 1884 he went to Vienna to study with the famous teacher Leschetizky*, who found on him so many deep-rooted technical faults that he advised him to give up his career as a pianist. But after two more years of intensive study he returned to the same maestro in Vienna who finally accepted him. His indefatigable contribution for the development of musical life, and his many concert tours, made of him one of the most prominent musicians of his time. He owed also, to a large extent, his fame to his concentrated expression, aristocratic appearance, beautifully cut cloths, graceful movements and personal elegance. He was awarded many high decoration, among them the Grand Cross of the Légion d'honneur*, Great Cross of the Order of the British Empire, and the Cross of Virtuti Militari, the highest decoration in Poland. All of these would have enshrine him as one of the best pianist in history; but his telltale recordings show us quite a different picture, and we realize that he does not live up to his reputation: he blasphemously uses rubato in Schubert and Beethoven, while in his fast tempos he appears as hasty and nervous as a beginner. They come to corroborate his teacher's (Leschetizky*) fears, when he recommended him to give up his career as a pianist. The bulk of his merits as a pianist lay, alas!, on sheer fashion. But as musicologist and music promoter he was of the first magnitude. Among his works towers the edition of

Chopin's complete works. Composed several works for piano, orchestral and chamber music and an opera, *Manru*.

-PADRE MARTINI, GIOVANNI BATISTA. (1706 Bologna; d. Id 1784) Italian composer and musicologist, one of the most famous figures in the whole history. His renown throughout Europe was absolute. A man of a highly remarkable culture and of a singular affability, he became the advisor and confident of the most relevant figures of his time, as is patent from the extensive correspondence he has left, mainly, Frederick the Great, Gluck**, Metastase, Quantz**, Burney*, Rameau, Jomelli*, Tartini**, several popes, and last, but certainly not least, W. A. Mozart. Burney* said: *He joins to innocence of life, and simplicity of manners, a native cheerfulness, softness, and philanthropy. Upon so short an acquaintance I never liked any man more; and felt as little reserve with him in a few hours, as with an old friend or beloved brother; it was impossible for confidence to be more cordial* (The Present State of Music in Italy. P. 193) And Mozart: *I never cease to grieve that I am far away from that one person in the world whom I love, revere and esteem most of all.* He composed a great amount of sacred and secular music, including several sonatas for string instruments. He heaped up a huge library of 17,000 volumes, and numerous letters received from the most distinguished personalities of his century.

-PAER, FERDINANDO: (1771 Parma; d. Paris 1839) Italian composer. Maestro di capella* of Parma (1792), Kapellmeister* in Dresden (1801), Maître de Chapelle* of Napoleon (1807) Director at the Kärntnertor-Theater in Vienna (1797) where he met Bthvn, Director of the Opéra-Comique and Théâtre Italien in Paris, Directeur de la Musique de la Chambre de Louis-Philippe, he was one of the most important composers of his time. Among his works we must highlight his operas *Camilla*, his masterpiece, *Griselda, Achille, Agnese, The Father and the Daughter, Leonora* and *Sargino*. He wrote also cantatas, oratorios and instrumental music with equal success.

-PAGIN, ANDRÉ-NOEL (1721 Paris; d.? 1785) French violinist. Studied with Tartini** in Padua, he was considered in France his best pupil (Burney*, State of Music in France and Italy. Pag 43) . Made his debut at the Concert spirituel* in Paris in 1747 playing one of his own sonatas, being praised as the ultimate perfection in violin technique. He played mainly Italian music, either Tartini's, Vivaldi's, or his own. He became one of the most salient virtuosos in Paris, particularly praised for his adagios* and cantabiles, extreme bow agility and just intonation, but his career was very short indeed. At the Concert spirituel* on Easter Sunday *he had the honour of being hissed for daring to play in the Italian style* (Burney*, Op. cit. p. 43) Having played since his debut in Paris only Italian works, he was utterly disenchanted by such an unexpected chauvinistic reaction from an audience which would not hear but French music, and he never returned to the Concert spirituel*. He turned instead to play at the luxurious private concerts of the Comte de Clermont, with a staggering salary of two hundred and fifty pounds sterling a year. (See Concert spirituel*). The bigot chauvinism of the French led them to stuck stubbornly to the music of Lalande, Lully, and Rameau until the beginning of the Romantic era with Viotti, repudiating systematically any Italian music, *so that the greatest crime of which the Italians seem guilty was having dared to compose a species of music more delicate and refined, than the rest of Europe can boast.* (Burney*. Present State of Music in Italy. p. 388.)

-PAISIBLE, LOUIS-HENRY (1748 St Cloud, Western residential suburb of Paris; d. S. Petersburg 1782) French violinist and composer, was a pupil of Gavinies**, one of the best in his youth, to the point that La Laurencie* says he surpassed his master. He gave many successful concerts in the Concert spirituel*, but after 1776 he ceased to appear. An extraordinary precocious victim of the barrier of the 50s, he lost faculties at 28 years only. After several concerts in Europe with little success he settled in St Petersburg. His play was worsening by the day, and in the end, unable to earn his life, and overwhelmed by debts, he shot himself in despair.

-PALAIS GARNIER See Opera de Paris, Paris opera.

-PARIS CONSERVATORY: It digs its roots into two older institutions (its forerunners) that merged to become the conservatoire: i) the *Ecole royale de chant* et de déclamation* and ii) the *Ecole supérieure de musique de la garde nationale**. Until the French Revolution, musical knowledge was taught in the "maîtrises", choirs and music schools, looked after by the clerical chapters of the different local churches. Upon their closing by the Revolution, another system had to be put in place to substitute them. This reform took two ways, that of the Ecole royale, and that of the Ecole supérieure of the National gard. A) The *Ecole royale de chant* et de déclamation* was founded as part of the Académie Royale de Musique* (Paris Opera*) in 1784, thanks to the efforts of the French musician François-Joseph Gossec* (b. Vergnies, Hainaut 1734 – d. Passy, annexed to Paris, XVI arrondissement 1829) who was its first director. Its aim, as its name implies, was the training of opera singers and theatre declamation, to which the teachings of string and keyboard instruments were added. B) *École supérieur de musique de la garde nationale*. The task to replace the old church schools by secular ones was entrusted to the formidable musical administrator Bernard Sarrette*, who became the head of the Ecole supérieur de music de la garde nationale, and later, the first director of the Paris conservatoire. His nation-wide plan included the creation of 30 (first degree) musical schools, 15 (second degree) ones, in replacement of the maîtrises, and a few (third degree) others, providing refreshment courses, plus an Ecole supérieur in Paris. All of them should provide free tuition. None of them were created with the exception of that of Paris: the Ecole supérieur de music de la garde nationale. One day prior to the demolition of the Bastille by the populace, the 13th July 1789, Bernard Sarrette* was named captain of the National Guard, entrusted with the responsibility to organise a band within the regiment, which he did by creating the Ecole supérieur de music de la garde nationale, with the double task to give open air concerts in patriotic and civic festivities, and to train the musicians of the Garde nationale. This new body of the Gard nationale took part in many public, patriotic events, as well as in the main civic festivities, not least, the transference of Voltair's ashes to the Paris Panteon in 1791. In order to produce new recruits for the band and increase its size, Sarrette* drew up a plan for a school of military music, which was accepted in 1792, founding the Ecole gratuite de la gard national, where 120 pupils, sons of soldiers of the Gard nationale, were given free tuition, establishing the first school for wind instruments in France. The gard national was abolished by the Commune de Paris*, but Sarrette* profited of the opportunity to increase the size of the Ecole supérieur de music de la garde nationale, reaffirming its goals, and redefining its statutes, obtained a decree (1793) that would transform the old École de la garde nationale into the Institut national de musique*. Sarrette*, wishing to extend the teachings of the Institut to singing, and string and keyboard instruments, took-over the existing Ecole royale de chant* et de déclamation, incorporating it to the Institut, in 1794. The following year this enlarged Institut national de musique* became the Conservatoire de Paris*.

-PARIS OPERA (See Académie royale de musique)

-PARTITA: (Italian divided) Means the same as suite* and sonata*. See Triosonata.

-PASDELOUP, JULES ETIENNE (1819 Paris; d. Fontainebleau, 50 Km S. of Paris, midway Paris-Auxerre, 1887) French violinist, conductor and administrator. Son of François Pasdeloup, conductor of the Opéra-Comique, he got a premier prix in violin in 1832. Violin teacher at the conservatoire since 1847 he founded with his pupils the Société des Jeunes Artistes, replaced in 1861 by the Concerts Populaires with the aim to bring classical music to a public that until then had not enough money to hear it, by selling cheap tickets. They became extremely popular, performing music of the not so well known German composers, and promoting, too, contemporary musicians such as Saint-Saëns, Massenet and Lalo. He was also director of the Théâtre de L'Athénée and Director of studies of the conservatoire. In 1869 he succeeded Léon Cavalho at the head of the Théâtre-Lyrique, where he premiered, in France, Verdi's Ballo in Maschera and Wagner's Rienzi.

-PEDAL (Sustaining pedal [in the piano]) See damper.

-PERRIN, PIERRE: (c 1620 Lyons; d. 1675 Paris) French poet and librettist. His life was an uninterrupted series of failures due to his weak character, from his early marriage, very young, to a wealthy widow of 61 years, to his verses, criticised and ridiculed by many. It is thanks to him that we owe the creation of the Paris Opéra, the Académie royale de musique*. He managed to convince Colbert* of the necessity of having an Opera genuinely French, both in music and verses, as the Italians had. At Colbert's* instigation Louis XIV issued a decree creating the Académie Royale de Musique* and entrusting Perrin with the sole privilege to establish Académies d'opéra in Paris and in the other cities of France for the performance of operas in French music and verse, similar to those of Italy. Although a mediocre poet he inaugurated his Académie de Musique, with a pastorale, Pomone, words by him and music by Cambert*, that had an enormous success, being performed 146 times. But his unscrupulous managers pocketed all the receipts and Perrin was incarcerated for debts. Much in need, he finally sold his privilege on the Académie d'opéra to Lully**. Pomone is considered to be the first complete opera in French.

-PERUGINO, PIETRO DI CRISTOFORO VANNUCCI, called IL (c1450 Citta della Pieve, nr Perugia, [Romagna]; d. Fontignano nr Perugia 1523) First magnitude Italian painter of the Umbrian school, early Renaissance, teacher of Raphael. Painted frescoes in the Sistine Chapel* of the Vatican. His most mature works are in Florence: "Madonna and saints" "Pieta" and his best portrait "Francesco delle Opere".

-PETIT: First name unknown (flourish in the middle of XVIII century) French violinist cited by la Laurencie* as pupil of Leclair**. He gave two superb concerts on Christmas day at the Concert spirituel* in 1741and 42. Titon de Tillet (Premier Supplément au Parnase français) puts him among the best violinists in

France. <There is nothing extraordinary in the fact that such a good violinist has remained almost unknown. In much more recent times (1838) Liszt, in his letter to Lambert Massart**, (Léttres d'un bachelier es music) affirms categorically that *Poggi* is the best tenor in Italy. (Which, given the supreme importance of Italian opera at the time, can be interpreted as being the best tenor in the world) Well, Poggi is not even mentioned in the monumental New Grove Dictionary.

-PIAF, EDITH: Byname of Edith Giovanna Gassion (1915 Paris;d. id 1963) French singer and supreme actress of the first magnitude, she is the most mytical singer of the French *chanson* or ballad. With a tragic childhood, she was abandoned by her mother, and became blind as the result of a meningitis for four years, all the tragedy of her life is reflected in her singing style, dramatic, and deeply moving. She started singing in the streets of Paris and was discovered by Louis Leplée, a cabaret manager. Encouraged by another mythical singer, Maurice Chevalier, she made her theatrical debut in 1935 and within a few years she was at the top of all singers. Her perfect voice emmission, just from the chest (Italian "ben impostata" well placed) with a splendid vibrato*, propelled right from her diaphragm, not artifically produced by the throat, as the bleating of a sheep, has no peer in her style and her abundant discography attest to it. She was the author of unforgetable songs like *La vie en rose, Le Vagabonde* and among her top successes we may name *Non, je ne regrete rien, Milord, Hymne à l'amour*.

-PIANO: [Intensity of sound volume] :Expression to denote the volume of a musical sound, meaning that it must be quiet or soft. It is marked with a *p* on the score. Derives from Italian piano: soft. It has three degrees of intensity: 1) *p* Piano, is standard soft. 2) A softer sound is marked *pp*, and 3) very soft *ppp* (*Pianissimo*). Its opposite (loud) is *Forte*.

-PIATIGORSKI, GREGORG (1903 Ekaterinoslav, now Dnipropetrovsk, by the River Dnieper, in its confluence with Samara River. [South Central Ukraine]; d. Los Angeles 1976) American cellist of Russian origin. Studied at the Moscow conservatory. Played at the Lenin Quartet, and was cellist of the Bolshoi Orch. In 1921 he left Russia and went to Leipzig for further studies. From 1924-28 he is selected by Fürtwangler as solo cello at Berlin's Philhar. Orch. Played in duo with Schnabel*, and in trio with this one and Flesch**. Played also frequently with Horowitz, and Milstein*. From 1949 on he played in trio with Arthur Rubinstein and Heifetz**. Created with Heifetz the chamber musical concerts in Los Angeles. Taught at the Curtis Institute of Philadelphia (1941-49) and from 1962 on at the University of Los Angeles. Played on three Strads: the Aylesford of 1696, owned also by Giardini** ans Starker*; the Batta of 1714, and the Baudiot of 1725). He also had a Nicola Amati of 1670.

-PIATTI, ALFREDO (1822 Bergamo; d. Crocetto di Mozo 1901) Italian cellist and composer. Entered the Theatre orch. of Bergamo at the age of eight. Entered the Milan conservatory in 1832 graduating in 1837, when his debut took place with great success. He toured Europe with equal success but his finances were disastrous and in 1834 he had to sell his cello to cure a sever illness. Liszt was impressed by him and sent him to Paris, where he had a sensational debut with a borrowed instrument. A few months later Liszt presented him with a Nicola Amati cello. He went to London in 1844 where he was acclaimed as an exceptional artist. He toured

Great Britain and Russia (1844-6) He had a profound influence on the cello history, particularly in G. B. He owned the following Strads: two violins, the Piatti, Ashley of 1717; and the Piatti, Arkwright of 1732, and the cello Piatti, the Red, of 1720, owned also by Mendelssohn, a present from General Oliver, which in wood and varnish surpasses even the mythical Strad Spanish Bass of 1713.

-PICCINI, NICOLA: (1728 Bari; d. Passy, annexed to Paris, to the XVI arrondissement, 1800) Italian composer of the first magnitude. He wrote more that 50 operas, and sacred and instrumental music. He flourished in Paris. He is an indisputable master of the opera "semiseria". He was at the head of the famous dispute between the *gluckists* (those in favour of the dramatic opera) and the *piccinists* (in favour of the musical opera) that took place mainly in Paris (1776-79)

-PISTOCCHI, FRANCESCO ANTONIO (1659 Palermo; d. Bologna 1726) Italian composer and castrato* singer. Prodigy child he started singing in public at age of 3, and published his first work, *Capricci puerili* at 8. Kapellmeister* to the Margrave of Brandenburg (1686-95), he made several tours with Torelli** to Berlin and Vienna. In 1702 he was named virtuoso da camera e di capella* to prince Ferdinand of Tuscany. His voice was magnificent, with a soprano pitch that later turned to contralto. Tosi* regarded him as the best singer of all times.

-PIZZICATO: From italian pizzicare, to pinch. To pluck, instead of bowing, the strings of a bow instrument (violin, cello).

-POGGI, ANTONIO (1806 Castel San Pietro, Bologna; d. id 1875). Italian tenor. Made his debut at Bologna in *Il Falegname di Livonia* by Pacini*. Sang in all the major opera houses including Paris, London, Vienna and, of course, Italy. His voice was particularly sweet and flexible, with a passionate, vibrant phrasing very appropriate for the romantic operas of Verdi, Donizetti, Rossini and Bellini. Was role creator of Carlo VII in *Giovanna d'Arco* (Verdi), Roberto in *Torquato Tasso* (Donizetti), and Ghino in *Pia de'Tolomei* (Donizetti). He was famous also for his role in *The Gazza Ladra* by Rossini. When he sang *I Lombardi alla prima crociata,* in the summer of 1844, he added nine notes to the cabaletta. He married the famous diva Frezzolini, but they parted soon. According to Liszt, who is not an ignorant, he was, categorically, the best tenor in Italy. He was honoured as Cavaliere dell'Ordine Piano by Pope Pio IX.

-POLYAKIN, MIRON BORISLOVICH (1895 Cherkassi, 165 Km SE of Kiev, along an immense reservoir in the River Dnieper, central Ukraine; d. Moscow 1941) Ukrainian violinist and teacher. After having studied violin with his father and with Bonsovsky at the Lysenko Music School in Kiev, he went to Auer** in S. Petersburg. Made frequent tours in Europe and USA. Professor at the conservatory of Leningrad and Moscow. Another of the best pupils of Auer, with Heifetz**, Zimbalist** and Elman**.

-POLYPHONY: All the music of Asian, Middle East and Arab countries was and is monophonic, meaning that their music is composed for one voice only, one single melody, which can be as ornamented and swinging as you wish, but that is only one melody, and if there appear other voices, they are exclusively to accompany the melody, without proper personality of their own. One single melody, one single part, which can be accompanied by others voices which have not a melody of their own, but are merely accompanying sounds, is what characterises the monodic or monophonic or homophonic music of these countries. By contrast, in the Western countries, around 1250 appeared the Rota of Reading {pronounced "red-ding"} (Main town of the bourogh [county] of Berkshire, 60 Km W of London. England) "Summer is icumen in", in which music was split into more than one part. The accompanying voice reaches the status of another independent part, with its own melody, which mingles and is interwoven with the treble melody, to form two parts (of equal importance) that dialogue among themselves. This polyphony* soon developed to include more than two parts, arriving to four or more independent parts, but which blend into each other to make a perfectly harmonious piece of music. And so, for example, all the piano pieces, from the Classical to our Moderns, passing through the Romantics, are written for four parts, four independent, yet harmonious, voices that dialogue among themselves. Since the essence of polyphony* is to have at least two independent parts, the fugue*, which make two parts dialogue in delayed imitations*, became the basis of all the science of harmony*.

-POLLEDRO, GIOVANNI BATTISTA (1781 Piova, nr Turin; d. id 1853) Italian violinist. Pupil of Pugnani**, he was violinist at the Royal orch. of Turin under the direction of Pugnani. Spent five years in Moscow at the orch. of prince Tatishchev. Was acclaimed in Germany, and played with Bthvn in 1812. In 1814 became leader* of the orch. of the Dresden court with the same salary as Weber. From 1824 to 44 he was maestro di capella* at the court of Turin.

-PONCE, MANUEL (1882 Fresnillo (Zacatecas), midway Durango and San Luis de Potosí, 50 Km NW of Zacatecas; d. Mexico D. F. 1948) Mexican pianist and composer. Studied at the conservatories of Mexico, Bologna and Berlin. Piano professor at the conservatory of Mexico, became its director in 1934-35. Music critic at La Habana 1915-17. From 1925-35 he lived in Paris working with Paul Dukas. His music is a balance between modern techniques and the folkloric tunes of his country. Among his works we must cite the Balada Mexicana, Poema Elegiaco, Concierto del Sur for guitar and orchestra inscribed to Andrés Segovia, and his last great work, the violin concerto where he introduces his song Estrellita, which he published in 1914 that became the greatest success in Latin America.

-PONTICELLO (*sul ponticello*) An indication to the violinist to bow the strings very near the bridge (Italian: ponticello) As a consequence, it is produced a sound of a high metallic tone, slightly rough and scratchy in the *Forte**, and silvery in the *Piano**

-PORTAMENTO: see glissando.

-POSITION: The positioning of the left hand on the fingerboard of the violin to play a certain set of notes on all strings without shifting the thumb that remains fixed on the neck. The fingerboard is divided normally into seven positions, being the first the one which is closer to the scroll and which plays the lowest notes on the violin. The thumb is placed firmly on the back of the neck, and the remaining fingers stop* the strings they can while the thumb remains immobile. For the second position the hand, or rather the thumb, moves down a certain distance on the fingerboard towards the bridge, and a new set of higher notes can be stopped*; the third position brings the thumb even closer towards the treble, and so on until the seventh position, the highest in pitch, and closest to the bridge. On each position the left hand fingers move and stop* the different strings while maintaining the thumb fixed in the same position on the neck. The moving from one position to another is called to shift position, whereby the thumb goes to its new position on the neck from where another set of different notes, higher or lower can be played. This is a general outlook, but there are even higher positions up to 12th and 13th, acrobatic positions very near the bridge. On the other end (low) there is a **half position** between the scroll and the first position. <Professor Galamian describes positions very well: "The building of good intonation rests mainly on the sense of touch in combination with the guidance of the ear. The fingers are like blind people who guide themselves through a sightless existence by touching objects which mark their paths from place to place. The analogy is pertinent to the training of the fingers on the violin. The hand learns gradually to orient itself, to find its proper location by the feel of the neck (and the body of the instrument in upper positions*) From the hand position* thus secured, the fingers in their turn learn to acquire, through the sense of touch, the feeling for correct placement and for proper stretch. In this they are continually helped, guided, and controlled by the ear" Principles of Violin Playing and Teaching. Second edition, 1985, 1962. Prentice-Hall Inc. A Simon & Schuster Company. Englewood, New Yersey 07632. Printed in the United states of America. Chapter two: The left hand. Intonation. Page 19. ISBN 0-13-710773-0>

-POUGIN, ARTHUR (1834 Châteauroux 1834; d. Paris 1921) French violinist and writer on music. Studied violin in the Paris conservatoire* with Alard**. He played at the orch. of Musard and the Opéra Comique, and was conductor of the Theâtre Beaumarchais, and assistant conductor at the Follies-Nouvelles. As a writer he concentrated on biographical studies and wrote the musical articles of the Larousse Dictionnaire Universel. He was feuilletonist of *Le Soir, La Tribune, L'Evenement* and *Le journal Officiel*, and made many contributions to *Le Menestrel, La France Musical, Le Théâtre, Chronique musicale*. He became chief editor of Le Menestrel in 1885. He owned the Strad Hall, Viotti of 1709

-POUPLINIÈRE de CHEVIGNÉ, ALEXANDRE-JOSEPH le RICHE, de la: (1693 Chinon, along River Vienne, a tributary of River Loire, midway Poitiers-Le Mans; d. Passy, annexed to Paris, XVI arrondissement, 1762) a wealthy French financier, "Fermier Général" and writer, famous for the extreme luxury of his social life and as promoter of Fine Arts [The *Fermier Général* was, in the ancient regime, an official who, against an advanced payment to the king of an annual amount, was authorised to collect the indirect taxes of the kingdom, being his salary the difference between the said amount and the actual sum collected. <Petit Robert>]. He had a private orchestra which had been directed by such important musicians as, Rameau, Gossec* and Johann Stamitz**. His musical soirées in Paris were most fashionable. As a writer he made a collection of tales entitled *Datra*, and the novel *Moeurs du siècle*.

-PRIMROSE, WILLIAM (1903 Glasgow; d. Provo, along Provo River, near Utah lake, 65 Km S of Salt Lake City. Utah, USA) Scottish violist. Studied, first, violin in Glasgow, then at the Guildhall School of Music in London and later in Belgium with Ysaye**, who encouraged him to change to the viola. Soloist with the main orchestras, Toscanini chose him as principal viola in the NBC Orch. (1930-35) Founded his Primrose quartet in 1939. Teacher at the University of Southern California (1961-65). Indiana University in Bloomington (1965-72) Tokyo and

Suzuki Institute in Musumoto. He played on a viola Amati of 1600. Published *Technique is Memory, Art and Practice of Scale* Playing, Violin and Viola*, with Menuhin, and *Playing the Viola*.

-PRINCE OF THE CHURCH: The cardinals of the Roman Catholic Church, so called because they are the successors of the Pope, viz, one of them will become, through election, the next Pope.

-PRIX DE ROME: See Villa Medicis*

-RAPPOLDI, EDUARD (1831 Vienna; d. 1903 Dresden) German violinist, conductor and composer. He played both the piano and the violin from the age of seven. He was violin pupil of Hellmesberger* Sr. at the Vienna conservatory (1851, to 54) and of Joseph Boehm. Played at the Vienna court orch (1854-61) He was leader* of the orchestras of Rotterdam (1861-6), Lübeck 1866, Stetting 1867, and the German Theatre in Prague 1869. Joachim** took him to teach at the Berlin conservatory (1871-7) He was leader* of the court orch. of Dresden 1877, and professor of its conservatory, giving memorable concerts there (1877-9) Excelled as teacher and chamber music player, and had an astonishing left hand technique, being in the words of Andreas Möser* "*one of the most musical persons I have ever met*". It was he himself who wrote to Massart a letter imploring to enter his classes "*to learn some aspects of violin playing from whom I consider the best teacher in the world*". Rappoldi played on the Strad. Rappoldi of 1719.

-READE, CHARLES (1814 nr Ipsden, Oxfordshire; d. London 1884) English author whose novels describe with passionate, vivid indignation, the social injustices of his days. In his early youth he was very active in the violin business at Soho, being himself a good performer on this instrument. Wrote several plays for the theatre, but had little success, and several more successful novels, such as *Hard Cash* denouncing the ill treatment of mental patients in private asylums; *Put Yourself in his Place* deals with the terrorism of unionists; *It is Never Too Late to Mend*, attacking the bad condition on prisons. But his masterpiece is *The Cloister and the Hearth*, where he brilliantly relates the adventures of the unknown father of Erasmus. He gave his name to his Guarneri del Gesu "Charles Reade" of 1733. As for the violin, he wrote four indispensable essays for any one who is interested on this instrument: "Cremona Violins. *Four letters Descriptive of Those Exhibited in 1873 at the South Kensington Museum*", in which he describes meticulously the beauties of all those fiddles. After reading it, I felt extremely perplexed, with the most strong sensation of being totally silly, followed by a severe depression. Poor old me! I thought I liked violins and could appreciate them for their contour, shape, proportions, and colour, but this is nothing, really nothing. He looks for beauty, and finds it in the most unexpected, unimaginable little details, that make you feel like a fool. To add to your mortification he says: *the minutiae of work in Stradivarius are numerous and admirable, but (they) are too well known to need discourse.* As a luthier Reade traded with formidable Strads such as the Dragonetti of 1707; the Sammons of 1704; the cello Bass of Spain of 1703; the Cessole of 1706; the Messiah of 1716; the Le Comte of 1725; and the viola Gibson of 1734, passing his name to all.

-RÉCAMIER, JULIE, MADAME DE: (1777 Lyon; d. Paris 1849) The daughter of a rich banker she doubled her fortune by marrying another wealthy banker. She was famous for the luxury of her salon, where she entertained all the cream of politicians and artists in Paris. She was praised for her charm and wit, having among her habitués great figures like Bernardotte, future king of Sweden and general Moreau opposed to Napoleon. This infuriated Napoleon who in 1805 ordered her exile. She went to Geneva, Rome and Naples. Returned to Paris after Napoleon's defeat, she resumed her receptions at the Abbayé-aux Bois. Her closest friends were Madame de Staël and François Chateaubriand. There are two famous portraits of her by François Gérard and J. L David. In the latter's she is lying on the sofa that took her name: *Récamier*. Within the fortune of Madame Récamier we find two valuable Strads: the Récamier, Molitar of 1697, owned also by Napoleon; and the Récamier, Elman of 1727, owned also by Napoleon.

-RECITATIVE: They constitute the very beginning of the opera, where a drama in words for the theatre was put into music. At the start, it was music which was subordinated to the verse, following its rhythm of long and short sillabs. Later the aria* became the most important part of the opera, where the most beautiful and ingenious songs were sang by the main singers, leaving the dialogues to be said in the ancient recitative way. The dialoguing parts of the opera, are not spoken, but half sung half recited, in a style that resembles the declamatory speech, but with a certain musical intonation, something similar to the Gregorian chant. It has a great advantage for singers: because opera singers are not at ease speaking on the stage, and their voice becomes more audible if it has a certain musical accent upon which they can support their powerful voice, this recitative is very convenient for them. It is a fact that an opera singer has ten times more volume in his voice singing than reciting. These recitatives have not attractive, melodious, easy to remember, tunes like the aria*, but they rather resemble the Gregorian chant. This is the reason why to compose an attractive recitativo is something notorious and extraordinary indeed.

-REICHA, ANTONIN (1770 Prague; d. 1836 Paris) Czech composer and theorist. He lived in Hamburg 1794-9, Paris 1799-1802, Vienna 1802-8 and definitively Paris from 1808, naturalizing French in 1829. Professor of composition at the Paris conservatoire* from 1818 had as pupils Vieuxtemps**, Berlioz, Liszt, Gounod and Franck. He wrote operas, orchestral and religious music, piano pieces, etc. but his main contribution was his wind quintets with prophetic harmonic and rhythmical discoveries.

-REIGN OF TERROR: see TERROR.

-RELLSTAB, LUDWIG (1799 Berlin; d. Id 1860) German music critic and poet. In his youth he played the piano, excelling in keyboard performances of Mozart and Bach. Met Bthvn and Schubert who set ten of his poems into music: (*Schwanengesang*). Critic for the *Vossische Zeitung*. Editor of the periodical *Berlin und Athen* and founder of the *Iris im gebeite der Tonkunst*. Very conservative he criticised Spontini and above all Rossini. He was the one who dubbed Bthvn sonata Op 27-2 "Moonlight". *A boat visiting, by moonlight, the primitive landscapes of the Vierwaldstättersee in Switzerland.*

-REMENYI, EDE (1828 Miskolc, county city 165 Km NE of Budapest; d. San Francisco, USA 1898) Hungarian violinist. He studied at the Vienna conservatory with Joseph Boehm** (1842-5). He made his debut in Pest playing later in Paris and London with great success. He met Liszt in Weimar, who encouraged him and composed the *Epithalam* for him. Made several tours through the main cities of the world. He had a great command of his technique, a beautiful tone and a remarkable individuality. He died while playing a concert in S. Francisco. He owned the Strad Titian, Remenyi, of 1704, owned also by Grumiaux.

-RÉMY OR ROEMY, GUILLAUME-ANTOINE (1858 Ongrée, Belgium; d. Nantes 1932) Studied at the conservatory of Liège winning the diploma and the Ysaye prize. He then went to Paris to study with Massart, winning premier prix in 1878. Played at the orch. of Eduard Colonne*, and frequently as soloist. Also in duo with Fauré and Saint-Saëns. Founded a string quartet bearing his name of deserved fame. The rival of Ysaye at the conservatoire de Liège, he was professor at the Paris conservatory 1896-1929.

-RIES, FERDINAND (1784 Bonn; d. Frankfurt am Main, 35 Km NE of Mainz, by River Main, Germany 1838) The most celebrated member of the Ries family, he became one of the best piano pupils of Bthvn, who secured for him appointments as pianist to Count Browe in Baden in 1802, and to prince Lichnowsky in 1805. From 1809 he was constantly on tour to Kassel, Hamburg, Stockholm and Copenhagen, touring also Russia. He was in England for 11 years, being justly celebrated by the Harmonicon. He collaborated with Wegeler in the *Biographishe Notizen über Ludwig van Beethoven*, one of the most important early biographies of the genius.

-RIES, FRANZ-WILHELM (1846 Berlin; d. Naumburg by Saale River, near mouth of Unstrut River, Saxony-Anhalt Land. 1932) German violinist and music publisher, son of Hubert (Pieter) Ries. Studied violin first with his father, then with Massart** and Vieuxtemps** in Paris. He started at the Crystal Palace in 1870, but soon his promising career was cut short by a nervous disease in 1873, which prompted him to enter the music trade, founding with Hermann Erler the RIES & ERLER publishing house in 1881. Owned the Strad Ries, Prieto, of 1693.

-RIES, HUBERT PIETER(1802 Bonn; d. Berlin 1886) German composer and violinist. After having studied with his father for a while, he went to Spohr becoming one of his best pupils. Settled in Berlin from 1824 he entered the Königstad Theater Orchestra and the Court Orchestra. In 1935 he was appointed director of the Berlin Philharmonic Society, becoming its leader* the next year. Fellow of the academy of Arts (1839). As composer he wrote two violin concertos, some string quartets and a *Violin School* for beginners.

-ROBESPIERRE, MAXIMILIEN FRANÇOIS MARIE ISIDORE DE (1758, Arras, Fr; d. 1794 under the guillotin*, Paris) One of the principal figures of the French Revolution. He made more than 500 speeches at the National Assembly. He presided over the ultra left party of the Jacobins*, and the Committee for Public Safety which instituted the Reign of Terror*. The terror excesses increased notably his enemies, and eventually he was declared outlaw by the National Convention, and arrested the 9 thermidor an II (see calendar* French Revolution) 27 July 1794. He tried to commit suicide wounding himself severely with a pistol in the jaw, but he was unsuccessful. On the evening of 10 thermidor (see calendar* French Revolution) -July 28- Robespierre and 20 of his followers were guillotined* before a cheering mob on the Place de la Révolution (Place de la Concorde).

-ROBINEAU, ALEXANDRE-AUGUST, L'ABBÉ (1747 Paris; d. id 1828) French violinist, composer and painter. Pupil of Gavinies** he went to Naples to study with

Lolli** (1762) Here his success was enormous to the point that he had the sobriquet of "il Lollinelli". Appeared often at the Concert spirituel*, he was *secretaire des menus plaisirs* from 1785 till the Revolution. He was also leader* of the orch of the Théâtre Français 1789-92.

-RODOLPHE, JEAN-JOSEPH (1730 Strasbourg; d. 1812 Paris) Alsatian violinist, horn player and composer. He studied violin with Leclair**, and counterpoint* with Traetta* and Jomelli* . Composed several operas and ballets. Professor of the Ecole Royale de Chant et de Déclamation, he passed to the Paris conservatoire* on its creation as solfège professor. He was a virtuoso of both horn and violin.

-ROLLA, ALESSANDRO (1757 Pavia; d. Milan 1841) Italian violist, violinist teacher and composer. From 1782 to 1802 he was first violist, first violin* and director to the court of Parma. He then moved to Milan where he was first violin* and director of the orch. of La Scala (1803-33). In 1808 he was the first professor of violin and viola at the new Milan conservatory. He was a composer of great renown, and a first rank teacher. Owned the Strad Rolla, Pannier of 1722.

-ROMBERG, ANDREAS (1767 Vechta, 30 Km SW Bremen-115Km NW Hannover; d. Gotha, 25 Km W Erfurt 1821) Belonging to a celebrated family of German musicians, learnt the violin from his father. He toured with his cousin Bernard Romberg, a cellist, to Frankfurt am Main and Paris where they appeared successfully at the Concert spirituel*. They went later to Bonn where they met the young Bthvn, and to Vienna where they made friends with Haydn, making later a long tour through Italy 1795-96. His style was robust but cold, and inexpressive. As a composer his setting of Johann A. Hiller's* *Lied von der Glocke* had international renown, reaching New York. Composed also operas, songs and choral works.

-ROSE, LEONARD (1918 Washington; d. White Plains, New York 1984) One of the best cello teacher and player of the century. American cellist. Studied at the Miami Conservatory, and later in New York. He passed then to the Curtis Institute of Philadelphia. Joined the NBC SO under Toscanini, the Cleveland Orch and the New York PO; toured widely as soloist. He is also a good chamber player, in ensembles with Stern** and Istomin*. He plays a cello of 1662 by Nicola Amati. A superb teacher he was head of the cello department of the Julliard School till his death. Among his pupils towers Yo Yo Ma. By his will a Rose scholarship has been founded. He died in the White Plains Hospital, New York, after a long illness. He was 66 years old and lived in Hastings-on-Hudson, N.Y.

-ROSENTHAL, MORIZ (1862 Lemberg [now L'vov, 460 Km W of Kiev, 90 Km from the border of Poland]; d. New York 1946) Ukrainian pianist. He studied first in his native country and later went to Vienna to improve his technique. In 1877 he met Liszt and was under his direct tuition for the following nine years. He played remarkably well the romantics. In his last years he specialised in Chopin. He had a prodigious quick finger action. His mazurkas are played with such a rhythm that they represent, perhaps, the authentic Chopin's style to play them. No other great pianist of the XX century has ever produced such a syncopated rhythm. To figure out what was the rhythm of Chopin we must read Sir Charles Hallé's* Autobiography where he reports the following conversation with Chopin himself: *"I once ventured to observe him that most of his Mazurkas (those dainty jewels) when* *played by himself, appeared to be written, not in 3-4, but in 4-4 time, the result of his dwelling so much longer in on the first note in the bar".*

-ROSSI, SALAMONE (1570 Mantua; d. id c 1630) Italian composer and instrumentalist. He spent all his life in Mantua with long periods at the service of the duke of Mantua. Composer of madrigals and sacred vocal music, he is specially important for his contribution to the triosonata*. Much influenced by Monteverdi.

-ROSTAL, MAX (1905 Teschen, Silesia) British violinist of Austrian birth. Studied with Flesch in Berlin. Appointed assistant to Flesch, he became later the youngest professor of the Berlin Hochschule für Musik (1930-33). Professor of the Guildhall School of Music and Drama, London (1944-58) and the Cologne Academy and Bern. Owned a Strad Cator of 1697, now known as "Max Rostal" and a Guarnerius of 1733, the "Charles Reade*".

-RUBINSTEIN, ANTON (1829 Vikhvatintsy, Moldavia; d. Peterhof, nr S. Petersburg 1894) Russian pianist, composer and pedagogue. Not to be mistaken for Artur Rubinstein of the XX century, he was one of the greatest pianists of his time, together with Liszt. From 1850 his dedication as advocator for musical activities in Russia was notorious, creating an Academy of Singing in S. Petersburg 1858 and above all the Conservatory of S. Petersburg in 1862, of which he was director. As pedagogue he managed to impose in Russia a more international teaching method, opposing the traditionalist Russian trend in vogue at the time, creating a Musical Society whose concerts he conducted. He made also a triumphant tour on North America with Wieniawski**, giving more than 200 concerts in the years 1872-73. Rubinstein has always been a legendary figure as pianist. Of him Wieniawski** had declared that "his best music teacher had been Rubinstein".

-RUST, FRIEDERICK WILHELM (1739 Wörlitz, nr Dessau, midway Berlin Halle; d. Dessau 1796) German violinist and composer, belonged to a renowned family of musicians and editors. While he studied law at Halle he studied music with W. F. Bach. In 1763 he entered the retinue of prince Leopold III of Anhalt-Dessau. In 1763-64 he was in Potsdam, studying the violin with Benda**. He managed to turn Dessau into one of the most prominent musical centres in Germany. He was a first rank virtuoso of the violin. His compositions were arranged posthumously by his grandson Wilhelm (1822-1892) who presented them as notoriously original, anticipating some aspects of Romanticism. But Neufeldt, who compared them with the manuscript, discovered they had been entirely rewritten and updated by the grandson. This scandal was one of the most execrable hoaxes in the history of music

-RUZICKOVA, ZUZANA (1928 Plzen[Pilsen]) Czech harpsichordist. Studied at the Prague Academy, becoming a teacher there. Won the Munich International Competition in 1956. Won a Grand Prix du Disque in 1961 with Benda's* G major concerto. Also the Supraphone Grand Prix in 1968 and 1969. Cofounder of the Prague Chamber Soloists. In 1963 she formed a duo with violinist J. Suk.

-SAINT EUSTACHE: The second church in importance of Paris (1532-1637). It is here that Mozart's mother is interred. Note worthy are its rose window over the main entrance door in heavenly blue colours, and its singing choir, one of the best in the world. They all sing sight reading any score put before them. Berlioz sang with them to cover his most urgent needs when he had just arrived in Paris, with a ridiculous paternal pension, to study medicine. Berlioz tells us that when he went for the entry examination, he was asked what song he had prepared to sing, to what he replied: "Give me any score and I will sing it for you" Note worthy, as well, is one of the most typical restaurants in Paris, opened 24 hours, with excellent oysters, sea-food, *soup à l'oignon* and *crêpes suzettes*, just opposite to the main door: *Au Pied de Cochon*. During the 50s and the 60s it was quite in fashion among the *"chic"* people of the City of Light* to mingle with the working classes of a celebrated market, Les Halles, after a night on the town, all in evening dresses, in a splendorous show off of equalitarian, democratic, and brotherly affability, not lacking some affected paternalism, and great doses of sheer vanity, ending, almost always invariably at dawn, by having a succulent *soupe à l'oignon* precisely in this restaurant which was within the market, at 6 rue Coquillière (lane of the shell fish). The site of Les Halles is now occupied by the Centre Pompidou.

-SAINT-GEORGES, JOSEPH Boulogne, Chevalier de. (c 1739 Basse Terre, Guadeloupe; d. Paris 1799). A mulatto, son of a French councillor in the parliament of Metz and of a negress of Guadeloupe, he was a French composer, violinist and swordsman. He excelled also in skating, dancing, riding and swimming. He might have studied with Gossec* (composition) and Leclair**. His virtuosity was outstanding but he had also great expressiveness. He started playing at the orch. of les Amateurs, under Gossec's direction. When Gossec was promoted director of the Concert spirituel* in 1773 he advanced to musical director of the Orch Des Amateurs, under whose direction they became one of the best orchs. in France.

-SALAZAR, ADOLFO (1890 Madrid; d. Mexico D. F. 1958) One of the most renowned Spanish musicologists, he had relevant posts in *Revista Musical hispano-Americana, diario El Sol, Sociedad Nacional de Música, Ateneo de Madrid, International Society of Musicology* in The Hague, *International Society for Contemporary Music, Société Française de Musicologie.* He exiled himself during the Spanish Civil War to Mexico D. F. where he taught al the Colegio de Mexico and the National Conservatory. He wrote more that 30 books and many essays of deserved fame, among others *Juan Sebastian Bach, Teoría y Práctica de Armonía Moderna, La Música en el siglo XX, Los Grandes Periodos en la Historia de la Música.*

-SANTLEY, SIR CHARLES: (1834 Liverpool; d. London 1922) English baritone. In 1855 he went to Milan to study with Gaetano Nava. In 1857 made his debut in La Traviata in Pavia, returning soon after to England to study with Manuel García* Jr.(Sitches). Sang mainly in the UK, and in 1871 toured the USA. Although not endowed with a natural beautiful voice he sang with great expression and was a good actor on the stage.

-SARRETTE, BERNARD (1765 Bordeaux; d. Paris 1858) French musical administrator, founder of the Paris Conservatoire*. Captain of the Garde Nationale he formed within this body a school of music in 1789, the *École supérieur de musique de la garde nationale* with the double goal to grant free tuition of wind instruments to young soldiers and to participate in the celebration of patriotic events. Thus the first free school for wind instruments was founded in France. The Commune de Paris* abolished the Garde Nationale in 1792, but Sarrette profited of the occasion to obtained in 1793 an authorisation to found a new, enlarged musical school where the old military musicians of the Garde Nationale became the new teachers; this was the *Institut nationale de musique**. Later, wishing to enlarge the teachings of this Institut to singing, and keyboard and string instruments, he obtained the incorporation to the Institut of the old *École royal de chant** in 1794. Finally, by a law of the Convention of the 16 Thermidor year III [see calendar* of French Revolution] (August 3, 1795) the Paris Conservatoire* was founded, entrusting its direction to Sarrette. He headed the Conservatoire for 20 years, in which period he organised the institution, creating the library and a museum. His qualities of organisation and creativity made of him a first rank personality of the musical life under the Revolution and the Empire.

-SAURET, EMILE (1852 Dun le Roi; d. London 1920) French violinist and teacher. Prodigy child. He studied with Vieuxtemps** and Wieniawski** taking from the latter his most individual, expressive vibrato. As a performer he played in all the major cites in Europe and made several triumphant tours in America. He taught in the Royal Academy of Music and Trinity College of Music in London; in The Musical College of Chicago; in Berlin at the Kullaks Akademie and at the Stern Conservatory. He published the *Gradus at Parnasus du violoniste*, a famous teaching work. His pet instruments: Strads: Sauret of 1702; Sauret, Cobbet of 1703; Sauret, Joachim of 1723, and a Guarneri del Gesu "Sauret" of 1744. This superb, stunningly beautiful, bright orange coloured instrument has been acquired by Perlman** in 1986.

-SAUZAY, EUGENE (1809 Paris; d. id 1901) French violinist. He entered the Paris conservatory* in 1824 to study with Baillot**, wining first prize in 1827. He replaced his indisposed teacher at the first Concert du conservatoire, playing a concerto by Rode**; thereafter he appeared frequently as soloist. He played the second violin and the viola in Baillot's string quartet. Later he formed his own group of chamber music. He taught at the Paris conservatoire from 1860 to 1892. He wrote *Etudes sur les quatuors de Haydn, Mozart et Bthvn* 1861, *L'Ecole d'accompagnement* 1869 (R 1972) and *Le violon harmonique* 1889. Had three valuable Strads: the Thibaud of 1709 owned also by Baillot; the Titian of 1715, owned also by Grumiaux and Zimbalist; and the de Baillot of 1732, owned also by Kreisler.

-SCALE: The ascending sequence of notes that go in a determined order of pitch from a principal note (tonic*) to its repetition in double frequency. They conform the octave* and the tonality* or the key* of a certain piece of music and are the basis of all western musical systems. It can also go in a descending order, of course. The normal diatonic* scale, in major* mode* , is: do, re, mi, fa, sol, la, si, do. Each note is separated from the other by one full tone (two semitones) except for the intervals* mi-fa, and si-do, that are apart only one semitone. For more details see octave.

-SCORDATURA: Any tuning of the violin other than the established g-d'-a'-e''. *(sol, re', la', mi''.* Spanish mnemonic: "sol relamido").

-SCHERING, ARNOLD (1877 Breslau; d. Berlin 1941) German musicologist. He began studying the violin and he even went to Berlin to work under Joachim** (1896) with the intention to become a virtuoso, but in 1898 he decided on an academic career, taking his PhD at Leipzig. He soon became associated with several musical periodicals: *Neue Zeitschrift für Musik; Bach-Jahrbuch*. Professor at the

University of Leipzig, Leipzig conservatory, Halle and Berlin. His main interest was ancient music, particularly Bach. His main work is *Geshichte der Musik in Beispielen*, 1931. He overreached himself in his efforts to explain how Bach should be interpreted (*an unattainable endeavour, for Bach is essentially awe inspiring and impenetrable, and therefore difficult to translate in music, for he lies somewhere in the middle of his two, far away, opposite extremes: his inflexible, almost mechanical tempo (strict time) on the one side, and on the other, his extreme, passionate "stilo rappresentativo*". To follow the strict time without falling into a frigid, heartless measurement, and to reflect passions and feelings without the exuberant excesses of Romanticism, here lies the secret.*<Neither a tarte à la crème, nor a computerized soulless mechanical tempo> (This is my personal view).

-SCHMELZER, JOHANN-HEINRICH (? c 1623; d. Prague 1680) Austrian composer and violin virtuoso. Said to have been teacher of Biber** He was chamber musician at the imperial chapel* in Vienna. Then he became vice Kapellmeister in 1671 and Kapellmeister* in 1679. Pupil of Antonio Bertali he published a series of solo violin sonatas in the Italian style, and many other *triosonaten** characterized by a rich contrapunctistic writing, and the use of scordatura*, which will be later developed by Biber**. He created a distinct Austrian style of sonatas with emphasis in a melodic cantabile with colourful ornamentation. He was considered one of the most salient composers of his time.

-SCHNABEL, ARTUR (1882 Lipnik, midway Brno-Ostrava, Austria [now Czech Republic]; d. Axenstein, Switzerland 1951) Austrian pianist and composer, naturalised in USA. One of the most salient pianists of all times he has become a legend. He studied the piano with Leschetizky* (teacher of Paderewski*) who oriented him towards a conception more musical than virtuosistic, encouraging him to play Schubert, totally neglected at the time. He told him this very significative compliment: "you will never become a pianist: you are a musician". Married to Therese Behr, a contralto renowned for her interpretations of Schubert's lieders*, they gave together memorable Schubertiades. He was also a fantastic chamber pianist, playing with Pablo Casals*, Flesch**, Primrose*, Fournier*, Szigeti**. Teacher at the Academy of Music in Berlin. He was the first to record the complete piano sonatas by Bthvn. His favourites authors were Mozart, Bthvn and Schubert. Particularly in the latter he plays with such a fire, stamina, rhythm, passion and romanticism, that even the most abused of his moments musicaux becomes new under his fingers. It is also in Schubert that Schnabel uses the pedal* with more intensity than in any other composer, pioneering thus the modern way to play the piano immersed in all the sonorities and harmonics* that the use of the pedal allows. If I were compelled to choose only one of his records I would not hesitate to buy the Marche Militaire D 733-1 in D (the most abused). It is here that he towers among others.

-SCHOELCHER, VICTOR (1804 Paris; d. Houilles, 11 Km NW of Paris 1893) French writer, musicologist and critic of art, he devoted the bulk of his writings to put an end to slavery in the empire. He became so famous that he was appointed under-secretary for the navy. In this capacity he prepared the famous decree that abolished slavery in the colonies.

381

-SCHRAMMEL, JOHANN (1850 Neulerchenfeld, nr Vienna; d. Vienna 1893) Austrian violinist and composer. Studied with Hellmesberger* Jr in Vienna. Played in the orchestras of the Harmonie and Josephstadt theatres. Wrote many popular dances, song and marches for the Schrammel trio. His *Wien bleibt Wien* is most popular in Austria. His brother Joseph (1852 Ottakring nr Vienna; d. id 1895) violinist and composer, studied also with Hellmesberger Jr. and was the founder and manager of the trio bearing his name. Composed many songs and dances for his trio, although with less success that his brother.

-SCHUBART, CHRISTIAN FRIEDRICH DANIEL (1739 Oberstonheim, Swabia; d. Stuttgart 1791) German composer, poet and writer on music. His exceptional talents for music showed very early but his parents wanted him to study theology. In a pendulum reaction he led a dissolute life that ended in his imprisonment for ten years, during which time he wrote the majority of his works, that include poems to be put in music (lieds), musical essays, and his main work *Ideen zu einer Ästhetik der Tonkunst*. His ideas and chronicles reflect vividly the musical life of his time. For him, expression is the axis around which the aesthetic of music turns. He was one of the first writers of his generation to comprehend the true value of J.S. Bach. His poem of "The Trout" put in music by Schubert has a perennial place in the lieder* literature.

-SCHUMANN, CLARA. Née WIECK*. (1819 Leipzig; d. Frankfurt am Main, 35 Km NE of Mainz, by River Main, Germany 1896). One of the most mythical musicians of all times, she was the wife of Robert Schumann, and one of the most formidable pianists of her day. Inspiror of R. Schumann and Brahms, her romantic struggle to marry Schumann against the fanatic opposition of her father became one of the most moving Romantic episodes in history, described in countless books. She was also a remarkably good composer.

-SCORDATURA: Any tuning of the violin other than its established g, d, a, e.

-SERKIN, RUDOLF (1903 Eger, Bohemia; d. Guildford, Vt USA 1991) American pianist of Austrian origin. Studied in Vienna with Richard Robert (piano) and Schönberg (composition). In 1920 he met Adolf Busch* a determinant influence in his musical life, whose daughter he married. With the Busch brothers he plays chamber music and discovers Bach. He worked at Darmstadt and Basel before settling in the USA, after a staggering debut with the Philhar. of New York under Toscanini. Piano teacher at the Curtis Institute of Philadelphia, and director of the Marlboro festival in Vermont, USA. With a splendid touch, and a fine musicality, he is one of the greatest pianists of the XX century.

-SERWACZYNSKI, STANISLAW (1791 Lublin; d. Lwow 1859) Polish violinist, conductor, teacher and composer. Studied with his father, a professional musician. Travelled in concert through Italy. Leader* of the theatre orchestras in Vienna and Budapest. He taught Joachim and Wieniawski.

-SEVEN HILLS, CITY OF THE: See City of the Seven Hills.

-SHARP: An accidental* sign put to the left of a note on the stave* which makes its conventional pitch increase by one semitone. If we add a double sharp, it will be increased by two semitones, or one tone. A single sharp is marked # on the staff*, and the double sharp is marked *x*. The notion of tones and semitones are so basic, that we take it for granted that the reader knows it, or will easily learn it.

-SINFONIA: Although it has great resemblance with the word "Symphony" it does not mean the same, but, a) either the overture of a vocal or operatic work, or b) an instrumental piece often analogous to the canzona* or the sonata*, suite* or partita*.
-SINGSPIEL: A typical German operetta in which singing alternates with spoken dialogues. It corresponds to the *zarzuela** in Spain and the *opera comique** in France. To make easier its study we will consider separately Germany and Vienna.
A) **Germany**: Although already Haydn had composed *Der Krume Toifel* (1751, performed in Vienna) among others, and Standfuss staged his *Der Toifel ist los* in Leipzig 1752, which originated a battle of pamphlets, and its second part *Der Lustige Schuster* (Lübeck 1759), the father of the singspiel in Germany is unanimously considered to be Johann Adam Hiller*, who made a revision of both in Leipzig in 1770- 71; after these, he reached its peak with *Die Liebe auf dem Lande* (1768), and *Die Jagd* (1770). The singspiel in Germany did not quite catch its full popularity until it was already in full swing in Vienna. We must name also Georg Benda's** *Walder* (1776), and *Romeo und Julie* 1776); Johann André's *Der Töpfer* (1773) *Elwin und Elmir* (Goethe, 1755), *Leonore* (1775); Neefe's *Heinrich und Lyda* (1776); Reichardt's *Jery und Bätely* (Goethe, 1801), and his best *Die Geisterinsel* (1798); Zumsteeg's *Das Tartarische Gesets* (1780), *Der Schuss von Gänzewig* (1781); Himmel's *Fanchon, das Leyermädchen* (1804); E. T. A. Hoffmann's *Die Maske* (1799), *Scherz, List und Rachel* (Goethe – 1801), *Die lustigen Musikanten* (1805) ; Conradin Kreutzer's *Jery und Bätely* (Goethe, 1810), *Baron Luft* (1830); Weber's *Die Macht der Liebe und des Weins* (1789), *Abu Hassan* (1810), *Der Freischütz* (1817), *Oberon* (1825). B) **Vienna**: The most important period starts in 1778 with the institution of the German National-Singspiel in Vienna by Joseph II. The first singspiel staged here was Umlauf's *Die Bergknappen* (1778, with over 30 perform.); He composed also *Die schöne Schusterin oder Die pücefarbenen Schuhe* (1779, with over 60 perform.), and *Das Irrlicht* (1782, with more than 30 perform.); We must mention also Carlo d'Ordonez's *Diesmal hat der Mann den Willen* (1778); Dittersdorf's* *Doctor un Apotheker* (1786), *Betrug durch aberglauben* (1786), *Die liebe im Narrenhause* (1787), *Hieronymus Knicker* (1789); Johann Schenk's *Im Finstern ist night gut tappen* (1789), *Der Dorfbarbier* (1796); Peter von winter's *Jery und Bäteli* (Goethe – 1790), *Das unterbrochene Opferfest* (1796), and his best, *Der Bettelstudent oder Das Donnerwetter* (After Cervantes, 1785); Gyrowetz's *Der Augenartz*; Weigl's *Die Schweitzerfamilie* (1809); Wenzel Müller's *Das verfehlte Rendezvous, oder Die weiblichen Jäger* (1782) and *Die Schwestern von Prag* (1794); Schubert's *Fernando* (1815), *Die Freunde von Salamanca* (1815), *Die Zwillinggsbrüder* (1889); Beethoven's *Fidelio*, and, last, but certainly not least, Mozart's *Die Entführung des Serail*. The supreme Singspiel is Mozart's **The Magic Flute.**
-SIRMEN, MADDALENA, née Lombardini. See LOMBARDINI
-SLUR: 1) Corresponds to the Italian notation *legato** meaning that the notes under this signature must be played with a most close continuity and unity, joining their sound together so that the sound of one note is followed by the next without break between them. The sound of one note is almost incorporated into the sound of the next, and will not stop until the next sound is audible, and so on with all the slurred notes, resulting in a musical phrase in which all notes are closely related in a single

sound impulse. It is the opposite of the stacatto* where between every note there must be a silence so that they become all well detached from one another. Slur is indicated on the stave* by a curved line over the notes that are wanted to be slurred. 2) In bow instruments it also means notes that must be played within one bow direction.

-SOCIÉTÉ DES CONCERTS DU CONSERVATOIRE DE PARIS: Created in 1828 at the request of Habeneck*, the members of the orch. are recruited exclusively among pupils or former pupils of the Paris conservatory*. Its first director was Habeneck*, who had the merit to introduce in France Bthvn's works, little known at the time. Among the renowned artist to play here were Chopin, Liszt, Ernst**, Berlioz, Pauline Viardot*, Clara Schumann*, Saint-Saëns, Sarasate**, Paderewski*, Joachim**, Enescu**.

-SONATA: At the beginnings of instrumental music, sonata meant the same as suite* and partita*. The sonata began as a piece of instrumental music for two violins and basso continuo*, in what the Germans call, more specifically, *Triosonata*, directly derived from the vocal canzona*. The first instrumental pieces for violin were not for a violin solo but consisted in works for several parts, to be played by two treble (two violins) in fugal* imitation* and a basso continuo* (harpsichord, organ). We find thus sonatas in trio by Schmelzer*, Valentini*, Fux*, Kerll*, Couperin, Vitali*, Bononcini*, Cazzati*, Rossi*, Ucellini* and Marini*. These sonatas basically consist of compilations and collections of small musical pieces, generally the transcription of vocal and dance music, disposed in series, that are played in succession, as a whole, in the same sitting. These sonatas are divided into two main groups: 1) Sonata da chiesa. 2) Sonata da camera. These two types of sonatas have something in common, the alternance of a certain number of contrasting movements, so that we may say that they differ more by the type of the pieces they contain, than by their general disposition. 1) The sonata da chiesa is more inspired by the stern polyphonic* style of church vocal music, and is divided into pieces of different tempos that contrast with each other like largo, allegro, adagio* and vivace, and where the use of the fugue* is almost constant. 2) The sonata da camera, on its side, consists mainly on a series of dances, in which the grave, solemn tone of the Sarabande alternates with the more gay of the Courantes and Giges. It will be this sonata da camera which will develop and progress more rapidly. The sonata da camera turns around three main, basic dances: Allemande, Courante and Sarabande, the essential triptych. To it other dances can be added, such as the Menuet, Bourrée, Gaillard, Gigues and Pavane. If we make a further effort we will arrive to the sonata for violin solo, without basso*. Bach during his Köthen period (1717-1723) writes three suites* and three sonatas* for violin solo which according to Spitta* are the first of their genre. But Adolfo Salazar* singles out those of other composers prior to Bach such as Baltzar*, Walther**, Biber**, Matteis*, Geminiani**, Pisendel**, and Telemann, the excellent characteristics of them all were gathered by Bach, and largely exceeded, reaching that greatest possible perfection, the search for which was the ultimate and central concern of Bach's method of composition. Nevertheless the extreme difficulties of these kind of sonatas make of them a rare specimen in the violin literature. As for the suites* and partitas* we will only say that they are but two more names to designate the same instrumental genre: the sonata. So sonata, suite and partita are equivalent. Suite is derived from the French "de suite": in succession, in a row; and partita, from the Italian "partita": a musical piece divided into parts. See trio sonata.

-SONATA FORM: It is a most sophisticated form of composition, which requires a high knowledge of harmony*, which presents very different formats, which are not specified in strict rules, but leave the composer an infinite variety of choice. Notwithstanding, we may say that, basically, it lies on the principle of double tension, both between the tonic* and other different keys* into which the composer ventures, and between the different themes, which contrast among themselves, viz, tragic versus sweet, virile v. delicate and feminine, bucolic v. triumphant, sad v. gay. The contrast between keys* is produced by modulating* ever to more remote tonalities* from the tonic*, which create in the ear a pressing desire to return to the tonic. When this distance is at its maximum, the sonata reaches its "Climax". When at the end the sonata returns to the tonic, a sensation of comfort and relieve fills up the listener's ears. It is divided, always broadly speaking, into three main parts: 1) Exposition: The main theme is "exposed" in the tonic*, and another theme may come, which modulates* generally to the dominant (see octave*). 2) Development: There come new themes, in new keys*, ever more distant from the tonic, which produces an eager desire to return to the tonic, but this return is delayed by the appearance of these new themes and keys*) 3)Recapitulation: The long desired return to the tonic takes place, but to make this relieve sensation more agreable there is, also, a return to the first, main, theme, in what is called *double return* of tonality* and theme. Being so intricate and complicated, I renounce here to explain it in a few words.

-SPITTA, PHILIPPE (1841 Wechold, Hanover; d. Berlin 1894) first magnitude German musicologist and music historian. Founder of the Bachverein in Leipzig (Bach Society) In 1875 he was appointed professor of Musical History at the university of Berlin and in 1875 he was Director of the Berlin Hochschule für Musik (conservatory). His monumental work Johann Sebastian Bach deals with his life and technical aspects of his work. Similarly important are his editions of the works of Buxtehude and Schütz. Co-founder of the great edition of German composers *Monuments of German Music* and of the first important journal of musicology *Viertljahrsschrift für Musikwissenschaft (*Quarterly Journal of Musicology).

-STACCATO: (Italian "staccare": to detach) A series of short, clearly separated notes, very much detached from one another, written in the score with a dot on top of them, performed on a single bow stroke direction, either up or down. There are two forms of it: 1) The "flying (or bouncing) staccato" in which, after every accentuated note, the bow is permitted – and encouraged – to leave the string, marking thus more vividly the detachment of every note. The bounces in this staccato are, nevertheless, constantly supervised by the right hand. 2) The "solid staccato" performed while the hair of the bow remains in permanent contact with the string; the bow is set firmly for each stroke, and the pressure is released after the accent has sounded on each note.

-STAFF (see stave)

-STAINER, JAKOB (?1617 Absam, Tyrol; d. id 1683) Austrian luthier*. His violins were the most reputed of all, their fame surpassing even that of the Cremona masters (Amati, Guarneri, Stradivarius). His first violin was made in 1638 and his last in 1682. Their reputation lasted well until the end of the 18th century, when a change in what was considered the ideal sound, made the Cremona instruments to be preferred. During the 19th century they completely superseded the Stainers. Today the Absam violins have only a historical value.

-STARKER, JANOS (1924 Budapest) American cellist of Hungarian birth. Graduated from the Budapest conservatory in 1935. After being first cellist in the Budapest PO 1945-6, he escaped to USA. First cello in the Dallas SO (1948-9) Metropolitan Opera Orch (1949-53) and the Chicago SO (1953-58). Cellist of great reputation has toured around the world. Played in trio with J. Suk** and Julius Katchen*. Professor at the Indiana University from 1958. Plays a Matteo Gofriller cello (Venice, 1706) called the "Star", The Strad ex Aylesford of 1696, owned also by Giardini and Piatigorski*, and a Guarneri del Gesu Nova of 1707.

-STAVE. [also staff] A grouping of five parallel lines on which the musical notations are written on the score.

-STILO RAPPRESENTATIVO: A musical style where music should express, (represent) the feelings and meanings of the words in vocal music, more specifically, in opera. As in so many other fields it was Monteverdi its creator. It implies the will of an extreme expressiveness with which, music by itself, without any help from the actors, is to describe an action or the emotion of a feeling. It aims at the perfect fusion of words with music, privileging music over action in the sempiternal dispute between words and music in opera.

-STOCKHAUSEN, JULIUS (1826 Paris; d. Frankfurt am Main, 35 Km NE of Mainz, by River Main, Germany 1906) German baritone, conductor and teacher. He began learning with his parents and in 1847 started private lessons with Manuel García* Jr., who was teaching at the time in the Paris Conservatoire*. He followed García Jr. to London where he performed for Queen Victoria. He travelled around Germany, Austria and Denmark until he settled in Frankfurt am Main in 1878, where he taught in the new conservatory, and at his own school of singing (1880). He did not sing many operas but preferred oratorios, and above all lieders* of Brahms, Schumann and Schubert, giving the first performance of Schubert's "Die shöne Müllerin" in Vienna. He made a good friendship with Brahms and the Schumanns. Brahms's *Magelone Lieder** are dedicated to him.

-STOP: To press firmly a string of the violin against the fingerboard to make it sound (vibrate) partially from the finger to the bridge, as opposed to *open* strings that vibrate freely all along their length.

-STOPS: double, triple, quadruple, multiple stops. See multiple stops.

-STRADELLA, ALESSANDRO (1644 Rome; d. Genoa 1682) Italian composer of the first magnitude. Of noble ascendance, he was wealthy enough to live as he wished. He was singer in S. Giovanni dei Fiorentini and the Oratorio del Crocifisso. After having been accomplice on a theft to the church, soon discovered, he was forced to leave Rome. He was hired by a distinguished member of a powerful family of Venice, Alvise Contarini, to teach music to his mistress. He instead wan her heart and flew in her company. Constantly pursued by hired hooligans to kill him, he was seriously injured in Turin. He continued his rover existence until he was assassinated for another intrigue with another woman, this time involving the most influential family of Lomellini in Genoa. He was one of the most inventive composers of his time, with a melodic lyricism, easily recognisable. His works include all major categories: instrumental: like many concerto grosso*, of which he is one of the inventors (with Torelli** and Corelli**) sonatas* da camera and da chiesa. Vocal: like cantatas, operas and oratorios.

-STRATICO, MICHELE (c 1721 Zara, [now zadar, Yugoslavia]; d. 1782 ?) Italian violinist and composer. He came from an aristocratic family of Venice. Pupil and friend of Tartini**, he was a dilettante.

-SUE, MARIE-JOSEPH, called EUGÈNE (1824 Paris; d. Annency 1857) Eugène was his pseudonym. The most popular French writer of the XIX century. Born into a wealthy family he was a very bad and turbulent student and his father took him out of school to send him for a long, long journey on board a ship to practice medicine. He went to La Martinique, Spain and Greece. After three years he returned with a lot of exciting experiences which he put down into novels. First, sea life stories like *Plik et Plok*, and *Atar Gull*. Having inherited a fortune from his father, he became one of the most well-known dandies in the City of Light*. His extravagant life, with fashionable official mistress included (Olympe Pelissier) made of him the talk of the whole Paris. He was the leading figure of the *Roman-Feuilleton* (newspaper serial) which highly increased the circulation of the newspapers in which they appeared. He described the high life in Paris in *Mathilde, Mémoires d'une jeunne femme*, which was his best seller, *Arthur, La Coucaratcha* and *La Vigie de Koatven*. Among his adventure novels we must name *Kernok le pirate* and *El gitano*. He denounced the injustices of the industrial revolution in *Les mystères de Paris*, which inspired Victor Hugo for his *Miserables*. He wrote also an *Histoire de la marine française*.

-SUITE: several musical pieces that are to be played in a row. [French "de suite"] Means the same as partita* and sonata*. See triosonata*

-SUN KING: Louis XIV of France. (le Roi Soleil).

-SUSTAINING PEDAL (see damper)

-SZEKELY, ZOLTAN: (1903 Kocs, midway Gyor-Budapest) Hungarian violinist. Pupil of Hubay in Budapest, he toured widely and was leader of the Hungarian String Quartet from 1935 until it disbanded. Good friend of Bartok he played in duo with him and was the dedicatee of his violin concerto 2, premiering it in Amsterdam with the Concertgebouw. Since 1950 he settled in the USA. Played on the Strad. Michelangelo, Szekely, Zoltan, Deschamp of 1718.

-SZERYNG, HENRYK (1918 Zelazowa Wola, small village 45 Km W of Warsaw [Chopin's birth place]; d. Kassel 1988) Mexican violinist of Polish birth. Studied in Berlin with Flesch, and in Paris with Thibaud and six years with Nadia Boulanger. Sent to Mexico to find homes for refugees on World War II, he started teaching at the University of Mexico in 1946. Has recorded all the Mozart works for violin and orch. His salient violins: Guarneri Sanctae Theresiae of 1685; Guarneri del Gesu Leduc* of 1743; a Strad king David ?; and a Guadagnini* of 1752.

-T'SONG, FOU (1934 Shanghai, China) British pianist of Chinese birth. Born into a cultivated family he first received lessons from Mario Paci. He won third prize at the Bucharest Piano competition, 1953, and third prize also at the Chopin Contest in Warsaw, 1955. He later studied with Drzewiecki. He has recorded a considerable amount of CDs and has toured the main cities of the world. His delicate sensibility makes of him an excellent interpreter of Debussy, Chopin and Mozart.

-TARISIO, LUIGI (Fontanetto, nr Novaro, Piedmont; d. Milan 1854) Italian luthier*, dealer and collector. Of a very humble origin he started as a carpenter before devoting to violin making. Very intelligent, he collected a numerous amount of valuable fiddles that remained unused in the towns of Northern Italy. He then started his business, taking to Paris some of the finest violins for sale in 1827. In this same year he made his greatest coup, buying an important collection from count Cozio of Salabue, among them his gem, a Strad of which he spoke every time he went to Paris, but would never take there, which no money would buy. So anxiously desired it became in the City of Light* that it was dubbed the "Messiah". After his death it was the turn of the Paris luthier* Vuillaume* (father in law of Alard**) who hurried to Italy to buy from his inheritors no less than 20 Strads (including the "Messiah") and more than 120 other masterpieces, all hidden in a dingy attic in Milan.

-TAUDOU, ANTOINE, ANTONINE BARTHÈLEMY ((1866 Perpignan [Pyrènnèes-Orientales]; d. Saint Germain en Laye, nr Paris, 1925) French violinist. Studied two years in the Paris conservatoire with Reben and later with Massart, with whom he got the first prize in 1866. Won the Prix de Rome* in 1869. Violin professor at the Paris Conservatory 1883-1913.

-TELMANYI, EMIL (1892 Arad, Hungary, now Oradea Romania, d. ? 1988) Pupil of Hubay** won the Remenyi* prize in 1906. His reputation began in Berlin with the Elgar's concerto. He is also reputed as conductor. His interest centred in Baroque music, inventing a special bow called the "Vega", which had not any particular success and, although practical, its use has not become widespread.

-TEMIANKA, HENRI (1906 Greenock, Just west of Glasgow, Scotland) American violinist and conductor of Scottish birth. Few violinists have had such cosmopolitan beginnings as him. After 8 year studies with Blitz in Rotterdam, 2 years with Willy Hess* in Berlin, 2 more years with Boucherit in Paris, and finally some more with Flesch** at the Curtis Institute, he graduated here in 1930. Leader* of the Scottish Orch and the Pittsburgh SO. He embarked on a soloist international career. He entered the most famous of all the Wieniawski** International Competitions, that of 1935, where he got a third prize after Neveu** 1st and Oistrakh** 2nd sic. Founded the Paganini** String Quartet in 1946, so called because all the Strads they played were once owned by Paganini, and the California Chamber SO in 1960. Professor at the University of California in Sta. Barbara (1960-64) and California state University at Long beach (1964-76) Has made several educational films and published *Facing the Music* (New York, 1973)

-TERROR, REIGN OF: the bloodiest period of the French Revolution (Sept 5, 1793-July 27, 1794) under the direction of the Committee for Public Health, where Robespierre* was its main figure. The terror took extreme harsh measures against any possible enemy of the Republic, priests, nones, nobles, hoarders, and in the end, anyone whatsoever. (In this indiscrimination consisted precisely the essence of the terror) and a wave of executions followed. The number of detainees was more that 300,000, and 40,000 were executed. The Hungarian born British novelist Baroness Emmuska Orczy, wrote a novel based on the Terror, *The Scarlet Pimpernel*, relating the elusive, risky adventures of a British noble, Sir Percy Blakeney, whose mission was to smuggle out of the terror to safety, French aristocrats. It has been brought to the movies several times with world wide success, to the extreme distaste of the French.

-TESSITURA: Range of voice from the lowest to the highest pitch of a singer. In a more concise meaning, it denotes the most used margin of notes of a certain piece, not its maximum extremes, but within which zone of that range it is most used. So, for instance, if we say that an aria* has a high tessitura, it means that most of it must be sung in the higher range. i.e. from 0 to 10 it would go most frequently within margin 6 to 8, or to say it more technically: if the total range of a tenor is from c to c'', two octaves*. The aria* would be in high tessitura if it makes him sing, more frequently, between e'' and a'' of the second octave*.

-THOMAS, AMBROISE (1811 Metz; d. Paris 1896) French opera composer. Son of a music teacher he had a solid formation in music and by the age of eight he was a good violinist and pianist. At the death of his father the family moved to Paris, where he entered the Conservatoire. He had private piano lesson with Kalkbrenner*. He won the Prix de Rome going to the Eternal City*, where Ingres directed Villa Medicis*, making a good friendship with him and playing frequently with him with delight. He rivalled constantly with Gounod. He enjoyed succes in his life time thanks to his uncritical acceptance of the chavinistic tastes of his time. Excelled in opera comique*, with great successes like *Le Caïd, Le Songe d'une nuit d'été;* but his master pieces were *Mignon* and the opera *Hamlet*. Director of the Conservatoire he was made Chevalier de la Legion d'honneur* in 1845, and on the occasion of the 1000th performance of Mignon, he was the first composer to receive the Grand Croix of this Order.

-TOLBECQUE. Belgian family of musicians settled in France. Jean Baptist Joseph (1797 Hanzinnen, Namour; d. Paris 1869) Violinist and composer. Studied violin with R. Kreutzer** at the Paris conservatory*. Played in the orch de l'Opéra Italien (1820-25) Founder-member of the Société des concerts du Conservatoire*. His dance composition were in great demand. Auguste Joseph (1801 Hanzinnen; d. Paris 1869) Violinist and composer. Studied with Kreutzer. Won premier prix in 1821. Played in the Opera orch. (1824-31) Member of the Société des Concert du conservatoire*, he played also at Her Majesty's theatre in London. Charles-Joseph (1806 Paris; d. id 1835) Violinist, conductor and composer. Studied with R Kreutzer; won premier prix in 1823. Played at the Société des Concerts du Conservatoire*. Was named conductor at the Théâtre des Variétés in 1830 where he composed music to be performed there.

-TOMASINI, ALOIS (1779 Eszterháza; d. Neustrelitz, midway Rostck-Berlin, 1858) Austrian violinist and composer. He studied with his father Alois Luigi. He was accepted at the Estherhazy Kapelle* in 1796. Haydn considered him a *rare genius*. He became Konzertmeister* at Neustrelitz in 1809. Owned the Strad Caroli, Corti, owned also by Teresina Tua, of 1709.

-TONALITY: also called key*. See scale and octave.

-TONIC: The main note of the diatonic* scale*, it gives the name to the key* or tonality* in which a piece of music is played, and governs all the rules of the diatonic* system.

-TOSI, PIER FRANCESCO: (c1650 Cesana, 70 Km W of Torino; 5 Km E of the frontier with France; d. Faenza 1732) Italian castrato*, teacher of singing, music writer and diplomat. One of the best singers of his time, he is remembered mainly for his treatise *Opinioni de' cantori antiche e moderni, o sieno Osservazioni sopra il canto figurato*. Bologna 1723. (opinions on ancient and modern singers)

-TOUCHEMOULINS, JOSEPH (1727 Chalone sur-Saône, midway Macon-Dijon; d. 1801 Ratisbon [Regensburg] along Danube River) French violinist and composer. We know little of this violinist. Pupil of Tartini** he worked all his life outside France, as "hof Musikus" and Kapellmeister* of the court of the Saxon elector Clemens Augustus, disputing this post with Ludwig van Beethoven the father of the great genius. When Beethoven was admitted to the post, he went to the court of count Tour und Taxis in Ratisbon.

-TRAETTA, TOMASSO (1727 Bitonto, Episcopal see and town 20 Km W of Bari; d. Venice 1779) First magnitude Italian composer of opera seria; his successes include *Ippolito ed Aricia, I Tindari, Armide*. But his masterpiece was *Antigona*. His work lies in the junction between Rameau, Gluck and Mozart.

-TREMAIS, DE (Flourished 1735-50) French violinist and composer. We know nothing about this mysterious, but remarkable violinist and composer, who does not appear in any newspaper or chronicle of his time. Only M. Huet says that he was pupil of Tartini**. Nevertheless his works for violin appear in Leclerc's catalogue of 1740.

-TREMOLO: It has three meanings: a) that which is produced by the left hand, either by trembling the stopping* finger without lifting it from the string (vibrato), either by making tremble two different notes with an interval* of less than one third, using two fingers, or an open string and one finger that stops* and releases the string in a very fast motion (trill*). b) the trembling effect can be produced, also, by a quick and continuous repetition of the same note, by bowing very fastly up and down on the same note, or on two notes being apart an interval* of more that one third, to distinguish it from the trill*. Here the trembling effect is produced by the fast and trembling motion of the bow up and down. It produces a highly dramatic effect, and was first introduced at the beginning of the 17th century. We find the first examples in B. Marini's* *Affetti Musicali* (1617) and in Monteverdi's *Combatimento di Tancredi e Clorinda* (1624). c) The vibration of the voice in singing is called also tremolo*.

-TRILL: a rapid alternation of two notes one tone or a semitone apart, imitating the warble of a bird.

-TRIOSONATA: the violin plays solo in the sonatas*, suites* and partitas* . Like all the instrumental music, the sonata for violin, or rather for two violins, derives directly from the vocal music, and more specifically from the **canzona***. The canzona is distinguished by two main features: A) It is a four-four time composition, with its typical rhythm: a minim followed by two crotchets, or its variant: minim, two quavers, and two crotchets. B) It is arranged in fugal* imitations*. These fugues* were basically assigned to two or more treble choirs, supported by one or more basso continuo* choirs. When these canzonas were transformed into violin sonatas the fugue* was assigned to two violins which dialogued among themselves, supported by a basso continuo* (organ or harpsichord). The first innstrumental pieces for violin were not for a violin solo but consisted in works for several parts, in what the Germans call, more specifically, *Triosonaten**, works to be played by two treble (two violins) in fugal* imitation* and a basso continuo*. We find thus sonatas in trio by Schmelzer*, Valentini*, Fux*, Kerll*, Couperin, Vitali*, Bononcini*, Cazzati*, Rossi*, Ucellini* and Marini*. But being the organ and the harpsichord polyphonic* instruments in themselves, it soon became evident that the second treble voice of the fugue* could be assigned to their right hand, reducing the two violins to a single one. This origin of the solo violin sonata* has been clearly highlighted by Arnold Schering* in his *Zur Gersighte der Solosonaten in der ersten Halfte des 17 Jahrhunderts* (Rieman Festschift, pp 309 and following). Notwithstanding the influence of the trio sonata* will be immense, and we can see Leclair and Gavinies composing trio sonatas even at a time when the solo sonata was already in full swing. In fact the trio sonatas will remain alive until Viotti, the founder of the Romantic school. For more details see sonata.

-TUA, TERESINA (1866 Torino; d. Roma 1956) Born to an impoverished good family, her father Antonio was a strolling violinist. She learnt from him the beginnings, becoming soon a prodigy child, playing in the cafes and piazzas of Liguria, Piemonte and the South of France. Thanks to a patroness she was able to go to Paris to study with Massart, winning premier prix in 1880. She immediately started her international soloist career, playing at the main cities of Europe and USA. In Berlin she captivated Joachim. She toured Russia 1895-1898. Played in duo with Rachmaninof, Rosenthal* and the cellist Popper. Teacher at the Milan Conserv. 1915-24, and later at that of Rome. She abruptly left her teachings to enter the convent dell'Adorazione Perpetua at Rome, with the name of Suor Maria di Gèsu. The way she extracted the notes from her violin was remarkably expressive and had a penetrating poetry. What do they have all pupils of Massart, that they all are tender, melancholic and have that poetry of their maestro? Was he as much contagious as that? How singular, indeed, to be able to teach your pupils to play with poetry instead of technique! It must be very difficult indeed, because, whereas to teach technique is rather easy, for it involves mechanical drilling and physical abilities, poetry, on the contrary, is a faculty of the soul, much more difficult, if not impossible, to teach! To teach poetry is like to teach good taste, or elegance, something unteachable *per se*, for they come with you from your cradle, and cannot be taught. Just another miracle of maestro Massart. Violinists with the sublime taste and poetry of Tua*, Flesch, Hassid, Wieniawski, Enescu, Thibaud and Kreisler can only have come within the Massart family. Teresina owned two valuable Strads: the Tua, Soldat of 1708; and the Caroli, Corti, of 1709, owned also by Tomasini.

-TUILERIES*: French royal chateau adjacent to the Louvre Palais in Paris. It was commissioned in 1564 by Chaterine de Medici, who wished to have an independent "room" from the Louvre. It took more than 200 years to his total completion. It was destroyed by arson in 1871 by the populace of the Commune*.

-UCCELLINI, MARCO (? 1603; d. Forlimpopoli nr Forli 1680) Italian composer and instrumentalist. After studying in Assisi, he was maestro di capella* at the cathedral in Modena, and later Maestro di capella* at the Farnese court in Parma. His most important contribution was the development of the triosonata*. His style would be later followed by Cazzatti*, Vitali*, and Bononcini*. His virtuosity reaches the highest point before Schmelzer* and Biber**. He was teacher of Bononcini*.

-UFFENBACH, JOHANN FRIEDERICH (1687 Frankfurt am Main, 35 Km NE of Mainz, by River Main, Germany, d. Id 1769) German amateur musician and writer on music. His abundant letters to relevant musicians, and his memoires of his extensive travels in Europe, bequeathed to the University of Göttingen, are of great interest. Goethe spoke of his skill in organising concerts, and of his collection of music in *Dichtung und Wahrheit*.

-VALENTINI, GIUSSEPPE (c1680 Florence; d. Paris 1760) Italian violinist and composer; he is supposed to have studied with Corelli**, having frequented the circles of Corelli in Rome. Published a set of triosonatas*, and several violin concertos*. His compositions are full of difficulties, with extreme leaps, very high positions* and the use of remote keys* and abrupt harmonique shifts.

-VAN LOO, CARLE: (1705 Nice; d. Paris 1765) Belonging to a family of artists of Flemish origin, he was one of the best rococo painters in France. His religious and historical paintings are famous, as well as his many portraits. We must name the *Life of St. Augustin*, in Notre Dame des Victoires in Paris, and the *Resurrection* in the cathedral of Besançon. He was a prominent teacher at the Academy of painting and later its director as well. On his first visit to Italy he married the daughter of Somis** Anna Maria Cristina. (See Van Loo, Madame)

-VAN LOO, MADAME (née ANNA-MARIA CRISTINA SOMIS) Daughter of Somis**, little is known about her, except for two highly complimentary accounts: That of president de Brosses*; and that of Arthur Pougin*. a) De Brosses in his *Lettres écrites d'Italie* (Letters written from Italy, letter 55 to M. Neuilly. [Bibliothèque Nationale de France]) allow us to kill two birds with one stone. 1) He heard a concerto specially played for him by Somis in the Turin chapel and says that "Somis made a mistake…and that he preferred Tartini** and Veracini** to him". This is of capital importance for us, for it corroborates my theory of the barrier of the 50s for violinists. De Brosses heard Somis in 1740 when Somis had 54 years of age. He had been a victim of the syndrome of the 50s and had, consequently, lost his faculties. On the contrary, neither Tartini nor Veracini were 50 when he heard them, and consequently they still played perfectly well. But immediately after he says: *Oh! Que je le troquerais bien (Somis) pour avoir sa soeur, la charmante, la céleste Vanloo, dont aucune voix que j'aie entendue en Italie me fait perdre l'idée! Il y en a beaucoup de plus grandes et de plus sonores, mais on ne trouve nulle part plus de grâces ni plus de goût, ni personne qui mette autant qu'elle de vie et de joie dans son chant.* <Oh! That I would swap him by his sister, the charming, the heavenly, Vanloo, that no other voice in Italie makes me forget her. There are certainly many others, louder and greater, but one cannot find anywhere more gracefulness, nor a better good taste, nor any other one who give as much life and joy to their singing.> (de Brosses makes a mistake: Madame Van Loo* was not Somis sister, but his daughter) b) Arthur Pougin* (Le Violon, les Violonistes et la Musique de Violon. Paris

1924) on his side informs us that "she married Carle Vanloo on his first visit to Italy, and that from her arrival to Paris she excited the admiration of the court and of the high society for the beauty of her voice and the charming manner with which she sang the Italian music. [Both accounts can be seen in Pougin's* book, pag 91]

-VAUDEVILLE: A satirical small verse of popular origin put in music, that was much in vogue in the light operatic genre. It is the forerunner of the opéra-comique*.

-VEGH, SANDOR (1905 Koloszvar [now Cluj-Napoca]; d. Salzburg 1997) Hungarian violinist. Studied with Hubay** and composition with Kodaly. Leader of the Hungarian String Quartet. Founded his own Vegh quartet in 1940. Violin professor at Liszt Academy in Budapest. Often appeared at the Casals's* Prades Festival. Professor also in Düsseldorf, Freiburg, Basle, and Salzburg. Specialises in programs of Bach. He played on the Strad "Earl of Harrington" of 1724, called also *Bentick* and *Paganini*.

-VEICHTNER, FRANZ ADAM (1741 Regensburg; d. Klievenhof [now Kalnciems] Courland 1822) German violinist and composer. Son of a luthier*, Johann Georg Veichtner, studied the violin with Benda** at Potsdam. He worked for count Hermann von Keyserling. In 1765 he was Konzertmeister* at the Courland court at Mitau. He was one of the leading figures of Courland's musical life.

-VERACINI, ANTONIO (1659 Florence; d. id 1733) Italian violinist. Uncle and first teacher of Francesco Maria Veracini**, he worked for Grand Duchess Vittoria of Tuscany, was maestro di capella* of S Michelle in Florence, and directed his father's music school.

-VERLAINE, PAUL (b. 1844 Metz; d. Paris 1896) French poet. French for his origin and nationality, but universal for his fame, his works have been translated into all the main languages of the five continents. There is nothing to say about this divine poet except that, as Anatole France said, "poets like him do not appear one in a century".

-VIARDOT, PAULINE. (1821 Paris – id 1910) French mezzo-soprano of Spanish origin. The younger daughter of the renowned teacher of singing Manuel (del Popolo) García* Sr., she took her name from her husband Louis Viardot, a distinguished French writer. (as a curiosity Monsieur Viardot was the first to translate into French *Don Quixote*) As a child she studied singing with her father, composition with Anton Reicha* and piano with Franz Liszt. One of the best of her time had extended her voice into the soprano and contralto register, having particular dotes of dramatic interpretation on the stage. Meyerbeer wrote specially for her *Le Prophète*. She reached her peak with Berlioz's edition of Gluck's *Orfeo*. She was also an excellent pianist, composer and teacher of singing. Paulina was rather plain, as is evident from her photographs, but she was such a good actress on the stage, that she transfigured herself into a most attractive and fresh creature.

-VIBRATO (VOICE): We are, by now, expert connoisseurs of the vibrato on the violin. We are going to study it on the voice. Also called "tremolo". As we know, it was forbidden, just as was in the string instruments. And we know, also, that it followed suite to the violin, very shortly, being its first great representative Caruso. The "true" vibrato must be sustained, or produced, by the thrust or the emission of a strong column of air comming from the diaphragm. If it is produced in the throat, it becomes "artificial", false, similar to the bleating of a sheep. The art of a maestro of singing centres, mainly, on two aspects: 1) the "placing" of the voice, so that its emission comes propelled from the diaphragm, and 2) the equalisation of all the notes of the tessitura, or range of the voice (from lowest to highest note). Once the voice is well placed or "impostata" it is easy to command a perfect vibrato, with a wide range of almost a full tone, like in the modern violin, strong, forceful and sensuous. Pavarotti and Caruso are the greatest examples of a good vibrato, together with Callas.

-VILLA MEDICIS: As part of the vast programme of patronage of fine arts, Louis XIV established in 1666 an Academy of Arts in Rome, the *Académie Français*. Students winner of the Grand prix de Rome*, in every fine art, would obtain a five-year scholarship to complete their studies in Rome. To lodge them all, the government bought Villa Medicis, a magnificent palace built in 1557 by Annibal Lippi (villa: A rural or suburban residence, especially one that is large and pretentious. <Webster Dictionary>); Villa Medicis became very significant because Michelangelo added one of its wings and some embellishing improvements; it is located upon the hillside of Monte Pincio, overlooking Rome. Ingres* was director of the Académie (1835-41) when Liszt paid him a visit in the last stage of his *Annés de Pélérinage*, and played with him the Bthvn sonata "Kreutzer" (the scene is reproduced in book four, Paganini. Also in Lettres d'un bachelier ès musique. A Hector Berlioz. San Rossore, October 2, 1839). For a more detailed description of Villa Medicis see Berlioz. Memoires. Chapter XXXII.

-VILLE LUMIÈRE: see City of Light

-VIOLON D'INGRES: In France means the favourite hobby of a person, and it was so indeed, Ingres being the best painter of his time in France, and having, as his best hobby, the violin, which he played "charmingly" in the words of Liszt: in a letter to Massart** from Rome March 1, 1839 he says: *I see very often M. Ingres who is very kind with me. We play a lot of music together. Did you know he plays very charmingly the violin? We have the project to play together all the music by Mozart and Bthvn.*(Franz Liszt. L'Artiste, le Clerc. Letter VII. P. 51. Jacques . Vier. Editions du Cèdre. Paris 1950) This say, originated in France at the end of the XIX century, was coined by journalist Emile Bergerat, who used it for the first time in 1871, alluding to the regrets of his father in law, Téophile Gautier, for not having devoted to painting. As for the violin itself, it is a small French instrument of the XVIII century, of an unknown luthier, which the painter bequeathed to the museum of Montauban in 1867.

-VITALI, GIOVANNI BATTISTA (1632 Bologna; d. id 1692) Italian composer. Taught by Cazzati* in Bologna he is famous for his contribution to the development of the triosonata*. Maestro di capella* di S. Petronio he was also member of the Academia Filarmonica. As pedagogue he published the famous *Artifice Musicali*. He influenced such eminent composer as Corelli** and Torelli**.

-VOLUMIER, JEAN BAPTISTE (c1670 Spain?; d. 1728 Dresden) Educated at the French court, he went to the Elector of the Brandenburg's court chapel* in Berlin, as violinist, becoming later Konzertmeister* and director of dance and ballet.

Having been dismissed after a dispute in 1708 he entered the service of the Saxon court in Dresden, becoming Konzertmeister* in 1709. He introduced the French sober, precise style in the orchestra, which distinguished it among the rest of Europe. He shared the first violin* post with Veracini**, and both played on his majesty's Strad. "King Augustus" of 1715. Quantz** said of him: "I never heard an orchestra better than the Dresden's under Volumier." He was a superb violinist and a good friend of Bach.

-VUILLAUME, JEAN-BAPTISTE (1798 Mirecourt, *midway Nancy-Vesoul, renown for its lutherie*; d. Paris 1875) French luthier* and violin dealer. He excelled in imitating the old violins of the Cremona region: Guarneri, Amati, Stradivarius. But his violins were not fakes, simply imitations, and very successful indeed. As dealer he traded the most fine violins of his time, towering the incomparable "Messiah" Stradivarius of 1716. He was the father in law of Alard**.

-WALLER, FATS (1904 New York City; d. Kansas City, Missouri 1943) American black jazz pianist, composer, singer and entertainer. One of the greatest of all times, his true name was Thomas Wright Waller. Born into a very religious family he started by playing the organ at the local church services. He was interested also in the piano from the age of six. His really first job was playing the organ to accompany silent films at the Lincoln Theatre Cinema. As composer he started making piano roles, with which he earned lots of money, and later, he earned even more publishing his own compositions. Fats enjoyed fully his musical life: his shows lasted until early morning, and provided he had whisky to drink, good food to eat, and an audience to entertain with his jokes and amusing songs, he was absolutely happy. But this kind of dissolute life infuriated his wife who broke up with him. He agreed to pay a settlement to keep her and their son. He was continually harassed by his ex-wife, who sued him as many times as she could, demanding always more and more alimony, but his "easy come - easy go" finance attitude did not leave much room for savings, and he never could pay his instalments, and eventually she managed to send him to jail for non payment. When a radio broadcaster announced that Fats was behind bars, a spontaneous collection was organised throughout the USA that in a record time helped to pay his debt and set him free. He appeared in films such as *Hooray for Love*, and the famous *Stormy Weather*; composed musicals like *Keep Shuffin'*, *Hot Chocolates*, and *Early to Bed*, and unforgettable songs like *Ain't Misbehaving* (where he alludes to his troubles with the jealousy of his wife. ("No one to talk with, all by myself, I'm thro' with flirtin, 'It's just you I'm thinkin' of, ain't misbehaving, I'm saving my love for you") *Huneysuckle Rose*, *Im Gonna Sit Right Down and Write Myself a Letter*, and *I've Got a Feeling I'm Falling*.

-WASIELEWSKI, Wilhelm JOSEPH VON (1822 Grossleensen; d. Sonderhausen 1896) German violinist, conductor and writer on music. He was one of the first pupils of the Leipzig conservatory studying with David**. First violin* in the Leipzig Gewandhaus* he gave several concert tours before settling in Düsseldorf. In 1852 he went to Bonn where he directed the Bthvn Verein. Member of the Accademia Filarmonica of Bologna.

-WELL WORTH A MASS CITY: Paris. This famous phrase was attributed to Henry IV of France. A fanatic Protestant, his presumptive rights to the throne run against the ancestral Roman Catholic faith of the country. A long period of religious wars between Protestant (Huguenot) and Catholic forces ravaged France for more than 30 years. To prevent a Protestant King reigning in France a Holy League of Catholic countries in Europe was organised to fight him, and Pope Gregory XIII excommunicated him, declaring him devoid of any right to inherit the crown. After two unsuccessful fake conversions to Catholicism and ten long years of civil and external war against the League, in which his attempts to siege Paris (the stronghold of the League) were in vain, his army exhausted, and the country devastated, he realized that the war had to be ended at any price, and he made a final definitive conversion to Catholicism in 1593. This conversion removed any legitimate pretext for resistance, and Paris finally gave up in 1594. He was then quoted to say: *"Paris is well worth a mass"*.

-WESTHOFF, JOHANN PAUL von (1656 Dresden; m. Weimar 1705) German composer and violinist. After having received a good education he became tutor of the two princes of Saxony. Member of the Dresden Hofkapelle* (1674-97) he toured frequently, playing for the Sun King* in Paris in 1682. Professor of French and Italian music at the court of Weimar. Great virtuoso, he shared with Walther and Biber the leading posts of Germany's virtuosi.

-WIECK, FRIEDERICH (1785 Pretzsch, 50 Km NE of Leipzig; d. Loschwitz, nr Dresden) Music teacher, father of Schumann's wife Clara, née Wieck. Famous piano teacher, he had among his pupils Bülow and Schumann, although his most notorious pupil was his own daughter Clara. His fanatic opposition to her marriage to Schumann made of their romance one of the most "romantic" love stories of all times. He composed several songs and studies for piano, wrote a book, *Klavier und Gesang*, (piano and singing) and a collection of aphorisms, *musikalische Bauernsprüche*.

-WILHELMJ, AUGUST (1845 Usigen; d. London 1908) German violinist of first category. He was recommended by Liszt to F. David**: "let me present you the future Paganini". International tours sent him to America, Australia and Asia with great success. He (violin soloist) and Wagner (conductor) played in London three memorable concerts in 1877. With a fabulous technique, rich tone, and strong personality, he was one of the best violinists of his time. On his most brilliant career he played one of the most impressive collection of valuable instruments: Strads such as the Wilhelmj of 1711; the Wilhelmj of 1721; the de Chaponay of 1722, owned also by Maurin; the Wilhelmj of 1725; the Weissheimer, Wilhelmj of 1728. And the Guarneri del Gesu Heifetz, ex David of 1740.

-WOLLF, EDWARD (1816 Warsaw; d. Paris 1880) Polish composer and pianist. After a period of studies in Warsaw, completed later in Vienna, he made his debut there in 1834, and in 1835 he settled in Paris. Very much influenced by Chopin he earned his living both as pianist and as composer with more than 300 works, some in collaboration with Beriot, and Vieuxtemps.

-WYSEMAN: *A worthy English music master, who is well known and esteemed by all the English at Rome, where he has so long been an inhabitant, that he has almost forgot his native tongue. He lived in the Palazzo Rafaele, without the gates of Rome; where, during the first winter months, he had a concert every week till the* *operas begin. It was here that the great Raphael lived, where there are still some of his paintings in fresco.* (Burney*. The Present State of Music in Italy. p. 373. Foot note.)

-ZANETTI, GASPARO (Flourished in Milan 1626-45) Italian composer and writer on music. He contributed to the reduction of several canzonas* for the *"Flores praetantissimorum virorum"*, but he is most celebrated for having written the first didactic book for the violin: *Il scolaro per imparare a suonare di violino...* all in first position*.

-ZARZUELA: A typical Spanish operetta, similar to the Singspiel* in Germany and the opera comique* in France, in which singing alternates with spoken dialogues. The most important of them are: *El Barberillo de Lavapiés* (1874) by Barbieri; Chueca's *La Canción de la Lola* (1880) which run for two uninterrupted years, one of its songs being taken by Falla in "El Sombrero de Tres Picos" 40 years later, *La Gran Via* (1886) played one thousand consecutive times, and *Agua, Azucarillos y Aguardiente* (1897); Chapí's *La Bruja* (1887) and *La Revoltosa* (1897); Manuel Fernandez Caballero's *El Duo de la Africana* (1893), *La Viejecita* (1897) and *Gigantes y Cabezudos* (1898); Tomás Bretón's* *Los amantes de Teruel* (1889), *La Dolores* (1895) and his master piece *La Vervena de la Paloma* (1894); Jerónimo Jimenez's *La Boda de Luis Alonso* (1897) *La Tempranica* (1900) Amadeo Vives's *Bohemios* (1904) *Doña Francisquita* (1923); José Serrano's *La Reina Mora* (1905) *La Canción del Olvido* (1918); Guridi's *El Caserío* (1926) *La Meiga* (1928); Usandizaga's *Las Golondrinas* (1914); and Federico Moreno Torroba's *Luisa Fernanda* (1932)

INDEX

399

Burney, 39, 40, 41, 42, 50, 52, 56, 57, 58, 59, 60, 62, 63, 64, 71, 75, 77, 78, 79, 80, 81, 83, 85, 272, 274, 314, 315, 321, 332, 335, 342, 345, 354, 358, 360, 363, 367, 397
BURNEY, 315
Busch, 248, 315, 382
BUSCH, 315
Busoni, 236, 237, 311, 326

C

CADENZA, 315
CALENDAR, FRENCH REVOLUTION, 315
Callas, 76, 279, 291, 394
Cambert, 35, 308, 369
CAMBERT, 316
Cambridge, 133, 345, 362
Campagnoli, viii, 74, 94, 95, 97, 302, 305, 309, 342
CAMPAGNOLI, 64, 94
Camposelice, 186, 258
Campra, 116
CAMPRA, 316
Canavas, 89
Cannabich, vii, viii, 71, 72, 74, 302, 305
Canon, 17, 125, 130, 247, 260
canzona, 28, 316, 334, 383, 384, 390
Capet, 102, 243
CAPET, 316
CAPILLA, 316
Capron, 69, 92, 342
CAPRON, 316
Carbonelli, 41
Carminati, 64
Caroli, 390, 391
Carrodus 1743, 16
Cartier, 85
CARTIER, 316
Caruso, 145, 334, 362, 394
Casadesus, 109, 242, 279, 294
CASADESUS, 317
Casals, 230, 265, 317, 324, 334, 381, 393
CASALS, 317
Casella, 116, 231, 237
CASELLA, 317
Casini, 58, 60, 331

D

E

F

G

GEWANDHAUS, 339

Giardini, viii, 26, 41, 42, 50, 51, 52, 56, 74, 77, 78, 79, 80, 81, 265, 302, 305, 315, 332, 363, 370, 386

Gibson, 251, 375

Gieseking, 326, 351

Ginastera, 250

Gingold, 102, 358

GINGOLD, 339

GITLIS, 339

Glazunov, 204, 233, 245, 246, 281

glissando, 56, 98, 137, 149, 208, 209, 224, 340, 372

GLISSANDO, 340

glissandos, 98, 116, 138, 149, 206, 208, 331

Gluck, viii, 72, 74, 75, 81, 95, 110, 233, 302, 305, 308, 328, 338, 340, 342, 344, 349, 354, 362, 364, 367, 390, 393

GLUCK, 74, 279, 290

Godowski, 310

Goethe, 115, 309, 383, 392

Goffriller, 334

Gofriller, 386

Goldberg, 55, 215

Goldman, 246

Goldschmidt, 198, 341, 357

GOLDSCHMIDT, 340

good taste, 51, 209, 259

Good Taste, 56

Gossec, 92, 100, 329, 355, 368, 373, 379

GOSSEC, 341

GOUBAUX, 341

Gounod, 175, 321, 324, 355, 356, 375

GRÄDNER, 341

gramophone, xiii, 144, 145, 147, 193, 204, 207, 210, 214, 235, 238, 248, 265, 266

Grand Prix du Disque, 258, 268, 378

Grande Bande, 34

Graun, 58, 64, 342, 345, 362

GRAUN, 342

Greville, 229

Grumiaux, x, 141, 176, 234, 265, 271, 280, 289, 294, 303, 305, 376, 380

GRUMIAUX, 232, 254, 291

Grün, 215, 231

Guadagni, 78, 338

GUADAGNI, 342

Guadagnini, 187, 258, 263, 346, 388

Guarneri, 16, 107, 125, 130, 138, 140, 141, 191, 212, 237, 251, 254, 256, 258, 260, 262, 266, 340, 343, 386, 395
Guarneri del Gesu, 16, 42, 130, 140, 141, 186, 187, 229, 232, 235, 240, 247, 249, 251, 263, 265, 327, 353, 360, 374, 380, 386, 388, 396
Guarneri Sanctae Theresiae, 388
Guarnerius, 245
Guastarobba, 64, 94
GUASTAROBBA, 342
Guénin, 92, 101
GUÉNIN, 342
Guerillot, 101
Guérin, 175, 326
Guignon, 50, 66, 89, 91, 310, 342, 363
GUIGNON, 342
Guillemain, 50, 89, 342
GUILLEMAIN, 342

H

Haack, vii, 71, 72, 73, 302, 361, 364
HAACK, 343
Habeneck, 27, 108, 163, 168, 170, 175, 178, 184, 185, 316, 318, 327, 356, 361, 384
HABENECK, 343
Haddock 1734, 16
Haendel, 215
HAENDEL, 343
Haff, 353
Halir, 314
Hall, 107, 143, 218, 235, 236, 239, 244, 250, 253, 254, 255, 257, 260, 263, 268, 373
Hallé, 52, 161, 163, 183, 275, 310, 314, 343, 357, 358, 366, 378
HALLÉ, 343
Hamilton, 236, 237
Hammig, 191
Handel, vii, 35, 40, 47, 50, 51, 95, 216, 284, 285, 286, 289, 290, 292, 299, 302, 305, 313, 318, 325, 328, 332, 335, 342, 362
HANDEL, 47, 283, 291
harmonic, 64, 90, 111, 143, 331, 344, 345, 362, 363
HARMONIC, 344
harmonics, 90, 96, 111, 344, 363, 381
Harold, 118, 130, 134, 176, 183
Harrison, 81, 265
Harrisson, 42, 264

Hart, 242, 259

Hasse, 58, 362

HASSE, 344

Hassid, x, 63, 176, 190, 216, 234, 257, 265, 287, 289, 293, 294, 298, 299, 303, 305, 391

HASSID, 215, 256, 271, 284, 291

Hauptmann, 188, 345, 362

HAUPTMANN, 344

Hauteterre, 69

HAUTETERRE, 345

Hawkins, 41

HAWKINS, 345

Hawley, 247, 332

Haydn, 72, 105, 109, 196, 258, 266, 282, 283, 294, 299, 328, 336, 361, 377, 383, 389

Hayot, 180

HAYOT, 174

Healy, 357, 362

Hegar, 130

Heifetz, x, 16, 26, 46, 47, 63, 102, 133, 141, 144, 181, 190, 191, 204, 205, 214, 234, 239, 240, 264, 278, 280, 283, 288, 291, 294, 296, 297, 298, 300, 303, 305, 370, 371, 396

HEIFETZ, 204, 239, 271, 281, 282, 291, 292

Heifetz, ex David 1740, 16

Heine, 115

HEINE, 345

Hellemesberg jr, 135

Hellemsberger, Sr, 374

Hellmesberger, ix, 135, 158, 213

HELLMESBERGER, 217

Hellmesberger Jr, ix, 149, 231, 303, 341, 382

HELLMESBERGER Jr, 187

Hellmesberger Sr, ix, 135, 187, 188, 303, 328

HELLMESBERGER, GEORG, 135

Hellmesberger, Jr, 187, 314

Hellmesberger, Sr, 187

Hercules, 212

Hermann, 71, 263, 285, 298, 299, 376

Herrando, 41

HERRANDO, 345

Hertel, 71

HERTEL, 345

Hess, 236, 327, 352, 361, 388

HESS, 346

412

Hiller, 71, 383
HILLER, 346
Hochstein, 191, 240
Horowitz, 55, 127, 183, 245, 350, 370
Hortus Coelicus, 39
Hubay, x, 26, 55, 190, 208, 209, 213, 285, 286, 291, 292, 299, 303, 305, 327, 387,
    388, 393
HUBAY, 208, 236, 265, 286, 292
HUMAN TOO HUMAN, 23
HÜTTENBRENNER, 346

I

Il scolaro, 26
Imbault, 92
IMBAULT, 346
imitation, 28, 39, 56, 90, 335, 347, 384, 391
IMITATION, 347
Ingres, 124, 127, 128, 129, 163, 347, 389, 394
INGRES, 347
instant adjustment, 143
Institut national de musique, 101, 330, 348, 369
Institut National de Musique, 107
INSTITUT NATIONAL DE MUSIQUE, 348
Institut nationale de musique, 380
Istomin, 253, 377
ISTOMIN, 348
Italian school of violin, 42

J

JACOBI, 173, 348
Jacobins, 349, 376
Jakob, 95
Jambe de Fer, 127
Jambe-de-Fer, 21
JAMBE-DE-FER, 349
Jaques, 177
jazz, 18, 145
Jesuit, 82, 351
Jesuits, 71, 82
JESUITS, 349
jeté, 116

413

K

414

L

415

416

418

MILSTEIN, 245, 295
Minaloto, 332
Mingotti, 79, 80, 363
MINGOTTI, 362
modern, 128, 213
MODERN, 271
MODERN SCHOOL, 146
MODULATION, 363
Molitar, 375
Monasterio, ix, 138, 182, 194, 195, 196, 213, 247, 251, 261, 303, 306, 317, 354
MONASTERIO, 193
Mondonville, 86, 89, 90, 331, 342, 344, 363
MONDONVILLE, 363
Montagnana, 260
Monteux, 253
Monteverdi, 26, 306, 318, 360, 378, 386, 390
MONTEVERDI, 26, 278, 295
Montoya, 194
Montpensier, 33, 353, 363
mordente, 56
Morgan, 191
Morigi, 64
MORIGI, 363
Moscheles, 140
MOSCHELES, 363
Mosel, 64
Möser, viii, 72, 73, 74, 302, 306, 343, 374
MÖSER, 364
Mossi, 41
MOSSI, 364
Mozart, viii, 24, 34, 37, 53, 54, 55, 72, 74, 82, 84, 118, 123, 139, 190, 194, 196, 198, 230, 231, 241, 254, 258, 263, 276, 282, 285, 293, 295, 298, 299, 301, 302, 306, 318, 321, 322, 326, 328, 335, 336, 344, 346, 347, 351, 355, 357, 360, 361, 362, 367, 375, 378, 380, 381, 383, 387, 388, 390, 394
Mozart, Leopold, 336, 355
MOZART, LEOPOLD, 82, 278, 295
Mozarts, 72
Mullova, 131, 189, 279, 280, 287, 296, 300
MULLOVA, 295
Muntz, 332
musical, 25, 33, 44, 58, 60, 64, 84, 87, 96, 103, 114, 115, 117, 124, 126, 133, 138, 157, 158, 161, 176, 182, 185, 187, 189, 192, 208, 209, 215, 217, 231, 236, 238, 247, 257, 261, 263, 277, 310, 321, 354, 356, 362, 374, 375, 381, 386

420

N

O

P

Q

R

S

T

U

W

432

WILHELMJ, 396
Wollf, 192
WOLLF, 396
Wyseman, 62, 63, 76
WYSEMAN, 397

Y

Yardonoff, 186
Youssopov, 247
Ysaye, x, 17, 102, 137, 142, 144, 145, 147, 148, 159, 174, 176, 181, 182, 186, 191,
    193, 204, 206, 209, 210, 211, 212, 214, 218, 230, 237, 238, 245, 246, 254, 280,
    288, 290, 292, 300, 303, 305, 307, 311, 339, 374, 376
YSAYE, 209, 232, 236, 248, 271, 281, 284, 300
Ysaye 1740, 17

Z

Zahn, 259
Zanetti, 26, 307
ZANETTI, 397
zarzuela, 314, 383
Zarzuela, 197, 365
ZARZUELA, 397
Zigante, 131, 280, 296
Zimbalist, x, 204, 233, 303, 307, 340, 371, 380
ZIMBALIST, 233, 271
Zoltan, 387
Zukerman, xi, 102, 192, 230, 260, 263, 265, 282, 287, 288, 289, 290, 292, 295,
    296, 297, 303, 307
ZUKERMAN, 243, 265, 282, 301

Printed in the United States
34186LVS00002B/115

9 781581 126679